introduction to
communication
research

---

second edition

John C. Reinard

California State University, Fullerton

Boston, Massachusetts • Burr Ridge, Illinois • Dubuque, Iowa
Madison, Wisconsin • New York, New York • San Francisco, California St. Louis, Missouri

McGraw-Hill

A Division of The McGraw·Hill Companies

INTRODUCTION TO COMMUNICATION RESEARCH

 This book is printed on recycled, acid-free paper containing 10% postconsumer waste.

1 2 3 4 5 6 7 8 9 0   QPF QPF   9 0 9 8 7

ISBN 0-697-32730-2

Editorial director: *Phillip A. Butcher*
Sponsoring editor: *Marjorie Byers*
Marketing manager: *Carl Leonard*
Project manager: *Terry Routley*
Production supervisor: *Sandy Hahn*
Cover designer: *Jeff Storm*
Compositor: *Carlisle Communications*
Typeface: *10/12 Times Roman*
Printer: *Quebecor Printing Book Group/Fairfield*

Library of Congress Cataloging-in-Publication Data

Reinard, John C.
    Introduction to communication research / John C. Reinard. — 2nd ed.
        p.   cm.
    Includes bibliographical references and indexes.
    ISBN 0-697-32730-2
    1. Communication—Research—Methodology.   I. Title.
  P91.3.R38   1997
302.2'072—dc21

                                         97-21501
                                           CIP

For my mother, Billie Erich

CONTENTS

SECTION III DESIGN OF RESEARCH

PREFACE

In the preface to the first edition of this book, I wrote:

> Research is not library work.
> Nor is it statistics.
> Nor is it field observation.
>
> Research is an argument. In particular, communication research is a process by which we answer questions and try to draw conclusions from information gathered about message-related behavior.

With the advent of the information superhighway, these words are truer today than ever. The major task in learning research methods involves developing skills that help us sift through the information that is available so that we can make reasoned claims based on data. Solid research has lines of argument that are expected for different sorts of claims to be made legitimately. Students need to know how to evaluate these lines of argument and how to construct them. This concern is shared by many fields in modern colleges and universities, but it is central in the study of communication research methods.

Thus, this introductory volume provides information on the tools of scholarship (libraries, statistics, and fieldwork) to help students learn ways to find and assess high quality evidence. This book attempts to train students to gather research evidence, develop research arguments, and think critically about them. In short, this book is designed to teach students how to "do scholarship," make reasoned cases, and offer research conclusions.

Whereas the first edition of this book represented the product of many years of experimentation with these instructional materials, the second edition benefits from the formal feedback of instructors and students who praised the book's student-friendly approach and paid the author the compliment of recommending further refinements in the work's structure and coverage of concepts, especially relating to new technology.

Those familiar with the previous edition will note some changes in this book.

- Chapters on definitions and theory and on measurement of variables have been moved to an early location in the book. Now students can study the conceptual foundations of communication research and see the link to measurement of variables before immersing themselves in the specific methods of different research approaches.
- Scores of examples have been updated and many examples from communication research have replaced those drawn from other fields. References to examples unlikely to be in the experience of students have been replaced.
- Material on communication resources has been completely revised in light of the avalanche of new resources that have hit the field during the last few short years. New library and "electronic library" resources unimaginable in the past are items of everyday experience to modern students.

- Discussion of ethical issues in research, such as deception, confidentiality, and informed consent issues are expanded in the boxed discussions called "A Question of Ethics" found throughout the text.
- New material on the use of focus groups in research appears.

Surely the most exciting recent influence on students' research is the Internet. This second edition includes practical suggestions on how to use the Internet to enrich research efforts.

A Student Study Guide is now available with this textbook. The Study Guide includes

- information on writing and usage to promote effective communication in papers and scholarship
- information on applying the APA reference style
- sample student papers that illustrate the form that many research arguments may take (including not only typical examples, but at least one composite poor example)
- applied assignment study sheets that provide students with opportunities to develop skills in analyzing and composing research

Many things that teachers and students have found praiseworthy about this book remain. First and foremost, this book is written for—and to—students who are taking their first course in research methods, typically on the sophomore or junior levels. By the end of the academic term, students should know how to do at least a couple of things.

- Students should know how to present and evaluate a research argument. Since most classes that follow the research methods course require research-based writing by the students, students need to know how to complete the process of drawing conclusions and making arguments from the literature.
- Students should know how to deal with the brass tacks of research: how to isolate a problem statement; how to distinguish independent and dependent variables; how to criticize and evaluate definitions; what theories are and why they are important; how to use the library and electronic resources; how to apply methods of sound research and standards for evaluating and proposing worthwhile studies; how to compose scholarship; how to collect data and execute a rudimentary, but logical design; and how to analyze simple data.

Second, to avoid overwhelming students with detailed elements of each methodological twist in communication research, this textbook spends time teaching the "survival skills" that students need to know, supplemented with clearly identified enrichment information labelled as "Special Discussions." The topics covered in these discussions range from such things as ways of knowing to statistical packages for the analysis of data. Third, this book uses research examples from the broad range of communication studies. Since communication research courses serve students from several communication areas—including speech communication, journalism, telecommunications, public relations, and speech and hearing science—examples from all these areas are deliberately included in discussions of content. Fourth, to assist students, the textbook format is designed to promote efficient study and review. Each chapter

- starts with a preview of all major topics;
- opens with an orienting paragraph to describe the thrust of the chapter;
- ends with a list of key terms to review when studying the chapter;
- includes margin notes to point out important concepts covered in the text;
- highlights key terms in boldface the first time they appear;
- relies on tables when they may reduce otherwise extended text discussions;
- concludes with a summary that is an actual and detailed chapter synopsis, which students will find very helpful when reviewing for examinations.

In addition, a glossary is included to help students define critical terms swiftly (these terms appear in **boldface**).

This textbook is divided into four sections that correspond to the major units successfully taught in introductory communication research methods courses. The first section introduces the field of communication as a research area. Students are guided through two chapters that introduce communication research as a distinct form and that review the issues involved in composing communication research problems, using hypotheses, and isolating types of variables.

The second part of the textbook deals with the rudiments of research reasoning. This section begins with a chapter concerning conceptualizations in communication research including use of theory and definitions. A second chapter in this section describes measurement in communication so that students understand the transition from conceptualization to operationalization in research. A third chapter deals with "Using Communication Research Sources" and focuses on library research skills, strategies, and using the Internet. This chapter emphasizes hands-on skills that students need almost immediately. A fourth chapter emphasizes a point of view for the book by addressing methods to compose communication research, including understanding the anatomy of a research article and mechanics of writing different forms of scholarly and classroom reports. The final chapter in this section addresses the communication research argument with an emphasis on the critical thinking skills that are taught in the introductory research methods course. This chapter describes the nature of the research argument and ways to evaluate research reasoning and evidence.

The third section of the book emphasizes the design of both qualitative and quantitative research studies (though most space is spent on quantitative methods since neophyte students tend to be least conversant with these tools). The primary task in this section lies in presenting essential materials that students need to know most, without ignoring other unique applications that have invigorated the field.

Five chapters are dedicated to these research building-blocks. The first two chapters in this section deal with conducting textual analyses of messages and undertaking participant observation studies. The third and fourth chapters concern designing descriptive empirical research (including questionnaire and interview studies) and conducting experimental studies. The remaining chapter involves sampling in communication research. In each case, examples across the broad realm of communication studies are covered.

The fourth part of the book concerns statistical analysis of data. The individual chapters involve traditional topics of such an introductory treatment. The first chapter addresses beginning descriptive and correlational statistics. The second chapter introduces the logic of statistical hypothesis testing and applies it to the case of comparisons between two means. The final chapter extends significance testing to cases that go beyond two means, including analysis of variance and chi square tests. In this final chapter, special discussions include "survival guide" introductions to advanced statistics that students may read, but should not be expected to use in the introductory course.

Many people helped me develop this work. My sincere thanks must go to my own teachers of research methods. These teachers included not only those who provided instruction in empirical methods, but those who directed my studies in rhetorical theory, argumentation, and qualitative methods. My students of introductory research methods courses for more than a decade deserve thanks since this book and the Student Study Guide reflect the product of experimenting with them to find ways to teach this course most effectively. I am very grateful to the scholars and teachers who reviewed drafts of this work and provided invaluable advice and support for the direction of this project. Sharmila Pixy Ferris, William Peterson College, Wayne, New Jersey; Dr. Susan A. Holton, Bridgewater State College, Bridgewater, Massachusetts; and Rebecca Ann Lind, University of Illinois at Chicago offered invaluable insights in preparing this second edition, in addition to those who gave expert criticism and advice on previous versions—John D. Bee, University of Akron; Judith Dallinger, Western Illinois State; Lyle Flint, Ball State University; William J. Schenck-Hamlin, Kansas State University; Judy R. Sims, University of Wisconsin, Eau Claire. In particular, I must offer special appreciation to Kassie Radomski and Michelle Kelley for their extraordinary help in shepherding this project to completion and offering their wise counsel and assistance to create this second edition. Finally I wish to thank my family. Without their willingness to permit my dedication of many hours, it would not have been possible to complete this volume.

Introduction to the Field

1

The Role of Research in Communication

2

Communication Problem Statements and Hypotheses

CHAPTER 1

The Role of Research in Communication

If politics is the art of the possible, research is surely the art of the soluble.

–Sir Peter Medawar

BEFORE WE GET STARTED . . .

Welcome to communication research! Though you may be skeptical, "doing" communication scholarship is an exciting and very enjoyable personal experience. Rather than just accepting what others tell you, you will learn how scholars (a term that includes you now) draw conclusions in our field. You will see how research should look so that you can evaluate the stuff that often gets passed off to us. Along the way, you will learn how to improve your thinking, your scholarly writing, and your ability to evaluate research arguments. Getting there can be challenging, but it is well worth the trip. This book does not assume that you have any background in research methods—just an interest. To get started, you need to know why you are here and what communication research is. This chapter is designed to get you moving in the right direction.

WHAT IS RESEARCH IN COMMUNICATION?

A field defines itself by its research. Research determines what content is taught in courses, the social contributions the field makes, and the sort of publicity an area gets.

Research

Research is the systematic effort to secure answers to questions. These questions are not mundane ones, such as, Have you seen my keys? or Want to see a movie? Instead, research questions deal with issues requiring reference to data[1] and information, such as, Did Patrick Henry deliver the "Give Me Liberty or Give Me Death!" speech?[2] Do women self-disclose private information more often than men do?[3] and Do people who arrive "fashionably late" to parties receive higher credibility ratings than people who arrive on time?[4] Research is not an ivory tower activity conducted by a few elect scholars. It is a very practical effort to get answers for questions. Research usually requires examining past inquiry into an issue. We often rely on reports found in libraries to learn about related work and to avoid repeating past mistakes. Regardless of sources of information, all research involves gathering information that goes beyond personal feelings or hunches. We search for some light on the facts of matters when we do research.

research defined

Sometimes people distinguish two types of research. **Basic research** is completed to learn about relationships among variables, regardless of any immediate commercial product or service. Most things we call "pure" scientific research fall into this category. Though researchers hope to make useful contributions, no economic payoffs are imminent. **Applied research** is completed to develop a product or solve an immediately practical problem. When communication researchers survey employee attitudes as part of a consulting contract, the work is considered applied research. Even so, trying to separate basic and applied research causes problems. Regardless of whether pure or applied research is involved, the methods of inquiry *are identical.* Furthermore, last year's basic research may be today's source of new products. Work that aimed to find out how to store information in digital form is now the basis for patents on satellite transmission of television signals. Though the terms have their place, for our purposes it is enough to know that good research can be basic or applied.

basic research defined

applied research distinguished

Communication Research

Regrettably, some people have difficulty separating communication research from work in psychology, sociology, or literature. They figure that since "meanings are in people" (Berlo, 1960, p. 175), any study of people is communication research. Straightening out this exaggerated view has taken some serious thinking. In 1968 a group of communication scholars met in New Orleans under a grant from the National Science Foundation to wrestle with the basic issues of distinguishing communication research and instruction. They concluded that "research in speech-communication focuses on the ways in which messages link participants during

communication research defined in New Orleans conference

---

[1] Let's get something straight right now. The word "data" is plural. Thus, we have to say, "data *are*" and "data *were,*" NOT "data *is*" and "data *was.*" A single piece of data is called a datum, but people do not use that word very often. Instead they refer to a datum as "a piece of data," a usage which sounds natural to most people.

[2] He didn't.

[3] They do.

[4] We don't know.

SPECIAL DISCUSSION 1-1
Behavior of Researchers

It is possible to overstate the matter, but there is a set of norms—almost a culture—that distinguishes most people who do research. In his book *Foundations of Behavioral Research* (1986), Fred Kerlinger described these characteristics.

Universalism: Scientific laws are the same everywhere. A scientific law states a relation between phenomena that is invariable under the same conditions.

Organized skepticism: Researchers are responsible for verifying the results on which they base their work. [Researchers do not accept claims blindly. They question research claims and offer criticism for each other.]

Communality: Researchers are willing to share knowledge freely and contribute to public knowledge.

Disinterestedness: Researchers must ban ulterior motives and be relatively free from bias. Any known or possible biases must not be admitted. [*Disinterested* does not mean *uninterested*—it only means that one can be impartial because one does not have a financial or personal stake in the outcome. Certainly, researchers do not study matters without passion. They care. But, they must be willing to let their conclusions be influenced by the data and by the data only. If a researcher receives a grant from sponsors who specify the results they wish the researcher to find, the researcher loses the "disinterest" that separates research from ordinary pandering.] (Kerlinger, 1986, p. 9)

---

interactions" (Kibler & Barker, 1969, p. 33). The scope of our research area was clear. Other fields may study personality traits, trends in society, medicine, or the beauty of poetry. Communication research is a specialty that studies message-related behavior.

communication studies message related behavior as a specialty

Communication might be defined as "the process by which participants transact and assign meaning to messages" (Reinard, 1991, p. 4). You may be asked by a relative or acquaintance what your major is. If you answer "communication," you might receive a puzzled expression in response. Unless you explain, they may think you are learning to install telephones. Instead you might say you are training to be a "message specialist" or "message scientist." You may also explain that your concentration in communication prepares you in a specific area of communication. To be clear, you need to explain that a **message** is the set of verbal and nonverbal cues communicators exchange. **Verbal cues** are the words people use in communication. Sometimes people confuse "verbal" cues with "spoken" cues (as in the phrase *verbal agreement*). Yet, spoken cues are specifically called "oral cues" (from the "orifice" or mouth). **Nonverbal cues** are communication elements beyond the words themselves. Variations in voice, facial expression, gesture, movement, touch, timing, physical closeness, media treatments, and format are all nonverbal cues. Taken together, these verbal and nonverbal cues provide plenty for us to study.

messages composed of:
1. verbal cues

2. nonverbal cues

THE CHALLENGES OF COMMUNICATION RESEARCH

Communication covers a very broad set of topics, and no single research method is embraced by the field. To study communication—even its specialties of journalism, and speech and hearing science—we must have very broad knowledge. This breadth both challenges students and invites them to enter the field and make contributions.

The Breadth Challenge

The number of communication applications can seem enormous, but there really is a rational order to it. James H. McBath and Robert C. Jeffrey (1978) were asked to identify the professional areas in communication on behalf of the National Communication Association and the National Center For Educational Statistics, which were trying to organize information about careers in many fields. The list of communication specialties used by the NCES is shown in Table 1.1. The left column shows the official taxonomy.[5] In the column to the right you will see some of the sorts of research possible in each of these areas. As you can tell, each area is broad enough to promote many interesting studies.

communication covers a broad set of topics

TABLE 1.1 Communication Specialties

Communication Taxonomy (McBath & Jeffrey, 1978)	Description of Research Possibilities (Crawford, 1980, with permission)
1. The Broad Areas of Mass Media Communication:	
Advertising	The study of mass media methods of influence to promote a product, service, or cause
Communication Technology	The study of the mechanisms and technologies of mass media
Communication Policy	The study of public policy and regulation of mass media communication and freedom of speech
Film as Communication	The role of popular and technical cinema in society
Journalism	The study of the methods of reporting and organizing news for presentation in print media
Public Relations	The study of methods of managing publicity and press relations for an organization, person, or cause
Radio	The study of the methods and uses of radio
Television	The study of the methods and uses of televised communication
2. Specific Areas of Speech Communication Research:	
Code Systems	The study of the uses of verbal and nonverbal symbols and signs in human communication

[5] Well, almost. A couple of areas have been added here, including conflict management, journalism, radio and television, and public relations. In the original effort, mass communication careers already were distinguished from other careers in communication.

TABLE 1.1 —*Continued*

Communication Taxonomy	Description of Research Possibilities
Intercultural Communication	The study of communication among individuals of different cultural backgrounds
Interpersonal Communication	The study of communication interactions occurring in person-to-person and small group situations
Conflict Management	The study of the role of communication in the creation and control of conflict
Organizational Communication	The study of interrelated behaviors, technologies, and systems functioning within an organization
Oral Interpretation	The study of literature through performance involving the development of skilled verbal and nonverbal expression based on critical analysis of written texts (aesthetics of literature in performance, criticism of literature in performance, group performance, oral traditions)
Pragmatic Communication	The study and practice of communication, the object of which is to influence or facilitate decision making
Argumentation	The study of reason-giving behavior
Debate	The study of decision making in which adversaries present arguments for decision by a third party
Discussion and Conference	The study of methods of decision making in which participants strive by consensus to discuss and explore an issue
Parliamentary Procedure	The study of the means used to handle deliberation in large, legislative bodies through the use of formal rules and procedures to regulate debate and discussion
Persuasion	The study of methods used to influence the choices made by others
Public Address	The study of speakers and speeches, including the historical and social context of platforms, campaigns, and movements
Rhetorical and Communication Theory	The study of the principles that account for human communicative experiences and behavior
Communication Education	The study of communication in pedagogical contexts (communication development, oral communication skills, instructional communication)
Speech and Hearing Science	The study of the physiology and acoustical aspects of speech and hearing (biological aspects of speech and hearing, phonological aspects of speech and hearing, physiological aspects of speech and hearing)

The Multiple Methods Challenge

In studying literature, qualitative methods are most often used. In history, the historical method is employed. In psychology, the experiment holds a prominent position. Yet, communication researchers use all these methods to answer their questions. Thus, they expose modern students to many methods. Though single studies may use multiple methods, for the most part a piece of research relies on either qualitative *or* quantitative methods.[6]

communication uses both qualitative and quantitative methods

Qualitative Methods

Qualitative methods describe observations in predominantly non-numerical terms. Sometimes qualitative studies make passing references to statistics (as when TV critics refer to the Nielsen ratings of various programs), but statistics are largely secondary to the attempt to answer research questions. Table 1.2 lists some chief types of qualitative methods.

qualitative methods defined

TABLE 1.2 Types of Qualitative Studies

Description	Examples
Historical-Critical Studies: research designed to describe a period, person, or phenomenon for the purpose of interpreting or evaluating communication and its effects.	*Historical Studies*: • Studying whether Lincoln's Gettysburg Address really met with negative reaction at the time it was delivered • Studying the true impact on Americans from Orson Welles's 1938 "War of the Worlds" broadcast • Studying dominant methods of treating stuttering during the last two hundred years *Criticism*: • Evaluating the use of argument by Ronald Reagan in his presidential debates • Evaluating whether newspaper reports of the news gave politically balanced reports of the U.S. entry into the Iraq-Kuwait crisis • Evaluating the ethical use of surgery in the treatment of speech-handicapped patients in the nineteenth century
Qualitative Observational Studies: methods designed to use predominantly attribute-type data to interpret contemporaneous communication interactions. *Case Studies and Interpretive Studies*: intensive inquiries about single events, people, or social units (interpretive studies attempt to look for themes or stories that are helpful to *interpret* or understand the case.)	*Case Studies*: • Investigating the practice of a successful speech therapist to pick up some pointers • Studying the communication inside a newspaper that is in the process of being sold

---

[6] Reasonable people differ on the classification of some of these types of studies, but the perspective advanced here represents a mainstream view.

TABLE 1.2 —*Continued*	

Description	Examples
Participant Observation Studies: inquiries in which the researcher takes the role of an active agent in the situation under study (sometimes may be used to gather quantitative data).	*Case Studies*: • Studying the process of news writing for a television station by joining the writing staff to report events from the inside • Investigating the development of public strategy for a political campaign by joining a campaign as an active worker who makes observations from within the organization
Ethnomethodology: originally developed by anthropologists to study societies of humans, an approach (rather than a rigorous method) in which researchers find an ethnic group, live within it, and attempt to develop insight into the culture; emphasis is on ordinary behavior, which participants take for granted, to find hidden meanings and unwritten rules people use to make sense of their world.	• Investigating how people react to television by living with an isolated group of people without television and watching their reactions in the days and weeks that follow introduction of televisions • Inquiring into the special language of street gang members by moving around with a gang during an extended time period
Discourse/Conversational Analysis: a method of examining utterances people exchange, for the purpose of discovering the rules and strategies people use to structure, sequence, and take turns in speaking, to learn how people manage their interactions with others.	• Studying the structure of interpersonal arguments among husbands and wives • Examining judge and attorney communication by looking at the structure of the abbreviated exchanges • Inquiring into children's speech development by identifying language competency levels among six-year-old and eight-year-old school children
Creative Studies: use of the method of performance or demonstration to explore an aesthetic or creative experience.	• Examining the problems of communicating Renaissance poetry to modern audiences by undertaking special performances in oral interpretation to contemporary student audiences • Examining whether a public relations campaign using multimedia news releases is perceived as a suitable way to transmit information by designing such a campaign directly

approach of qualitative research methods:

description and interpretation

There is more to qualitative methods than the type of data—though the type of data plays a very big part. Most qualitative research in our field tends to *describe* or *interpret* communication exchanges. These studies try to describe the human condition by using general views of social action. They may critique communication by relying on standards derived from a body of existing theory. Researchers who use qualitative methods often try to interpret the meanings to be found in communication exchanges. They may look at individual examples of communication rather than searching for patterns that run across individuals. Our language is very broad here, but the differences in emphasis will become pronounced as we continue.

TABLE 1.3 Types of Quantitative Studies

Description	Examples
Survey Studies: techniques that involve carefully recorded observations which provide quantitative descriptions of relationships among variables.	
Descriptive or Observational Surveys: direct observations of behavior by use of some measurement (the researcher does not manipulate or change any variables).	• Discovering what sorts of things small group communicators say that predict their becoming group leaders • Identifying the relationship between the number of newspapers a person reads on a regular basis and the amount of fear of society rated on a measure of state anxiety
Content Analysis: "a systematic, quantitative study of verbally communicated material (articles, speeches, films) by determining the frequency of specific ideas, concepts, or terms." (*Longman Dictionary of Psychology and Psychiatry,* 1984, p. 176; used through courtesy of Walter Glanze Word Books.)	• Studying the amount of violence on children's television programs • Inquiring into the amount of newspaper space dedicated to stories about the women's movement • Analyzing of the types of speech defects shown by children in samples of spontaneous speech
Opinion Surveys: assessments of reports from individuals about topics of interest.	• Analyzing opinion surveys regarding which candidate people think won a political debate • Examining whether the public believes that speech correction therapy should receive increased funding in the public schools • Assessing surveys of the favorite television programs people watch
Experimental Studies: a method of studying the effect of variables in situations where all other influences are held constant. Variables are manipulated or introduced by experimenters to see what effect they may have.	• Studying the impact of the use of evidence completed by exposing one group to a speech with evidence and another group to a speech without evidence • Studying the effect of color in advertising by exposing one group to an ad with color printing and another group to an ad without color printing

Quantitative Methods

Some research data are in numbers. In fact, **quantitative research methods** are inquiries in which observations are expressed predominantly in numerical terms. As Table 1.3 shows, quantitative research has two major branches: surveys (of all varieties) and experiments.

Why would researchers in their right minds want to represent the world of communication as a bunch of numbers? Surely there must be something going on other than a love of numbers by some people. Though the type of data distinguish these methods from qualitative tools, the research issues probed also tend to be different. Quantitative research tends to be *explanatory,* especially when experiments

quantitative methods defined

approach of quantitative research methods:

explanation and prediction

some research skills are important regardless of the methods used

are involved, or it attempts to use precise statistical models to achieve comprehensive understandings of human communication (as in survey studies and polls of public opinion). These methods often try to explain communication behavior by looking at processes that allow researchers to *predict* future behavior, frequently using models of causal processes. Thus, quantitative research usually attempts to answer questions about how *many* people are involved in an activity. Hence, any statistical tools are means to ends—not ends in themselves. If researchers wish to have precise explanations that characterize processes, or if they wish to develop methods to study communication behavior, quantitative research methods are invited. Of course, the research question guides selection of methods, not the other way around. It is improper to decide that you want to be either a quantitative or qualitative researcher. You have to choose methods to suit research questions.

You, Forms of Research Methods, and This Book

All research requires the same basic skills to frame a question, look in the library (and check the Internet these days), and reason to conclusions from data. This book will start by helping you with these common tasks. The first section introduces the field as a research area, methods for isolating the research problem (a surprisingly difficult task, as it turns out!), and how to construct and use hypotheses. The second section, "Understanding Rudiments of Research Reasoning," deals with developing theories and definitions, understanding measurement, locating information in the library and on Internet, writing a logical research argument, and evaluating research evidence and arguments. As you can see, the first two sections of the book consider topics all researchers must know, regardless of the particular methods they eventually select to analyze data.

advanced studies of applied methods require coursework beyond the scope of the introduction to research class

The third section examines the "Design of Research," including participant observation methods and documentary studies that sometimes are considered qualitative methods (content and interaction analyses). Empirical methods are dominant in this section of the book since they reflect the sorts of things that can reasonably be learned in a one-term course on research methods, and they fit the major interests of current communication students. The use of other qualitative methods—such as conversation analysis, rhetorical analysis, and ethnography—are defined but not covered in depth. Completing such research requires that you first study sets of underlying theoretic orientations covered in other classes. Hence, after taking advanced coursework in linguistics you may demonstrate skills by completing a conversational analysis. After taking advanced coursework in rhetorical theory you can count on completing rhetorical criticisms. After completing work in social interactionism you may be expected to complete an ethnographic study (though rarely at the undergraduate level). Each of these methods presumes advanced study that you must complete elsewhere. This choice is not a judgment about the value of one method over another (no single method is best for all research questions), but a practical decision to make your learning reasonable. The final section of this book addresses "Statistical Analysis of Data" and introduces some fundamentals of these methods. The common theme throughout this book is that research is an argument in which scholars (including you) are supposed to employ their best thinking and available evidence. Both the merit of the data and worth of research reasoning must be evaluated. Therefore, research requires us to train our minds and our abilities to express ourselves—as well as to be familiar with tools for inquiry.

The Scholarly Rigor Challenge

Research must meet standards of excellence. In particular, we must conduct our research with the recognition of five key qualities (after Tuckman, 1978, pp. 10–12):

scholarly rigor:

1. *Research is systematic.* Productive research follows steps that carry out some sort of design. Researchers ask questions and implicitly agree in advance to search for answers by examining pertinent information. Unexpected results often emerge. The effect is called **serendipity** and refers to finding something valuable while looking for something else. It seems that systematic researchers stand the best chance of grasping the importance of unexpected findings.

1. systematic

serendipity defined

2. *Research is data driven.* Issues that ask us to investigate things that cannot be tested in this life (e.g., does God exist?) are not matters that we can settle by our research methods. As such, researchers are supposed to be willing to change their minds in light of new data. If data cannot be collected, or if we are unwilling to alter our opinions, the issue is not suitable for research.

2. data driven

3. *Research is a sound argument.* Though students are sometimes surprised to learn it, research actually is a process of advancing arguments. But this statement does not mean that researchers are just trying to win over others with clever appeals. Though in everyday life people can be persuasive by the force of their styles or personalities, research arguments reason from research data and information to draw conclusions. Thus, **arguments** in this context are defined as claims advanced on the basis of reasoning from evidence. Sound reasoning is vital for effective research. Flippant or sloppy thinking is not valued. Thus, logic and the methods to evaluate arguments are valuable tools to judge research.

3. sound argument

arguments defined

4. *Research is capable of replication.* By attempting to replicate or reproduce the research of scholars, we can tell if research findings are generally true or accidental. If research methods are so vaguely described that it is impossible to repeat the procedures in a study, the worth of the entire research project is questioned. Regardless of whether replications are actually completed, the ability to replicate studies is essential for any piece of sound research.

4. capable of replication

5. *Research is partial.* There is always more that could be added about a topic. Research findings are partial because we may discover new relationships involving other variables that make us modify or qualify the conclusions we have found. Thus, researchers do not claim to have discovered "The Truth" for all time. Instead, they advance tentative—but meaningful—insights for communication phenomena.

5. partial

The Personal Challenge

People who do research don't often tell you how much fun they have making new discoveries. In fact, they might be a little embarrassed to tell you about the rush they get when completing a successful research project. But for all the excitement that research provides (and it can be an addicting pleasure), it also can be demanding. As you begin to look at research methods, it might help to know that students who do well in research methods classes tend to consider these personal issues and needs:

1. orderly thinking

1. *The need to think in an orderly way.* Though learning research methods will help improve your critical thinking abilities, orderly thinking also is a key to success. Researchers quickly find that half-considered ideas are exposed as weak. We must train our minds to separate the relevant from the irrelevant, the observable from the unobservable, and the complete from the incomplete.

2. clear writing

2. *The need to write clearly.* Research includes communicating the effort to others. To succeed, you must write crisply and clearly. Writing research and scholarship is not the same as writing a typical essay, short story, or letter. Research writing is very precise, structured, and to the point. Effective writing does not mean writing beautiful prose, but using crystal clear language, grammar, and support. While we are on the subject, let's get something else straight: first drafts are not acceptable in research. Everybody's first draft of a paper is lousy. Despite what you may have been told in high school, you must revise, edit, and polish research to put it in proper form. You may be familiar with the writer William Faulkner. After he was awarded the Nobel Prize for literature, a reporter asked him what it felt like to be recognized as one of the world's greatest writers. He responded, "I am not one of the world's greatest writers, but I am among the world's two or three greatest *re*writers." Faulkner had to revise his work, and so do the rest of us. Taking a course in research should help you improve your writing abilities.

3. set aside prejudice

3. *The need to set aside personal prejudices in light of data.* In research and scholarship, we must be willing to let the data decide our conclusions, even if we do not like them very much. When Galileo first observed moons around planets other than earth, many Church fathers refused to look through his telescope. Church doctrine had decided that such things were impossible, and no data were allowed to contradict it. Galileo was persecuted for letting data—not prejudice—guide his conclusions. Though the world now respects Galileo's position, many people are still unwilling to let the data decide matters. They have a difficult time studying research methods since research methods place priority on the data, not on beliefs.

4. organized and follow instructions

4. *The need to stay organized and follow instructions.* Research requires following careful research protocols and methods. Thus, it is important for scholars—even those studying research methods for the first time—to follow directions and stay organized. Students must fight the urge to leave out steps, take shortcuts, or ignore instructions. There is much that is creative in research, but we must harness that creativity by being organized and following instructions in detail. Researchers know that details matter.

5. know reasons to study research methods

5. *The need to know the reason for studying research methods.* Students sometimes take a required class in research methods without knowing why. Yet, most effective students take time to learn the reasons for studying this subject (and all others, for that matter). Why study communication research methods? Among the most common reasons are

- to learn to think rigorously and critically, especially about research evidence that is advanced for acceptance in a variety of popular and scholarly applications

- to learn how to find answers to questions about communication
- to acquire survival skills to help read and use the field's literature
- to learn how to sort through research for answers to research questions.

Any of these reasons justifies looking at research methods. Your personal goals for approaching this subject can be a great resource to you.

The Ethical Challenge

Research is not amoral. Conducting research is bound up in the ethical standards our society has accepted. Research is judged not only by the rigor of procedures and the results obtained, but by the ethics of the researchers. The Archbishop of York challenged British scientists to consider the ethical consequences of their research by urging them to ask, "What applications will be made of my research?" before they undertake research.

Many organizations have developed formal codes of conduct to guide practitioners and researchers. Among the most well known of these guides is the Code of Conduct for the American Psychological Association. The American Association for Public Opinion Research developed a code of conduct for researchers involved primarily in public survey research. Others exist in our field as well. The American Forensic Association has a detailed code of conduct to guide debate and contest speaking activities. Regulations of the United States Office of Education, the Department of Health and Human Services, and some federal laws protect the rights of individuals who are subjects of research. Clear breaches of ethical standards are treated harshly in the field. Violations can—and have—resulted in termination of employment and virtual expulsion from the field. Ignorance of such codes is not considered an excuse. Reasonable adults are expected to think about the likely consequences of their conduct before they act. Paul Reynolds (1975) put together a composite list from twenty-four different organizations whose research touches on the social sciences. This list is found in Table 1.4 and involves a total of 78 prescriptions. In addition to this list, this book includes a number of "Special Discussions" dedicated to ethical issues (listed under the heading, "A Question of Ethics").

professional codes of conduct

The Structure of the Field Challenge

People in speech communication, speech and hearing science, journalism, and telecommunications work in a field structured across many departmental lines. Similarly, communication research has been promoted by many organizations whose members often cross the barriers created by organization frameworks at different schools. It is helpful to know what the major organizations in our field do to showcase our research.

National Communication Association

Founded in November of 1914, the National Communication Association (NCA) was the first organization to sponsor research publications.[7] Originally called the National Association of Academic Teachers of Public Speaking, it changed its name to the

---

[7] The Eastern Communication Association was founded before the National Communication Association, but it did not begin publishing a research journal until 1953.

TABLE 1.4 A Composite Code of Ethics for Social Science Researchers

The numerals in parentheses indicate the number of ethical codes that list the item.

Principles

General Issues Related to the Code of Ethics

1. The social scientist(s) in charge of a research project is (are) responsible for all decisions regarding procedural matters and ethical issues related to the project whether made by themselves or subordinates (7).
2. Teachers are responsible for all decisions made by their students related to ethical issues involved in research (1).
3. All actions conducted as part of the research should be consistent with the ethical standards of both the home and host community (1).
4. Ethical issues should be considered from the perspective of the participant's society (2).
5. If unresolved or difficult ethical dilemmas arise, assistance or consultation should be sought with colleagues or appropriate committees sponsored by professional associations (2).
6. Any deviation from established principles suggests: (a) that a greater degree of responsibility is being accepted by the investigator, (b) a more serious obligation to seek outside counsel and advice, and (c) the need for additional safeguards to protect the rights and welfare of the research participants (2).

Decision to Conduct the Research

7. Research should be conducted in such a way as to maintain the integrity of the research enterprise and not to diminish the potential for conducting research in the future (3).
8. Investigators should use their best scientific judgment for selection of issues for empirical investigation (1).
9. The decision to conduct research with human subjects should involve evaluation of the potential benefits to the participant and society in relation to the risks to be borne by the participant(s)—a risk-benefit analysis (2).
10. Any study which involves human subjects must be related to an important intellectual question (4).
11. Any study which involves human subjects must be related to an important intellectual question with humanitarian implications, and there should be no other way to resolve the intellectual question (2).
12. Any study which involves human participants must be related to a very important intellectual question if there is a risk of permanent, negative effects on the participants (2).
13. Any study involving risks as well as potential therapeutic effects must be justified in terms of benefits to the client or patient (2).
14. There should be no prior reason to believe the major permanent negative effects will occur for the participants (1).
15. If the conduct of the research may permanently damage the participants, their community, or institutions within their community (such as indigenous social scientists), the research may not be justified and might be abandoned (2).

Conduct of the Research

16. All research should be conducted in a competent fashion, as an objective, scientific project (4).
17. All research personnel should be qualified to use any procedures employed in the project (7).
18. Competent personnel and adequate facilities should be available if any drugs are involved (4).
19. There should be no bias in the design, conduct, or reporting of the research—it should be as objective as possible (4).

TABLE 1.4 —*Continued*

Effects on and Relationships with the Participants

Informed Consent

General

20. Informed consent should be used in obtaining participants for all research; investigators should honor all commitments associated with such agreements (10).
21. Participants should be in a position to give informed consent; otherwise it should be given by those responsible for the participant (2).
22. Informed consent should be used if the potential effects on participants are ambiguous or potentially hazardous (7).
23. If possible, informed consent should be obtained in writing (1).
24. Seek official permission to use any government data, no matter how it was [sic] obtained (1).

Provision of Information

25. Purposes, procedures, and risks of research (including possible hazards to physical and psychological well-being and jeopardization of social position) should be explained to the participants in such a way that they can understand (7).
26. Participants should be aware of the possible consequences, if any, for the group or community from which they are selected in advance of their decision to participate (1).
27. The procedure used to obtain the participant's name should be described to him or her (1).
28. Sponsorship, financial and otherwise, should be specified to the potential participants (2).
29. The identity of those conducting the research should be fully revealed to the potential participants (2).
30. Names and addresses of research personnel should be left with participants so that the research personnel can be traced subsequently (1).
31. Participants should be fully aware of all data gathering techniques (tape and video recordings, photographic devices, physiological measures, and so forth), the capacities of such techniques, and the extent to which participants will remain anonymous and data confidential (2).
32. In projects of considerable duration, participants should be periodically informed of the progress of the research (1).
33. When recording videotapes or film, subjects should have the right to approve the material to be made public (by viewing it and giving specific approval to each segment) as well as the nature of the audiences (1).

Voluntary Consent

34. Individuals should have the option to refuse to participate and know this (1).
35. Participants should be able to terminate involvement at any time and know that they have this option (3).
36. No coercion, explicit or overt, should be used to encourage individuals to participate in a research project (6).

Protection of Rights and Welfare of Participants

General Issues

37. The dignity, privacy, and interests of the participants should be respected and protected (8).
38. The participants should not be harmed; welfare of the participants should take priority over all other concerns (10).
39. Damage and suffering to the participants should be minimized through procedural mechanisms and termination of risky studies as soon as possible; such effects are justified only when the problem cannot be studied in any other fashion (8).
40. Potential problems should be anticipated, no matter how remote the probability of occurrence, to ensure that the unexpected does not lead to major negative effects on the participants (1).

TABLE 1.4 —*Continued*

41. Any harmful aftereffects should be eliminated (4).
42. The hopes or anxieties of potential participants should not be raised (1).
43. Research should be terminated if danger to the participant arises (3).
44. The use of clients seeking professional assistance for research purposes is justified only to the extent that they may derive direct benefits as clients (1).

Deception
45. Deceit of the participants should only be used if it is absolutely necessary, there being no other way to study the problem (3).
46. Deception may be utilized (1).
47. If deceit is involved in a research procedure, additional precautions should be taken to protect the rights and welfare of the participants (2).
48. After being involved in a study using deception, all participants should be given a thorough, complete, and honest description of the study and the need for deception (5).
49. If deception is not revealed to the participants, for humane or scientific reasons, the investigator has a special obligation to protect the interests and welfare of the participants (1).

Confidentiality and Anonymity
50. Research data should be confidential and all participants should remain anonymous, unless they (or their legal guardians) have given permission for release of their identity (15).
51. If confidentiality or anonymity cannot be guaranteed, the participants should be aware of this and its possible consequences before involvement in the research (4).
52. Persons in official positions (studied as part of a research project) should provide written descriptions of their official roles, duties, and so forth (which need not be treated as confidential information) and be provided with a copy of the final report on the research (1).
53. Studies designed to provide descriptions of aggregates or collectivities should always guarantee anonymity to individual respondents (1).
54. "Privacy" should always be considered from the perspective of the participant and the participant's culture (1).
55. Material stored in databanks should not be used without the permission of the investigator who originally gathered the data (1).
56. If promises of confidentiality are honored, investigators need not withhold information on misconduct of participants or organizations (1).
57. Specific procedures should be developed for organizing data to ensure anonymity of participants (1).

Benefits to Participants
58. A fair return should be offered for all services of participants (1).
59. Increased self-knowledge, as a benefit to the participants, should be incorporated as a major part of the research design or procedures (1).
60. Copies or explanations of the research should be provided to all participants (2).
61. Studies of aggregates or cultural subgroups should produce knowledge which will benefit them (1).

Effects on Aggregates or Communities
62. Investigators should be familiar with, and respect, the host cultures in which studies are conducted (1).
63. Investigators should cooperate with members of the host society (1).
64. Investigators should consider, in advance, the potential effects of the research on the social structure of the host community and the potential changes in influence of various groups or individuals by virtue of the conduct of the study (1).

TABLE 1.4 —*Continued*

Interpretations and Reporting of the Results of the Research

65. Investigators should consider, in advance, the potential effects of the research and the report on the population or subgroup from which participants are drawn (1).

66. Participants should be aware, in advance, of potential effects upon aggregates or cultural subgroups which they represent (1).

67. The interests of collectivities and social systems of all kinds should be considered by the investigator (1).

68. All reports of research should be public documents, freely available to all (4).

69. Research procedures should be described fully and accurately in reports, including all evidence regardless of the support it provides for the research hypotheses; conclusions should be objective and unbiased (14).

70. Full and complete interpretations should be provided for all data and attempts made to prevent misrepresentations in writing research reports (6).

71. Sponsorship, purpose, sources of financial support, and investigators responsible for the research should be made clear in all publications related thereto (3).

72. If publication may jeopardize or damage the population studied and complete disguise is impossible, publication should be delayed (2).

73. Cross-cultural studies should be published in the language and journals of the host society, in addition to publication in other languages and other societies (2).

74. Appropriate credit should be given to all parties contributing to the research (9).

75. Full, accurate disclosure of all published sources bearing on or contributing to the work is expected (8).

76. Publication of research findings on cultural subgroups should include a description in terms understood by the participants (2).

77. Whenever requested, raw data or other original documentation should be made available to qualified investigators (1).

78. Research with scientific merit should always be submitted for publication and not withheld from public presentation unless the quality of research or analysis is inadequate (1).

Note: From "Ethics and Status: Value Dilemmas in Professional Conduct of Social Science," by P. D. Reynolds, 1975, *International Social Science Journal, 27* (4), pp. 563–611. © UNESCO, adapted with permission of Blackwell Publishers, Ltd.

Speech Association of America, which remained the name until 1970 when the organization adopted the Speech Communication Association as its title. In March 1997 the organization adopted its current name, reflecting the breadth of the field. In addition to promoting research and employment networking at its annual convention, this organization publishes several journals that report research:

- *Quarterly Journal of Speech* (founded 1915). The oldest journal in the field, deals with general speech communication, focusing heavily on communication and rhetorical theory and criticism.
- *Communication Monographs* (founded 1934—formerly, *Speech Monographs*). Originally designed to publish lengthy research pieces, now dedicated to communication theory with emphasis on quantitative studies.
- *Communication Education* (founded 1952—formerly *Speech Teacher*). In the 1980s, this journal was divided into two publications: *Communication Education* and *Speech Communication Teacher.*

- *Text and Performance Quarterly* (founded 1981). Dedicated to oral interpretation of literature and aesthetics in communication.
- *Critical Studies in Mass Communication* (founded 1984). Dedicated to critical and interpretive study and analysis of mass media communication.
- *Journal of Applied Communication Research* (founded 1973, NCA sponsorship begun 1991). Dedicated to research on applied topics in field settings.

Two additional yearbooks are also published by NCA, the *International and Intercultural Communication Annual* and the *Free Speech Yearbook.*

SPECIAL DISCUSSION 1-2
Classical Roots of the Communication Field

Communication is one of the world's oldest academic fields. The first book on communication was written sometime around 2675 B.C.E. by Ptah Hotep, a teacher of the sons of Egyptian Pharoahs. The book was called *Precepts* and served as a textbook on communication for many centuries. Yet, widespread communication studies did not really begin until around 500 B.C.E, when the city-state of Athens instituted a democratic system and people found that they had to speak for themselves to exercise their rights. Athenian freemen were expected to participate in the popular assembly (if they gave consistently bad advice they could be banished outright) and on juries (ranging in size from a low of 51 members to a high of 1,501 members—though most were 501). People needed communication skills and they were eager to find teachers to help them. The first groundswell of teachers to make their way to Athens were called *sophists.* Today that term means a person who uses clever but fallacious arguments. In ancient times, however, sophists were teachers who traveled around instructing people wherever there was a market. These teachers gave very practical instruction that was useful to common folk who direly needed to improve their skills. Sometime around 470 B.C.E. a Sicilian named Corax (generally believed to be the earliest of these teachers) "invented" the study of communication (called *rhetoric*). At the very least, he wrote the first detailed work on the art of effective public speaking, *Rhetorike Techne,* including details on organization and uses of arguments from probability. Other sophists included Protagoras (the father of debate), Theodorus of Byzantium (who studied figures of speech such as puns), and Prodicus of Ceos (an early expert in the study of words or *philology*).

Surely the greatest contributor to communication studies in the classical age was Aristotle (384–322 B.C.E.). He made the first attempt to develop a complete rhetoric that was philosophically compelling. In his book *Rhetoric,* he defined our study as "the faculty of discovering in the particular case what are the available means of persuasion." Thus, rhetoric was not a *practice* but a *field of study*—an advance that still gives us intellectual integrity as a distinct field. Though Aristotle did not write about all "canons of rhetoric," he became associated strongly with them because he discussed many of them in detail. These canons were five major categories that may be studied to help understand communication: *invention* (types and sources of ideas); *arrangement* (organization of ideas); *style* (use of words); *delivery* (use of voice and gesture); and *memory* (ability to recall passages and examples for utterance). When universities were founded during the Middle Ages, three primary subjects were studied: logic, rhetoric, and grammar. Remnants of this tradition can be seen today in the speech communication student's wearing of a silver tassel at graduation ceremonies to symbolize the study of "oratory" in the silver age.

The study of speech and hearing science also had its roots in ancient times. Plutarch, the Greek biographer, recounted that Demosthenes had a monotonous voice and stammered when he spoke. Under the guidance of an actor named Satyrus (the oldest known speech therapist?) Demosthenes improved his diction by practicing a number of drills including speaking with pebbles in his mouth. Though the deaf were routinely put to death in ancient Rome and Greece, during the Middle Ages, speech and hearing science was pursued as a sacred duty. In the seventh century, when Bishop St. John of Beverly was successful in teaching a deaf-mute to speak, the Roman Catholic Church promptly declared it a miracle. Later, developing a code of charitable deeds, the Church promoted compassion for handicapped people in general, but it also unknowingly declared speech and hearing science not a profession, but an act of charity.

Journalism and mass communication professions also began in the classical period. At the order of Julius Caesar, the world's first "newspaper" *Acta Diurna* (*Daily Events*) was published in Rome during the first century B.C.E. In reality, the newspapers were little more than bulletins that were duplicated by hand and posted in the Forum, but large numbers of people made a daily routine of reading them. It would not be until the seventh and eighth centuries that the world's first printed newspapers would appear in Peking. The method of printing employed wood blocks—a time-consuming method since blocks were prepared individually for each issue and then discarded. Since the government controlled reporting the news, only a very limited form of journalism appears to have been practiced. When movable mitred type was developed in Europe during the fourteenth century, widespread and rapid spread of the news became possible and journalism emerged as a serious profession.

International Communication Association

Founded in 1949 as the National Society for the Study of Communication, the name was changed to the International Communication Association (ICA) in the mid-1960s. This organization encourages participation from all branches of communication (except for speech and hearing science), drawing especially strong links between those studying mass communication and those studying interpersonal communication. Every three years the annual convention is held outside the United States. It publishes three major journals:

- *Journal of Communication* (founded 1951). From 1974 through 1991 ICA turned over editorship to the Annenberg School for Communication at the

University of Pennsylvania. Designed to promote the broad study of communication, it is oriented primarily toward studies of mass media, television, and popular culture.

- *Human Communication Research* (founded 1974). A premier outlet for research in communication theory with emphasis on quantitative studies.
- *Communication Theory* (founded 1991). Dedicated to essays on theoretic and metatheoretic developments in communication.

Starting in 1980, ICAs Division of Political Communication and its sister division in the American Political Science Association collaborated to produce a journal titled *Political Communication* (previously called *Political Communication and Persuasion*). ICA also sponsors the *Communication Yearbook,* containing commissioned essays and research papers.

American Speech-Language-Hearing Association

Though once part of the National Communication Association, the American Academy of Speech Correction was founded in 1926. The organization changed its name four times after 1926, settling on the American Speech-Language-Hearing Association (ASHA) in 1979. ASHA is best known for its certification programs for practitioners of speech correction and speech and hearing science. It also promotes research and scholarship through its publications:

- *Journal of Speech and Hearing Disorders* (founded 1936). Called the *Journal of Speech Disorders* until 1948, this journal features research and theoretic essays across the realm of speech and hearing science.
- *Journal of Speech and Hearing Research* (founded 1958). Dedicated to research, measurement, and applied work in speech and hearing science.
- *ASHA* (founded 1959). Focuses on professional speech and hearing research issues and the administration of the organization.
- *Language, Speech and Hearing Services in Schools* (founded 1970). Attention paid to issues of interest to speech and hearing specialists with emphasis on speech-handicapped children.
- *American Journal of Speech-Language Pathology* (founded 1991). Focuses on clinical practice issues for therapists.

From time to time, the association also publishes a *Monograph* series and *ASHA Reports,* containing proceedings from annual meetings.

Association for Education in Journalism and Mass Communication

This organization is the largest national professional organization in mass communication. Founded as the American Association of Teachers of Journalism in November 1912, it adopted its current name in 1982. In addition to its annual meetings that showcase research, the organization sponsors these journals:

- *Journalism & Mass Communication Quarterly* (founded 1924). Originally called *Journalism Bulletin,* then *Journalism Quarterly,* it features predominantly nonquantitative studies of journalism.

- *Journalism & Mass Communication Educator* (founded 1945). Originally called *Journalism Educator,* it focuses on educational issues and essays related to instruction.
- *Journalism & Mass Communication Monographs* (founded 1966). Originally called *Journalism Monographs,* it includes extended studies in mass communication issues and theory.
- *Mass Communication Review* (founded 1973). Studies the influence of mass communication on society.
- *Newspaper Research Journal* (founded 1979). Includes commentary and research related to print communication.
- *Public Relations Research Annual* (founded 1989). Includes reviews of special research topics in public relations.

Interest groups also publish materials that have nearly the full status of journals including *The Journalist,* the *International Communication Bulletin,* the *Journal of Public Relations Research,* and *Media Law Notes.*

Broadcast Education Association

Called the Association of Professional Broadcast Education for many years, the Broadcast Education Association held its first annual convention in 1954 and focuses its attention exclusively on electronic media and its effects. This group publishes these journals:

- *Journal of Broadcasting & Electronic Media* (founded 1956). Originally called the *Journal of Broadcasting,* it features essays and research on broadcasting with emphasis on showcasing quantitative research and applied commentaries.
- *Feedback* (founded 1959). Includes essays and news on broadcast education.

American Forensic Association

Founded in 1949 by a group of debate coaches and teachers of competitive forensics, the American Forensic Association (AFA) is dedicated to issues surrounding competitive forensics. Through 1963, AFA published the *Register,* a quarterly newsletter that included some research. The *Journal of the American Forensic Association* began in 1964 and is now called *Argumentation and Advocacy,* reflecting the expansion in content beyond the traditional arenas of competitive forensics. The organization sponsors national forensic events and promotes research through a program of competitively awarded grants.

Special Interest Organizations

Many organizations have specialized concerns. Some have their own publications and conferences, whereas others meet along with other professional organizations. Though a complete inventory would be inappropriate here, the most prominent of these groups appear in the following list (grouped by interest).

- Intercultural and International Communication: International Society for Intercultural Education Training and Research (publishes *International Journal of Intercultural Relations,* founded 1977); International and Intercultural

Communication Association (founded 1983); World Communication Association (publishes journal, *World Communication,* founded 1972); Pacific and Asian Communication Association (publishes journal, *Human Communication,* founded 1996).

- Women and Gender Issues in Communication: The Organization for Research on Women and Communication (publishes journal, *Women's Studies in Communication,* founded 1977); Women in Communication, Inc.; Organization for the Study of Communication, Language, and Gender (founded 1978, hosts annual convention).

- Forensics: National Forensic Association (publishes journal, *National Forensic Journal,* founded 1977); Cross Examination Debate Association (publishes an *Annual*); Delta Sigma Rho-Tau Kappa Alpha, Pi Kappa Delta, Phi Rho Phi (honor societies—all publish their own journals); International Forensic Association; National Forensic League (high school, publishes journal, *Journal-National Forensic League,* founded 1991).

- General Communication: Association of Communication Administrators (publishes *Journal of the Association for Communication Administration,* founded 1972); American Communication Association (hosts annual research conference, plans to publish a journal); Lambda Pi Eta (national communication honor society); International Listening Association (publishes *Journal of the International Listening Association,* founded 1987); Religious Speech Communication Association (publishes *Journal of Communication and Religion,* founded 1978).

- Rhetorical Studies: Rhetoric Society of America (publishes *Rhetoric Society Quarterly,* founded 1971); International Society for the History of Rhetoric; Kenneth Burke Society.

- General Semantics: The International Society for General Semantics (publishes *ETC: A Review of General Semantics,* founded 1943).

- Media Use in Education: Association for Educational Communication and Technology (publishes *Educational Technology Research and Development,* founded 1953).

- Business Communication: Association for Business Communication (publishes *Business Communication Quarterly,* founded 1969).

- Journalism and Telecommunications: Alpha Epsilon Rho, Sigma Delta Chi (honor societies); Public Relations Society of America; National Association of Broadcasters; American Newspaper Publishers Association; American Journalism Historians Association (publishes *American Journalism,* founded 1983).

- Public Relations: Public Relations Society of America (publishes *Public Relations Journal,* founded 1945); Foundation for Public Relations Research (publishes *Public Relations Review,* founded 1975).

Regional and Local Organizations

Every region and nearly every state has at least one organization representing the interests of that area and publishing at least one journal. Become familiar with the organization that is dominant in your area. It will help your study of research methods.

TABLE 1.5 Regional Research Journal Names

Regional Association	Original Title	Revised Title
Eastern Communication Association	Today's Speech (founded 1953)	Communication Quarterly
	Communication Research Reports (founded 1984)	
Central States Communication Association	Central States Speech Journal (founded 1949)	Communication Studies
Southern States Communication Association	Southern Speech Bulletin (founded 1935)	Southern Speech Journal
	Southern Speech Journal	Southern Speech Communication Journal
	Southern Speech Communication Journal	Southern Communication Journal
Western States Communication Association	Western Speech (founded 1937)	Western Journal of Speech Communication
	Western Journal of Speech Communication	Western States Communication Journal
	Communication Reports (founded 1988)	

Your instructor can give you information about joining your regional organization. All these organizations have student membership rates and agreements with other regional organizations to give complimentary copies of their publications to sustaining members of the other regional associations. These organizations often change the names of the journals they publish. Table 1.5 indicates the various name changes of the journals published by the regional organizations. Such information may be helpful when you start reading research and wonder why all those old copies of journals are missing (in reality, the journals simply changed names).

It is beyond the scope of this book to list all the state and local organizations in the field. Ask your instructor about them, though, since many—such as the California Speech Communication Association, the New York State Speech Communication Association, and the Tennessee Speech Communication Association—regularly publish research of more than local interest. Many schools and departments also publish their own outlets for scholarship. For example, the *Columbia Journalism Review* was established in 1962 by the Columbia University School of Journalism, the *Howard Journal of Communication* was inaugurated in 1988, the University of Iowa Center for Communication Study began publishing the *Journal of Communication Inquiry* in 1974, and Washburn University started the *Journal of Radio Studies* in 1992. The trend toward numbers of school-sponsored publications seems to be growing, not diminishing.

Organizations Outside the United States

Interest in communication studies and research has been blossoming outside the United States. Furthermore, the growth has been worldwide. Thus, students of today must think internationally when they consider research questions. The following groups and ones like them represent the tip of the iceberg for this very exciting development in our field: the Canadian Communication Association; the European Communication Association; the International Clinical Phonetics and Linguistics Association (which publishes *Clinical Linguistics & Phonetics*); the European Speech Communication Association (which publishes *Speech Communication*); the European Institute for Media Research Projects; the Center for Global Communications (Japan); the Nordic Documentation Center for Mass Communication Research (which publishes the *Nordicom Review of Nordic Research on Media & Communication*); the International Telecommunication Society (which publishes *Information Economics and Policy*); the Japan Center for Intercultural Communications; the Center for Languages and Intercultural Studies (Denmark).

With the rise of the Internet, so-called "electronic journals" (such as the *Electronic Journal of Communication*) have emerged as very real research publication options. Newly formed organizations have been able to use the information superhighway to create new journals and promote their research interests. So, we should expect growth in the lists of research sources available to help us answer questions. Fortunately, the Internet allows us to get at such information sources rapidly and inexpensively.

To get in touch with the communication associations mentioned here, you may wish to search the Internet. To help you, the URL addresses available at the time of this writing are included on the disk supplied with this book.

SUMMARY

Research is the systematic effort to secure answers to questions. Research questions deal with issues requiring reference to data and information. Research regularly invites examining past inquiry into the issue. Basic research is completed to learn about relationships among variables, regardless of any immediate commercial product or service. Applied research is completed to develop a product or solve an immediate practical problem. Yet, regardless of whether pure or applied research is involved, the methods of inquiry are identical. In 1968 the New Orleans Conference concluded that "research in speech-communication focuses on the ways in which messages link participants during interactions." Thus, communication research is a specialty that studies message-related behavior. Communication might be defined as "the process by which partici-

pants transact and assign meaning to messages." A message is the set of verbal and nonverbal cues communicators exchange. Verbal cues are the words people use in communication (as opposed to oral cues, which are spoken). Nonverbal cues are communication elements beyond the words themselves.

There are many challenges in communication studies. First, the challenge of breadth involves the large number of communication applications. Second, the multiple methods challenge means that communication researchers use both qualitative and quantitative methods. Qualitative methods of study use descriptions of observations expressed in predominantly non-numerical terms. Most qualitative research in our field tends to *describe or interpret* communication exchanges. Quantitative research methods are inquiries in which observations are expressed predominantly in numerical terms. Quantitative research tends to be *explanatory,* (especially when experiments are involved), or it attempts to use precise statistical models to achieve comprehensive understandings of human communication (as in survey studies and polls of public opinion). These methods often try to explain communication behavior by looking at processes that allow researchers to *predict* future behavior, frequently using models of causal processes. Thus, quantitative research usually attempts to answer questions about *many* people involved in an activity. Third, the scholarly rigor challenge means that research involves recognition of five key conditions: research is systematic (though unexpected results often emerge—the effect is called serendipity and refers to finding something of value while looking for something else); research is data driven; research is a sound argument (arguments in this context are claims advanced on the basis of reasoning from evidence); research is capable of replication; research is partial. Fourth, the personal challenge means that successful students of

research tend to consider the following issues: the need to think in an orderly way; the need to write clearly; the need to set aside personal prejudices in light of data; the need to stay organized and follow instructions; the need to know the reason for studying communication research methods (to learn to think rigorously and critically; to learn how to find answers to questions about communication; to acquire survival skills for reading and using the field's literature; to learn how to sort through research for an answer). Fifth, the ethical challenge means that researchers must abide by formal codes of conduct (including guaranteeing confidentiality, which is the requirement that all information gathered from individual subjects is secret), and must act with professional responsibility (by following accepted rules of conduct with thoroughness and attention to concerns of subjects). Sixth, the structure of the field challenge involves recognition that communication research is promoted by many organizations whose members often cross the barriers created by organizational frameworks at different schools.

TERMS FOR REVIEW

Research
Basic research
Applied research
Communication
Message
Verbal cues
Nonverbal cues
Qualitative methods
Historical-critical methods
Qualitative observational studies
Case studies and interpretive studies
Participant observation studies
Ethnomethodology

Discourse/conversational analysis
Creative studies
Quantitative methods
Survey methods
Descriptive or observational surveys
Content analysis
Opinion surveys
Experiment
Serendipity
Arguments
Confidentiality
Professional responsibility

CHAPTER 2

Communication Problem Statements and Hypotheses

A prudent question is one-half of wisdom.

–Francis Bacon

QUALITIES OF PROBLEM STATEMENTS
    Useful Problem Statements
    Criteria for Sound Problem
      Statements
    Constructing Problem Statements
USING HYPOTHESES
    Using Hypotheses to Test
      Explanations

Requirements of Hypotheses
Constructing Sound Hypotheses
Types of Hypotheses in Quantitative
    Studies
IDENTIFYING VARIABLES IN HYPOTHESES AND PROBLEMS
    Isolating Variables in Hypotheses
    Independent Variables
    Dependent Variables

BEFORE WE GET STARTED . . .

Students who study research methods for the first time tend to think that the hardest part of inquiry is carrying out a study. In fact, one of the hardest parts is finding the right question to ask and the right hypothesis to advance. Accordingly, this chapter explains problem statements and hypotheses and provides steps to guide you in developing your own.

QUALITIES OF PROBLEM STATEMENTS

problems isolated

problem statements
1. set limits on
relevant information
2. structure inquiry

The **problems** we investigate are the questions we expect to answer through research. Hence, selecting and wording problem statements are vital parts of the research craft. Inexperienced researchers sometimes do not recognize how important problem statements are—until they have gotten in over their heads. There are two reasons problem statements must be specified before studies are completed. First, they set limits on relevant information. They allow researchers to know what information to examine and what information to set aside. Second, clear purposes structure inquiry.

Problem statements invite certain methods and techniques. If problem statements suggest an experiment, the inquiry will be structured to provide careful control and clear manipulation of the variables. The question we ask guides us to the methods that are relevant to its proper answer. Of course, problem statements may be revised—usually involving fine-tuning the language or adding qualifiers—after some inquiry into the topic. Yet, a working problem statement should be constructed to get the process rolling.

Useful Problem Statements

It is important to pose problem statements that are possible to answer. Thus, there are two prerequisites for useful problem statements.

Problem Statements Must Be Within the Researcher's Capabilities

Let's be honest about it: many questions you care about cannot be answered by you now—or ever. Some questions cannot be answered unless you have the money or special skills that may not yet be yours. You may be interested in learning if the disintegration of the Soviet Union led to an increase in the number of "underground press" publications in the independent states. But if you do not speak Russian, you probably cannot complete such a study. Furthermore, you may not have a way to get access to formal collections of underground publications. Fundamentally, you must choose problem statements that are "do-able" given your resources and abilities.

questions must be within the researcher's competence

Problem Statements Must Be Narrow but Not Trivial

Perhaps the biggest difficulty with problem statements is that some are either too broad to answer or too limited to be significant. Students are often assigned the task of composing problem statements to investigate at a later time. Without thinking, some students propose such problems as, the causes of stuttering, the rise of public relations as a profession, ways to increase communication among spouses, and the speaking habits of American preachers. Writing a term paper or research article on such large topics is unrealistic. Similarly, a subject can be narrowed down to the point where its answer is trivial. Under the appropriate heading, "Brilliant Deductions," comedian Jay Leno (1991, pp. 1–7) reported on newspaper accounts of studies that seemed to ask trivial questions:

questions must be narrow but nontrivial

> With investigative techniques that rival Sherlock Holmes's, today's scientists are peeling back the layers of knowledge—arriving at undreamed-of discoveries. Take the following headlines for example . . .
>
> Smaller families require less food [Leno's comment: So that would mean bigger families require more food? I'm confused.]
>
> Farmers buy most farmland [Leno's comment: Gee, I wonder what they do with it?]
>
> Ability to swim may save children from drowning [Leno's comment: I guess we'll just have to use bigger weights.]
>
> Sewers are not good playgrounds [Leno's comment: Sounds like just another overprotective mom.]
>
> Americans are unlikely to give up eating during recession [Leno's comment: "We thought about it, but then we got hungry" department.]
>
> Jail crowding caused by increase in criminals, new study concludes [Leno's comment: Let's not jump to any conclusions.]

Some communication problem statements are so insulated that researchers may forget the importance of studying meaningful message-related behavior. For instance, one student attended presentations made by applicants for a university job:

> As one successful candidate described her research into male reactions at baby showers . . . [the student] says she couldn't help but think, "What the hell does this have to do with anything?" (Kiefer, 1992, p. 10)

Good research questions must avoid extremes of breadth and triviality.

CRITERIA FOR SOUND PROBLEM STATEMENTS

Proper phrasing of problems is required to make them useful. We will consider some criteria for worthwhile research problems.

unambiguous statements, usually in question form

1. *Problem statements must be stated unambiguously, usually as questions.* These problem statements have been found in published research articles:

   - Does the Intercultural Communication Workshop significantly improve the American participants' intercultural communication competence? (Hammer, 1984, p. 253)
   - What differences in motivation for attendance are there between [sic] infrequent, occasional, and frequent movie-goers? (Austin, 1986, pp. 117–188)

   Sometimes problems have "subproblems" that narrow the issues into increasingly compact units. In some articles, the research problem is phrased as a purpose statement. In other research pieces, the problem statement emerges near the end of the literature review as a summary claim to be tested. A problem statement may or may not be followed by a question mark.

must include two variables

variable defined

constant defined

2. *Except for simple descriptive studies, problem statements must include at least two variables.* Researchers try to relate one variable to another. The term "variable" has a very special meaning in research. A **variable** is a symbol to which numbers may be assigned. This statement sounds as though it is restricted to quantitative studies, but it is not. The following question has clear variables in it: Has the number of threat appeals declined in American preaching from 1900 to 1990? To answer this question, we might survey manuscripts of preachers of each time period to count the number of such appeals at each time frame. The use of threat appeals is a variable. It is capable of taking on two numbers—either preachers use them in sermons or they do not (100 percent or 0 percent use). Of course, the number of such threats is an obvious variable. The time frame, 1900 to 1990, also is a variable. The opposite of a variable is a constant. A **constant** is a symbol to which only one number may be assigned. Many research questions ask about relationships between some variables while holding others constant. Look at this problem statement: Among upper-division college students, what is the relationship between communication apprehension and grades in public speaking? The class level of the college students is held constant, since it is restricted only to upper-division college students. You might sometimes hear researchers talk about the need to have control in their studies. What they mean is that they want to take variables that can be nuisances and make constants out of them.

Some problem statements involve such low-level questions that only one variable is involved, such as

- What proportion of their daily newspapers do people read?
- Which medium of advertising is most popular among small businesses?
- How many women chair communication departments in American colleges?

Though in the early stages of research such questions may be useful to characterize a process or field, they elicit rather low levels of information.

3. *Problem statements must be testable.* A testable problem must be capable of yielding more than one answer. Yet sometimes researchers ask questions that have only one answer. Look at these examples from the work of pupils and some established scholars:

problems must be testable

Example	**Deficiency**
How can politicians sell themselves to the public?	The example asks about a logical possibility— what *can* politicians do? Future options are nearly endless and there is no way to find an appeal that is *not possible* in the future.
Is there a pattern to the ways people watch television?	The example is answerable only by saying "yes." Anything forms a pattern, even if the regularity is random. The question answers itself by its own construction.
Do charismatic leaders increase group productivity?	This example cannot be answered because notions of "charismatic leaders" and "productivity" may be so broad that they cannot be pinned down. The problem is not in testable language.

4. *Problem statements must not advance value judgments.* Research can reveal whether computerized therapy reduces stuttering in children. But it cannot tell if computerized therapy should be used for stutterers. That choice requires moving beyond research and evaluating pragmatic choices. Research questions, therefore, may not substitute value judgments for appeals to facts, as in the following attempts: Is public speaking training better at reducing communication apprehension than counseling therapy? Should trials be videotaped? Is it a bad idea for newspapers to use unnamed sources for news reports?

problems make no value judgments

5. *Problem statements must be clear grammatical statements.* In the fever of enthusiasm, some scholars may compose incomplete or ungrammatical problem statements that are inevitably unclear. By expressing problem statements with great clarity, it is possible to promote thoughtful research that gets the job done efficiently. Using nonstandard grammar can also cause misunderstandings. A student turned in this problem statement: "Does humor make a speech more persuasive?" In standard English one cannot say *more* without following it with a *than*. Anything less than this form is a sentence fragment. *More* than what? one might ask. More than nothing? More than it once was? More than messages using other types of appeals? Indeed, all comparative forms (such as higher, lower, less, and fewer) require *than* to complete the sentence. It is wise to use standard grammar if problem statements are to be capable of standing on their own and guiding research.

must be grammatical

SPECIAL DISCUSSION 2·1
What Problem Statements Are Not

Though we may find some useful standards for research questions, it is also a good idea to know what are *not* useful research questions. The types of pseudo-problem statements may trick us into spending our time on them when, in fact, they may not be worth our time.

1. Questions asking for obvious yes or no answers (after Leedy, 1989, p. 49). It is not worthwhile to ask: "Do communication classes affect the skills of students?" Any stimulus has some kind of effect—even if it is an insignificant one. The answer may be trivial, such as: "Yes, the classes affect students very little."

2. Questions asking about applying a statistical tool (after Leedy, 1989, p. 48). These questions confuse the method of answering the question with the research questions themselves. Problem questions should ask for relationships, not statistical methods.

3. Questions proposing personal learning goals (after Leedy, 1989, p. 47–48). In fact, personal references have no role in productive research questions. The following example is inappropriate: "The purpose of this study is to learn ways advertisers sell products." Purpose statements do not "learn" anything. The research question should get to the point and ask about relationships.

4. Questions that have already been competently studied (after Auer, 1959, p. 64). If the question has already been answered effectively, there is little reason to repeat the research.

5. Questions that cannot really be solved (after Auer, 1959, pp. 66–67). Whether because of the lack of resource materials or because the question deals with broad, philosophical issues that cannot be resolved, such questions are not suitable for research.

Constructing Problem Statements

format for phrasing problem questions

Once a meaningful problem issue has been found, composing a problem statement can be handled with relative ease. The following format can be used to construct worthwhile problem statements. The format involves filling in the blanks in the following question:

> What is the relationship between _____ and _____ ?

By substituting variables of interest for the blanks, many research questions can be composed. Of course, this format is just a starting point, since statements may require great modification to put them in their final form. Some problems involve more than two variables. Even so, all problems ask about relationships between variables, and useful problems may be found in clear formal statements. Pupils sometimes advance first drafts of problem statements that are sentence fragments (little more than topic titles). Yet, useful problems can be developed through thoughtful revisions as in these examples:

First Draft Example	**Revised Example**
(from a student of mass communication) "The image of girls in children's programming"	"What is the relationship between the frequency of girls as characters in children's programming and their portrayal in submissive or dominant roles?"
(from a student of interpersonal communication) "Self disclosure and relationship development"	"What is the relationship between the amount of self disclosure among romantic partners and their level of communication satisfaction?"
(from a student of speech and hearing science) "Adult aphasia and therapy"	"What is the relationship between the use of group or individual therapy for adult aphasic patients and their use of correct initiation and response to questions?"

Sometimes problem statements are overwritten. Difficulties emerge when problem statements include motives or explanations of observations, as in the following example: "In an effort to avoid potential charges of sexual harassment, do male managers avoid socially oriented interpersonal communication episodes with female employees?" The introductory phrase is not a meaningful part of the problem statement, but a possible *interpretation* of results. Eventually the question became, "Do male managers in complex organizations report fewer socially oriented interpersonal communication episodes with female employees than with male employees?"

problems should exclude interpretation of results

Now that we have noticed that problem statements play a vital role in research, it is obvious that each area in our field makes great use of them. Table 2.1 shows examples of the sorts of research questions we might probe. Both qualitative and quantitative research efforts require full problem statements to guide efforts. It is not surprising that questions such as those listed might be asked regardless of research. You should look at the list of sample questions to see if any stimulate your interest or give you some ideas for directions you may wish to take on your own.

USING HYPOTHESES

Whereas problem statements ask about relationships, hypotheses suggest direct declarative answers. A **hypothesis** is "an expectation about events based on generalizations of the assumed relationship between variables" (Tuckman, 1978, p. 27). Here is an analogy that might explain how research is completed (after Auer, 1959, p. 72–73). Suppose you were a detective solving a murder. Before you answered the question, "Who killed Mr. Body?" with a formal hypothesis, you might explore several tentative **working hypotheses:** Colonel Mustard did it in the ballroom with the candlestick; Mrs. White did it with the revolver in the kitchen; Professor Plum did it with the rope in the library. Each working hypothesis could by tested against available information. Then you could eliminate each working hypothesis until one reasonable explanation emerged. You might finally conclude that Mr. Green did it in the bedroom with the knife. This hypothesis could be used as a formal criminal charge against Mr. Green.

hypothesis defined

working hypotheses as tentative answers

You may have heard that a hypothesis is an "educated guess." Unfortunately, most people using that definition place emphasis on the word *guess* rather than on the

TABLE 2.1 Examples of Problem Statements in Communication Research

Qualitative Research	Quantitative Research
Speech Communication	

Qualitative Research	Quantitative Research
In what ways have studies of the use of facial expressions changed since 1600 through 1996? What methods of speech preparation were used in the Lincoln-Douglas debates? What communication training areas were most prominent for the founders of the American Society for Training and Development?	What is the relationship between the use of facial displays of interest and interpersonal attraction? What is the impact of heckling of a speaker on audience sympathy for the speaker? Do managers who use responsive listening behaviors with subordinates report greater communication satisfaction than other managers?

Speech and Hearing Science

Qualitative Research	Quantitative Research
What were the major sources of influence on the development of the modern phonetic alphabet? What events led to the founding of the American Speech-Language-Hearing Association's certification processes for educational institutions? What trends in the role for speech therapists in the treatment of brain injured patients have taken place from 1925 through 1996?	What is the relationship between the use of visualization therapy and traditional drills on reduction of stuttering in adults? Do speech handicapped school children report lower self-esteem than other children? What is the relationship between timing of therapy for aphasic patients and their levels of phonological skill following therapy?

Mass Communication

Qualitative Research	Quantitative Research
What changes in public funding have contributed significantly to the rise of the educational use of television? What major justifications have been used by the Federal Communications Commission to deny license renewals to radio and television stations? What is the relationship between the establishment of ethics codes for public relations professionals and the rise of public relations as an academic discipline?	What is the relationship between the use of satellite television in developing nations and changes in literacy rates? What is the relationship between the amount of television watched by adults and the level of anxiety about personal safety? Do saturation advertising campaigns on television significantly increase product name recognition more than saturation advertising campaigns using newspapers?

Special Application Areas

Qualitative Research	Quantitative Research
What phases were important to the development of communication education in the Western regions of the United States from 1880 through 1940? What was the role of oral interpretation of literature in the practice of elocution of Dr. James Rush? What conditions in education led to the development and spread of tournament debating in America?	What is the relationship between the use of videotaped speeches in public speaking classes and perceptions of speaker delivery? What is the relationship between the size of oral interpretation programs in U.S. universities and the number of ethnic minority students involved in the activity? What is the relationship between the sex composition of debate teams and their win/loss records?

word *educated.* In fact, a hypothesis takes a general expectation—perhaps from a fully developed theory—and predicts what would be expected in the research project's new application. Furthermore, a hypothesis must have some kind of a rationale provided for it. There is a lot more education than guesswork in hypotheses.

      Some experts claim that hypotheses are the working tools of theory. They recognize that theorists apply their theories by developing hypotheses based on them (Giere, 1979, pp. 69–70). Though many hypotheses are based directly on applications of formal theories, some are not. Sometimes informal thinking is used to develop initial hypotheses.[1]

hypotheses are more than "educated guesses"

hypotheses often are working tools of theory

Using Hypotheses to Test Explanations

Although a formal presentation of the role of logic in using hypotheses to test theories is beyond the scope of this book, a few basics can be shared. Hypotheses allow us to contrast one theory against another by reasoning with tools of formal logic. A theory explains how concepts or constructs are related to each other. A hypothesis relates the theory to specific observations of variables. In logic, the structure that permits us to examine the soundness of "if . . . then" statements is called the "conditional syllogism." A **conditional syllogism** is a formal logical system in which the major premise makes an "if-then" statement. In fact, when applied to the logic of hypothesis testing, the major premise of a conditional syllogism may state that if a theory is true, then a hypothesis derived from it will be supported by data. The conditional syllogism takes one of two valid forms:

hypotheses are used to examine theories in conditional syllogisms

Major Premise	If the theory is true, then the hypothesis will be supported by data.	**MP:** If the theory is true, then the hypothesis will be supported by data.
Minor Premise	The theory is true.	**mp:** The hypothesis is not supported by data.
Conclusion	(Therefore) the hypothesis is supported by data.	**C:** (Therefore) the theory is not true.

Researchers test hypotheses by gathering data to see if either of these two valid forms appears in fact.[2] Though both are valid, the first one is fairly rare in practice. If you know a theory is true, why would you need to test hypotheses derived from it? Researchers with supported hypotheses probably want to know if the underlying theories are tenable, not the other way around. The second example is very interesting since it helps researchers test whether a theory is bogus. In this way, hypotheses let

---

[1] There is controversy regarding whether all hypotheses are applications of theories. Ray and Ravizza (1988) state that hypotheses are "developed in relation to an explicit or implicit theory" (p. 370). Similarly, the authors of the *Longman Dictionary of Psychology* (1984) believe that all hypotheses are "based on theory" (p. 361). Yet, others think that hypotheses sometimes come from very casual speculation (Mason & Bramble, 1989, p. 72). The second view seems most typical of the facts and it is endorsed here.

[2] The first example is a valid form called *modus ponens,* which is the method of affirming (from the Latin *ponere* which means "to affirm"). The second is called *modus tollens,* which is the method of denial (from the Latin *tollere* which means "to deny").

hypotheses let researchers examine and disprove unsound theories

researchers get evidence to falsify theories if they are untrue. Thus, hypotheses can help test theories by determining when they need to be rejected in light of the facts. Logically, it does not work the other way around. We do not use hypotheses to prove a theory is true—we use hypotheses to find out if the theory has or has not survived one additional test. So, when we say that research is sound and logical argument, we *do not* mean that researchers are in the business of *proving* their favorite theories. If you hear someone say that they are trying to "prove" a theory, you know they got the concept a trifle confused.

Reasoning from hypotheses often involves comparing different theoretic expectations and eliminating options. Arthur Stinchcombe (1968, p. 22) explained,

> The basic logical process of science is the elimination of alternative theories (both those we know and those we do not) by investigating as many of the empirical consequences of each theory as is practical, always trying for the greatest possible variety in the implications tested.

hypotheses used to eliminate alternative theories

Since hypotheses allow us to eliminate alternative explanations, Stinchcombe suggested the desirability of pitting the predictions of one theory against another in "crucial experiments." Though there is some difficulty in doing so, the idea that we make progress by attempting to eliminate unacceptable theories by testing hypotheses remains central in our studies.

Requirements of Hypotheses

hypothesis requirements:

To have worthwhile research hypotheses, scholars must meet several obligations, including the following:

1. state relationship between variables

1. *Hypotheses must state relationships between variables.* Hypotheses make statements or predictions. They are not simple statements of definitions. It is not a hypothesis to state: "Intercultural communicators speak with different cultural influences." Similarly, the statement "Intercultural communicators speak differently" is not a hypothesis. "Speak differently" is not a variable. What does it mean? Speaking rapidly? Speaking with an accent? Speaking with great reserve? We do not know.

   Sometimes hypotheses appear that really are just circular predictions about one variable. For instance, one student submitted a hypothesis that "Stutterers will exhibit greater disfluencies than nonstutterers." Though different words are used, the hypothesis actually has only one variable. Stutterers are identified because of their disfluencies. To predict that they have such disfluencies is circular—actually a definition. Another hypothesis took the form "The more media literacy instruction students receive, the more instructional information students will report knowing about media literacy." The more information you hear, the more information you hear. Such matters really are what researchers call "manipulation checks," not substantive research hypotheses. Such hypotheses do not advance our understanding very much.

2. consistent with literature

2. *Hypotheses must be consistent with what is known in the literature.* Hypotheses often are derived directly from theories. Hence, hypotheses should be rooted in past knowledge. If past research has shown that the amount of television violence

has been increasing, it would not be consistent to advance a hypothesis predicting that the amount of violence in prime-time television has been decreasing.

3. *Hypotheses must be testable.* Though powerful, research methods cannot deal with matters beyond observations that can be made in this life. Consider this "wannabe" hypothesis: "Public speaking instruction improves self-confidence better than oral interpretation instruction." This hypothesis asks the researcher to make a personal value judgment. One could advance a testable hypothesis by stating the issue as: "Public speaking instruction increases self-confidence more than oral interpretation instruction." Research questions must deal with matters that can be resolved by examining information. Of course, hypotheses can deal with evaluations people make. Researchers frequently study attitudes and values. But in these cases, the hypotheses still are matters that can be tested by gathering specific information.

4. *Hypotheses must be clear, grammatical, and unambiguous declarative sentences.* Since a hypothesis answers a research question, we expect it to be a crisp declarative statement. Declarative statements are sentences that make claims, rather than ask questions, give commands, or express wishes. Even so, you might be surprised at the number of beginning research students who compose hypotheses that are not full declarative sentences. Table 2.2 provides a sample of such hypotheses submitted to the author by students. In addition to the examples, you can see a brief statement of the flaw in the hypothesis.

> **3. testable**
>
> **—hypotheses may deal with attitudes and values as variables**
>
> **4. clear, grammatical, and unambiguous declarative sentences**

Constructing Sound Hypotheses

After—and *only* after—you have developed a worthwhile problem question, you can begin to think about the methods that might be most appropriate to help answer it. Indeed, by the time you construct hypotheses, it is a good idea to have a rough notion of the research methods you wish to use. Sometimes researchers will compare two groups to look for differences (as in typical experiments and some surveys). Sometimes researchers will look for associations and simple relationships. Thus, since hypotheses are potential answers to research questions, they should be stated in words that are related to the methods that will be later employed.[3]

> **researchers should think ahead to study methods when phrasing hypotheses**

Two formats can help you compose and develop worthy hypotheses. The first predicts that a difference will be observed between groups and has the following form:

> **format of hypotheses predicting differences**

> Subjects {or people} who are
>> high in {or low in, characterized as, exposed to, etc.}
>>> (*insert favorite input variable of interest*)
>> will have higher {or more, or greater, or less}
>>> (*insert favorite output variable of interest*)
>>>> than others {or others who are high in, or low in, or not characterized as, not exposed to, etc.}
>>>>> (*insert favorite input variable of interest*).

---

[3] When writing research proposals many researchers find it helpful to pose a research question, outline a study method to answer the research question (as put forth in the problem statement), and then return to complete their literature reviews and compose formal hypotheses. Of course, they often find they must revise their first thoughts in light of their reading, but that's no big deal.

TABLE 2.2 Hypothesis Phrasing Difficulties

Submitted Hypotheses	Comment
Stuttering rate and age of onset.	This hypothesis is not even a sentence!
A journalism student earns more money after graduation than their peers.	This statement is an insult to grammar. "A journalism student" is predicted to differ from "*their* peers." Singular or plural pronouns are required for grammatical construction.
People who own computers have less communication satisfaction with their wives.	The construction has two flaws. (1) Language is vague, though some specific meaning must be intended. People who own computers could be male or female, single or married. But this writer has assumed that people who own computers are husbands. (2) The sentence is a fragment. In English, one cannot use the word "less" without the word "than" appearing in the sentence somewhere else. As stated, the sentence leaves us hanging. It states that computer owners have "less communication satisfaction with their wives" than what? than whom? We do not know because the sentence is not complete.
Communication teachers who grade on the curve increase difficulties for students.	The hypothesis is ambiguous. "Difficulties" could mean almost anything. Specific observable difficulties must be identified instead of the current vagueness.
Communicators in Latino families differ from communicators in Anglo families.	The ambiguity of this hypothesis makes it unacceptable and untestable. "Differ" is not a variable. Thus, this hypothesis does not have two variables put into relationship. Furthermore, the form of the difference is hopelessly vague.
Because women have been stereotyped, they are not credible television news broadcasters.	This double-barreled statement did not ask about a relationship, but asked us to *explain* a relationship when it is found to exist. It would not test the hypothesis if one found that women newscasters in the major television markets *were not* perceived as lowly credible sources. Neither would it test the hypothesis if women newscasters *were* perceived as lowly credible sources (only the reasons are asked).

This format is found in such hypotheses as the following:

> Subjects who are high in self-esteem will have greater attitude change in response to a persuasive message than others who are low in self-esteem.

format for predicting simple relationships

A second way to phrase hypotheses involves statements of simple relationships and commonly has the following form:

> There will be a direct {or positive, or negative, or inverse, or curvilinear} relationship
> between (*insert favorite first variable of interest*)
> and (*insert favorite second variable of interest*).
>
> or
>
> As (*insert favorite first variable of interest*)
> increases {or decreases, etc.}
> the (*insert favorite second variable of interest*)
> decreases {or increases, etc.}.

Such a hypothesis could be phrased as follows:

As the amount of eye contact used by speakers increases, the credibility ratings of the speakers increase.

One also could phrase this statement in a slightly different form:

There will be a direct relationship between the amount of eye contact used by speakers and credibility ratings.

Though you probably will need to revise your final wording somewhat, these patterns are simple ways for you to begin constructing your own hypotheses.

Types of Hypotheses in Quantitative Studies

In quantitative research, we often subdivide hypotheses into two forms: material hypotheses and null hypotheses. Sometimes called the *research hypothesis* or just *the hypothesis,* the material hypothesis states what the researcher predicts will be found by gathering data. There are two forms of research hypotheses to consider.

distinguishing material hypotheses

Nondirectional material hypotheses simply state that there will be some kind of relationship between variables (they are sometimes called "two-tailed" hypotheses because of the way statistics are used to test them). Suppose, for example, that we wished to compare the amount of television watched by children from Protestant and Catholic homes. A nondirectional hypothesis would predict the existence of a difference, but would not specify which children watched the most television. This nondirectional hypothesis can be abbreviated by using the Greek letter mu (μ) to represent the population average of each group. We could use μ_1 to represent the average amount of TV viewing by children in Protestant homes, μ_2 for the average TV viewing by children in Catholic homes. The nondirectional research hypothesis would appear as

nondirectional hypotheses

$$H_1: \mu_1 \neq \mu_2.$$

Directional material hypotheses state the form of the differences. Suppose a researcher suspected that Protestant children watch more television than Catholic children. The directional hypothesis would appear as

directional hypotheses

$$H_1: \mu_1 > \mu_2.$$

The symbol $>$ means "greater than" and the symbol $<$ means "less than."[4] This hypothesis predicts the direction of the differences.

As the name suggests—null, nil, *nada*—a **null hypothesis** states that there is no relationship between variables. Using the same abbreviations as previously employed, the null hypothesis would be represented as

null hypotheses

$$H_1: \mu_1 = \mu_2.$$

When dealing with directional hypotheses, researchers often expand the null hypothesis to include all results that would oppose the material hypothesis. Thus, if the

---

[4] In English grammar, of course, one can say "less than" only when the things identified *cannot* be counted. If things can be put in numerical terms, one grammatically is required to say "fewer than." Thus, the signs at the supermarket *should* say "Use the Express Lane if you have 10 or *fewer* items"—but they don't. Yet, we still say "less than" when translating the term $<$, recognizing that it is not English.

research hypothesis is: H_1: $\mu_1 > \mu_2$, the null hypothesis might be expanded to state H_1: $\mu_1 \leq \mu_2$.

used as a statistical hypothesis

What good is such a hypothesis for researchers? Null hypotheses are used in quantitative research as statistical hypotheses. Researchers try to find data that reject null hypotheses. In a nutshell, here is the logic behind it. Testing our material hypothesis requires that we present a case for it. But any data we find could be dismissed by our opponents as atypical. They may say, "You haven't found a *relationship* with your samples; in fact, if you kept sampling you would find that there are no differences at all." So, we reason the other way around. We pretend—just for the sake of argument—that the null hypothesis is true. Then we ask if data we have gathered are so inconsistent with the world of the null hypothesis that it is improbable that the data could be found if the null hypothesis were true. Thus, researchers support research hypotheses by rejecting null hypotheses as improbable.

one argues for material hypotheses by rejecting null hypotheses

null hypotheses like the presumption of innocence in criminal trials

So, by a process of elimination we can conclude that the research hypothesis is tenable. This language may seem a bit strange because of all the negative words we have to use. But the situation is much like the presumption of innocence we have in our court system (Erickson & Nosanchuck, 1977, pp. 145–149). We start with a null hypothesis that the defendant is not guilty. Then the prosecution tries to show that facts make it unlikely that the defendant has acted like someone who is not guilty. People are not found innocent—there is no way to get positive evidence to show that evil acts have not occurred. Instead, a defendant is found either "guilty" or "not guilty" of the specific charges. As you can see, we use null hypotheses all the time. Technically, we are not allowed to say that a null hypothesis is "accepted." You can think it, but don't say it or write it. We cannot logically accept a statement without evidence, but the null hypothesis claims there is no evidence of anything to begin with. So, if we do not reject the null hypothesis, we can only say that we "failed to reject the null hypothesis." Similarly, we never can claim to "prove" or "confirm" a research hypothesis. Another future study might destroy our research hypothesis. The strongest statements we are allowed to make are that research hypotheses are "supported" or "found tenable." The hypothesis actually only survived one more test—so these claims are fairly strong ones to make. If you read an article where the researcher oversteps these bounds, you know that the article has at least one flaw and may contain other mistakes as well.

cannot "accept a null", but can "fail to reject"

IDENTIFYING VARIABLES IN HYPOTHESES AND PROBLEMS

Hypotheses put variables into relationship with each other. They identify the roles of variables and their functions in research.

Isolating Variables in Hypotheses

distinguishing variables from levels of variables

When looking at hypotheses, it is important to identify the chief variables involved. Yet, students sometimes confuse the *number* of variables in the hypothesis with the *levels* of a variable. For instance, how many variables are there in this hypothesis?

H_1: People with high self-esteem read newspapers more often than people with low self-esteem.

If you think that there are two variables, self-esteem and amount of newspaper reading, you are correct. Some look at this example and see three variables: high self-esteem, low self-esteem, and amount of newspaper reading. But, high and low self-esteem are merely *levels* or degrees of the same variable, self-esteem. It is important not to confuse levels of a variable with a completely new variable. How many variables are in this hypothesis?

H_1: Women are persuasive sources.

Assuming that persuasiveness is measured on a standard attitude scale, there is no second variable in the hypothesis. Sampling only women holds constant the potential variable of sex. We suspect that the author really wanted to know if women and men differed in their persuasiveness. But the author didn't say so. It is as important to spot the difference between a constant (a control) and a true variable in a hypothesis as it is to resist confusing levels of variables for variables themselves.

distinguishing variables from constants

Hypotheses use variables to make predictions. Some variables are used to start predictions and others are predicted effects. Examining hypotheses lets us identify the role of variables. There are two major variable types, independent and dependent.

Independent Variables

Independent variables predict outcomes (dependent variables) posited in hypotheses. These variables are easy to remember. The *in*dependent variables are the same as *in*put variables. These independent variables are starting points for making predictions.

independent variables identified

Sometimes researchers refer to **moderator variables.** Moderators are variables that mediate the independent variable's prediction of the dependent variable. In reality, moderator variables are just additional independent variables that help predict the effects of chief independent variables. For instance, look at the following hypothesis:

moderator variables identified

H_1: Female communication students who study research methods pursue graduate studies more than male communication students who study research methods and female communication students who do not study research methods.

The independent variable in this study is whether one takes research methods courses. A moderator variable has been added: student sex. Moderator variables permit subtle relationships to be explored.

Dependent Variables

Dependent variables are variables whose values or activities are presumed to be conditioned on the independent variable in the hypothesis. The dependent variable is the consequent, the *predicted* variable, and the *output* variable. If the hypothesis is tenable, changes will be seen in the dependent variable. Thus, in our research hypothesis, the dependent variable is the degree to which students pursue graduate studies.

dependent variables identified

It is important to identify independent (input) and dependent (output) variables by looking at a hypothesis. Yet, many students may have some initial difficulty with this skill. It may be useful to have some examples to work with as you develop your skills. Table 2.3 shows some hypotheses along with identification of independent and

---

TABLE 2.3 Hypotheses and Variable Identification

Hypothesis	Variable Identification
H: Anglo speakers will stand a further distance away from receivers than will Asian speakers.	independent variable: national background of speaker dependent variable: distance from receivers
H: Stuttering children will report higher levels of anxiety than nonstuttering children.	independent variable: stuttering level of children dependent variable: anxiety
H: The voting behavior of lowly educated people exposed to negative political campaign advertisements will be affected more than will the voting behavior of highly educated people exposed to positive political campaign advertisements.	independent variables: (1) type of political campaign advertisement; and (2) level of voter intelligence (NOTE: depending on the rationale, level of voting behavior could be identified as a moderator variable) dependent variable: voting behavior
H: Regardless of level of ego-involvement, newspaper readers with sophisticated listening skills will have greater critical thinking ability than newspaper readers with unsophisticated listening skills.	independent variable: sophistication level of listening skills dependent variable: critical thinking ability (ego-involvement is a constant, not a variable)
H: National politicians will use more metaphorical language and more examples of ambiguity than will local politicians.	independent variable: type of politician (national or local) dependent variables: amount of metaphorical language and number of examples of ambiguity
H: Students who are high in communication apprehension will show higher levels of communication competence when presented with teachers using nondirective styles than will highly communication apprehensive students exposed to teachers using directive styles.	independent variable: type of style used by teachers dependent variable: communication competence (high communication apprehension is a constant, not a variable)
H: Computer literate people will initiate fewer conversations than will computer illiterate people.	independent variable: level of computer literacy dependent variable: amount of initiation of conversations

---

dependent variables. You should cover the right side of the table to see if you can identify the independent and dependent variables accurately. After time you will find it easy to identify these two forms of variables.

SUMMARY

Problems we investigate are the questions we expect to answer through research. There are two reasons that purpose statements must be specified in advance of completing studies. First, purpose statements set limits on relevant information. Second, clear purposes structure inquiry. Research questions invite certain methods and techniques. Useful problem statements must satisfy two prerequisites: (1) problem statements must be within the researcher's capabilities; (2) problem statements must be narrow but not trivial. Criteria for phrasing worthwhile research problems include five requirements: First, problem statements must be stated unambiguously, usually as questions. Second, except for simple descriptive studies, problem statements must include at least two variables. A variable is a symbol to which numbers may be assigned. The opposite of a variable is a constant. A constant is a symbol to which only one number may be assigned. To control variables, researchers take variables that can be nuisances and make constants out of them. Third, problem statements must be testable. Fourth, problem statements must not advance value judgments. Fifth, problem statements must be clear grammatical statements.

A hypothesis is "an expectation about events based on generalizations of the assumed relationship between variables." Though sometimes called an "educated guess," a hypothesis takes a general expectation—perhaps from a fully developed theory—and predicts what would be expected in the research project's new application. Furthermore, a hypothesis must have a rationale provided for it. Hypotheses are the working tools of theory. Hypotheses allow us to contrast one theory against another by reasoning with tools of formal logic. A conditional syllogism is a formal logical system in which the major premise makes an "if-then" statement. When applied to the logic of hypothesis testing, a conditional syllogism's major premise states that if a theory is true, then a hypothesis derived from it will be supported by data. Researchers test hypotheses by gathering data to see if valid forms of the conditional syllogism appear. Hypotheses may compare different theoretic expectations to eliminate options. Pitting one theory's prediction against another is called conducting "crucial experiments."

Worthwhile research hypotheses must (1) state relationships between variables, (2) be consistent with what is known in the literature, (3) be testable, (4) be clear, grammatical, and unambiguous, usually in the form of a declarative sentence. There are two generic ways to phrase hypotheses. The first predicts that a difference will be observed. A second way to phrase hypotheses involves statements of simple relationships. In quantitative research, we often subdivide hypotheses into two forms: material hypotheses and null hypotheses. First, the material hypothesis states what the researcher wishes to support by gathering data. There are two forms of material or research hypotheses to consider: (1) Nondirectional material hypotheses state simply that there will be *some kind* of relationship between variables (they sometimes are called "two-tailed" hypotheses because of the way statistics are used to test them); (2) directional material hypotheses state the form of the differences. Second, the null hypothesis states that there is no relationship between variables. The null hypothesis is used in quantitative research as a statistical hypothesis and actually is the hypothesis that a researcher tries to get data to reject. Quantitative researchers start with assuming the truth of the null hypothesis (just for the sake of argument) and then ask if data that have been gathered are inconsistent with the world of the null hypothesis. If it is improbable that our data could be found if the null hypothesis were true, we conclude that it is unreasonable to continue presuming that the null hypothesis is true.

Hypotheses put variables into relationship with each other and identify their roles and functions in research. There are two major forms of variables. Independent variables predict the outcome (dependent variable) posited in the hypothesis. Moderator variables mediate the independent variable's prediction of the dependent variable. Dependent variables are variables whose values or activities are presumed to be conditioned upon (variables that are consequent to) the independent variable in the hypothesis.

TERMS FOR REVIEW

Problem
Variable
Constant
Hypothesis
Working hypothesis
Conditional syllogism

Nondirectional hypothesis
Directional hypothesis
Null hypothesis
Independent variable
Moderator variable
Dependent variable

Understanding Rudiments of Research Reasoning

CHAPTER 3

Conceptualizations in Communication Research

There is nothing so practical as a good theory.

–Kurt Lewin

DEVELOPING THEORETIC CONCEPTUALIZATIONS IN COMMUNICATION
    Is Communication "Scientific" Enough to Have Theories?
    Anatomy of Theories

Functions of Theory
Applications of Theory
DEVELOPING DEFINITIONS FOR CONCEPTS
    Using Conceptual Definitions
    Using Operational Definitions

BEFORE WE GET STARTED . . .

Research is guided by the conceptualizations scholars use. Theories play a central role in scholarship and give us ways to organize bodies of knowledge. Indeed, one purpose of research is to develop theoretic explanations for things. Yet, using concepts requires defining them so that they can be studied. Thus, this chapter explains what theories are, the forms of coherent definitions, and standards you can use to evaluate them.

DEVELOPING THEORETIC CONCEPTUALIZATIONS IN COMMUNICATION

importance of theory   Research attempts to find relationships and explain them. Theories are used to help us understand these relationships. Whether we are aware of it or not, most significant claims we make rely on theory-oriented statements. Moreover, formal and informal theories are sources of research hypotheses. In fact, theory construction is a purpose of all research, scholarship, and science. Some have made this goal central to research. Look at these typical statements about theory in research:

- Research is guided by theory and contributes to theory (Tucker, Weaver, & Berryman-Fink, 1981, p. 14).

- The basic aim of science is theory (Kerlinger, 1986, p. 8).
- We found the fundamental aim of science to be the development of explanatory conceptualizations, called *theories* (Mason & Bramble, 1989, p. 29).
- A researcher's aim . . . is *to generate theoretical explanations for observed patterns of human communication* (M. J. Smith, 1988, p. 10).

In general, research is a means to an end, not an end in itself. The goal of research is to develop theories and explanations. Thus, we should consider whether communication is scientific enough to have true theories, the anatomy of theories, and the roles communication theories have for us.

Is Communication "Scientific" Enough to Have Theories?

To decide whether communication can be approached as a science (or social science), it makes sense to define **science** and remove some myths about it. Then, we can ask if communication is a science (though you may have a good idea about the position taken here).

Prerequisites for Science

Science is as much a frame of mind as it is anything else. Stuart Chase (1954) described science as "a label for our attempts to find out how the universe works by means of careful observation rather than armchair speculation" (p. 110). Though this description is accurate, there are several competing views of science that you may have heard. Horace and Ava English, in their *Comprehensive Dictionary of Psychological and Psychoanalytical Terms* (1958), reviewed the major approaches along with comments about each one's usefulness, starting with

science as an attitude

meanings of science:

1. The study of natural phenomena by the methods of the physical and biological sciences (p. 479)

1. science as something done in science departments

The first view claims that science is what people in the natural sciences do. Yet, the definition excludes things properly included as sciences. English and English explained:

This usage, while common, arbitrarily excludes most investigations and systematizations of knowledge in the psychological and social disciplines. Such a division is not warranted either by historical development or by the contemporary state of affairs, and it gives to science in English a narrower connotation than that of related expressions in other European languages (pp. 479–480).

The word "science" comes from the Latin word *scientia,* which means "knowledge." Thus, it would seem that other systematic ways to obtain knowledge about the facts might bear some relationship to science. Yet, the first definition excludes them. A second definition of science holds that it is

2. Organized and systematic knowledge (p. 480)

2. science as any organized knowledge

Yet, many projects that do not reference data to check expectations (part of the scientific method) would be included in this definition's view. English and English criticized this definition as follows:

This usage, though occasionally useful, is as much too broad as the first is too narrow (p. 480).

SPECIAL DISCUSSION 3-1
Making Knowledge Claims in Research

Scholarship and research are not the only ways to answer questions and draw conclusions. In fact, sometimes reasonable actions are based on nonresearch methods. The most well-known nonscholarly methods include the following (after Peirce, 1955, esp. ch. 2):

- The method of **tenacity**, in which we claim to know something because we have always known it (the method of tenacity may be correct most of the time, but it is misguided when facts change and decisions need to be revised);
- The method of **authority**, in which we accept a claim because authority figures have accepted it (though this method leads people to correct conclusions most of the time, under some conditions, it may be flawed);
- The **a priori** (Latin for "from the earlier part") *method,* in which we claim knowledge before having any experience with it (thus, we believe a priori that "all men are created equal" without needing to gather data on the matter—this method usually leads to timeless conclusions that are beyond research);
- The method of **trial and error**, in which we claim knowledge after making repeated trials to eliminate unacceptable answers (eventually, persistent failures disprove so many alternatives that an answer will emerge—though trial and error provides very sure knowledge, "learning through experience" is a very slow and inefficient way to develop claims about things we know).

Research, on the other hand, makes claims by using the tools of scholarship and science, which involve two processes: making observations of things and using the tools of reasoning to evaluate different explanations of observations. There are two ways the research method may be used to help draw conclusions:

- Developing claims from reviews of literature uses documents such as past studies to help compose problem statements. Such a literature review permits us to draw research conclusions from research documents previously unrelated to each other. A variation in the research literature review argument is **meta-analysis,** which combines quantitative results from many studies to reveal the overall sizes of effects that exist among variables.
- Using the scientific approach to guide development of claims involves applying the scientific method. Though the scientific method has been described by different scholars as including various numbers of steps, at minimum the scientific method involves collecting data and establishing "a functional relationship among these data" (Bachrach, 1981, p. 4). Some others list as many as seven steps (Jones, 1973). The steps are not necessarily followed in order. In fact, most researchers find that they cycle back from one step to another. The important thing is that the scientific method forces scholars to stay close to the facts of a matter. We will suggest four steps to the scientific method:[1]

  1. Observing facts either casually or formally leading to developing a fundamental research question
  2. Developing a working hypothesis or theoretical solution to guide the research (though researchers may revise their ideas and develop formal explanations)
  3. Testing expectations against information
  4. Establishing a conclusion or functional relationship based on deciding whether the working hypothesis or theoretic solution is supported

In fact, any time researchers check expectations against information, they are applying the scientific method. Indeed, both quantitative and qualitative research can be completed by using the scientific method.

---

[1] This listing is based on the one provided by Auer (1959, p. 25) which, in turn, was based on the writing of John Dewey (1910).

A third view holds that science is the use of particular methods to develop knowledge (across subject fields).

> 3. A particular body of knowledge—for example, physics, physiology, psychology—distinguished by the special set of operations employed in gathering empirical facts and by a distinctive set of constructs employed in interpreting the data (p. 480).

3. science as the application of the scientific method

This definition tells us that a field becomes a science when it uses the scientific method. After time, as well, each field concentrates on some key concepts of its own to study. In our field, we have focused on such concepts as communication apprehension, speech and hearing disorders, and broadcast of messages through television and radio. Using the scientific method makes a field a science even before a great deal of information exists on it. For instance, we could ask when chemistry became a science instead of a magician's bag of illusions. Chemistry is certainly a science now. Yet, how many chemistry studies had to be completed before we recognized chemistry as a science worthy of the name? The question sounds a bit silly. The reason is that chemistry—as with all fields that qualify as sciences—became a science when the scientific method was used in research. The method to gather information defines a field as a science, not simply the results of applying the method. Thus, we can define **science** as a way of testing statements by systematic application of the scientific method.[2]

science defined

Is Communication a Science?

Since science has been defined as the use of the scientific method to gather information, we might ask if communication can be considered a science. It all depends on the method a researcher chooses to use. If a communication scholar relies on nonresearch methods of knowing about communication—tenacity, authority, *a priori* belief, and trial and error—then the scholar is not "doing science." If communication scholars rely on the method of aesthetics or art to explore communication (as is often done in oral interpretation of literature studies), then the inquiries would not be defined as science. On the other hand, if the scholar uses research methods to know things about communication, then communication is a science. All communication research states problems, sets criteria for permissible interpretation, and makes careful observations of communication transactions. Thus, using research methods in communication makes communication a scientific study area.

communication is a science if the scientific method is used to study it

To say that communication is a science if the methods of science are used to study it, however, should not be misinterpreted. We are only talking about the *study* of communication, not the *practice* of communication by artists and practitioners. The study of communication is a science if one chooses to use the scientific method to inquire into it. The practice of communication remains an art to be performed and refined.

yet the practice of communication is an art

---

[2] This statement is not a circular definition. The term *scientific method* has been defined here by the distinctive steps of the approach. There has been no reference back to science in the definition of *scientific method*. It should also be noticed that the definition does not use the term defined since the term *scientific method* is a single term that cannot be broken down into smaller units of *scientific* and *method* without also dissolving the meaning it has been given here.

SPECIAL DISCUSSION 3-2
Models, Laws, Rules and Metatheories

Theory construction has developed a language of its own. Though these terms often are mixed together, they are actually different things.

- **Model**   Though a model (such as a communication model) is often just a picture used to explain a concept, a model is actually an expression that not only states relationships but displays them. All mathematic statements (e.g., $E = mc^2$) and physical prototypes are models since they display relationships.

- **Law**   "A verbal statement, supported by such ample evidence as not to be open to doubt unless much further evidence is obtained, of the way events of a certain class consistently and uniformly occur" (English & English, 1958, p. 288). Of course, all laws have limits (e.g., the laws of falling bodies apply to objects in a vacuum) and communication laws often hit their boundaries vary rapidly.

- **Rule**   "A theory that explains a pattern of effects by referring to human intentions, reasons, or goals" (M. J. Smith, 1988, p. 354). Rules express patterns of expected activity, though changing intentions, reasons, or goals may make people occasionally appear inconsistent (people break rules on occasion, but the rules are a regularity nonetheless).

- **Metatheories**   Ways we think about theories are called "metatheories" to indicate notions beyond the theories themselves. These matters influence issues to explore, definitions, and designs in research. Some prominent metatheories include positivist/atomist views, phenomenology, general systems theory, and constructivism.

Anatomy of Theories

**"theory"
misinterpreted**

We had better get rid of a common misconception. Theories are not just wild ideas people have. When somebody tells us that he or she has a theory about something, it is usually just a bold, unsupported claim. Theories worthy of the name must meet certain obligations and standards. Theories allow us to organize and—if we do it right—understand communication phenomena. Kenneth Hoover (1979, p. 37) explained this role for theory:

> Science rests its claim to authority upon its firm basis in something called "reality." We occasionally described science as, simply, reality testing. Since everybody thinks they

[*sic*] know what reality is, science acquires a fundamental appeal. Yet the necessary partner of realism in science is that wholly imaginary phenomenon, theory. Without the many roles that theory plays, there would be no science (and, some would argue, there would be no understandable "reality" either).

It would help if we understood what a theory truly is and what its elements are.

Definition of a Theory

A **theory** is "a body of interrelated principles that explain or predict" (*Longman Dictionary of Psychology,* 1984, p. 744). Obviously, theories are not just wild ideas people have. A theory is a logical system that organizes and explains the facts. Though theories are often modified as they develop and reflect research, they are still composed of elements that have a fairly fixed form. Theories help answer research questions. Furthermore, their development and modification are objectives of research.

theory defined

Components of Theory

Suppose a theory ran over you in the street. What kind of description could you give? To provide details, you need to know its characteristics and features. All theories must have three characteristics: an abstract calculus, theoretic constructs, and rules of correspondence (after Deutsch & Krauss, 1964, ch. 1).

elements of a theory

An **abstract calculus** is simply the logical structure of relationships. The word "calculus" refers to any deductive system. What is a deductive system? A deductive system is a logical method in which conclusions are drawn from premises. Researchers often use the logical form called the "conditional syllogism," for example:

1. abstract calculus defined

> Major premise: If p, then q
> Minor premise: p
> Conclusion: (therefore,) q

The relationships in the theory are its abstract calculus. This example states that as one event occurs another event should also occur. The exact form of the relationships defines the nature of the theory. For instance, suppose we have a little theory with a principle stating that as a speaker's physical attractiveness increases, the speaker's persuasiveness also increases. The theory has this major premise

> Major premise: If a speaker's physical attractiveness increases, then the speaker's persuasiveness will increase.

To test the soundness of the theory, we could gather data to see if we could complete the rest of the argument. We might plan an experiment that has a persuasive message given by an attractive source (and for control purposes, an unattractive source as well). If the theory has any merit, the results of the experiment should be reflected in facts that are consistent with the logical conclusion that must follow from the premises. For instance,

> Major premise: If a speaker's physical attractiveness increases, then the speaker's persuasiveness will increase.

Minor premise: (An experiment is completed in which) a speaker's physical attractiveness increases.

Conclusion: (Therefore, the experimental results must show that) the speaker's persuasiveness increases.

If the facts do not support the conclusion that must logically follow, then no valid argument could be made for the theory.

The abstract calculus is just the relationship expressed in the statement, "if p, then q." The statement that as one increases, the other does, too, is the statement of relationship, regardless of the terms involved in the relationship. But, to have a theory we do need some specific terms. These terms are the second element of theories.

2. constructs defined

Theoretic constructs are the terms that we substitute into the abstract calculus of a theory. Specifically, **constructs** are "generalizations about observables according to some common property" (Deutsch & Krauss, 1964). Constructs are general terms that group many instances of activity together into meaningful units. But constructs are the generalizations, not the events themselves. For instance, self-esteem is a construct. So is source credibility. So is newspaper sensationalism. But nobody has ever seen your self-esteem. Nobody has ever seen your source credibility. Nobody can see your newspaper's sensationalism. These terms are used to describe a collection of variables that have been found. Though nobody has seen your self-esteem, there are behaviors—variables—that people have seen about you. People could say that you have been observed: (1) stating that you trust your own opinions; (2) setting high goals for yourself; and (3) stating that you believe you are competent in many ways. But people don't talk that way. Instead, these variables in your activity may be summarized by the useful general term "self-esteem." So, constructs are summary descriptions about collections of specific variables.

In the little theory we have been considering, two constructs have been identified: physical attractiveness and persuasiveness. These key terms cannot be seen. Instead, there are collections of variables that share attractiveness in common (such as measurable evaluations of personal appearance, style of dress, and ratings of personal beauty) and there are collections of variables that share persuasiveness as a common feature (such as variables of measurable attitude change, reported behavioral intentions to perform future activities, and changes in reported value systems). These key terms—constructs—are the matters related by the abstract calculus of a theory.

hypothetical constructs defined

Even though constructs are general terms, it is possible to get full definitions for them. You sometimes may hear of things called "**hypothetical constructs**" or concepts. These terms refer to constructs for which we cannot make related observations directly. Such things as cognitive consistency, motivational inertia, and individual needs, are examples of matters that have been axioms employed in some very interesting theories. They cannot be seen, but they can often be useful as starting assumptions to get us thinking in interesting ways.

3. rules of correspondence defined

Rules of Correspondence show how well the theory's constructs and abstract calculus can be applied to actual experience. They are used to apply theories. We occasionally hear people say that something "looks good in theory" but won't work in practice. But if a theory won't work in practice, it's a bad theory. It is a contradiction in terms to say that a theory won't work in practice. All theories must have sound rules of correspondence.

The three components of a theory are like the legs of a three-legged stool. If any one of the legs is knocked away, the entire structure falls. Similarly, if any element of a theory is missing, we do not have a theory that can stand. In the theory on source physical attractiveness we have been examining, rules of correspondence are fairly strong. Among methods to study physical attractiveness, some research has shown people pictures of speakers who varied in physical attractiveness (for review see Berscheid, 1985). Persuasion has been studied in a host of ways, ranging from measures of attitude change to reviews of historical trends. Of course, in some cases, we must wait for rules of correspondence to catch up to the theory.

all elements required for theory to exist

Requirements of Theory

Some strange things may masquerade as theories. It is important to recognize them so that we are not misled. Fortunately, there are two requirements that help separate true theories from counterfeits.

1. *The requirement of falsification* holds that any theory must deal with statements that could be falsified by data and information if the theories were untrue.[3] For a time during the seventeenth century, it was believed that fire was caused by something called *phlogiston*. This substance had to be present to cause a fire, but it was completely combusted (leaving no trace) by fire. So, if you rubbed two sticks together and got a fire, you knew phlogiston had been present, even though you could not prove it. If you could not start a fire by rubbing sticks together, then there simply was no phlogiston in the sticks (you could look and you wouldn't find any). The problem, of course, is that the theory of combustion was incapable of falsification. Today we know that phlogiston does not exist, but in those days there was no acceptable evidence that could disprove the phlogiston theory. Phlogiston, then, was not a true theory. Today, similar problems abound and articles of faith sometimes are advanced as scientific theory. Sometimes students say they hope to prove a theory true. In reality, they are attempting to falsify alternative theories. We must recognize the difference if we are to avoid wasting our time.

   theories must be capable of being falsified if they are incorrect

2. *The requirement of tentativeness* demands that scholars recognize that a theory's answers are provisional. Theories can only describe part of the reality that exists. Other theories may emerge at a later time that provide improved explanations. We do not mean that existing theories are proven wrong by new ones. Instead, relationships are redefined by new theories. Sometimes existing theories are shown to be special cases of the new theory's applications. Using theories means that a

   theories are only tentative explanations

---

[3] Sir Karl Popper wrote in detail on the importance of falsification in scientific research (1968a, b; 1972). He took the view that the ability of a theory to be falsified if it is untrue distinguishes scientific propositions from nonscientific propositions. He did not believe that only scientific propositions are meaningful, but he was most concerned that we not be misled by people who claim to advance scientific theories that are really counterfeit theories.

researcher's explanations are not the only ones that will be found. Thus, conclusions should be developed with a certain amount of tentativeness.

Functions of Theory

Theories can serve four different but interrelated purposes. These purposes are a sort of hierarchy of theory, and they all play an important role in scholarship.

1. description

1. **Description** is the lowest level of theorizing, in which behavior is characterized into different forms. For instance, there has been continuous interest in identifying what are called "compliance gaining message strategies." Much of the original theorizing by Marwell and Schmitt (1967) attempted simply to identify the sorts of methods that people use to influence others. A dozen years later, Jacobs and Jackson (1979a, 1979b) dedicated much of their time describing patterns of conversations in actual and potential exchanges people can have. They found that interpersonal conflicts include the additional categories of hints, prompts, and projections from other people. Such work can challenge ways people think about basic concepts.

2. explanation defined

2. **Explanation** involves taking an event and treating it as an instance of a larger system of things (after Homans, 1961, p. 10). In general, we attempt to explain things that have occurred. Logical explanations occur when a behavior is shown to be a logical application of theory. The Uses and Gratifications theory, for instance, has been used to explain the reasons people use the Internet as a mass media source (Walther, 1992).

3. prediction

3. **Prediction** describes what can be expected in the future. Prediction sometimes is considered a separate step for theories, but as one writer put it:

> Predicting events that will occur in the future and explaining events that have occurred in the past are, except for a difference in temporal perspective, essentially the same activity as long as scientific statements are abstract. (Reynolds, 1971, p. 5)

prediction may be one means for explanation

In fact, being able to predict is one useful way to explain things. Attempts to predict future events are prominent in many theories in communication. For instance, Berger and Calabrese (1975) developed a theory of initial interactions people have with each other. The theory submits that we communicate in ways that help us reduce our uncertainty when we meet new people. One specific prediction in this theory has received a lot of attention: "High levels of uncertainty cause increases in information seeking behavior" (p. 103). This statement has guided researchers' expectations for future studies. Moreover, it allows ordinary folks a way to predict what might happen when they meet new people as well.

4. control identified

4. **Control** is the power to direct things. Some theories provide information to influence our own personal environment. Thus, control really is the degree to which we can find useful additional applications for the explanations of a theory. Certainly if people know what is expected to occur in the future, that information might be used to affect the environment.

Applications of Theory

The ways researchers use theories reflect their preferences. Developing theories involves setting priorities and making some choices.

Data First Versus Theory First Inquiry

In general, there are two approaches to theory and inquiry. Sometimes called the "inductive approach" to research, the first method involves gathering information and then developing theoretic explanations. Rather than becoming locked into a formal theory, we gather information on an open canvas of observation. Researchers doing exploratory work often employ this approach. In addition, scholars who study samples of naturally occurring conversations tend to use this approach (they often try to gather samples of conversation to develop theories rather than to test existing theories). The second approach is just the opposite: we develop theoretic thinking and then gather data to test it (particularly its limits). Table 3.1 shows the advantages and disadvantages typically claimed for each approach. As you can see, some of the advantages argued for the data-first method involve the flexibility of the approach. Similarly, most of the advantages of the theory-first method deal with the rigor and logic it provides.

> **data first inquiry identified**
> **theory first inquiry identified**

Scholars are engaged in a hot controversy about the desirability of each approach. For all the division drawn between them, however, the two approaches share many elements in common. When first developing theories, researchers make informal notes about activities they find interesting. Such unstructured data collection leads to thinking that may evolve into tentative theories for testing. Thus, to develop theories, some sort of data collection (though we may not want to call it formal research) enriches the effort. Similarly, it is hard to imagine how researchers could select variables to study unless they had some hunches that stimulated them to look at some activities instead of others. Arthur Bachrach described how these little undeveloped (and unstated) theoretic orientations appear: "I think all investigators make these on-the-spot hypotheses. Some call them hunches: I choose to call them hypothesitos, which is semi-Spanish for 'little hypotheses'" (1981, p. 70). Thus, it really may be impossible to have "theory free" research. There is always some idea behind selecting concepts and variables for study. But some researchers prefer not to work from fully developed theoretic statements at the beginning of their inquiries. Theory development *both* follows and precedes researchers' observations. Thus, it is clear that theory and observation go hand in hand in the research craft.

> **both approaches share much in common**

> **data first researchers use theories or little hypotheses to select variables for study**

Normative, Ethical, and Rhetorical Theories

Predictive theories are not the only sorts of theories we have in communication. We often hear about such things as "rhetorical theory," "information theory," or "argumentation theory." Such theories are known as normative or ethical theories. In communication studies, you are likely to see references to both predictive and normative theories. Furthermore, these two categories have promoted very different sorts of research efforts.

Normative and prescriptive theories are those whose principles involve defining the qualities that make communication meaningful or desirable. The area of normative theory comes from work in what sometimes is called **normative science,** which is "a discipline that systematically studies man's [and woman's] attempts to determine what is correct, valuable, good, or beautiful" (English & English, 1958, p. 349). Though they are called normative theories, you should not think that they are just a bunch of value judgments made by eggheads. Instead, these theories explore

> **normative and prescriptive theories identified:**

TABLE 3.1 Theory First Versus Data First Research

	Theory First	Data First
Advantages	1. "Theories may develop from any source and are not limited to phenomena that can be observed with current measuring instruments" (M. J. Smith, 1988, p. 13).	1. One does not enter research with predetermined expectations.
	2. One may be free to take advantage of serendipity since unexpected findings are readily identified.	2. One may be free to follow the unexpected directions.
	3. Promotes efficient research since key variables of interest are identified early.	3. One stays close to data and avoids tendencies toward reification (the fallacy of thinking that abstract concepts are concrete things).
Disadvantages	1. Researchers may force theoretic explanations on information even if it is inappropriate to do so.	1. "Explanations are limited to phenomena that can be observed with current measuring instruments" (M. J. Smith, 1988, p. 13).
	2. Theories may become articles of faith to their followers, even after the theories have outlived their usefulness.	2. Does not test alternative theoretic explanations, but develops suggestions for theory.
	3. Theories are difficult to construct and require exhaustive thinking beyond the energies of most scholars.	3. Promotes inefficient research since key variables of interest are not identified early.

activities that try to explain correct patterns of behavior. For instance, the theories of logic, ethics, and mental health are examples of normative theories (Chaplin, 1985, p. 307), because they involve explanations of behavior that when applied by other people, have the potential to improve our ability to reason and to adapt to each other. Because these behaviors seem to invite theorists to give advice based on their theories, they are called normative theories.

Ethical theory and rhetorical studies have gone hand in hand. In specific terms, **ethical and rhetorical theories** consist of principles that describe worthy and effective communication respectively. The rhetorical theories developed by Aristotle, Cicero, Campbell, Whately, and Perelman are examples of rhetorical theories. Though these theories contain some statements that make predictions (such as Aristotle's proposition that "*ethos* is the most potent of all means to persuasion"), most statements are meant to organize principles of communication that describe appropriate and effective communication. Rather than predict relationships alone, these theories try to define how communication may be suitable and worthy. Ethical theories posit standards of what are considered to be good actions of people. As applied to communication, ethical theories are used to explain whether communicators (called rhetors) used suitable and worthy methods to influence others.

ethical and rhetorical theories identified

DEVELOPING DEFINITIONS FOR CONCEPTS

Theories provide relationships among concepts, but if a concept cannot be defined, it cannot be studied. Thus, early in the research process terms must be defined to identify variables clearly. Careful definitions determine if research can be understandable and coherent.

Not only do definitions give us a shorthand for research, definitions may be taken as premises for research. They also may suggest ways to complete studies and the sorts of information that might be collected. Thus, the definitions a researcher selects can be premises for later decisions. For instance, the concept of source credibility has been the object of several definitions. One view defined credibility as the "*image* of a source in any communication situation" (Mortensen, 1972, p. 147 [italics added]). Adopting this definition, a host of researchers identified handfuls of credibility factors, ranging from source competence to source tallness (the latter found in a clever study by McCroskey and Young, 1981). On the other hand, an alternative definition of source credibility explained it as "the *attitude* toward a source of communication held at a given time by a receiver" (McCroskey, 1972, 63, [italics added]). When researchers have adopted this definition, only the attitude factors of source credibility (character and competence) have been studied. In very real ways, a scholar's definitions are premises for subsequent research selections.

definitions as premises for research

You probably have thought that definitions were things found in *Webster's* or *Random House* dictionaries. But these dictionaries were developed to provide accounts of the ways people have used words, not technical meanings for terms. In scholarship, we mean something very precise when we use the term "definition." Scholars consider a **definition** to be a statement asserting that one term may be substituted for another. One way or another, definitions tell us what concepts and variables really mean by isolating their essential qualities. These definition statements are not shown to be "true" in a strict sense because they are not tested against data. But we test the degree to which definitions are truly useful, reasonable, and applicable in research. To grasp the use of definitions, it is helpful to look at two forms: conceptual and operational definitions.

definition defined

Using Conceptual Definitions

A **conceptual** (or constitutive) **definition** relies on other concepts to describe a term. Most of the time what we call "dictionary definitions" are conceptual definitions. For instance, "salience" may be defined as the "prominence" of something. This type of definition gives us a feeling for a term by relating it to other terms.

conceptual definitions

Levels of Conceptual Definition: Daily, Poetic, and Scholarly

People define things on three general levels: daily, poetic, and scholarly.[4] Much difficulty people sometimes have in understanding research results from confusing these three types of definitions. Thus, we should distinguish among them.

---

[4] This discussion benefits from the writing and headings developed by Arthur J. Bachrach (1981, pp. 80–84). Though Bachrach calls the third type of definition "the scientific definition," here it is called a scholarly definition, reflecting the breadth of research methods.

Many communication research projects could not be done without a sponsor's funding. Researchers naturally have to seek financial support for some of the work they wish to do. There is no problem—unless one of the following problems occurs.

First, some sponsors may be interested only in research that advances their own limited pet theories. As a result, sometimes other critical viewpoints do not get a fair hearing. Christopher Simpson's history of mass communication research, *Science of Coercion: Communication Research and Psychological Warfare 1945–1960* (1994), describes the link between early communication studies and government-sponsored psychological warfare efforts during the Cold War with the Soviet Union. Simpson noted,

> Leading mass communication researchers were not "bought off" in some simplistic sense during the 1950s; they instead internalized and reflected the values of the agencies they had been hired to assist for reasons that seemed to them to be proper, even noble. (p. 94)

Most of the research was designed to help the U.S. government influence citizens of both the United States and foreign nations as part of a means of social control. Such sponsorship led to the dominance of some scholars in research publication, preference for some theories and variables in publications, and prominence of sponsored pet theories—such as the "two-step model" of communication—which were the basis for largely counterproductive propaganda programs in

> Guatemala, Nicaragua, El Salvador, the Philippines, Turkey, Indonesia, and more recently Panama and the Soviet Union . . . [leaving them] today, both materially and spiritually, less democratic, less free, and often living in worse health and greater terror than before this purportedly benign form of intervention began (Simpson, 1994, p. 116).

By the late 1950s, even labels for variables changed to match official desires. Studies of propaganda were published without ever using the clear term. Instead, only studies that used such antiseptic words as "social influence" and "attitude change" were tolerated.

Second, an ethical problem emerges when a sponsor is unwilling to be identified as the funding source. Such concealment of support has often been followed by a sponsor's claim to have found "independent evidence" to support that sponsor's position. In 1954, to avoid charges of violating international law and United Nations' conventions by carrying out psychological warfare during peacetime, the United States Central Intelligence Agency filtered research funds to mass communication researchers through the Voice of America and an unnamed government agency (American Association for Public Opinion Research, 1954–55; Simpson, 1994, p. 88). Such failure to identify sources of funding is generally considered an ethical breach.

Third, researchers face an ethical difficulty when the sponsor indicates the study results that are desired. A scholar who agrees to complete such research gives up a willingness to be guided by the data, rather than prejudice. Yet, it is surprising how many times sponsors issue "rewards" for researchers who can "prove" the existence of parapsychology phenomena, the existence of the soul as a physical element, and support for assertions that cigarettes are not harmful.

Daily definitions are statements generally adopted by members of a society. Consider a term used extensively in intercultural communication studies: "culture." A daily definition of this word might be the customs, arts, and crafts of people in a society. This definition is almost general knowledge and can be useful when we talk to each other. Yet, for research purposes it may not be detailed enough to serve as a premise for study.

daily definitions distinguished

Poetic definitions are statements that involve figurative interpretations of objects. We sometimes hear of "poetic license" or exaggerations. These exaggerations are examples of poetic definitions. A poetic definition of "culture" might be "the civilizing tradition that elevates and invigorates society." The definition cannot be taken literally because it makes a poetic judgment of the term. We understand that poetic definitions are not to be taken as highly specific statements. Yet, we sometimes can confuse poetic definitions with other sorts of definitions.

poetic definitions distinguished

Scholarly definitions are highly specific statements that have technical meanings for a group of scholars. Intercultural communication is a major part of our field. "Culture" has been defined in this manner as "the peculiar and distinctive 'way of life' of a group or class, the meanings values and ideas embodied in institutions, in social relations, in systems of belief, in mores and customs, in the uses of objects and material life" (Hall & Jefferson, 1975, p. 10). This definition certainly is technical. It is useful to researchers, however, because it identifies elements to be examined (and perhaps measured) when studying culture.

scholarly definitions distinguished

The Problem of Clarity

One difficulty scholars have in being clear involves some sorry compromises researchers often make involving interchanging definitions, using circular definitions, and assuming "mutual understanding."

Inappropriateness of Interchanging Definitions.

It is dangerous to use daily, poetic, and scholarly definitions interchangably. Yet, many times researchers do just that. Psychologist Arthur Bachrach (1981, p. 81) explained,

interchanging nonscholarly definitions with scholarly definitions is a difficulty

> a major error is the transference of a daily definition (or, less likely, a poetic one) to scientific usage. . . . It might also be observed at this point that the transfer of scientific communication to the daily or poetic realm would be equally inappropriate.

In research, we must rely on scientific definitions, rather than daily definitions. To summarize research accurately, we must know when scholarly definitions are used and when research is based on very different definitional premises.

The Problem of Using Circular Definitions.

Circularity occurs when definitions simply repeat things. We must attempt to avoid the circularity that comes with many daily definitions. Rather than explain concepts, most daily definitions refer us to other concepts which, after definition, often send us back to the term we started with! For instance, returning to a previous example, a daily definition of "culture" might be the "society" of a group of people. So, what is the society of a group of people? Answer: It's their culture. You probably have seen the flag of the

circular definitions are to be avoided

Olympic games in which five circles intersect. Circular definitions are Olympic flag statements. One term moves us to another term, which then cycles back to give us the first term again. We must be careful about permitting daily definitions to be used where scholarly definitions are required. It is not acceptable to say that speeches are dull since they are boring, that speakers are credible since they are respected, or that audiences are attentive since they are alert. These statements merely state equivalently that speeches are boring since they are dull, that speakers are respected since they are credible, and that audiences are alert since they are attentive. Each statement uses Olympic flag circular definitions that refer us back to our original terms. Technically, circular definitions are flawed because they are illogical. They commit the fallacy of begging the question in which the conclusion of an argument is used as a premise for the argument. Thus, using circular definitions is unreasonable for researchers. Useful definitions must not be circular.

circular definitions are illogical

Assuming Mutual Understanding. Researchers sometimes mistakenly assume that "everybody knows" what they mean, even though there is no useful scholarly definition. Former U.S. Supreme Court Justice Potter Stewart asserted that although he could not define obscenity, "I know it when I see it." Such assumption of common understanding is dangerous in research. If we cannot define what we mean, we probably cannot make important statements about it. Furthermore, as philosopher Willard Quine commented: "The less a science has advanced the more its terminology tends to rest upon an uncritical assumption of mutual understanding" (1946, p. 84). Using daily definitions often boils down to our assuming that "everyone knows" what we mean, even though scholarly definitions are not available. The problem, of course, is that everybody does not really know what we mean precisely. If communication is to be recognized as a mature area of inquiry, it is vital that the assumption of common understanding *not* be made in research.

relying on assumption of common understanding is a difficulty

Sources of Conceptual Definitions

To find definitions you will need to use a library and find how scholars have defined terms. Definitions can be found in many different places. For instance, Mark H. Wright explored the competing foundations for the concept of "identification" between speakers and audiences in an article called "Burkean and Freudian Theories of Identification" (1994). Sometimes research articles have titles indicating that they contain definitional discussions. For instance, Gilda Parrella (1971) discussed the rather gnarled concept of "empathy" in an article titled "Projection and Adoption: Toward a Clarification of the Concept of Empathy." Similarly phrased titles can reveal when articles deal with conceptual and definitional issues. Yet, most articles do not get into detailed discussions of definitions. There are three additional types of sources where you can find useful definitional treatments:

where to find definitional treatments

- Handbooks and collected essays. Many conceptual essays regularly appear in handbooks and annual reviews.
- Textbooks. Many textbooks you have used in your classes take the time to define their terms and explain their choices by reviewing competing defini-

tions (if you have sold your books, shame on you!—you will need to visit the library to renew your acquaintance with them).

- Specialized dictionaries. Surely the quickest way to find definitions is by searching specialized dictionaries, such as the *Longman Dictionary of Psychology and Psychiatry: A Walter D. Glanze Book; The Communication Handbook: A Dictionary* by Joseph A. DeVito; *The Broadcast Communications Dictionary,* edited by L. Diamant; *Terminology of Communication Disorders: Speech, Language, and Hearing* by Nicolosi, Harryman, and Kresheck; *Diagnostic and Statistical Manual of Mental Disorders* published by the American Psychiatric Association (includes all speech and hearing disorders). Some of these dictionaries provide only one definition for each concept, reflecting the best choice in the opinion of the editors. Thus, you will need to examine several sources.

Criticism of Conceptual Definitions

In research literature you will find more than one meaning for the central core of a concept. These meanings may have very different implications for ways you may study the concept. So, it is important to evaluate the meaning of these definitions in some detail. Sound conceptual definitions are found by sifting competing alternatives. This sifting requires relying on standards to judge whether definitions are useful and reasonable. Five of the most useful of these guidelines are (after Auer, 1959, p. 70):

standards to evaluate conceptual definitions:

1. Conceptual Definitions Must Include All Situations or Instances Properly Included in the Term Defined. Conceptual definitions cannot leave out examples of the concept that might be found. The term "persuasion" is sometimes defined as an intentional use of messages to change attitudes and behaviors. Some criticize this definition since it seems to exclude examples of accidental or unintended persuasion. Since they view accidental persuasion as a part of persuasion, they think that the suggested definition is unreasonable.

1. must include all proper situations or instances

2. Conceptual Definitions Must Exclude Situations or Instances that are Not Properly Included in the Term Defined. Definitions must have limits. After all, if something is defined as everything, it is uniquely nothing. Some definitions are so broad that the constructs are left terribly confused. For instance, Paul Cozby defined "self-disclosure" as "any information about himself which Person A communicates verbally to a Person B" (1973, p. 73). This definition makes nearly anything a person says to another "self-disclosure," including public speeches, sales persuasion, and insincere exchanges. But the literature of the field usually describes self-disclosure as a "risky" process in which one person "reveals" potentially damaging information that the other person would not know otherwise. Since too much is included in Cozby's definition, it has doubtful value.

2. must exclude situations or instances not properly included

3. Conceptual Definitions Must Not Use the Term Defined. It is not very helpful to define a "fear appeal" as "an appeal that arouses fear." The term is used to define itself! This sort of definition creates big logical difficulties. Consider the paradox created by using the term defined as part of the definition. In developing

3. must not include the term defined

his theory of types, Bertrand Russell showed the following square (Bachrach, 1981, p. 83):

> Every statement
> in this square
> is false.

The situation is a paradox. If the statement in the square is true, then it has declared itself to be false. If the statement in the square is false, then it must be true. It turns into an intellectual mess. In our field such statements are occasionally found in only slightly more subtle forms. At a recent convention one scholar presented a paper advocating that researchers adopt a postmodern view of their research. Correctly or incorrectly, this person explained that a starting point for this view was accepting the statement that "there are no true statements." If the statement is true, then it is not true. But if it is false, it must be true. In one form or another, when a term defined is included in the definition, the potential for this sort of pointless paradox is very great.

4. must be more precise than the term defined

4. Conceptual Definitions Must Be More Precise than the Term Defined. Definitions try to get specific with terms. Accepting definitions that are broader (and more vague) than the original term defeats the entire process of trying to define terms precisely. One textbook defined "power" as "a quality inherent in the relations between two or more people" (Myers & Myers, 1982, p. 196). The new terms were even broader than "power." Eventually, the authors proposed a list of requirements for power. As it was, the definition was difficult to use since it was not more precise than the term defined.

5. must exclude loaded language

5. Conceptual Definitions Must Exclude Loaded Language. Definitions should avoid making value judgments. The extra emotional language means the definition is not strictly equivalent to the term defined. Definitions should stick to specifics. For example, "democratic group leadership" could be defined as "exercise of direction that respects the individual while promoting the greatest good for the greatest number." We can hope so, of course, but it does not actually *characterize* democratic leadership. Definitions must avoid loaded language to be reasonable.

Using Operational Definitions

operational definitions distinguished

An **operational definition** describes what is to be observed by specifying what researchers must do to make observations. An operational definition does not, however, give you a "feeling" for the concept. Instead, it tells you the steps that must be followed to make an observation. It usually takes the form of a description of research methods to isolate or measure variables or specific examples of types of observations. An operational definition is like a recipe. The recipe tells you steps to follow in preparing food, but it does not tell you conceptually how the dish tastes. Similarly, a restaurant guide could describe the appearance and taste of meals, but operational definitions for them may be the steps taken by the chef to create the dish.

Researchers know the importance of having both conceptual and operational definitions. They make it possible to shuttle back and forth between two worlds: the conceptual and the empirical. As you might imagine, there is probably only a small number of reasonable constitutive definitions for a concept. But there can be many potential operational definitions from which the researcher may select. For instance, we might define communication competence as: "the ability to interact well with others" (Spitzberg, 1988, p. 68) or "the extent to which judgments about the observed communicator match conceptions of the 'ideal' " (Pavitt, 1990, p. 9). These definitions describe communicator competence by relating it to other concepts. Operational definitions, on the other hand, identify observations by describing the methods to make an observation. For instance, we could state that communicator competence is operationally defined as one's score on Wiemann's communicative competence scale (1977) or any other numerous measures of competence that are widely available. Thus, the use of constitutive and operational definitions go hand in hand in isolating research for further study.

though only few constitutive definitions, there may be many operational

An Attempt at Precision of Definition

After one has reasonable conceptual definitions, researchers who want to get specific must use operational definitions. Although operational definitions sometimes are used in the absence of conceptual definitions, doing so is a mistake. When used in combination with conceptual definitions, however, operational definitions help us get specific. The more specific we can be, the more precise our research evidence will be. Operational definitions take conceptual definitions and describe the methods that would be used to make direct observations of instances and examples of the variables. In research dealing with the effects of the speaker's use of notes on attitude change, operational definitions of "attitude change" would include descriptions of attitude scales to be used. Since operational definitions are attempts to get specific, the desire for precision requires their use.

operational definitions promote precision

After identifying the problem statement, it should be possible to restate it with operational definitions substituted for the variable names. For instance, look at the problem statements in Table 3.2 and the translations into operational terms. In each case operational definitions were used for each variable. Restated, each problem may be specifically isolated. By doing so, the link between the general understanding provided by constitutive definitions and those provided by the operational definitions can be seen.

definitions for terms in the problem statement

Operational definitions are not entire definitions by themselves. Thus, we require researchers to cover *both* conceptual and operational matters. Researchers should use operationalizations that are consistent with their constitutive definitions. Without stating constitutive definitions first, though, it may be very, very difficult to tell if operational definitions make sense. If the researcher provides references to sources where constitutive definitions may be found, there may be little harm since you can look at the original if you wish. None of this discussion means that researchers actually re-member to define their terms in research articles. Regrettably, the facts are quite the contrary, depending on the publication and its editor. Nevertheless, operational definitions should be fitting exemplifications of the concepts or variables defined.

operational definitions must be used with conceptual definitions

TABLE 3.2 Operational Definitions and Problem Restatements

Problem: Does the Intercultural Communication Workshop significantly improve the American participants' intercultural communication competence? (Hammer, 1984, p. 253)

Variable	Operational Definition
Intercultural Communication Workshop	The Intercultural Communication Workshop taught at the University of Minnesota
Intercultural communication competence	Scores on a set of scales used by observers to rate behaviors of workshop participants as they describe their reactions to potential situations involving people of different cultures

Restatement: Does the Intercultural Communication Workshop taught at the University of Minnesota significantly increase the scores on a set of scales used by observers to rate behaviors of American participants as they describe their reactions to potential situations involving people of different cultures?

Problem: What differences in motivation for attendance are there between [sic] infrequent, occasional, and frequent movie-goers? (Austin, 1986, pp. 117–188)

Variable	Operational Definition
Motivation for attendance	Scores on a 70-item measure of motivation for attendance
Types of movie-goers (infrequent, occasional, and frequent)	Scores on a checklist indicating the frequency of subject movie going

Restatement: What differences in scores on a 70-item measure of motivation for attendance are there among subjects' scores on a checklist indicating the frequency of subject movie-going?

Forms of Operational Definitions

Operational definitions can be of three forms. Furthermore, these types may be used in combination in a single study.

manipulated independent variables identified

1. **Manipulated independent variables** are sometimes called "stimulus variables" because researchers introduce and control them in experiments. In a classic study, for instance, a researcher wanted to see the effects of source credibility on student audiences at Northwestern University (Haiman, 1949). The independent variable, source credibility, was manipulated by having speeches advocating national health insurance introduced as having come from different sources: Thomas Parran, then Surgeon General of the U. S.; a Northwestern University sophomore; and Eugene Dennis, then Secretary of the American Communist Party. This manipulated independent variable was effective in showing that credible speakers are most persuasive.

assigned or measured variables identified

2. **Measured/assigned variables** are not introduced or controlled by the researcher, but are carefully observed and/or measured. Often these variables are characteristics that can be identified, though it would be impossible (or unthinkable) to manipulate them. If we wanted to learn if women were more persuasible than men,

it would be impossible to manipulate the sex of the receiver (get serious!), but we could identify men and women and *assign* their persuasibility ratings to distinct categories for analysis. If we want to know if highly dogmatic people talk more in small group discussions than lowly dogmatic people, researchers might *measure* the degree of dogmatism using established scales.

3. **Direct classification variables** are operational definitions that rely on simple identification or classification of observable characteristics of information. The direct assignment operational definition describes what information must be observed for the presence of a variable to be claimed. For instance, Stephanie Greco Larson (1991) explored whether the portrayal of sexual violence on television soap operas, specifically *All My Children,* sent a message that "when women say 'no' they really mean 'yes' [which] contradicts overt attempts to demonstrate the seriousness of sexual aggression" (p. 156). To operationalize sexual violence, Larson used the method of direct assignment to identify whether kisses between romantic partners were forced or not forced. "A forced kiss was any kiss accompanied by a physical struggle which demonstrated resistance, even if this resistance was [*sic*] temporary" (p. 157). This matter was not measured. Instead, the method of direct assignment was completed by identifying the information that would have to exist for the variable to be operating.[5]

direct classification variables identified

Standards for Operational Definitions

Operational definitions are examined in detail when measurements are involved. Direct tests of the consistency and accuracy of measures are parts of the process of describing measurement tools. Yet, operational definitions are expected to meet some minimum standards. Herbert Feigl (1945) established criteria for sound operational definitions that give useful guidance.

1. *Empirically Based and Definite.* The word "empirical" means observable (though many people think that it refers to scientific information). For operational definitions to make sense, they must be specific, and they must be related to something that can be identified through observation.

standards for evaluating operational definitions

2. *Logically Consistent.* If operational definitions are inconsistent with constitutive definitions, then the operationalizations may be irrelevant to the concept under investigation. One study included a variable known as "ethnic identity" of African Americans. Yet, the operational definition consisted only of terms that African Americans preferred as the label for their race. One might raise questions about how related racial labels are to one's total sense of ethnic identity. In sum, the operational definition must have clear relationships with conceptual definitions.

3. *Intersubjective.* **Intersubjectivity** is the degree to which different researchers with essentially different beliefs draw essentially the same interpretations of the meaning of observations. Certainly different people have different views, but they

---

[5] She found support for her expectation. It seemed that the soap opera rewarded "persistent men" and sent mixed messages about sexual violence generally.

also share some common interpretations. This area of shared agreement on meaning is what we mean by intersubjectivity. A useful operational definition should be one that different scholars could identify as related to the concept at hand. Therapists have different favorite definitions for the concept of stuttering. But when presented with the same set of patients most therapists still show strong agreement when identifying the behaviors that distinguish stuttering from nonstuttering patients. Indeed, their consistent use of the same sort of operational definitions across studies is one (though fallible) index of the degree of intersubjectivity for the operational definition.

4. *Technically Possible.* A good operational definition should be capable of being put into direct application in research. If an operational definition requires technologies that are not yet available or that are not morally or tactically possible, the operationalization's usefulness is cast into doubt. For instance, if we wanted to study the impact of persuasive messages on the electrical resistivity of the left hemisphere of the brain, it might not be possible to do such research in the absence of technology (and surgery) that is not available.

5. *Repeatable.* Operational definitions must be capable of repeated use by different researchers. Sometimes therapists claim they can tell operationally whether a patient is responding positively to therapy by looking at the patient's "general demeanor." If the therapist is asked how he or she is able to draw conclusions from that vague operationalization, the therapist may respond that it is based on his or her own experience. Such a defense of an operational definition—even if true— means that a scholar is using a vague method that probably cannot be employed by others. But, if others cannot duplicate a scholar's methods, the operationalizations fail to meet the standard of repeatability.

6. *Suggestive of Constructs.* Operational definitions are examples of constitutive definitions put into direct observation and experience. But operational definitions can also point researchers toward new concepts. To advance theory, operational definitions should stimulate attention to other concepts. Thus, the ability of operational definitions to suggest other constructs can be helpful to advance comprehensive theory building by scholars.

SUMMARY

Theory construction is a purpose of all research, scholarship, and science. A science is a particular body of knowledge—for example, physics, physiology, psychology—distinguished by the special set of operations employed in gathering empirical facts and by a distinctive set of constructs employed in interpreting the data. Thus, we can define science as a way of testing statements by systematic application of the scientific method. Since all communication research states problems, sets criteria for permissible interpretation, and makes careful observations of communication transactions, using

these methods makes the study of communication a scientific study area, though the practice of communication may remain an art.

A theory is a body of interrelated principles that explain or predict. Theories have three components: (1) an abstract calculus, which is the logical structure of relationships; (2) theoretic constructs or generalizations about observables according to some common property ("hypothetical constructs" or concepts refer to constructs for which we cannot make observations directly); (3) rules of correspondence, which show how well the theory's constructs and abstract calculus can be applied to actual experience. Two requirements help separate theories from counterfeits: (1) the requirement of falsification holds that any theory must deal with statements that could be falsified by data and information if the theories were untrue; (2) the requirement of tentativeness demands that scholars recognize that a theory's answers are provisional. Theories can operate for four interrelated functions: (1) description, in which behavior is characterized into different forms; (2) explanation, which takes an event and treats it as an instance of a larger system of things; (3) prediction, which describes what can be expected in the future (prediction is also a way to explain things); (4) control, which is the power to direct things.

There are two approaches to theory and inquiry. Sometimes called the "inductive approach" to research, the "data first" method involves gathering information and then developing theoretic explanations. The second approach, "theory first" develops theoretic thinking and then gathers data to apply and test it. In actual practice, theory development *both* follows and precedes researchers' observations since theory and observation go hand in hand. Normative and prescriptive theories are those whose principles involve defining the qualities that make communication meaningful or desirable. The area of normative theory comes from work in what sometimes is called "normative science," which is a discipline that systematically studies humanity's attempts to determine what is correct, valuable, good, or beautiful. Ethical and rhetorical theories consist of principles that describe good and effective communication respectively.

If a concept cannot be defined, it cannot be studied. Not only do definitions give us a shorthand for research, definitions may be taken as premises for research, suggest ways to complete studies, and invite some sorts of information for collection. Definitions are statements asserting that one term may be substituted for another. There are two forms of definitions: conceptual and operational. A conceptual (or constitutive) definition relies on other concepts to describe a term. There are three general levels people use to define things: daily definitions

(statements generally adopted by members of a society); poetic definitions (statements that involve figurative interpretations of objects); scholarly definitions (highly specific statements that have technical meanings for a group of scholars). One difficulty scholars have in being clear involves some sorry compromises researchers often make: interchanging daily, poetic, and scholarly definitions; using circular definitions; and assuming "mutual understanding." Conceptual definitions can be found in many different places including some articles, handbooks and collected essays, textbooks, and specialized dictionaries. To criticize conceptual definitions we can apply the following guidelines: (1) conceptual definitions must include all situations or instances properly included in the term defined; (2) conceptual definitions must exclude situations or instances that are not properly included in the term defined; (3) conceptual definitions must not use the term defined; (4) conceptual definitions must be more precise than the term defined; (5) conceptual definitions must exclude loaded language.

An operational definition describes what is to be observed by specifying what researchers must do to make observations. Researchers know the importance of having both conceptual and operational definitions since they make it possible to shuttle back and forth between two worlds, the conceptual and the empirical. Though there is probably only a small number of reasonable constitutive definitions for a concept, there can be many potential operational definitions from which the researcher may select. Operational definitions are not entire definitions by themselves. Thus, we require researchers to cover *both* conceptual and operational matters since without stating constitutive definitions first, it may be very, very difficult to tell if operational definitions make sense. Operational definitions can be of three forms: (1) manipulated independent variables (sometimes called "stimulus variables" because researchers introduce and control them in experiments); (2) measured/assigned variables (not introduced or controlled by the researcher, but carefully observed and/or measured); (3) direct classification variables (operationally defining concepts by simple identification or classification of observable characteristics of information). Operational definitions are required to be: (1) empirically based and definite; (2) logically consistent; (3) intersubjective (different researchers with essentially different beliefs draw essentially the same interpretations of the meaning of observations); (4) technically possible; (5) repeatable; (6) suggestive of constructs.

TERMS FOR REVIEW

Science
Meta-analysis
Theory
Abstract calculus
Theoretic constructs
Constructs
Hypothetical constructs
Rules of correspondence
Description
Explanation
Prediction
Control
Normative and prescriptive theories

Normative science
Ethical and rhetorical theories
Definition
Conceptual definition
Daily definition
Poetic definition
Scholarly definition
Operational definition
Manipulated independent variable
Measured/assigned variable
Direct classification variable
Intersubjectivity

CHAPTER 4

Measurement in Communication Research

When you cannot measure, your knowledge is meager and unsatisfactory.

–Lord Kelvin

**THE ROLE OF SOUND
MEASUREMENT IN
COMMUNICATION RESEARCH**
  Measurement as a Foundation for
    Research
Levels of Measurement
**OPERATIONAL DEFINITIONS
AND MEASURES**

  The Requirement of Reliability
  The Requirement of Validity
**POPULAR TOOLS IN
COMMUNICATION STUDIES**
  Methods to Measure Judgments
  Methods to Measure Achievement

BEFORE WE GET STARTED . . .

So far, we have taken a problem statement and theorizing through the level of conceptually and operationally defining variables. To take the next step in communication research we need to consider how to measure variables. Indeed, if you can't measure variables of interest, it is difficult to investigate communication very well. Researchers are expected to describe the measurements they use and to provide evidence that the measures are good ones. In this chapter we will describe how variables are measured, how evidence of good measurement is provided, and popular tools in communication studies.

THE ROLE OF SOUND MEASUREMENT IN COMMUNICATION RESEARCH

The ways researchers identify and measure variables are important factors in determining the integrity of a study. You may have heard of the expression "Garbage In, Garbage Out" or "GIGO" for short. This concept reminds us that our conclusions are only as good as our data. If researchers have sound and accurate data, they can draw meaningful conclusions. Poor measurement and poor isolation of variables produce studies from which only weak claims can be drawn.

Measurement as a Foundation for Research

Less-than-accurate measurement works against researchers—it never works in their favor. This fact is because imperfect measurement introduces additional variation or background noise into a study besides the variation that already exists in samples. Thus, relationships that truly exist in the data may get lost in the background noise.

imperfect measurement creates attenuation of results

This problem is called **attenuation** of results, which means that there is a reduction in the size of observed effects because of measurement imperfection. The lack of adequate measurement of variables, then, creates a bias against the researcher's finding relationships (even if they really exist).

Levels of Measurement

Measurement involves assigning numbers to variables according to a system. Even in qualitative studies, variables are classified and identified on some level of measurement. It is important to understand the many ways numbers can be assigned to different kinds of variables. We should understand them because the levels of measurement dictate the sorts of statistical tools that can be used to analyze data.

nominal level measurement defined

- **Nominal level measurement**—The term *nominal* comes from the Latin word *nomen,* which means "name." Hence, nominal level measurement uses numbers as simple identifications of variables. Any number is used to identify or "name" a category. Numbers on football jerseys are examples of nominal level measurement since the numbers are used just to name the players. Studies that compare men to women, stutterers to nonstutterers, speeches with evidence to speeches without evidence, and newspapers to television broadcasts all use the nominal level of measurement. You could assign numbers to each category (such as calling men "category 1" and women "category 2"), but the numbers are only labels for the categories. There is no measure of the *degree* to which a variable is present. Nominal level measurement is often called the lowest level of measurement. You might suppose that nominal level measurement is of limited use to researchers. But you should avoid this judgment. Nominal level measurement is used to identify the attributes of the variables we study. Hence, nominal level measurement is used whenever we are interested in qualitative variables. In qualitative research most variables are identified (or not) on this nominal level of measurement. Other sorts of research also use nominal level measurement. For instance, experiments take nominal categories (an experimental group vs. a control group) and check for effects on an output variable.

ordinal level measurement defined

- **Ordinal level measurement** uses rank order to determine differences. Thus, if you were ranking a speech competition, you could rank the best speaker as "number 1," the second best as "number 2," the third best as "number 3," and so forth. This method will not tell you *how much* difference exists between speakers. For that information you must add a rating scale.

- **Interval level measurement** assigns numbers to items as a matter of degree. "Specifically, the intervals between the numbers are *equal* in size" (Cozby, 1989, p. 149). Most exams you have taken fall into this category. Most rating scales tend to be interval data as well.

  interval level measurement defined

- **Ratio level measurement** extends interval measurement to include an "absolute zero." An **absolute zero** indicates that the property measured is completely absent. For instance, when you measure your weight, you use ratio level measurement since a score of 0 would mean that you had no weight at all. Suppose you got up one morning and the outdoor temperature were 0 degrees Fahrenheit. Would that number indicate the absence of heat outside? Of course not—even though it might feel like it. But 0 on the Kelvin scale *is* the complete absence of heat since 0 Kelvin is the theoretic point at which thermal motion of atoms of molecules ceases—the point at which there would be no heat. If we measure the number of newspaper column inches dedicated to news stories about the Internet, we use ratio level measurement. When therapists count the number of dysfluencies by a client during a 5-minute period, ratio level measurement is involved.

  ratio level measurement defined

Interval and ratio levels of measurement allow us to use meaningful arithmetic to examine data. Even so, some writers have doubted that most popular measurement tools actually use scales with equal intervals (Stevens, 1951). Other researchers, however, have studied the impact of violating assumptions of pure intervals, and they found the alleged difficulties to be trivial on eventual statistical analyses of data (e.g., Baker, Hardyck, & Petrinovich, 1966). At least, we can follow the lead of scholars who have decided to call most of our popular tools "quasi-interval" measures, because they act enough like interval measures to permit using statistical tools designed for them (Hopkins & Glass, 1978, p. 13).

many of our measures are "quasi-interval"

It should be mentioned that measurement levels depend on the tools that may be available. For instance, a speaker's voice pitch could be identified in simple nominal categories (speakers with high-pitched voices, speakers with low-pitched voices) or voice pitch could be measured with an oscilloscope to identify ratio level cycles. In many studies researchers often start with interval level variables, and then group them down into nominal level categories. For instance, groups of highly intelligent and lowly intelligent people might be created out of a sample that originally measured each person's IQ on an interval scale. Thus, measurement levels are often determined by the methods researchers choose.

researchers often collapse variables down into lower levels of measurement

OPERATIONAL DEFINITIONS AND MEASURES

Once researchers have chosen variables to study, they select operational definitions for them. To determine if wise selections have been made, two interrelated characteristics are argued for the operational definitions: reliability and validity. Though in a broad sense these concerns influence all researchers, the rest of this chapter emphasizes applications predominantly to quantitative research.

The Requirement of Reliability

As a standard requirement in scholarly journals, empirical researchers are expected to produce evidence showing that their measures are reliable.

SPECIAL DISCUSSION 4-1
The Fallacy of Misplaced Precision

Researchers know that the results of a study can only be as good as the data. Some researchers, however, may claim precision that goes beyond the data. Sometimes labelled **false precision** (Kaplan, 1964, p. 204), the basic idea is that researchers claim more precision in analyzing data than was present in the original data.

Here is how it works. Suppose a researcher collects data from 500 people to find out how they feel about the statement, "Third party candidates should not be elected U.S. president." Subjects give their reactions on 5-point scales ranging from "strongly disagree" (scored as 1) to "strongly agree" (scored as 5). The researcher might find that the average response is 4.26667. In reality, this precision is bogus since the original rating system is a 1 to 5 scale. Carrying out general data to incredibly precise points is meaningless. It is a false precision because the numbers researchers compute cannot be better than the data themselves.

So, what should researchers do? One school of thought holds that researchers should round back to the level of precision in the original data. But this method may introduce great rounding error when other statistics are computed from the data. A second method advises carrying out computations no more than two digits beyond the level of precision in the original measures. In our example, we would be permitted to carry out our computations no more than two decimal places. Thus, we might report an average of 4.27. Researchers are warned to avoid the temptation to commit the **fallacy of misplaced precision.**

Defining Reliability

reliability defined

Reliability is the internal consistency of a measure. A consistent measure tends to produce the same measurements over time. Thus, reliability is really a test of the stability of a measure. Unreliability can be introduced many ways. Items on a measure may be inconsistent with each other because they are vague, confusing, or simply irrelevant to common concepts. But individuals who take a test can also introduce sources of unreliability. Bruce Tuckman explained (1978):

ways unreliability is introduced

> Among the factors which contribute to the unreliability of a test are (1) familiarity with the particular test form (such as a multiple choice question), (2) fatigue, (3) emotional strain, (4) physical conditions of the room in which the test is given, (5) health of the test taker, (6) fluctuations of human memory, (7) amount of practice or experience by the test taker of the specific skill being measured, and (8) specific knowledge that has been gained outside of the experience being evaluated by the test. A test which is overly sensitive to these unpredictable (and often uncontrollable) sources of error is not a reliable test. Test unreliability creates *instrumentation bias,* a source of internal invalidity in an experiment. (p. 161)

For the most part, standardized tests—such as IQ tests, personality tests, and placement tests sold by commercial testing firms—have been examined for reliability.

The tests are often accompanied by reports and manuals that describe how such reliability has been established. Though there is controversy about the accuracy or validity of some of these measures, there has been enough evidence to permit researchers to use them.

Assessing Reliability

Researchers can determine a measure's reliability several ways. All these methods are comparable. The methods differ in their data collection methods, rather than in the sorts of information they provide. All these methods take information about the consistency of a measure with itself and compute a **reliability coefficient.** This coefficient is actually a correlation, which measures the amount of association or coincidence of things. Without getting into the details here, let us just say that a reliability coefficient can range from 0 (no reliability) to 1 (perfect reliability). But you will not see many coefficients of 0 or 1. Instead, you will see numbers with decimal points, such as .82, .91, or .77. A measure with *really* good consistency should have reliability of .9 or higher. A good measure may have reliability in the .80 to .89 range. A fair measure should have reliability of at least .7. As a matter of publication policy, the American Psychological Association has decided that tests with coefficients below .6 should not be analyzed in studies. The following methods assess reliability:

> **reliability coefficients identified and interpreted**

> **methods to assess reliability**

- **Test-retest reliability** involves giving a measure twice and reporting consistency between scores. If a measure is consistent, then a person should have pretty much the same score each time. Of course, people can change from one testing time to another. But a reliable test should give tolerably consistent results from one occasion to the next. An audiometer used in speech and hearing science might be tested one week against standard pitches. The next week the process might be repeated. If the observed pitch drifted, this degree of unreliability could be noted and an adjustment made in the machine. Test-retest reliability is time consuming since two data collections are involved. This method is often useful when measures contain single items or when test items combine matters that are largely independent of others on the same measure. For instance, Ritchie and Fitzpatrick (1990) developed the Revised Family Communication Patterns Instrument and found test-retest correlations ranging from .64 to .82 for the subscales that composed the scale.
- **Alternate forms reliability** (also called "parallel-forms technique") involves constructing different forms of the same test from a common pool of measurement items, giving each of the different forms to the *same* group of people, and determining the degree of consistency between them. You may remember taking standard achievement tests in high school or before attending college. You may have noticed that the tests had different forms (such as Form A, Form B, and Form C) so that people sitting next to each other did not have the same test. Professional test designers often combine alternate forms reliability with other reliability methods.
- **Split half reliability** divides a test into two parts, scores them separately, and checks the consistency between the two scores. Research such as Wheeless, Frymier, and Thompson's (1992) examination of the 16-item Communication

Satisfaction Scale found very high reliability by use of split-half reliability methods. You might suppose that researchers with a 40-item true-false test create halves by scoring the first 20 items as one test and the second 20 items as the second test. But they don't. People may become fatigued near the end of a test and score worse than they did on the first part. So, researchers may create halves by scoring the even numbered items as one test and scoring all the odd numbered items as the other test. Hence, sometimes this method is called "odd-even reliability."

- **Item to total reliability** computes the correlation of items with the total test. Here is the idea. If you take an exam and answer the first test question correctly, you would expect to get a higher overall test score than somebody who got the first answer wrong. There should be a high correspondence or correlation between your score on a test *item* and your score on the *total* test. Using this method, researchers drop unreliable items and keep the remaining test (often recomputing reliability). Under what circumstances could your score on a test item correlate zero with the total? (That's exactly zero—no rounding.) There are only two ways such a thing is possible: either everybody passed the item or everybody failed it. In either case, your score on that item would give no information about whether you did well or poorly on the test as a whole. Sometimes a test item is related inversely with the total test score. This condition means that if you pass an item you are likely to get a lower score on the rest of the test than did someone who failed the item. These sorts of test items must be measuring something completely apart from the rest of the test. Therefore, researchers automatically delete them from their final measures.

- **Intercoder reliability** takes a slightly different approach to reliability. Sometimes people will look at behavior and categorize it by using some sort of check sheet. The basic question becomes, "Do different people rate things the same way?" If researchers complete a content analysis of communication, any check sheet categories used by researchers can be examined for reliability. We can look at the way two (or more) researchers (also called "raters") complete the same check sheets to rate the same communication. The more ratings are the same between raters, the more reliable the check sheet is. Though one could use some applications of correlations to get the job done, scholars have made things easy for us by developing shortcut formulae that give us intercoder reliability. Though there are several forms that have been used, prudent researchers tend to rely on either Cohen's *kappa* (Cohen, 1960), which compensates for the number of times rating categories are used, or Scott's *pi* (Scott, 1955), which also compensates for the rates of agreement that would be expected by chance alone. Table 4.1A illustrates the use of Scott's *pi* in a typical example. Though this example involves a case of two coders, the formula can be extended to any number of coders (see Fleiss, 1971). This method permits researchers to identify how reliably content analysis check sheets are used to code communication. (Cohen's *kappa* involves some cumbersome computation, we do not include it here. A good review of these different methods is found in Fleiss, 1981).

Cohen's kappa and Scott's pi for reliability of content analysis categories

TABLE 4.1 Statistical Reliability Formulae

A. Intercoder reliability for content analysis or diagnostic categories: (Scott's *pi*)

Formula

$$pi = \frac{\text{proportion observed agreement} - \text{proportion expected agreement}}{1 - \text{proportion expected agreement}}$$

where:

$$\text{proportion observed agreement} = \frac{(\text{number of raters}) \times (\text{number of same ratings made})}{\text{total number of ratings by all raters}}$$

proportion expected agreement = sum of the squared proportions in each category

EXAMPLE: Coders rated the proportion of violence in children's TV programs observed during a two-week period. They reported the proportion of agreement among themselves at .80 (leave in the decimal point). The violence was categorized into five categories:

threatening violence	.40
punching others	.10
slapping	.30
using weapons	.10
off-screen violence	.10

$$pi = \frac{\text{proportion observed agreement} - \text{proportion expected agreement}}{1 - \text{proportion expected agreement}}$$

$$= \frac{.80 - (.40^2 + .10^2 + .30^2 + .10^2 + .10^2)}{1 - (.40^2 + .10^2 + .30^2 + .10^2 + .10^2)}$$

$$= \frac{.80 - (.28)}{1 - (.28)}$$

$$= \frac{.52}{.72}$$

$$pi = .72$$

B. K-R 20: used when a test deals with correct and incorrect answers

Formula

$$\text{K-R 20} = \frac{k}{k-1} * \left(1 - \frac{\text{sum of P} * \text{Q of each test item}}{s^2 \text{ of the total test score}}\right)$$

where:

k = the number of items on the test
P = the proportion (keep the decimal point in) of people who answered the item correctly
Q = the proportion (keep the decimal point in) of people who answered the item incorrectly
s^2 = the variance (a measure of variability [see chapter 13])

TABLE 4.1 —Continued

EXAMPLE: A measure of retention of information in radio ads was assessed by use of a five-item true-false test. The first item was answered correctly (P) by 70% of the people, the second item was passed by 65%, the third item was passed by 50%, the fourth item was passed by 60%, and the last item was passed by 80%. The variance of the total test was 2.4.

$$= \frac{k}{k-1} \quad * \quad \left(1 - \frac{\text{sum of P * Q of each test item}}{s^2 \text{ of the total test score}}\right)$$

$$= \frac{5}{5-1} \quad * \quad \left(1 - \frac{(.7 * .3) + (.65 * .35) + (.50 * .50) + (.60 * .40) + (.80 * .20)}{2.4}\right)$$

$$= 1.25 \quad * \quad \left(1 - \frac{(.21) + (.23) + (.25) + (.24) + (.16)}{2.4}\right)$$

$$= 1.25 \quad * \quad \left(1 - \frac{1.09}{2.4}\right)$$

$$= 1.25 \quad * \quad (1 - .45)$$

$$= 1.25 \quad * \quad (.55)$$

K-R 20 = .69

C. Coefficient alpha: used when a test does not have correct and incorrect answers

Formula

$$\alpha = \frac{k}{k-1} * \left(1 - \frac{\text{sum of } s^2 \text{ of each test item}}{s^2 \text{ of the total test score}}\right)$$

where:

k = the number of items on the test
s^2 = the variance (a measure of variability [see chapter 13])

EXAMPLE: A measure of speech fluency rating scale containing five seven-point scales. The variance for the first scale item was 3.2, the variance for the second item was 3, the variance for the third item was 3.8, the variance for the fourth item was 2.5, and the variance for the fifth item was 3.4. The variance of the total test was 38.

$$\alpha = \frac{k}{k-1} \quad * \quad \left(1 - \frac{\text{sum of } s^2 \text{ of each test item}}{s^2 \text{ of the total test score}}\right)$$

$$= \frac{5}{5-1} \quad * \quad \left(1 - \frac{3.2 + 3 + 3.8 + 2.5 + 3.4}{2.4}\right)$$

$$= 1.25 \quad * \quad \left(1 - \frac{15.9}{38}\right)$$

$$= 1.25 \quad * \quad (1 - .42)$$

$$= 1.25 \quad * \quad (.58)$$

$$\alpha = .73$$

- Statistical shortcuts are not really different forms of reliability. They are simply ways to get reliability coefficients rapidly, especially when major computer programs are used. It should be remembered, however, that these different tools are mathematically equivalent and can be interpreted similarly. There are two options that are most often used. As Table 4.1B shows, one tool is called **K-R 20,** which is shorthand for Kuder-Richardson formula 20 for reliability. This method is used when researchers want to determine the reliability of a measure that has items that are scored as correct or incorrect answers. Most exams that you have taken in classes, and tests of comprehension and skills use this sort of method for reliability. But suppose we measure perceptions or ratings that people may have—such as attitudes, self-esteem, ratings of speech intelligibility, or ratings of newspaper sensationalism. Under these conditions there is no "correct" answer. The consistency with which people react to such items on the measure may be tapped by using **Cronbach's coefficient alpha**[1] (α) (Cronbach, 1970, pp. 160–161) as illustrated in table 4.1C.

*(margin note: **K-R 20 identified for tests with correct or incorrect answers**)*

*(margin note: **coefficient alpha**)*

An interesting fact about measurement is that the longer a test is, the more reliable it becomes. With increasing length, variation from item to item tends to balance out. A mathematic proof of this relationship is called the Spearman-Brown prophecy formula. Thus, major statistical formulae for reliability tend to be corrected for test length so that comparisons of different measures can be made regardless of their length.

The Requirement of Validity

Imagine a stairway in your home. If the stairway were not firm and stable, the stairs would become shaky when you tried to stand on them, and you could not get to your destination. That's an example of an unreliable stairway. When a measure is unreliable, it is unstable, and you can't use it to get where you want to go. Now, suppose the stairway were sturdy. It would be reliable, and you could use it the same way every time you walked on it. But what if the carpenters built it to lead to the roof, and you want to go to the upstairs rooms? The stairway could still not get you where you want to go. This stairway is not a valid path to the upstairs rooms because it is pointed in the wrong direction. That's the notion of reliability and validity in a nutshell: reliability means the measure is stable; validity means the stable test truly measures what is intended (it's pointed in the right direction).

Defining Validity

Validity is the consistency of a measure with a criterion. In plain terms, validity is the degree to which a measure actually measures what is claimed. Reliability is determined by looking at the *internal* consistency of a measure. Looking at internal

*(margin note: **validity defined**)*

---

[1] Cronbach developed a "shortcut" formula called coefficient alpha$_k$ for tests that have correct and incorrect answers. In fact, as Cronbach explained (1970, p. 161) this formula is the same as K-R 20. Similarly, Kuder and Richardson developed a formula called K-R 21, which is equivalent to Cronbach's coefficient alpha. Yet, researchers usually report coefficient alpha for measures that don't have correct answers and reserve K-R 20 for tests that feature correct and incorrect answers.

SPECIAL DISCUSSION 4-2
Use of Self-Report Measures

Much communication research relies on the reports and evaluations of people who were participants in communication under investigation. The problem is that such reports may or may not be valid. Researchers have to be careful with self-report measures. There are two sorts of these measures that have raised concern: personal evaluations by participants and recall of past communication exchanges by participants.

CONCERNS WITH DIRECT ACCOUNT REPORTS

Sometimes research subjects cannot give accurate reports of their reactions to communication. They may not know what they are being asked, they may not know how they feel about issues, or they may feel pressure to answer so that they look good. One researcher called such research "illusory research" since analyzing such data is far removed from the variables the researcher originally wished to study (Sypher, 1980). With such tools as semantic differential scales, for instance, "measures may be tapping semantic similarity rather than actual communication behavior" (p. 80).

Many times people make reports that exaggerate the frequency with which they do socially desirable things. For instance, public opinion surveys of church attendance in the United States are quite high with over 40% of Americans reporting that they attend church services regularly. Yet, one study found that actual observed attendance at churches was much lower (Hadaway, et al., 1993). In one county, 33% of the Protestants said they went to church, though only 20% really attended. Among Roman Catholics, 51% reported going to church, whereas only 28% did.

To assure valid measurement with self-report data, researchers often add "control checks." As a form of predictive validity, one may determine whether self-reports accurately reflect what people really do. For instance, Duncan and Lieberson (1959) examined self-reports of social distance among different ethnic groups in Chicago. To check on the validity of the self-reports, they examined the relationship between social distance scores and the degree to which the members different ethnic groups physically segregated themselves from each other. They found a high correlation between these variables. Thus, they had evidence that gave them "confidence that the subjective measure (social distance) was a valid measure of respondents' feelings" (Schutt, 1996, p. 96). By using such validity checks, limitations on self-report validity claims may be made.

CONCERNS WITH "RECALL" STUDIES

Some studies ask subjects to recall recent communication encounters and to report what occurred and their feelings about them. Naturally, these studies introduce another limitation on results—the ability of subjects to recall accurately what occurred. For instance, Trapp and Hoff (1985) asked people to recall arguments in which they had been involved and to describe the results of the arguments. Trapp and Hoff found that people reported that the arguments rarely were resolved.

consistency, however, will not reveal if a measure is "pointed in the right direction." To assess validity, researchers need to find some *external* evidence to allow researchers to believe they are measuring what they intended. Thus, validity is the consistency of a measure with some outside criterion or standard by which to judge the test.

Reliability versus Validity

As you can tell, it is possible to have a reliable measure without its being valid (you can have a stable stairway that does not go where you intended). But you cannot have a valid measure without its first being reliable. Thus, validity presumes reliability. Hence, if you have a valid test, you have a reliable one.

validity presumes reliability

Assessing Validity

There are four major ways to determine validity, though researchers usually combine some of them to argue for their measures: face validity, expert jury validity, criterion validity, and construct validity.

methods to assess validity

- *Face validity* involves researchers' looking at the content of the measurement items and advancing an argument that on its face the measure seems to identify what it claims. Sometimes arguments about content can be quite reasonable. Furthermore, this method has been the most common approach taken by researchers to argue the validity of their measures. It is limited, however, by the absence of additional direct evidence and, of course, by the reasoning powers of the researcher.

- *Expert jury validity* involves having a group of experts in the subject matter examine the measurement and judge its merit. Researchers sometimes report the number of positive assessments received from the experts. Most often, experts give advice to help the researcher make improvements. Thus, expert juries frequently are consulted to help develop measures. As a method of validation, the expert jury method boils down to face validity that involves additional people.

- **Criterion validity** consists of methods that assess a measure's worth by examining its relation to some outside criterion. There are two forms of this method.

  1. **Concurrent validity** correlates a new measure with a previously validated measure of the same construct. This method is commonly used when a traditional research area is extended with updated measures. For example, as part of her work on the measure of Teacher Affinity-Seeking, Danielle Dolin (1995) validated her new measure by concurrent validity with a previously validated measure of student affect for the teacher.

  2. **Predictive validity** is the degree to which a measure predicts known groups in which the construct must exist. Thus, if you were developing a measure of one's tendency to self-disclose private information about oneself, you might find a group of people and see if this test predicts whether self-disclosure actually occurs. Rubin and Shenker (1978) used this technique to show that their self-disclosure scale successfully predicted whether self-disclosure was actually received by college students' roommates. If you developed an instrument to measure successful sales communication, you might find a group of successful salespeople and a group of not-so-successful salespeople. After administering the test to both groups, you could see if it distinguished between the two known groups. If so, then a claim of predictive validity could be made.

- **Construct validity** studies are among the most impressive works in communication research. Construct validation requires that a new measure be administered to subjects along with at least two other measures. One of these measures should be a valid measure of a construct that is known conceptually to be directly related to the new measure (that is, as scores on the new measure increase, scores on the related construct also should increase). For instance,

  > if a physiological measure of heartbeat is supposed to be indicative of communication anxiety, then it would be reasonable to expect people in high stress communication situations to have more rapid heartbeats (higher measured communication anxiety) than would be expected of people in low stress communication settings. (Emmert, 1989, p. 114)

  Another of these measures should be a valid measure of a construct known conceptually to be inversely related to the new measure (that is, as scores on the new measure *increase,* scores on the related construct should *decrease*). Some researchers add a third variable known to be unrelated to the construct measured by the new instrument. Yet, most construct validation studies exclude this final comparison. If the new measure is valid, it should produce significant findings in the correct directions. Obviously, the conceptual bases for the measures must be very well understood and the theoretic foundations clear. Such studies are not easy, and they are major inquiries in and of themselves. One influential effort was completed by James McCroskey (1978) to validate the "Personal Report of Communication Apprehension" (also known as the PRCA).[2] Since communication apprehension is one's "fear or anxiety associated with either real or anticipated (oral) communication with another person or persons" (McCroskey, 1977, p. 78), he isolated a valid measure of "verbal reticence," which was known to have a direct relationship to communication apprehension. He also found valid measures of three constructs that were known to have theoretically inverse relationships with communication apprehension: extroversion, self-esteem, and self-acceptance. When all the measures were administered, the patterns were as predicted. Though it does not always work out so well for researchers, construct validation was completed for the PRCA and it has become a very popular research tool.

POPULAR TOOLS OF MEASUREMENT

Some major measurement techniques have been popular in our field. Two major categories include measures that express judgments of some kind and measures that identify achievement.

Methods to Measure Judgments

Communication researchers often ask people to report their attitudes or rate some behavior. These judgments can be measured in many ways, but the most popular tools in communication have been Thurstone scales, Likert scales, Guttman scalograms, and semantic differential-type scales.

Thurstone Equal Appearing Interval Scales

Named for their creator, L. L. Thurstone, these scales are actually called "equal appearing interval" scales. They are composed of statements related to some topic. For instance, if you wanted to rate the bias in newspaper coverage of political campaigns, you might use a Thurstone scale with statements such as, "Newspapers are very biased," "Newspapers do not tell the truth," and "Newspapers have a hard time being impartial." Respondents would be asked to identify the statements with which they agree. Then, unbeknownst to the subjects, you would determine a total score by adding up the point values for each of the statements with which the subjects agreed. How do we get the point values? That's the time-consuming part. The researcher typically puts together a list of fifty to one hundred statements (on cards) and then asks a group of people (from the same population that will later use the scales) to sort the cards on a scale ranging from 1 to 11 indicating how extreme the statements are. For instance, the statement "Newspapers are very biased" is more extreme than the statement "Newspapers have a hard time being impartial." So, these statements would be placed at different locations on the scale. After the raters are finished, the researcher identifies statements that have consistent ratings. Then these statements are given an average score based on their ratings. In using the scales in a study, the researcher simply tallies up the total points of the statements with which each person agreed. Table 4.2 shows such a scale.

Thurstone scales identified

---

[2] This study actually relied on information from other published and unpublished works to make its case. Furthermore, a section of additional personality correlates is excluded from this description.

TABLE 4.2 Examples of Rating Scales

THURSTONE SCALES

Place a check mark in the blank next to each statement with which you agree.

_____ 1.	This class in research methods is more challenging than other courses I am taking this term.	(9.8)
_____ 2.	This class in research methods teaches me valuable information.	(10.1)
_____ 3.	This class in research methods is what I expected.	(6.0)
_____ 4.	This class in research methods is interesting.	(8.9)

NOTE: Numbers in parentheses indicate the point value for each statement. The scale is scored by adding the points for all items for which the respondent indicates agreement.

SEMANTIC DIFFERENTIAL-TYPE SCALES

Rate the concept "The President" according to the way you perceive it or feel about it by placing an X on each of the seven-point scales to indicate your evaluation.

The President

reliable	___:___:___:___:___:___	unreliable*
uninformed	___:___:___:___:___:___	informed
unqualified	___:___:___:___:___:___	qualified
intelligent	___:___:___:___:___:___	unintelligent*
valuable	___:___:___:___:___:___	worthless*
inexpert	___:___:___:___:___:___	expert
dishonest	___:___:___:___:___:___	honest
unfriendly	___:___:___:___:___:___	friendly
pleasant	___:___:___:___:___:___	unpleasant*
selfish	___:___:___:___:___:___	unselfish
awful	___:___:___:___:___:___	nice
virtuous	___:___:___:___:___:___	sinful*

NOTE: Items followed by asterisks (*) indicate reverse scoring. Scores on the first six items are added together to produce a "competence" score. The remaining items are added together to produce a "character" score.

Source: From Table 3, McCroskey, J.C. (1966). Scales for the measurement of ethos. *Speech Monographs, 33,* 72. Copyright by the Speech Communication Association. Used by permission of the publisher and James C. McCroskey.

GUTTMAN SCALOGRAM

Consider a person who is Chinese and circle the number next to each of the situations listed below in which you would accept a person from this group.

1. as visitors to my country
2. to citizenship in my country
3. to employment in my occupation
4. to my street as neighbors
5. to my club as personal friends
6. to close kinship by marriage

NOTE: This scale is an adapted version of the Bogardus Social Distance scale (Bogardus, 1933). The number of items circled is the score received by the individual.

TABLE 4.2 —*Continued*

LIKERT SCALE

Personal Report of Communication Apprehension (PRCA-24)

Directions: This instrument is composed of 24 statements concerning your feelings about communication with other people. Please indicate in the space provided the degree to which each statement applies to you by marking whether you (1) Strongly Agree, (2) Agree, (3) Are Undecided, (4) Disagree, or (5) Strongly Disagree with each statement. There are no right or wrong answers. Many of the statements are similar to other statements. Do not be concerned about this. Work quickly, just record your first impression.

_____ 1. I dislike participating in group discussions.

_____ 2. Generally, I am comfortable while participating in group discussions.

_____ 3. I am tense and nervous while participating in group discussions.

_____ 4. I like to get involved in group discussions.

_____ 5. Engaging in a group discussion with new people makes me tense and nervous.

_____ 6. I am calm and relaxed while participating in group discussions.

_____ 7. Generally, I am nervous when I have to participate in a meeting.

_____ 8. Usually I am calm and relaxed while participating in meetings.

_____ 9. I am very calm and relaxed when I am called upon to express an opinion at a meeting.

_____10. I am afraid to express myself at meetings.

_____11. Communicating at meetings usually makes me uncomfortable.

_____12. I am very relaxed when answering questions at a meeting.

_____13. While participating in a conversation with a new acquaintance, I feel very nervous.

_____14. I have no fear of speaking up in conversations.

_____15. Ordinarily I am very tense and nervous in conversations.

_____16. Ordinarily I am very calm and relaxed in conversations.

_____17. While conversing with a new acquaintance, I feel very relaxed.

_____18. I'm afraid to speak up in conversations.

_____19. I have no fear of giving a speech.

_____20. Certain parts of my body feel very tense and rigid while giving a speech.

_____21. I feel relaxed while giving a speech.

_____22. My thoughts become confused and jumbled when I am giving a speech.

_____23. I face the prospect of giving a speech with confidence.

_____24. While giving a speech I get so nervous, I forget facts I really know.

SCORING

Group = 18 − (1) + (2) − (3) + (4) − (5) + (6)

Meeting = 18 − (7) + (8) + (9) − (10) − (11) + (12)

Dyadic = 18 − (13) + (14) − (15) + (16) + (17) − (18)

Public = 18 + (19) − (20) + (21) − (22) + (23) − (24)

Overall CA = Group + Meeting + Dyadic + Public

The method is quite sound and continues to be used in many studies in communication. Researchers who study effects of stress on communication often use a rating scale of stressful life events that is a Thurstone scale of events (Reinard & Boster, 1978). Subjects receive a total stress score by adding up the points associated with the events that they report happening to them in the recent past. Yet, the method can often be tedious, time consuming, and expensive. The scales also must be done anew every time the topic of evaluation is changed.

Likert Scales

This technique presents statements that reflect clear positions on an issue and then asks subjects to indicate their responses on five-point scales: strongly agree, agree, neither agree nor disagree, disagree, disagree strongly. A few researchers use four-point scales, leaving out the middle position entirely. Occasionally researchers have added additional scale positions, "disagree slightly" and "agree slightly," but the basic system is not defined by the number of points used. Instead, items that have high reliability with each other are combined by adding up the ratings that respondents give. Unlike Thurstone scales, which assign a value for each item with which a person agrees, Likert scales simply gauge the degree to which there is agreement or disagreement with statements representing a common issue.

You have filled out Likert scales on teacher evaluation forms and, very probably, on some surveys you have completed in your classes. These scales are very popular because it is relatively easy to develop them (a researcher can determine reliability at the same time the data are collected, for instance). Yet, a total score sometimes hides specific details of the response from a person. Moreover, if researchers change their topics, the items on the Likert scale may have to be composed all over again.

Guttman Scalogram

Developed by Louis Guttman, this scale presents a series of statements dealing with one topic and arranged according to their level of intensity. Surely the most popular Guttman scale has been the Bogardus "Social Distance" scale (see Table 4.2). This

scale has often been featured in studies of racial and ethnic prejudice. The more prejudiced a person is, the reasoning goes, the fewer circumstances this person would find acceptable. Because the statements are arranged on a single continuum, if we know the number of statements with which a person agrees, we probably also know which statements the person accepts. For instance, if a respondent rates it acceptable for a person to have employment in one's profession, that respondent also probably finds it acceptable for the target person to be a citizen in the country and to visit the country. Thus, the number of statements with which a person agrees also lets us know *which* particular statements they probably were.

The Guttman scale is scored by counting the number of statements with which a respondent agrees. In our example, the fewer items circled, the more "socially distant" the respondent is from others. Of course, some people may not follow a set pattern in their responses. Thus, Guttman developed a criterion called the "coefficient of

reproducibility" to assess the reliability of these "scalograms." To compute a coefficient of reproducibility, the researcher arranges the statements in order, ranging from the most frequently agreed items in a sample through the least frequently agreed to items. Then, the researcher looks at each subject's total scores to count the proportion of the time that the respondent answered as expected. That is, if people agreed with three statements, they should have answered the three most frequently accepted statements. Any time an answer appears outside the predicted pattern, an exception is noted. Guttman recommended that consistent responses be observed at least at 90% of the time, or a coefficient of reproducibility of .90.[3]

This scaling method is highly useful when there is a clear continuum of responses that people could make on some issue. Yet, the stringent requirements for such a scale may make it challenging to come up with new Guttman scales. Furthermore, they are specific to topics and must be developed from scratch each time a new topic is investigated.

applications, advantages, and limitations

Semantic Differential-Type Scales

In 1957, Charles Osgood, George Suci, and Percy Tannenbaum wrote *The Measurement of Meaning* in which they reported research to discover how people assign meaning to words. To help them along the way, they developed a type of scale that involved using pairs of "bi-polar" adjectives (often separated by seven points, sometimes six, sometimes five) that could be used by people to indicate their reactions (see table 4.2). Since they were studying semantics (the study of the relationship between words and their meanings), they called their scale the "Semantic Differential." The method became popular among researchers who were not studying semantics. Thus, these applications to other subjects resulted in their being called Semantic Differential-*type* scales.

semantic differential-type scales identified

This scale method has become the most popular measurement approach in communication studies. An object of evaluation is presented to people who indicate their responses by checking or circling scale positions. A total score is obtained by assigning values from 1 to 7 to each item and simply adding up items on the same dimension. To measure a concept—such as competence or character perceptions of a source—researchers use a set of adjective pairs. Then they use standard tools to show reliability for the items used to measure each common dimension.

This method is very convenient to use and, unlike other tools, can be employed almost regardless of the topic under evaluation. For instance, the same scales can be used to assess credibility of any source. Researchers don't need to construct new scales to evaluate each different source. Yet, the responses on each dimension give only a composite reaction, rather than information about the contours of responses. For instance, suppose a person received a score of 16 on four semantic differential-type scales. The person might have "flip flopped" from one extreme positive position to an extreme negative position and back again. Or, the response might have emerged if the

applications, advantages, and limitations

---

[3] The coefficient of reproducibility is computed by counting the number of "errors" and dividing by the total number of responses. Then this proportion is subtracted from 1.0. Originally Guttman (1944) stated that a coefficient of .90 was required for an acceptable scale. At a later time, Guttman permitted the scale to be used if the coefficient of reproducibility were .80 or higher (since one imperfection created two potential errors to count—one for the "incorrectly" used scale and one for the scale that "incorrectly" should have been used but was not). But the requirement of .90 has remained as the most typical standard.

person neither agreed nor disagreed on all items. A simple total may miss such differences in response patterns. Overall, however, the method seems to have gained popularity because of its great versatility.

Methods to Measure Achievement

Researchers often obtain data on achievement or knowledge of some content. The formats to measure such information provide a repertoire that researchers can use repeatedly. On one level, achievement or knowledge of content can be tested by such methods as true-false or multiple-choice tests. Sometimes researchers give respondents questions that ask them to choose between two alternatives. Called the "forced choice format," the researcher gives subjects two statements, one of which they must choose. This method is useful to help identify how individuals make choices, but sometimes the choices are difficult for respondents to complete accurately (Hale, Boster, & Mongeau, 1991).

A variation of sorts is the paired comparison method. In this format, subjects receive alternatives with all possible combinations given two at a time. This method is invaluable for ranking alternatives that may seem to have a great overlap in quality. If you were asked to rank a list of 10 newspapers for general credibility, it might be difficult to rate them all at once. Instead, you could be given two newspapers and asked to choose which of the two is the most credible. Then all other combinations would follow, a pair at a time. The final ranking could be found by counting the number of times each paper was preferred.

SUMMARY

Accurate measurement is vital to sound research. Measurement imperfections introduce additional variation or background noise into a study in addition to variation that already exists in samples. This problem is called attenuation of results, which means that there is a reduction in the size of observed effects because of errors in measurement. There are four measurement levels for data: (1) nominal level measurement uses numbers as simple identifications of variables; (2) ordinal level measurement uses rank order to determine differences; (3) interval level measurement identifies items as a matter of degree (the intervals between the numbers are equal in size); (4) ratio level measurement extends interval measurement to include an "absolute zero" (in which a score of 0 indicates that the property measured is completely absent).

Reliability is the internal consistency of a measure. There are several ways researchers can determine a measure's reliability. All these methods take information about the consistency of a measure with itself and compute a reliability coefficient, which is a correlation that measures the amount of association or coincidence of things. Test-retest reliability involves giving a measure twice and reporting consistency between scores. This method is time consuming but often is useful when measures contain single items or when test items combine matters that are largely independent of others on the same measure. Alternate forms reliability (or parallel-forms technique) involves constructing different forms of the same test from a common pool of measurement items and correlating scores that sample groups receive on both. Split half reliability divides a test into two parts, scores them separately, and checks the consistency between the two scores for a sample group (sometimes this method employs odd-even reliability). Item to total reliability computes the correlation of items with the total test. Intercoder reliability examines the degree to which different raters consistently categorize things by using some sort of check sheet (in content analysis of communication, prudent researchers tend to rely on either Cohen's *kappa,* which compensates for the number of times rating categories are used, or Scott's *pi,* which also compensates for the rates of agreement that would be expected by chance alone). Statistical shortcuts are ways to get reliability coefficients rapidly using such methods as K-R 20 (used when researchers want to determine the reliability of a measure that has items that are scored as correct or incorrect) or coefficient alpha (when correct answers are not identified).

Validity is the consistency of a measure with a criterion. In plain terms, validity is the degree to which a measure actually measures what is claimed. Though it is possible to have a reliable test without having a valid one, one cannot have a valid measure without its first being reliable. Thus, validity presumes reliability. There are four major ways to determine validity. Face validity involves researchers' looking at the content of the measurement items and advancing an argument that on its face the measure seems to identify what it claims. Expert jury validity involves having a group of experts in the subject matter examine the measurement device and judge its merit. Criterion validity assesses a measure's worth by examining its relation to some outside criterion, such as (a) concurrent validity that correlates a new measure with a previously validated measure of the same thing, and (b) predictive validity, which is the degree to which a measure predicts known groups in which the construct must exist. Construct validation requires that a new measure be administered to subjects along with at least two other measures, one of which is known to be directly related to the concept, and one of which is known to be inversely related to the concept (if the new measure is valid, it should produce significant findings in the correct directions).

Communication researchers often ask people to report their attitudes or rate some behavior. The most popular methods to use are Thurstone equal appearing interval scales (that have assigned point values for each of the statements with which subjects agree), Likert scales (that consist of statements for which subjects indicate their agreement or disagreement on five-point scales), Guttman scalograms (involving a series of statements dealing with one topic and arranged according to their level of intensity), and semantic differential-type scales (7-point scales bounded by bipolar adjectives). Researchers often obtain data on achievement or knowledge of some content by using such formats as true-false or multiple-choice tests. Sometimes researchers give respondents "forced choice format" items that request them to choose between two alternatives. A variation is the paired comparison method in which subjects receive alternatives in all possible combinations taken two at a time.

TERMS FOR REVIEW

attenuation
nominal level measurement
ordinal level measurement
interval level measurement
ratio level measurement
false precision
reliability
reliability coefficient
test-retest reliability
alternate forms reliability
split half reliability
item to total reliability
KR-20

Cronbach's coefficient alpha
validity
face validity
expert jury validity
criterion validity
concurrent validity
predictive validity
construct validity
Thurstone equal appearing interval scales
Likert scales
Guttman scalogram
semantic differential-type scales

CHAPTER 5

Using Communication Research Sources

In the last analysis, research per se constitutes a method for the discovery of truth which is really a method of critical thinking.

—Clifford Woody

BEFORE WE GET STARTED . . .

Why? What? When? How? and Where? This chapter addresses these questions to prepare you for effective research. To do any kind of research, you must gather information about past work related to the subject. Thus, you need to spend some time in the library. These days, you also need to be familiar with using the Internet and electronic information sources. This chapter addresses these basic questions so that you can make fast work of library and electronic inquiry. It provides practical help on how to use—not simply examine, but *use*—research sources to build research arguments. Hence, you will learn how to structure your initial forays in the library and on the Internet. This chapter offers not a comprehensive list of information sources but an outline of the survival skills you should apply in your work.

APPROACHING RESEARCH MATERIALS

Research involves sifting materials to make cases. This section will answer some questions about three research dimensions: why? what? when?

The "Why?" Research Uses Past Work to Develop Arguments

Looking at past work helps us build research arguments. In this sense, an **argument** is the process of advancing conclusions based on reasons and evidence. Research argues to conclusions from the raw materials of information. In turn, the reasons may be tested with established standards of sound argument. Past inquiry guides us in several ways. **argument defined**

- *Past Research Gives Premises for Argument.* A **premise** is a statement in a logical argument that is the foundation for others drawn from it. Therefore, you can use past research as a premise for new research arguments. The reasoning does not prove the conclusion is true, of course. Yet, we can justify advancing some possible directions for future research. **1. finding premises for arguments**

- *Past Research Gives Evidence for Argument.* Many issues—even in a field as wide open for research as communication—have been studied successfully in the past. You can look at both the results and at the theories that have guided research. Past research also help you learn when a theory's limits have been found. Such information and criticism can be recorded for later use in your own arguments. **2. finding evidence for arguments**

- *Past Research Helps Balance Reliance on Authority and Empirical Data.* When reviewing literature you will encounter many different opinions. When an authority's interpretations stay close to the facts, you may feel justifiably comfortable accepting them. But when an authority ignores the facts or refuses to stick to them, you can feel justifiably suspicious. Since research is an argument, the papers you write are also arguments. Some inexperienced researchers believe they can ignore past work and use entirely new ideas and methods. Keith Stanovich calls this misguided approach the "**Einstein syndrome**" (1986, chap. 8) since researchers who suffer from it fail to connect their "sudden breakthrough" with lessons from others. By discarding previous lessons as irrelevant (hardly ever a justifiable claim), they fail to learn from the successes of others. So, it is useful to spend time looking at ways writers and scholars have conceptualized, justified, studied, and interpreted a research area. **3. balancing scholarly opinions against data** **"Einstein syndrome" defined**

The "What?" Purposeful Library Research

Though you must take the time getting to know the specialized language of a subject, your library research—traditional library or electronic library—will be most productive if you know what you want to find. Don't interview experts, go to the library, or surf the Internet unless you have first decided what you are looking for. Don't worry about closing your mind to new information. You will find unexpected material along the way, and you will want to take advantage of it. Do not just look for "background information." What is background anyway? When do you know when you have enough background? Experienced researchers know that background materials flow **research should be conducted with a goal or purpose**

topics to look for in library research

naturally from a search for specifics. Regardless of your problem statement, some of the most obvious things to seek at the library are

- definitions of key concepts and variables
- ways concepts and variables have been measured and studied
- summary statements that people (especially textbook writers) seem to make about the subject
- classic research studies on a subject (the studies that all the textbooks seem to reference)
- research that shows what methods to use
- research that shows what mistakes to avoid

absence of information is important to know

Sometimes you may find surprisingly little on your subject. That absence is very useful information. It suggests that the subject cries out for research. It may also indicate that most people have found the subject uninteresting (so what? most people may not have thought about the subject the way you have). Get used to finding that past research has not answered your particular research question. The field is wide open and you may find valuable things to investigate for yourself.

Where do you find information to answer your questions? Table 5.1 lists sources that can help to answer many questions (along with a rating of the usefulness of each source). Sometimes you will not find what you wish in these sources. For instance, we usually expect textbook writers to define their terms, but there are exceptions. Wayne C. Booth wrote an entire book called *The Rhetoric of Fiction* (1964) without ever defining the term "rhetoric." Research articles rarely state definitions. Instead, they may refer to sources with acceptable definitions. Thus, you should consider the resources indicated in table 5.1 when you seriously explore the library. Aside from looking at textbooks and articles (for which guidance will be given later in this chapter), there are three types of resources you should examine:

encyclopedias

- *Encyclopedias.* You may find useful context, reviews of general issues, and definitions in encyclopedias. In mass communication, for instance, encyclopedias can be useful sources *early* in the search effort, since many provide annual updates that describe new technologies and changes in communication law. You may also wish to check specialized encyclopedias available for each field.

handbooks, yearbooks, and annual reviews

- *Handbooks and Annual Reviews.* Although you may think of a handbook as the same thing as an employee manual, the term has been enlisted by scholars to refer to books containing summaries of literature and brief reviews of common topics. Most handbooks offer both summaries and criticisms of controversial issues.

dictionaries

- *Specialized Dictionaries.* Dictionaries of usage (such as Webster's) are poor sources for technical definitions because they are usually not written by people in the applied field you investigate. On the other hand, dictionaries of psychology, communication, mass media, and speech and hearing science attempt to provide correct technical definitions.

As you read, you will see references to other sources that you can track down later. Students sometimes read a literature review from a book and accept it as

TABLE 5.1 Sources Useful for Obtaining Information in Library Searches

Ratings of Sources*

Matters to Investigate	Categories of Sources			
	Textbooks	**Handbooks, Yearbooks, and Annual Reviews**	**Specialized Encyclopedias and Dictionaries**	**Articles**
Definitions of key concepts and variables	A	B	A	C
Ways concepts and variables have been measured and studied	C	B	D	A
General summary statements about the subject	A	A	F	C
Classic research studies in the field	A	A	F	B
Research that shows what methods to use	C	B	F	A
Research that shows what mistakes to avoid	C	B	F	A

```
*  These subjective ratings indicate   A: excellent source
                                        B: often useful source
                                        C: occasionally useful source
                                        D: rarely useful
                                        F: forget it
```

SOURCES FOR INFORMATION

Source	Comment
Encyclopedias	
Hudson, R. V. (1985). *Mass media: A chronological encyclopedia of television, motion pictures, magazines, newspapers, and books in the United States.* New York: Garland.	Covers mass media history from 1638 through 1985 in the United States.
International encyclopedia of communications. (1989). New York: Oxford University Press. (4 vols.).	Precis of over 500 topics of interest to communication
Sills, D. L. (Ed.). (1968). *International encyclopedia of the social sciences.* New York: Macmillan. (18 vols.).	Dated but useful background with emphasis on classic work in the social sciences
Dictionaries	
General	
Chaplin, J. P. (1985). *Dictionary of psychology* (2nd rev. ed.). New York: Dell.	Particularly useful for presenting definitions relatively free of jargon
DeVito, J. A. (1986). *The communication handbook: A dictionary.* New York: Harper and Row.	Definitions of terms and essays on broad communication topics
English, H. B., & English, A. C. (1958). *A comprehensive dictionary of psychological and psychoanalytical terms.* New York: McKay.	An oldie but goodie; contains clear explanations and criticisms of different schools of thought
Longman dictionary of psychology and psychiatry. (1984). New York: Longman.	Definitions of over 21,000 terms; among the largest of such dictionaries
Marriot, F. H., & Kendall, M. G. (1990). *A dictionary of statistical terms* (5th ed.). New York: Longman.	Definitions of concepts and formulae in statistical analysis of data

TABLE 5.1 —*Continued*

Source	Comment
Dictionaries	
General	
Vogt, W. Paul. (1993). *Dictionary of statistics and methodology: A nontechnical guide for the social sciences.* Newbury Park, CA: Sage.	Descriptions of terms in research design, methods, and statistical analysis; frequent examples given
Wolman, B. B. (Ed.). (1988). *Dictionary of behavioral science.* (2nd ed.). San Diego: Academic Press.	Broad review of terms in the social and behavioral sciences
Mass Communication	
Diamant, L. (Ed.). (1989). *The broadcast communications dictionary* (3rd ed.). New York: Greenwood Press.	Listings limited to broadcast terms, definitions on mass media operations, and technology
Ellmore, R. T. (1991). *NTC's mass media dictionary.* Lincolnwood, IL: National Textbook.	Terms in journalism and telecommunications
Fletcher, J. (1988). *Broadcast research definitions.* Washington, DC: National Association of Broadcasters.	Definitions of terms related to television and radio broadcasting
Longman dictionary of mass media and communications. (1982). New York: Longman.	Definitions of terms used across mass media specialties
Urdang, L. (Ed.). (1992). *The dictionary of advertising.* Lincolnwood, IL: NTC Business Books.	Emphasis on layout, public relations, art design, and advertising jargon
Watson, J., & Hill, A. (1993). *A dictionary of communication and media studies* (3rd ed.). London, UK: Edward Arnold.	Definitions of concepts in the broad realm of mass communication studies
Weik, M. H. (1989). *Communications standard dictionary* (2nd ed.). New York: Van Nostrand Reinhold.	Definitions of concepts and terms involving mass mediated communication and technology
Weiner, R. (1990). *Webster's New World dictionary of media and communications.* New York: Webster's New World.	Coverage of technical terms in journalism and telecommunications
Speech and Hearing Science	
Morris, D. W. H. (1988). *A dictionary of speech therapy.* London, UK: Taylor and Francis.	Terms related to treatment and measurement in speech correction
Nicolosi, L., Harryman, E., & Kresheck, J. (Eds.). (1996). *Terminology of communication disorders: Speech, language, and hearing* (2nd ed.). Baltimore: Williams and Wilkins.	Terms emphasizing speech, hearing, and language diagnostic items for the therapist and clinician
Travis, L. (Ed.). (1971). *The handbook of speech pathology and audiology.* New York: Appleton-Century-Crofts.	A classic work detailing contributions in speech and hearing science

TABLE 5.1 —*Continued*

Source	Comment
Handbooks, Yearbooks, and Annual Reviews	
General	
Arnold, C. C., & Bowers, J. W. (Eds.). (1984). *Handbook of rhetorical and communication theory.* Boston: Allyn and Bacon.	14 topics covered, of interest to general communication theory and rhetorical studies
Berger, C. R., & Chaffee, S. H. (Eds.). (1987). *Handbook of communication science.* Newbury Park, CA: Sage.	28 chapters with essays covering major aspects of social science communication research
Communication yearbook. (1977–). Newbury Park, CA: Sage.	Essays and comprehensive literature reviews in broad areas of communication (sponsored by International Communication Association)
Isaac, S., & Michael, W. B. (Eds.). (1981). *Handbook in research and evaluation* (2nd ed.). San Diego: EdITS.	Designs and critical standards for evaluating research
Lindzey, G., & Aronson, E. (Eds.). (1985). *The handbook of social psychology* (3rd ed.). New York: Random House. (2 vols.)	Syntheses of theory and research on areas in social psychology, often communication related
Rubin, R. B., Palmgreen, P., & Sypher, H. E. (Eds.). (1994). *Communication research measures: A sourcebook.* New York: Guilford.	62 measurement tools related to communication described, their validity discussed, and critiqued
Tardy, C. H. (Ed.). (1988). *A handbook for the study of human communication: Methods and instruments for observing, measuring and assessing communication processes.* Norwood, NJ: Ablex Publishing Corp.	15 measurement tools in communication described, and their validity discussed
Mass Communication	
Gerbner, G., & Siefert, M. (Eds.). (1984). *World communications: A handbook.* New York: Longman.	Reviews of communication technology globally, emphasizing international development
Mass communication review yearbook. (1980 through 1987). Newbury Park, CA: Sage.	Studies on mass communication and applied areas (no longer published)
Rosen, P. T. (Ed.). (1988). *International handbook of broadcasting systems.* New York: Greenwood Press.	Mass media publications and associations for each nation with emphasis on those hosting UN Centres
World media handbook. (1990). New York: United Nations.	Descriptions of global systems of radio and TV broadcasting
World radio TV handbook: A complete directory of international radio and television. (Annual). New York: Billboard Publications.	Global listing of radio and TV broadcasting organizations including much technical detail
Special Topics	
Intercultural Communication	
Assante, M. K., Gudykunst, W. B., & Newmark, E. (Eds.). (1989). *Handbook of international and intercultural communication.* Newbury Park, CA: Sage.	Collected essays on intercultural, international, and interethnic communication variables
International and intercultural communication annual. (1974–). Newbury Park, CA: Sage.	Articles, research summary essays, and book reviews

TABLE 5.1 —*Continued*

Source	Comment
Interpersonal Communication	
Duck, S. (Ed.). (1988). *Handbook of personal relationships: Theory, research and interventions.* New York: Wiley.	Concern with interpersonal relationships from psychological, sociological, and communication views
Knapp, M. L., & Miller, G. R. (Eds.). (1994). *Handbook of interpersonal communication* (2nd ed.). Newbury Park, CA: Sage.	Emphasis on reviews of interpersonal communication since the 1960s
Spitzberg, B. H., & Cupach, W. R. (1989). *Handbook of interpersonal competence research.* New York: Springer-Verlag.	Conceptualization, research, and measurement concerns regarding communicator competence
Organizational Communication	
Goldhaber, G., & Barnett, G. A. (Eds.). (1988). *Handbook of organizational communication.* Norwood, NJ: Ablex Publishing Corp.	Reviews of methods and application areas in organizational communication
Jablin, F. M., Putnam, L. L., Karlene, H. R., & Porter, L. W. (Eds.). (1987). *Handbook of organizational communication: An interdisciplinary perspective.* Newbury Park, CA: Sage.	Chapters on organizational communication contexts, structures, issues, and processes across academic fields
Ruch, W. (1989). *International handbook of corporate communication.* Jefferson, NC: McFarland.	Essays on business communication applications to international public relations and communication in multinational corporations
Political Communication	
Nimmo, D. D., & Sanders, K. R. (Eds.). (1981). *Handbook of political communication.* Beverly Hills, CA: Sage.	First handbook on subject with primary emphasis on U.S. politics
Swanson, D. L., & Nimmo, D. (Eds.). (1990). *New directions on political communication.* Newbury Park, CA: Sage.	Companion to 1981 handbook; includes bibliography of post-1981 materials
Public Relations	
Dilenschneider, R. L., & Forestal, D. J. (1987). *Dartnell public relations handbook* (3rd ed., rev.). Chicago: Dartnell.	Review pieces on applications of internal and external public relations including many case studies
Lesly, P. (Ed.). (1991). *Lesly's handbook of public relations and communications* (2nd ed.). Chicago: Probus.	Reviews of applied issues in public relations and related mass media applications
Public relations research annual. (1989–). Hillsdale, NJ: Lawrence Erlbaum.	Original research in public relations and publicity
Other	
Nussbaum, J. F., & Coupland, J. (Eds.). (1995). *The handbook of communication and aging research.* Hillsdale, NJ: Erlbaum.	Essays on issues in communication and the aging process, needs of senior citizens, and challenges of aging
Free speech yearbook. (1960–). Carbondale: Southern Illinois University Press.	Reviews of free press/free speech issues and case studies

sufficient. Unfortunately, literature reviews tend to be dated by over a year by the time a book is published. Furthermore, some authors may summarize literature inaccurately or with a biased point of view. By checking original sources you can find out what the research really discovered. Furthermore, by browsing through journals published shortly after the original articles, you can tell if serious objections and reactions were raised to them.

dangers of relying on secondary reviews of literature

The "When?" Guiding Yourself with a Research Outline

Sometimes new students hear horror stories from other students about long hours spent in the library. The stories tell more about the inefficiency of some students than the use of resource materials. The easiest way to use time effectively is to create a research planning outline—a very efficient way to help you complete your research. Because we recommend this method so strongly, we will tell you how to use a research outline and later show you an actual search completed with one. Table 5.2 shows a research outline to plan library work for a paper on credibility of newspaper sources. Here's how to put one together:

use of a planning outline

- Divide a large piece of paper into three columns (you may wish to turn your paper sideways to have enough room).
- Title the first column, "Paper Outline," title the second column "Research Items," and the third "Sources to Check."
- In the column labeled "Paper Outline" put together a very rough outline of the paper or assignment you plan to write (these things give you a reason to visit the library). You cannot know every detail of the paper, of course, but you know the instructions you were given by your teacher. Dedicate at least one main point to each broad topic you were assigned to cover. In Table 5.2 the student was told to write a paper about the credibility of newspaper sources, making sure to define terms and to summarize research on the topic. So, a main point has been dedicated to each issue. Make sure to leave plenty of space so that new items can be added if necessary.
- In the column labeled "Research Items" list the information you need to get so that you can write each section of the paper.
- In the column labeled "Sources" list library sources to review. The sources identified in Table 5.1 can be useful resources to examine early in your work. The last part of this chapter, on library and Internet tools, introduces some major sources that you can review to complete the third column.

At the library, start at the top of your outline and work your way through. Instead of spending hours looking for random information, you can find materials in an orderly fashion without getting sidetracked into interesting but irrelevant areas. It may seem obvious to plan your time efficiently by making some notes, but next time you visit a library watch the other students. You won't see many people who have organized their time. Some of them may look very frustrated. They will spend more time than you in the library—but they will have less to show for it. Plan your time and you will have all you need.

managing time with research planning outlines enhances efficiency

TABLE 5.2 Research Planning Outline		
Paper Outline	*Research Items*	*Sources to Check*
Credibility of Newspaper Sources		
I. Definitions		
A. Source Credibility	→ Definition of Source Credibility	→ Handbooks of Communication, Mass Communication
	(check other terms: ethos, prestige)	→ Books: persuasion Dictionaries: Longman of Psych and Mass Communication
B. Kinds of Source Credibility	→ Dimensions of Credibility (check measurement methods)	→ Articles: Abstracts: Psychological Abstracts, Journalism Abstracts, Index to Journals in Communication Studies through 1990
II. Credibility Research in Newspapers		
A. Impact of Newspaper Credibility	→ Studies of credibility by readers (not TV or radio studies)	→ Unpublished work, Resources in Education
B. Levels of Credibility of Different Newspapers	→ Surveys of credibility ratings of readership pool	→ Unpublished work, Resources in Education, Internet search

Setting limits on the scope of your research is critical before you look for resources. If you have an exhaustive literature review for which a month's preparation time is provided, you may set limits very broadly. If you have only a week to complete a review of chief definitions, you may need to limit your examination to key books, specialized dictionaries, "think piece" articles, and articles that have summarized related research.

THE "HOW?" MANAGING RESEARCH MATERIALS

Learning from experience is an effective way to develop research skills, but it is very inefficient. Thus, it would be a good idea to develop some survival skills to *prepare* for your first literature searches.

Techniques for Bibliographic Research

Searching for source material is dominated by assembling bibliographic materials of one sort or another. You must remain flexible to find and record information as it comes your way.

Mastering the Library

Each library has some unique qualities. Take a tour of your local library and find out its approaches. You will find that the person at the reference desk is ready and willing to help you. But don't ask the librarian how to read an index or how to do a project you have been assigned. This book and your instructor are supposed to teach you those skills. Remember, you will want the librarians to help you if you run into a special problem—don't burn them out with questions you can get answered in class or by reading this book. You will soon grow comfortable with the layout of things and will be able to make library searches with ease.

learning local library qualities

Tactical Skills in Bibliographic Research

To be effective, bibliographic research requires developing some basic skills:

- Take notes in brief form. Your working notes or cards (containing quotations and summary information) should be selective and to the point. Long quotations or lists of statistics can often be summarized since you rarely will report such specifics in your projects.

  take notes in brief form

- Practice good note-taking skills. Since examining information requires you to summarize materials, it is vital to take notes accurately. Most people either take too many notes or too few. Instead you should get the main ideas first. Then, you can add appropriate details or explanations.

  importance of good note-taking skills

- Follow proper reference form. In different branches of communication, the proper citations follow the current editions of the *MLA Handbook for Writers of Research Papers* or the *Publication Manual of the American Psychological Association*. By the late 1980s nearly all communication journals accepted the latter style sheet (hence, this book uses it). All materials should be quoted fully and in context. You may wish to photocopy key pages just to be safe. If other sources are referenced in quoted material, you must obtain full citations for them. Though you should avoid editing others' words, if a portion of a quotation must be omitted, use ellipses (. . .) in its place. If words or phrases must be added to make a statement clear, the additions should be placed within brackets [ ]. If you notice a grammatical or spelling error, leave the words as in the original statement and follow the offending passage with the word *sic* within brackets (*sic* means "thus" or "so" in Latin).

  proper quotation and reference form

SPECIAL DISCUSSION 5–1
Ten Commandments of Library Use

Librarians can be very helpful, but many students do not know how to work with them. "The most common complaint heard among reference librarians about their work is that few people know how to ask reference questions" (Katz, 1982, p. 16). Two librarians (Gardner & Zelevansky, 1975) suggested these 10 commandments:

I. Thou shalt be prepared with a valid, logical and/or reasonable query and not an inchoate question, without form and void.
II. Thou shalt request all information in the beginning.
III. Thou shalt be honest and true with thy librarian in revelation of what though seekest, much as thou wouldst not hold back symptoms from thy physician.
IV. Thou shalt exhibit the patience of Job in waiting at the librarian's desk (or at the other end of the telephone) so that when the answer to thy query is divined, the search shall not have been in vain.
V. Thou shalt express thine appreciation of labor well done by thy librarian through written testimony to his/her supervisor.
VI. Thou shalt not designate the "Source," but rather utter clearly that which is sought.
VII. Thou shalt not require thy librarian to be accountable for that which is not yet published.
VIII. Thou shalt not require thy librarian to interpret data in chapter and verse.
IX. Thou shalt not scorn a wise referral, for surely any sage counsel cannot lead thee far astray and may indeed bear fruit.
X. Thou shalt not steal.

Source: Reprinted from *Special Libraries*, v. 66, no. 7 (July 1975), p. 326. © by Special Libraries Association.

Library Research Strategies

selecting a library search strategy

Getting started in the library can be invigorating. Plunge in with your research issues list, note cards, laptop computer (if you have one), and plenty of writing materials. But plunge in with a strategy to guide you. Look at your research outline sheet. Then, go wherever you need to trace down that information. Two major library research strategies can help give you a starting place.

General to Specific

general to specific described

Starting with general sources and then finding leads to specific sources is useful when you do not have an extensive background on the subject. At the beginning of your research career, that condition will occur most often. Furthermore, if the topic is fairly broad, you may wish to start with the general-to-specific method, just to make sure that you do not omit important theoretical foundations of the work. If you do not know enough to be sure about which strategy to use, this one is for you.

SPECIAL DISCUSSION 5-2
A Question of Ethics: Avoiding *Inadvertent Plagiarism*

Plagiarism refers to "the false assumption of authorship: the wrongful act of taking the product of another person's mind, and presenting it as one's own" (Lindey, 1952, p. 2). Most students realize that it is plagiarism to copy others' words without giving credit. But it is also plagiarism to express another person's *ideas* without giving credit.

> A writer who fails to give appropriate acknowledgment when repeating another's wording or particularly apt term, paraphrasing another's argument, or presenting another's line of thinking is guilty of plagiarism. You may certainly use another person's words and thoughts in your research paper, but the borrowed material must not appear to be your creation. (Gibaldi, 1995, p. 26)

Penalties for using uncredited sources are severe and may include academic punishment, failing grades, or expulsion. There is an obvious way to avoid plagiarism: document everything, except your unique interpretations and comments regarding research literature. The *MLA Handbook* explains (Gibaldi, 1995, p. 29):

> Of course, common sense as well as ethics should determine what you document. For example, you rarely need to give sources for familiar proverbs ("You can't judge a book by its cover"), well-known quotations ("We shall overcome"), or common knowledge ("George Washington was the first president of the United States").

Yet, if you make a statement you think is common knowledge, think again. What is "common knowledge" may be a matter of opinion. If there is any doubt possible, back up what you say with source materials—otherwise, omit the uncredited material.

Start your research with general textbooks, handbooks, yearbooks, and specialized encyclopedias. Sometimes students do not know what textbooks to grab. There is a simple method. Look at your problem and ask yourself the title of the class in which people usually study such a subject. Textbook publishers prefer using textbook titles that reflect names of courses for which they are intended. Write down keywords from the course title. Then, look up the books whose titles include those keywords. **Keywords** are terms under which information about the topic may be   **keywords defined** found. Hence, if you are interested in looking at communication styles of leaders in business, you may rightly think that this topic is usually covered in courses on organizational communication, business and professional communication, and management communication. Look up a few books to find their location in the library. Then, browse through them (starting at the index sections) to select the most useful sources.

Though general sources may not answer your research questions directly, start with them and copy down relevant statements. Most important, write down references the authors used in *their* general surveys. After looking at a handful of textbooks, you will probably have enough specific references to know where to go for further detailed information. Try to choose sources that have the most promising sounding titles. It is fairly easy to tell whether an article is worth reading since most scholarly articles have boring yet descriptive titles. Though there are exceptions, standard phrases used in titles (or subtitles) can tell much about an article. For instance, the following phrases often reveal what to expect:

- "A Case Study of . . ." (translation: a situation examined in detail)
- "An Experimental Study of . . ." (translation: a quantitative study—in the field or laboratory—in which variables were manipulated under controlled settings)
- "A Survey of . . ." (translation: a quantitative study in which an area is characterized but no variables are manipulated)
- "Theories of . . ." (translation: a review and critique of theories or orientations)
- "Measurement of . . ." (translation: a review/critique; or suggestions for a new method to measure a construct)
- "On the Meaning of . . ." (translation: a review/critique of major approaches to define a concept)
- "A Content Analysis of . . ." (translation: a quantitative analysis of some examples of communication)
- "A (Burkean, Aristotelian, Fantasy Theme, etc.) Analysis of . . ." (translation: a rhetorical critique of a piece of communication, a movement, or a source of communication)
- *Foundations of* . . . (translation: usually books covering the broad domain of a subject)
- *Handbook of* . . . (translation: a book containing essays and brief guides to literature and methods in an area of study)
- *A Theory of* . . . (translation: a book or an article—advancing a theory or fundamental orientation)

interpreting article titles

Most historical studies do not identify the method of inquiry in their titles. Instead, they just announce the object of the historical inquiry. Look at references you find in your searches to tell which articles may be most relevant. Do not just read citations. Try to consider what they are about.

Specific to General

specific to general described

Sometimes you may read an article or essay that grabs your interest. Perhaps you have asked your instructors about a specific topic. You may have received a reference to help you get started. You can begin with these specific sources and write down the citations to related research and theory identified in them. Then, you may repeat the process with the new sources. Soon, information snowballs as one reference leads to others.

You will find that different articles often reference the same "classic" research or theories. You will want to take the time to note such patterns across studies. You can also extend the search by using other abstracts and citation indices. This search method is effective when you have a specific starting piece or author name and are interested primarily in unearthing other general findings. Furthermore, the method can be helpful when you are uncertain about the most common keywords used to index the research.

uses of the specific to general pattern

SPECIAL DISCUSSION 5–3
Bibliographic Research Records: Elements of a Bibliographic Card

It is helpful to record key information on note cards. Such a card is shown below. In fact, you should have some blank 4- by 6-inch or 5- by 8-inch cards before you enter the library (don't use 3- by 5-inch cards—they are just too small to use flexibly). As you go through resource materials, keep track of your work by completing full bibliographic cards. If you have a laptop computer, you may have software to record note cards on disk for electronic sorting later. Regardless of the tools you use, some things that should be on all bibliographic cards are the following:

Bibliographic Card

Verbal Aggression Hurts Most from Friends Unless Teasing

Martin, M. M., Anderson, C. M., & Horvath, C. L. (1996). Feelings about verbal aggression: Justifications for sending and hurt from receiving verbally aggressive messages. *Communication Research Reports, 13,* 19–26.

"Clearly, receiving verbally aggressive messages from friends is considered more hurtful than messages from acquaintances. An exception was that no difference was found when the verbally aggressive message was in the form of teasing." (p. 23)

Study was a survey of the degree to which college students perceived justification and hurt from verbally aggressive messages in the abstract.

- *Title.* A newspaper-type headline title that summarizes information on the card and helps with filing material. Record only one thought on each card—to continue material, simply start another card.
- *Citation.* Use full citations in proper bibliographic form. Don't abbreviate this part since it will prove very time-consuming later (you may have multiple works from the same authors, or from authors who share the same last name, which you will have to sort out later).

SPECIAL DISCUSSION 5–3
(Continued)

- *Quotation or Abstract.* There are two types of bibliographic cards. If direct quotations are used, such material is placed within quotation marks. If materials refer to other sources, include the original citations on your note card (you will want to check on exact wording by going to the original source later). Using abstracts (summaries in your own words) of methods, findings, and conclusions will help you keep track of all sources you examine so that you do not visit the same sources repeatedly. Additionally, using cards allows you to compare recent work on a subject with previous thinking.
- *Commentary.* Add brief comments of your own about the work (placed within brackets to emphasize that they are not claims of the author of the original work). Such comments are also called "**annotations**" and offer additional explanations, comments, evaluations, or criticisms, to help you understand the material.

After collecting information on cards, you can sort them by key topics. Start with the general questions listed in this chapter:

- definitions of key concepts and variables
- ways concepts and variables have been measured and studied
- general summary statements about the subject
- the classic research studies in the field
- problems that researchers have struggled to solve
- research that shows what methods to use
- research that shows what mistakes to avoid

If you notice a void in any category, let that category be the object of a brief, intensive visit to the library. You may wish to use insert dividers between sections (do not buy dividers that have printed letters on them—you are filing information by topics, not by the alphabet). If you do an exhaustive literature search you may wish to compile a master "key" of any subdivisions. Of course, you should review your bibliography cards frequently to keep current on the status of your inquiry. Curiously, students who "do not have time" to put together bibliography cards nearly always need *more* time to complete projects than students who rely on this valuable tool.

THE WHERE: KEY LIBRARY TOOLS

Entire books have been written about library resources (e.g., Rubin, Rubin & Piele, 1996; Beasley, 1988; Paradis, 1966) and you probably already know how to find general materials. The best training to find scholarly research materials is brief guidance, followed by library experience. Rather than cover such matters exhaustively, we will guide you to *some* of the most helpful tools for communication studies. Library tools really boil down to two forms: hierarchical systems or keyword systems.

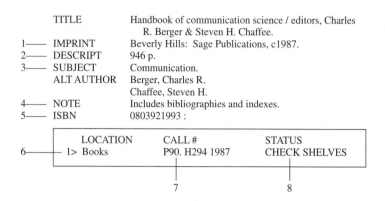

FIGURE 5.1
Sampling Catalog Listing

NOTES: This item was taken from the OPAC listing at the California State University, Fullerton Main Library.

1. The imprint contains information necessary for a citation including the city of publication, the publisher, and the date (the listing is in error; the city of publication was Newbury Park, CA at the time this book was published, as the book's title page clearly stated).*
2. The book is described as 946 pages long including indices and author biographies.
3. Since the subject matter was communication, you may use this keyword to browse other related topics.
4. Features of the book to help readers use it.
5. ISBN (International Standard Book Number) serial number assigned by book numbering agencies such as R. R. Bowker Co. in the United States.
6. Location of each copy of the book in the library. Copy number one is listed among the other ordinary books of the library.
7. The call number is the code number for the book and, in this case, follows the Library of Congress classification system.
8. The book is located on the shelves and is not checked out, nor in the reference room, overdue, on hold, or the like.

*There is a lesson for us in this example. When doing original library work, it is important to look at the books directly to check the details, rather than assuming (sometimes in error) that the catalog listing is correct.

Hierarchical Systems for Books and Collections

Hierarchical systems of filing tell you where common material is found—in the same location in the library. Such things as catalogs of books and special collections files are examples of these hierarchical guides. These guides help you locate where you can find books, handbooks, and other collections.   **hierarchical systems**

You may remember large wooden card files listing the books possessed by libraries. They are only a memory now. Currently, nearly every college library uses some sort of electronic catalog of books. The speed at which books can be identified is enhanced by using such systems. Of the many computerized library systems, the Colorado Alliance of Research Libraries (CARL) and Online Public Access Catalog (OPAC) have been adopted in most college libraries. Listings are available on book titles, names of authors, or subjects. A typical listing for such a search item appears in Figure 5.1. You may wish to read all the listings in a given subject heading to select the   **electronic book catalogs**

subject tracings identified

most recent books available, just to make sure that you do not miss recent contributions. You will also want to notice any **subject tracings** or keywords that list other subject headings under which the book is also listed. These headings can be used if you reach a dead end with your current keywords.

catalog systems often permit access to other search tools

These systems are more useful than they once were. In addition to listing books, they list journals held by the library and often permit you to use some on-line search systems. For instance, CARL permits you to access entries from the *Education Index,* the *National Newspaper Index, Newspaper & Periodical Indexes, Transcript,* and *UnCover.* This simplifying of search systems is progressing in leaps and bounds. It would be a good idea to make friends with some reference librarians at your school so that you can keep up with the latest time-saving tools.

the Dewey Decimal system

the Library of Congress system

To identify the call numbers of the works relevant to your topic, you will rely on one of the two major systems in use. The Dewey Decimal system was invented by Melvil Dewey in 1873 to help organize the library at Amherst College, when he was an undergraduate student (see Paradis, 1966, p. 4; Best, 1981, pp. 313–315). The method became dominant in public libraries, and many college libraries use it today. Yet, it became difficult to add new specialized topics gracefully. Over time, many libraries adopted the Library of Congress method first developed by Herbert Putnam pursuant to an 1880 act of Congress. Today, most college libraries and government-depositories (libraries that regularly receive copies of federal government documents) employ this system (see Table 5.3).

systems to identify holdings at other libraries

Most libraries also subscribe to electronic systems that list what books, journals, recordings, films, and nonprint media are available at other libraries. For instance, the Online Computer Library Center (OCLC) sponsors *WorldCat,* which catalogs holdings at hundreds of United States libraries. If your library does not have a book, the system tells you the other libraries that do. The Research Libraries Information Network (RLIN) performs virtually the same function for more than a score of America's largest libraries. Similar systems also are available regionally. Check your local library to see which systems are available to you (for free, that is).

indices and guides to books

Services are available that index critiques of new books. For trade publications—books that are likely to be sold at major commercial bookstores—some guides may be worth checking, depending on your topic. *Book Review Digest* presents summaries and critiques, and the *Book Review Index* lists the places where book reviews have been published. For speech and hearing scientists, the *Technical Book Review Index* can be particularly valuable. For rhetorical studies and film and mass media criticism, the *Index to Book Reviews in the Humanities* provides a guide to 685 related publications. In mass communication, the guides tend to be narrow and somewhat dated. Among the most popular has been *Basic Books in the Mass Media,* edited by Eleanor Blum and covering selected books through the late 1970s.

Keyword Systems

use of index and abstract sources

Keyword-based systems, such as *Psychological Abstracts* and *Communication Abstracts,* send you to different locations in the library to find articles and papers. The major guides to these materials are known as indices and abstracts. There are two major categories of such keyword guides to books and articles: computerized systems and hard copy systems. They are not different—they just list the same materials in different form.

TABLE 5.3 Dewey Decimal System and Library of Congress Classifications with Emphasis on Categories for the Communication Field

Dewey Decimal System	Library of Congress
000 General Works	A General Works
	B Philosophy, Psychology, Religion
070 Journalism	B Philosophy (General)
	BC Logic
100 Philosophy and Related Fields	BF Psychology (for social psychology, see HM), including communication theory
120 Epistemology, Causation, Humankind	BH Aesthetics
140 Specific Philosophic Systems	BJ Ethics
150 Psychology	C History
160 Logic	D World History
170 Ethics	E, F American History
	G Geography, Anthropology
200 Religion	H Social Science
	H Social Science (General)
300 Social Sciences	HA Statistics
310 Statistics	HE Transportation and Communication (telecommunication 7601–8688; radio and television (8689–8700)
340 Law	
350 Public Administration	HF Commerce (business administration and personnel management (5001–5549; advertising 5801–6191)
370 Education	
400 Language	HM Sociology (social psychology, 251–291)
	HQ Social groups (family and marriage 503–1064)
410 Linguistics	
420 English Languages	HS Societies
	HT Communities, Classes, Races
500 Pure Sciences	K Law
	L Education
600 Technology (Applied Sciences)	M Music
	N Fine Arts
610 Medical Sciences (including speech and hearing disorders 616.85)	P Language and Literature
	P Philology and Linguistics (general)
	PE English
620 Engineering	PN Literature (drama 1600–3299; oratory speech communication, debating, recitations 4001–4355; journalism, communication law, practical journalism, amateur journalism, by region or country 4699–5650)
650 Management and Auxiliary Services	
700 Arts and Recreation	
800 Literature	Q Science
	R Medicine
900 History	RC Internal Medicine (stuttering, speech correction, and therapies 423–430)
	RF Otorhinolaryngology
	S Agriculture
	T Technology
	U Military Science
	V Naval Science
	Z Library Science-Bibliography

Computer Searches and Databases

The computer age has come to most libraries. Some of the early awkwardness in the computer systems has been overcome and you will find electronic searches are fairly simple tasks. Communication databases make quick work of literature searches. Two forms of computerized materials are available, although additional forms are in the offing at the time this book is being written.

CD–ROM sources

CD–ROM Sources.   For students, the cheapest and easiest systems use **CD–ROM** form, translated as "Compact Disc–Read Only Memory." These CDs are the same sorts of disks found in music stores and in stereo sets, but instead of containing music in digital form, they contain databases that can be searched rapidly. They are called "Read Only Memory" because you cannot record onto them—you can only read from them. The CD–ROM systems run on personal computers in the library or on networks linked to terminals also used to find books in the library. After finding references, you can decide which citations, summaries, or texts you wish to have printed or stored on discs.

CD–ROMs contain indices and directories of sources. Thus, you may treat them as highly efficient substitutes for hauling around many volumes of abstracts and indices. Once you use these systems, you will wonder why anyone would ever use any other methods. There are limits, of course. First, in many CD–ROM systems, except for the most recent years (depending on the system that means 1990 or 1980 onward), you may have to use hard copy versions or repeat your search with a different set of discs. Second, many libraries are still developing adequate subscriptions to CD–ROM services and some subjects may not yet be supported locally. Unfortunately as well, many libraries must charge fees to use their search systems. Two significant breakthroughs in CD–ROM materials for much of the field are:

- *CommSearch95* (sold and distributed by the National Communication Association) features author and title indexes for 22 journals through 1994, keyword indexes for 19 communication journals, abstracts for NCA sponsored journals from 1972 to 1994, and full texts (with keyword search capabilities) for NCA sponsored journals from 1991 through 1994. Further improvements in the breadth of offerings are promised in future versions.
- *ComIndex* (sold by subscription to the Communication Institute for Online Scholarship) includes 55 journals and ancillary publications in the field. It handles keyword bibliographic searches of article titles but does not include full texts or abstracts.

If your library does not have copies of these sources, see if they are available in the department office that houses your academic major.

use of on-line databases

On-line Databases.   On-line database systems connect the researcher with a central computer and can be used to search for books, articles, and reports on key topics. The on-line search usually results in listing large numbers of entries in bibliographic format with many accompanying abstracts. Since on-line searches have been around for some time, there are many of them. Some require that you work through your local library, but others require only that you have a computer that can be connected to a telephone line. Table 5.4 lists some of the major database search systems. Many of these resources are also available on CD–ROM (most of the sources in Table 5.5 are on CD–ROM), some are also available on the Internet, and some are available only through direct on-line contact. You should keep in mind that—unlike CD–ROM systems that are free to library users—firms charge for on-line services, usually by the number of entries the search produces. Thus, you must plan these searches carefully.

Using Keywords

The following steps can make learning to use keywords fairly simple.

1. Select keywords from the problem statement. Pause before you look at electronic indices to jot down the keywords that describe topics you are investigating. Some common sense is required. If you look for information about the impact of televising a speech on the speaker's credibility, you may list such words as "television," "speeches," and "credibility." The on-line database *Dialog* includes automatic prompts, so that you can use the precise vocabulary of the system. In on-line searches, using very broad terms might produce long lists of irrelevant materials—a waste of time for you and potentially costly as well.

2. Develop alternative lists of descriptor terms. Unless you have a lot of experience researching a topic, your initial keywords may not be the same ones used by the index service staffs. You may need to think creatively. For instance, for many years the *Education Index* listed studies of "communication apprehension" under the subject heading "bashfulness." You need to prepare synonyms in case the first keywords do not work for you. Fortunately, many indexing services have guides to give you help in selecting keywords and CD–ROM systems have automatic prompts to help you.

3. Combine keywords. In an on-line search you need to see if you can combine keywords that you have already tested individually to make sure they are meaningful in the system. For instance, you might use the three keywords "television," "speeches," and "source credibility" (the latter is actually two keywords, but it serves as one for us). The computer system starts by looking for all the listings on "television." Then, the system subdivides the list to identify citations that also have the keyword "speeches." Finally, it makes a pass for listings that also have the term "source credibility." Eventually, the system produces a very focused list.

4. Undertake on-line activity. During the search, the computer will prompt you with questions and will respond to your input. The systems listed in Table 5.4 are a bit different from each other, but you will find that the prompting systems are very extensive and easy to use. You may wish to change databases and search different materials. Though it is admittedly a bother, it is vital to record (preferably on your research outline) sources you have searched and keywords you have used. Without such a record, you may find yourself examining the same materials more than once. In many cases you may wish to have the list of abstracts, citations, and references printed out or downloaded to a disk of your own. Make sure that facilities are set up for you when you request these services. It is frustrating to log off and then find that no hard copy system was attached. Take the time to consult with your local librarian to understand in advance the options available to you.

Margin notes:

electronic search steps
1. find keywords

2. find alternative keywords

3. combine keywords

4. undertake on-line activity

TABLE 5.4 Online Computer Search Systems

System	Content and Commentary	Useful for
I. *Full Text Listings or Abstracts*		
LEXIS	Legal research (full texts of court cases, laws, and significant pending legislation, as well as references to law journals and specialized library collections)	Communication and the law; mass communication law
Magazine ASAP	Information from popular magazines indexed in *Magazine Index*	Mass communication and historical background
National Newspaper Index	Abstracts and indexes of items appearing in the *New York Times, Los Angeles Times, Wall Street Journal,* and *Christian Science Monitor*	Mass media, public relations, and historical background
NEXIS	Full text of articles from newspapers, wire services, and many government publications	Mass media, public relations, and historical background
VU/TEXT	Information primarily from newspapers emphasizing business issues; also has *ABI/INFORM* materials	Organizational communication, public relations, and mass media
II. *Other Computerized Systems of Existing Hard Copy Index Services*		
CIS/Index	Same as hard copy version of *CIS/Index* (index and abstracts of congressional publications) (from 1970 forward)	Rhetoric and public address, mass communication
Dissertation Abstracts Online	Same as hard copy version of *Dissertation Abstracts* (from 1861 forward)	All fields
Education Index	Same as hard copy version of *Education Index* including nearly 400 publications broadly related to education (from 1983 forward)	Rhetoric, communication education, communication theory and processes
ERIC	Same as hard copy version of *Resources in Education* and *Current Index to Journals in Education* (from 1861 forward)	Most social science subfields in education and communication; particularly valuable for listings of unpublished sources, such as convention papers
Humanities Index	Same as hard copy version of *Humanities Index* (from 1984 forward)	Rhetoric, criticism, communication theory
Legal Resources Index	Index and some abstracts of articles from 800 law journals and over 3,000 ancillary publications (from 1980 forward)	Communication and the law and mass communications law
Linguistics and Language Behavior Abstracts	Same as hard copy version of *Linguistics and Language Behavior Abstracts;* index and abstracts of journals in language, communication disorders, and learning disabilities (from 1973 forward)	Speech and hearing science

TABLE 5.4 —*Continued*

System	Content and Commentary	Useful for
Management Contents	Indexes and abstracts from over 130 international publications in management and public administration (from 1974 forward)	Organizational communication
Newspaper & Periodical Indexes	Indexes and abstracts from over 25 newspapers, 1,600 periodicals, and 70 television news and information broadcasts (periodicals from 1986 forward; newspapers from 1989 forward; broadcasts vary)	Mass communication, journalism, criticism
Newsearch	Most recent two-to-six weeks of information in guides published by Information Access Inc. (includes *Academic Index, Legal Resource Index, Management Contents, National Newspaper Index, PR Newswire*)	Communication theory, communication and the law, mass communication law, organizational communication, journalism, mass communication, and public relations
PsychINFO	Same as hard copy version of *Psychological Abstracts;* index and abstracts of journals articles, books, and book chapters in psychology and other social sciences (from 1974 forward)	Social sciences, communication theory and processes, and psychology in applied areas
PsycLit	A CD–ROM version of *Psychological Abstracts*	Social sciences, communication theory and processes, and psychology in applied areas
SciSearch	Same as hard copy version of *Science Citation Index;* index of citations used in over 600 journals in the natural sciences (from 1975 forward)	Speech and hearing science; useful to find who is quoting whom and to find commentaries on published articles
Social Sciences Index	Same as hard copy version of *Social Sciences Index;* index of over 400 journals and magazines related to the social sciences (from 1983 forward)	Social sciences, communication theory and processes
Social SciSearch	Same as hard copy version of *Social Sciences Citation Index;* index of references used in articles from over 1400 social science journals (from 1981 forward)	Social sciences; useful to find who is quoting whom and to find commentaries on published articles
Sociological Abstracts	Same as hard copy version of *Sociological Abstracts;* index and abstracts of articles from journals and related publications throughout the social sciences including some communication journals (from 1963 forward)	Social sciences, communication theory and processes, mass communication
Trade and Industry ASAP	Information from *Trade and Industry Index*	Organizational communication and public relations

TABLE 5.4 —*Continued*

System	Content and Commentary	Useful for
Transcript (Journal Graphics)	A catalog of the *Transcript/Video Index;* listings and abstracts of transcripts of over 20,000 news and information television broadcasts for sale by Journal Graphics	Mass communication, political communication, and public relations
H. W. Wilson guides	Largely duplications of	
Wilson: Business Abstracts; Education Abstracts;	*Business Periodical Index* (from 1982 forward including abstracts from June 1990) *Education Index* (from 1983 forward including abstracts from 1994)	Organizational communication and public relations Rhetoric, communication education, communication theory and processes Rhetoric, criticism, communication theory
Humanities Abstracts;	*Humanities Index* (from 1984 forward including abstracts from 1994)	
Social Science Abstracts	*Social Sciences Index* (from 1983 forward including abstracts from 1994)	Social sciences, communication theory and processes
III. *Other Systems*		
Comserve	Internet version of *ComIndex CD-ROM (Communication Institute for Online Scholarship listing of 55 journals and publications)*	All aspects of communication except speech and hearing science (permits one free search to the public)
ABI/INFORM	Articles and abstracts in business and management	Organizational communication and public relations
Bibliographic Retrieval Services	Wide range of reference databases	Social sciences, mass communication, organizational communication
BRS/AfterDark	Highly popular private service; provides nondaytime access to multiple major database indices, including *PsychINFO, ERIC, ABI/INFORM,* and many others useful to communication	Social sciences, popular subjects, and access to major databases
CompuServe Information Service	News retrieval from newspapers and wire services, financial information, and corporate profiles	Mass communication, historical background, and organizational communication
Dialog	World's largest information retrieval system developed by Lockheed Corporation; Dialog accesses all the sources listed in section II of this table except for *SciSearch, Social SciSearch, Transcript,* and Wilson Guides (*Dialog* also operates *Knowledge Index*)	Full listing of materials in all fields
Dow Jones News/ Retrieval Service	Information from the *Wall Street Journal, Barron's,* and the *Dow Jones News Wire* (from 1979 forward)	Organizational communication and financial background
InfoTrac	Broad databases including book reviews and articles	Communication theory, mass communication, rhetoric, and organizational communication
Management Contents	Abstracts of periodicals in management and public administration	Organizational communication and public relations

TABLE 5.4 —*Continued*

System	Content and Commentary	Useful for
OCLC (Online Computer Library Center) *FirstSearch*	Comprehensive search system including indices and abstracts (for a fee, copies of publications may be ordered from First-Search); Among sources listed in section II of this table, *FirstSearch* includes *ERIC, PsychINFO, Social Sciences Index,* and *Sociological Abstracts*	All fields
Knowledge Index	Evening and weekend access to databases on almost every subject including over four million books, articles, convention papers, government documents, and technical reports	Full range of natural and social sciences
The Source	Specialized electronic bulletin boards on over 75 topics, UPI News Service, stocks, bonds, travel services	Organizational communication and public relations
System Development Corporation	Review of a large number of sources in the broad science	Social and natural sciences
UnCover	Tables of contents of nearly 15,000 journals and magazines in major libraries (from 1988 forward)	All fields (searchable through CARL system)
Wilsonline	Search guide to H. W. Wilson resources	Business, organizational communication, educational issues, humanities, and social sciences

Indices and Abstracts

Though computerized systems have collected indices and abstracts, you may have to rely on hard copy volumes to find some sources. An index lists locations of resource materials and articles. An abstract also provides a brief summary of the work. Since indices and abstracts are often found in companion reference works, we can describe them together. Regrettably, no single hard copy index covers the breadth of our field. So, you may wish to check different sources to find citations to the most valuable articles. Among the first you may wish to consult are the following:

use of index and abstract sources

- *Index to Journals in Communication Studies Through 1990,* edited by Ronald J. Matlon and associate editor Sylvia P. Ortiz (1992). The current edition covers major communication journals, excluding only those in speech and hearing science, public relations, and management communication.
- *Communication Abstracts,* a bi-monthly publication that lists abstracts of articles from over 200 communication-related periodicals (the December issues include subject and author indices).

Table 5.5 lists and briefly describes major indices and abstracts. Since these sources are organized differently from each other, you will need to spend a moment or two

TABLE 5.5 Indices and Abstracts to Scholarship in Communication for Major Divisions of the Field

Source	Description	Useful For
Business Periodicals Index	120 periodicals in business related issues	Organizational communication
Canadian Education Index	Canadian periodicals, books, and pamphlets	Speech and hearing science, communication education
Child Development Abstracts and Bibliography	Child development issues	Speech and hearing science
C.R.I.S.	Combined Retrospective Index to journals in Sociology	Communication theory, mass, organizational communication, group processes
Communication Abstracts	21 communication subfields indexed and summarized	All aspects of communication except speech and hearing science
Current Contents: Social and Behavioral Sciences (previously Current Contents: Behavioral, Social & Educational Sciences)	Reproduces tables of contents of 1,300 journals; articles from multi-authored books (other Current Contents available for other fields)	Communication theory, mass communication, organizational communication
Deafness, Speech and Hearing Abstracts	Listings and abstracts from 250 journals	Speech and hearing science
Education Index	Journal articles, book reviews, and chapters in yearbooks	Communication theory, mass, rhetoric and public address, communication education
Exceptional Child Education Resources	Journals in special education	Speech and hearing science
Index to Doctoral Dissertations International (also found with Dissertation Abstracts: Comprehensive Dissertation Index 1861–1972)	All doctoral dissertations in the U.S. and Canada	All fields
Index to Journals in Communication Studies Through 1990	19 journals in communication, speech, rhetoric, and mass communication	Major areas of the field except speech and hearing science
Index Medicus	Monthly reviews of medical journals	Speech and hearing science
International Indexes to Film & Television Periodicals	International listings of articles on television	Mass communication
Journalism Abstracts	Dissertations and theses on journalism submitted by cooperating institutions	Mass communication and journalism
Journal of Broadcasting: Author and topic Index to Volume 1 Through 25	Index of single journal from 1956 through 1981	Mass communication
Journalism Quarterly Cumulative Index	Index of single journal from 1924 through 1983	Journalism

TABLE 5.5 —*Continued*

Source	Description	Useful For
Linguistics and Language Behavior Abstracts	International journals related to linguistics	Language, speech and hearing science
Master's Abstracts	Master's theses across fields submitted by cooperating institutions (not as comprehensive as dissertation holdings)	All fields
Psychological Abstracts	Summaries of research in psychology	Mass communication, communication theory, group processes, organizational communication
Rehabilitation Literature	Material on physically handicapped people	Speech and hearing science
Resources in Education (formerly *Research in Education*)	Locally published working papers of otherwise unpublished convention papers and reports; copies available on microfiche	All subject matters, but dominant in social sciences
Social Science and Humanities Index (from 1974 divided into separate publications):	Publications within and outside the U.S.	Mass communication, organizational communication, communication theory, group processes
Humanities Index	Periodicals; reviews of books	Rhetoric, mass communication, journalism, communication theory
Social Science Index	Periodicals in broad range of social sciences	Mass communication, communication theory, intercultural communication
Sociological Abstracts	Research summaries from over 1,000 international journals	Mass communication, communication theory
Topicator	Unique titles in marketing, advertising, and communication	Mass communication, advertising

(it doesn't take long) to find out how each guide is arranged. Once you are comfortable with the major guides for your area, you will be surprised how easy it is to find information.

Sometimes you may wish to look at popular press treatments, such as when you need to find reactions to speakers or communication trends. The indices to nonscholarly literature have been omitted from the tables in this chapter. Surely the most popular of these sources is the *Reader's Guide to Periodical Literature,* an index that includes more than 130 general public interest magazines. For magazines published a very long time ago, you can check *Poole's Index to Periodical Literature, 1802–1906* and the *Nineteenth Century Reader's Guide to Periodical Literature 1890–1899.* For popular sources outside the United States, you might wish to review the *Canadian Index* or the *Subject Index to Periodicals* (for British periodicals). Major newspapers

guides to general periodicals

also index their publications. Similar guides can be found to government documents, regulations, and reports. Your local librarian can direct you to them.

Suppose you wonder if there is any commentary or criticism of a scholarly work. The *Social Science Citation Index* and the *Science Citation Index* list articles that have cited a particular reference. Sometimes the references are in passing, but sometimes the citations indicate extended critiques.

Special bibliographies can also help you find useful materials on many topics. Some of the most useful include the following:

Bibliographic Index. Lists publications containing at least fifty references on a subject (useful to find reviews of literature).

Freedom of the Press: An Annotated Bibliography (edited by R. E. McCoy, Carbondale: Southern Illinois University Press, 1968).

Freedom of the Press, a Bibliocylopedia: Ten-Year Supplement, 1967–1977 (edited by R. E. McCoy, Carbondale: Southern Illinois University Press, 1979).

Freedom of the Press: An Annotated Bibliography, Second Supplement, 1978–1992 (edited by R. E. McCoy, Carbondale: Southern Illinois University Press, 1993). Scholarship and legal discussions of freedom of speech and the press issues.

Global Guide to Media and Communications (edited by John A. Lent, Munchen, Germany: Saur, 1987). Bibliography of books, dissertations, articles, and monographs on mass media of specific countries or regions.

Journalism: A Guide to the Reference Literature (edited by Jo A. Cates, Englewood, CO: Libraries Unlimited, 1990). Selective bibliography of articles on broadcast and print journalism.

Mass Media Bibliography: An Annotated, Selected List of Books and Journals for Reference and Research (edited by Eleanor Blum and F. Wilhoit, 2nd ed., Urbana: University of Illinois Press, 1990). Includes over two thousand entries in applied areas of mass communication and broadcasting.

Mass Media Law: A Selected Bibliography (2nd ed.) (edited by D. M. Gilmor, 2nd ed., Minneapolis: University of Minnesota Press, 1990). References to legal issues in freedom of the press and mass communication law.

Political Campaign Communication: A Bibliography and Guide to the Literature (edited by L. L. Kaid, K. R. Sanders, and R. O. Hirsch, Metuchen, NJ: Scarecrow Press, 1974).

Political Campaign Communication: A Bibliography and Guide to the Literature, 1973–1982 (edited by L. L. Kaid and A. J. Wadsworth, Metuchen, NJ: Scarecrow Press, 1985). References to literature on campaigns and related political communication research.

USING THE LIBRARY

Practical library searching involves confronting challenges. The following methods will help you manage your search to solve problems.

SPECIAL DISCUSSION 5-4
Using Legal Resource Materials

Materials in the law must often be examined to study mass communication law, legal communication, and freedom of speech. Though you may not be at a school with extensive collections in the law, you are still not far from a county law library, which you can use. It is helpful to understand legal citations. For instance, a law in the *United States Code,* may be cited as: 12 U.S.C. § 724. The citation is read, "Title 12 of the *United States Code,* Section 724." The *U.S. Code Annotated* summarizes major laws, and the *U.S. Code Service* lists related court decisions, legislative history, and provides additional references in each category.

Supreme Court decisions are identified as, for example, *Roe v. Wade,* 410 U.S. 113 (1973). The case title lists the plaintiff and the defendant. The number following the title is the volume number of *U. S. Reports* in which the decision is located. The page number on which the decision begins is listed next. The date is placed in parentheses after the rest of the citation. The *Supreme Court Reporter* indexes cases with abstracts of legal issues raised in the case. *Lawyer's Edition of the U.S. Supreme Court Reports* provides a legal analysis and includes statements from the briefs and arguments actually made by the lawyers. As general collections, West's Digests are popular including: the *General Digest* that summarizes cases and the *Federal Practice Digest* organized by topic areas.

Many guides can help you find articles in the law. The *Index to Legal Periodicals* is the major guide to U.S. law journals, just as the *Index to Foreign Legal Periodicals and Collections of Essays* is the counterpart for law journals in foreign countries. The *Law Review Digest* provides bi-monthly summaries of law journal articles and the *Index to Periodical Articles Related to Law* covers sources other than law journals.

Conducting the Library Session

If you are armed with your research planning outline, you can be highly efficient. Box 5.1 shows a diary of an actual search using the outline from Table 5.2. Based on initial thinking, the student was able to list some potential sources to examine. As you can see, the library session can be quite efficient when a research outline is used. Without such a method, you might just tread water in the library. By the way, this search provided the student with all the information needed to construct a meaningful critical explication of a research area—and the paper got an *A*.

Troubleshooting in the Library

For all the fascination libraries hold—the collected wisdom of ages is just waiting there—inexperienced people can become frustrated. We will consider some student complaints, along with some suggested solutions.

BOX 5.1
Diary of a Library Search Using the Research Outline Method

Using a research outline is recommended for library research. The following shows a diary of the work during an actual library search in which the Research Outline found in Box 5.1 was applied.

10:10 A.M.   Entered library. Went to on-line system to find call numbers for *Handbooks of Communication* (P 90.H293), *Mass Communication* (not in library), *Mass Communication Review Yearbook* (P 87.M28 1987), books on persuasion (e.g., *Persuasion* by R. Bostrom: BF 637.P4 B6 1983), Longman Dictionaries of *Psychology* (BF 31.L66 1984—in reference room) and *Mass Media* (P 87.5 .L66 1982—reference room).

10:20 A.M.   Went to stacks section P 90.H293. Found *Handbook of Communication* edited by Poole, et al. in 1973 (OK for definitions). Looked up source credibility in index and on page 230 found definition of credibility as "believability" in chapter written by McGuire. Bibliography card prepared. Looked in *Mass Communication Review Yearbooks*—no discussions of definitions indicated in index. Quickly browsed shelf. Looked at *Handbook of Communication Science* (P 90.H294.1987) edited by Berger and Chaffee—checked index; no definition discussed but criticisms of factor analysis studies noted on pages 464–465 in chapter written by Gerald Miller. Made bibliographic note. Checked nearby series called *Progress in Communication Sciences*—no discussion of source credibility. Saw general communication books and looked in their indices. Mortensen's *Communication* (P 90 M65) had definition of credibility as "image of a source in any communication situation" (p. 147). Made bibliography card.

10:50 A.M.   Went to stacks for persuasion books. Found Bostrom book. Whole chapter on credibility—covers kinds of source credibility and dimensions in simple language; decided to check it out. Other books defined credibility in same way as previously found definitions.

11:15 A.M.   Went to reference room to find *Longman Dictionary of Psychology* (nothing) and *Longman Dictionary of Mass Communication* (nothing).

11:25 A.M.   Went to reference area to find indices to articles. CD–ROM for *Dialog* available including all materials for *Psychological Abstracts, Journalism Abstracts,* and *Resources in Education* (among others). Used menu on computer to find all works on "source credibility"—118 listed. Used menu to request "source credibility" and "mass communication"—none listed. Went back to search for source credibility. Requested screen listing of bibliographic references. Entries listed one at a time by pressing "Page Down" key on keyboard. Read titles of entries looking for keywords. Found studies of credibility by newspaper readers, surveys of newspaper credibility (sometimes comparisons to TV credibility), and surveys of credibility ratings.

BOX 5.2
(Continued)

Prepared bibliography cards on eight sources (two were unpublished sources listed in *Resources in Education*—library has these on microfiche next to the microfilm for newspapers—all numbers for the item written down). Found new conceptual articles (e.g., McCroskey and Young) and studies in newspaper credibility. Prepared bibliography cards on each source. Requested that the abstracts for these sources be listed on the screen to be sure the sources were the best to use). Given the length of the articles, chose not to print out full text.*

11:55 A.M.   Went to lunch

12:45 P.M.   Went to microfiche area to get two unpublished sources. Skimmed papers on microfiche reader. Made one bibliographic note on each article.

 1:25 P.M.   Went to journal holdings and found remaining articles. McCroskey and Young article photocopied, as was 1987 article by Gaziano and McGrath in *Journalism Quarterly.* Bibliographic cards taken on other sources.

 1:55 P.M.   Left.

Though the student may find that looking up citations found in the copied articles requires returning to the library, the search effort is pretty much done at this point—all in fewer than three hours. As it turned out, this search did not require a return visit to the library until the next class assignment. If a library search outline plan had not been followed, who knows how long the person would have stayed in the library?

---

*If the student had taken a PC disk with her, she could have downloaded copies of abstracts (or articles) to print out at a later time elsewhere.

When the Source is Unavailable

Sometimes a key source is not available at your library (it happened in our example in Table 5.6). The sources may have been checked out, the library may not own the resource, or the materials may have been lost or vandalized. There are two general ways around this problem. First, you may use an interlibrary loan program. Every library has such a cooperative venture. Through it you can ask other libraries to lend you the missing work. If an article is involved, other libraries will often send you a photocopy. Interlibrary loans are not as slow as often believed, but if you require instant information, you may need to seek another option. Another way around the problem involves reading other articles that offer some descriptions about the key source. By triangulating information from different sources, you may get an idea of what was done in the original piece. This method is dangerous, however, since writers are selective in describing others' work, and because secondary summaries may

when sources are unavailable:

interlibrary loan

triangulating reports of research

contain flaws. Furthermore, the method of triangulation is very, very time-consuming for the amount of benefit it might produce.

When There is "No Information on my Topic"

use the known to unknown search strategy

A word to the wise: do not say to your instructor, "There is no information on my topic." Your instructor knows that somewhere, someone has said *something* relevant to your topic. Your *specific* research question may not have been answered yet (much to your credit, since you are an original thinker), but there is always something out there related to your topic. To find materials you should try the "known to unknown" search pattern. With this strategy, you take your research issue, such as the impact of tele-conferencing on interpersonal attraction of group members, and then look at research into each concept separately. You might investigate the things that affect interpersonal attraction generally. Such material is *known.* But you may observe that there is little information about attraction in teleconferencing settings. This material remains *un-known.* You might decide from what is known generally to develop arguments about possible relationships that might exist between teleconferencing methods and attraction. By looking at the issue broadly, it is possible to unearth much valuable information.

When the Journals are Missing

missing journals: use microforms and check for changed journal names

Sometimes journals may not be on the shelves. Before panicking, find out if the library has microform copies. Sometimes journals are available, but the names have been changed. For instance, if you chase down a citation (from another source) to a journal called *Communication Studies* for 1983, you may grow nervous when the listing of publications shows that the library has this journal only from 1989 forward. In reality, this journal was called the *Central States Speech Journal* until volume 40 in 1989, though the call number remained the same. Titles change often enough that you should not give up at first. Yet, if you find that journals truly are not available, you will need to contact interlibrary loan services for help.

When the Material is Technical and Complex

dealing with very technical material: use specialized dictionaries

ask key questions

Research articles sometimes seem complicated and bewilderingly technical. Rather than get bogged down, you may wish to rely on some of the specialized dictionaries listed in table 5.1. Sometimes books and critiques are available to help you put some perspective on the matter. Most journal essays and articles place abstracts at the beginning of articles. These guides are good starting points with technical and complex materials. Begin by asking, What was the purpose of the research? By doing so, you can often grasp extended background discussions. Then ask, what method or reasoning was used to draw conclusions? Sometimes you may wish to outline these methods (briefly) in your own notes. Finally ask, what did the work find and conclude? Many times the conclusion is an afterthought, but sometimes it is the lion's share of the materials.

USING THE INTERNET

The Internet has its roots in the efforts of the U.S. Department of Defense to link military bases, the Pentagon, universities, and defense contractors in a system that could not be destroyed in a single nuclear attack. But it was not until the end of the cold war that the Internet became an information system that is estimated to grow from

12 million host computers in January 1997 to 187 million by January 2000 (Sachs & Stair, 1996, p. 6). The **World Wide Web** (WWW) is part of the Internet. It is the collection of computers around the world (called Web servers) "that organizes information using hypermedia. Each document can contain embedded references to images, audio, or other documents" (*The beginner's guide to the Internet,* 1995, p. 92). **Hypermedia** are information approaches "in which each page of information can contain embedded references to images, sound, and other pages of information. When a user selects an item, the hypermedia system follows the associated reference" (p. 89). How can you use the Internet to learn about communication research? Most important for researchers, many research libraries, special collections, and academic resources are available on the Internet. Thus, many of your reference searches can benefit by looking at the Internet. This section summarizes Internet tools you can employ in your research.

World Wide Web defined

hypermedia defined

Elements of the Internet

Internet elements fall into two basic sets of materials that can be accessed easily by one system. One set allows you to send messages and participate in discussions. It includes the following:

elements of the Internet

- E-Mail: Electronic mail or **E-mail** is a system for exchanging messages with other Internet users and "is the leading use of the Internet" (Kardas & Milford, 1996, p. 27). In most cases, E-mail arrives a few minutes after it is sent. In some international applications, the E-mail may take nearly a day to arrive.

E-mail defined

- Newsgroups: **Newsgroups** use E-mail to connect you to discussion groups composed of Internet users who share a common interest. Newsgroups concern nearly any subject you can imagine. A variation on newsgroups is called **"IRC" (Internet Relay Chat)** in which participants hold "conversations" with others in very nearly "real time" exchanges. You might get leads to some research information and criticism by following a specialized newsgroup, but it is not likely that chat groups will do much more than waste your research time.

newsgroups defined

IRC distinguished

The other set of materials allows you to find and retrieve information at Internet sites. The major tools for retrieving information are:

- FTP: **FTP** or "File Transfer Protocol" allows Internet users to move files from one computer on the Internet to another. Regardless of the system you use, FTP permits you to connect with another computer to transfer graphics, text, or computer programs.

FTP defined

- Telnet: **Telnet** permits Internet users to log on to a computer at some other location and run programs on it. You could use Telnet, for instance, to connect to the CARL system. You could then use the major search tools available through CARL using commands in that remote system just as if you were actually there (which, after a fashion, you are).

Telnet defined

- Browsers: **Browsers** are programs that let you search and display things on the Internet. Comprehensive browsers can help you get what you want without requiring you to learn different computer command systems. They provide nearly seamless access to many tools (including FTP and Telnet) and all parts of the Internet. The most popular browsers are Netscape Navigator and Microsoft Explorer.

browsers combine all Internet elements

SPECIAL DISCUSSION 5-5
Elements Needed for Internet Access from Your Own Computer

EQUIPMENT NEEDED FOR THE INTERNET

Without going into detail on the matter, to use the Internet on your own equipment you need the following hardware:

- An IBM compatible PC with at least a 386 microprocessor (486, Pentium, or Pentium MMX preferred), 4 megabytes of memory on the motherboard (8 or more preferred), and plenty of memory to store a browser program and files that you wish to download. (If you use a Macintosh system, requirements are similar.)
- A modem that will connect your computer to other computers through the telephone lines (modem speeds are constantly improving—so get the fastest modem you can reasonably afford; if you get a slow modem, you'll learn to your dismay why many people call the WWW the "World Wide Wait").
- (optional) A sound system so that you can download sound files and play them back.
- (optional) A high quality video card and monitor to capture detail in graphics and images you might wish to examine.

SOFTWARE BROWSER

Before using a comprehensive Internet browser on an IBM compatible PC, you need to install a version of Windows (3.1 or higher, including Windows 95). On Macintosh systems, browsers run directly from the resident operating system. Though many browsers are available, the most popular are from Netscape and Microsoft. Students and faculty members are permitted to use versions of Netscape for free, and anyone is permitted to use Microsoft Explorer for free. So, find the one you like best and make arrangements to download it from the Netscape or Microsoft Web site.

GETTING ACCESS TO THE INTERNET

To get on the Internet, you must find a source to give you access. You have some options.

- You can make arrangements through a commercial provider. These sources are very competitive. Keep an eye out for new companies and new deals. You can also contact these commercial providers for information and subscription offers (if you use the Internet very much, however, you may wish to use other providers): America Online (800) 827-6364; Compuserve (800) 848-8199; Prodigy (800) 776-3449. These sources all use their own Internet software.
- You can use the Internet through libraries or computer lab(s) at your school, usually for free (or for a small lab fee).
- You can use the Internet by telephoning your school's computer center from a computer you have at home. This step may require special account numbers that your local computer center can help you obtain.

How Do I Get on the Internet?

Most college libraries or computer laboratories have workstations that allow students Internet access. If you want to establish Internet access from your own personal computer, you will need to acquire some equipment, a software browser, and a phone connection (see Special Discussion 5-5).

Fortunately for you, as a student your school probably makes access to the Internet available to you for free (or nearly free). The direct way to get the job done is to contact your school's computer center.   **how to get:**

- Get an E-mail account and Internet access. It is very easy to get set up. At the author's school, to get an E-mail account students are simply directed to a   **E-mail**
  machine resembling a bank's ATM. Students insert their identification cards and enter the password they wish to use for their E-mail transactions.

- Ask what you must do to get access to a computer that lets you browse the World Wide Web. Most school computer labs will permit you to use their   **Web access**
  computers to browse the Internet (without the need for you to fill out additional forms or obtain other accounts). To use the Internet from a home computer, you might need to obtain a personal or class account number and password.

Conducting an Internet Session

There is a lot of talk about the Internet as some sort of "information superhighway." But the Internet is much more like a disorganized attic than it is a well constructed superhighway. Thus, researchers use comprehensive browsers to help get information they want. Figure 5.2 shows the opening screen that appears when you get on the Internet and use Netscape Navigator (version 2.02, also called Navigator Gold). You   **layout of Netscape**
can move to different locations on this "page" by using a mouse. When you wish to   **Navigator**
make a selection you click the left button on the mouse. Teaching you details of a
browser program is beyond the scope of this chapter, but you can find a handbook and   **handbook available**
answers to frequently asked questions by moving the mouse arrow to "Help" at the   **online**
upper right corner of your browser screen. When you click on "Help" a menu appears that contains several choices for you. If you use the mouse to click the option marked "Handbook," a very readable guide appears on your screen.

To help you get started, let's walk through part of an Internet search session. Browsers present Internet information as a series of "pages," starting with a "home page" from each source. To browse resources you use the buttons on the toolbar   **elements of basic**
(conveniently identified with such terms as: "Back" for moving to the previous page;   **Netscape commands**
"Forward" for moving to the next page; "Home" for returning to starting page for   **and options**
your browser; "Reload" for reloading a current page; "Images" for displaying any graphics that have not been automatically loaded; "Open" for opening new locations or files; "Print" for printing out the current pages you are browsing; "Find" for searching a page for particular words or phrases; "Stop" for halting transfer of information to the current page). The set of directory buttons (What's New!, What's Cool!, Upgrades, Net Search, Net Directory, and Newsgroups) send you to special places on the Internet.

FIGURE 5.2
Internet Browser Page

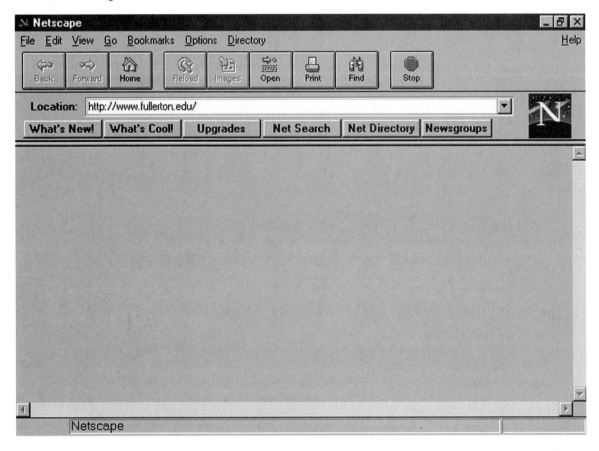

Surfing the Internet for Research Information

"surfing" the net

When you browse the Internet for information you are "surfing" the net (reminiscent of the CERFnet developed by Susan Estrada in 1988). You'll find that many library sources are available to you through the Internet. Keep track of your Internet sessions the same way you do other library work. Make sure you have a disk to copy materials you want as you go.

Suppose you want to find what information exists on the variable "verbal aggression." If you know the location of a source of such information, you can click the "Open" button and enter the source's address (called a **URL** or "Uniform Resource Locator"). If you don't know the URLs of sources concerning your topic, click on the "Net Search" button to find a list of search sites you can use to search the Internet for Web sites that contain keywords that interest you.[1] The screen will reveal a list of search sites including Yahoo!, a popular search tool, and a good place to start looking for information (we would select the Yahoo! site if it were not already identified). Next to the Yahoo! logo, a blank is provided for search terms. Suppose you enter "verbal aggression" and click on the "Search" button. The result of this effort may be found in Figure 5.3. As you can see, the Yahoo! search system found "no Yahoo! categories" the day this search was completed. So, the search system automatically shifted to the AltaVista search system and found a number of Internet sites, two of which fit into the window in Figure 5.3. The second reference may sound particularly interesting since it uses our keywords in the title. If you move the mouse pointer to the title of this source (often indicated by a different typeface or text color), and then click the left mouse button, you will be whisked to the other document itself. This highlighted or underlined material is called a **hyperlink** and allows automatic connections to other sources.

        net search example

        hyperlink identified

    You can read the document and decide if you would like to have a copy of it. This particular document is a text file (no pictures) and can be saved. Of course, you can always print it by selecting the "Print" button from the browser screen. If you want to save a copy of this document on a disk, you can simply select "Save" from the "File" command menu. This approach, however, saves not only the page you see, but all the programming commands that created it. So, if you want to save only the finished page, you must use a different approach. Select "Save As" from the "File" command menu. A menu will appear that has the name of your file followed by a dot and three letters, such as ".htm". Change this suffix to ".txt" (unless you want to save all the programming codes along with the file). On another part of the menu you will be asked to identify the "File Type" for the page(s) you wish to save. Choose saving it as a "Plain Text .txt" file by clicking on that option. When you click "OK," the file will be saved as a text file and you can edit it in a word processor later.[2]

        saving a copy of an Internet document

    If you find a picture or image you would like to save (perhaps to put in a term paper or essay), you can do so very easily. Simply place the mouse arrow on the image and press the *right* mouse key. When the menu appears, select the "Save This Image As" option. A new menu will appear that allows you to change the file name and the location where you would like it saved. Select "OK" on the menu and the image is saved. But you should know that pictures, as well as text, are copyrighted materials. Though copyright laws provide limited "fair use" for you, you do not have the right of further duplication and distribution of images without getting permission.

        saving an image

---

[1]Clicking on the "Net Directory" button will send you to locations where you can search the Internet for Web sites organized by categories. Clicking on the "Newsgroups" button will send you to locations where you may access newsgroups on various topics (you must first "subscribe" [for free] to newsgroups, which must be supported by your local "news server"). To find out what newsgroups are supported by your server, while running Netscape Navigator click on the "Options" command at the top of your browser, and click on "Show All Newsgroups." It will list all the supported newsgroups so that you can browse them.

[2]These text files are saved as ASCII (American Standard Code for Information Interchange) files that any word processor can convert to their own systems. Most recent versions of popular word processors also can import files written in html (hypertext markup language).

FIGURE 5.3
Searching the Internet for Items on "Verbal Aggression"

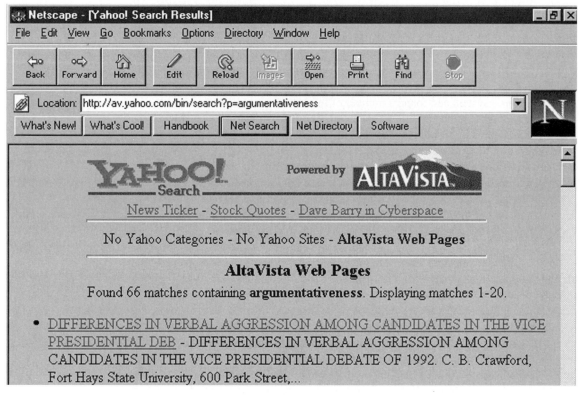

saving a location as a "bookmark"

If you encounter a really great Web site, you might wish to save its location. This task can be completed easily by clicking the "Bookmarks" menu box at the top of the screen. A file containing a list of your favorite sources will be created and you can add to it as you wish. After a time you can organize a list of sites to guide you to your most useful Internet sources. This list is your **bookmark file.**

Using Search Engines

search engines defined

Finding resources on the Internet is helped by using a **search engine** that can rummage through Internet resources for keywords and content areas (in the example just given, you used Yahoo!). There are some commercial sources (e.g., Comserve, Electric

SPECIAL DISCUSSION 5-6
Advice for Internet Searches

Using Internet technology invites some special words of advice. In their book, *Internet 101,* Alfred and Emily Glossbrenner offered the following pieces of advice (1996, p. 68):

1. Try to develop the Internet habit. [Many questions can be answered by searching the Internet early and by relying on its powerful search engines.]
2. Don't assume, however, that the Internet contains the sum total of humankind's knowledge. [Though many library resources are available on the Internet, it is not a substitute for traditional library work.]
3. The quality of the information available on the Net these days is impressive. But the very best stuff is either not on the Net, or if it is, it is not available for free.
4. Just because it's on the Net doesn't mean it's either accurate or true. [Since there is no quality control of the Internet, many things on it are inaccurate, incorrect, or deliberately misleading. Apply tests of evidence and reasoning to evaluate the integrity of Internet materials.]
5. Most people on the Web are trying to promote themselves or sell you something, not help you do research. Therefore, Internet searching will require some additional effort to collect keywords, examine listings, and set limits on Internet sessions.

Finally, remember to document your sources completely. Though citation formats for Internet materials are still under development, you will need to save data on URLs, dates (of the document and your search), and Web page titles.

Library, FirstSearch) that charge for searches, but this discussion does not include them. The major search tools tend to fall into three categories:

1. *Automated Search Systems.* Yahoo! and AltaVista are examples of automated search systems that index Internet sites. There are more than 40 different search engines available[3] and the number is growing all the time. On Netscape, the search functions automatically send you to any of 21 search tools, ranging from AccuFind to Yahoo! Microsoft Explorer relies on a reduced list of search systems, though others can be accessed by using their URLs. These systems are usually compiled by computerized searches of the Web and they are incredibly comprehensive and helpful.

automated search systems available on browsers

---

[3]A nearly exhaustive set of hyperlinks to search engines may be found on the Web site "VCN's Forty Ways to Search the Web" at the URL, "http://www.vcomm.net/guides.html".

gopher systems defined

2. *Gophers.* A **gopher** system uses a collection of menus or catalog listings on a topic. When you select an item from the list, you are either sent to it, or you are sent to another menu. Unlike pages on the World Wide Web, gophersites do not use graphics and colors. They rely on text-based links. Developed to help you "go for" information, this approach to Internet searching was developed at the University of Minnesota (whose mascot is the golden gopher). Each gopher system looks a little different from others and some are dedicated to limited topic areas. It would be tedious to review all of them. Fortunately you need not do so. Many search engines previously described provide links to gophers. Furthermore, a database called Gopherspace—containing menus from over 5,000 gopher systems—can be searched using a software tool called "Veronica."[4] Some gophers let you search the system with a tool known as "Jughead." Another system called "Archie" was invented to search FTP files by name, but it is not as popular these days.

indexing gopher systems

alternative collections and guides to:

3. *Other Systems.* Over time, you will find some search tools that are really helpful when you investigate topics in your communication specialty. Some of the most helpful collections of guides to sources are: Special Internet Connections sometimes known as the Yanoff List; Perry Rovers's list of FTP sites; the Clearinghouse for Subject-Oriented Internet Resource Guides, listing over 400 guides and including extensive listings in business, science, and the social sciences; and the World Wide Web Virtual Library.

1. Internet sources

2. newsgroups available to you

A fairly recent development has been the emergence of "electronic journals" that publish research without ever printing a journal. Some of these journals are edited with scholarly rigor, but others are really newsletters with some articles of varying quality. There has been more activity in this area in other social sciences than in our field. But the trend seems to have become an established one with the availability of such electronic journals as the *Electronic Journal of Communication, Current Research in Social Psychology, The Web Journal of Modern Language and Linguistics,* and *Computer-Mediated Communication Magazine.* You can get a listing of electronic journals through LC Marvel, a resource supported by the Library of Congress.

emergence of electronic journals

Using Standard Sources

availability of standard library sources through Internet

One nice thing about the Internet is that it makes available the resources of major libraries. For instance, suppose you wish to hear what President Grover Cleveland or Theodore Roosevelt really sounded like. If you have a sound card in your computer you can surf to the Vincent Voice Library (see Figure 5.4) and click on "Sound Samples from US Presidents - from Cleveland to Clinton" (http://web.msu.edu/vincent/index.html). After you identify a president, you will have to wait for a moment for the file to be transferred to you. Then you will actually hear a voice that you might

---

[4]An easy way to access Veronica is through Yahoo, which you can reach by clicking on the "NetSearch" button. Select "Computers and Internet" and then "Searching the Net" as the topic area. Select "Veronica" and choose from the menu of servers.

FIGURE 5.4

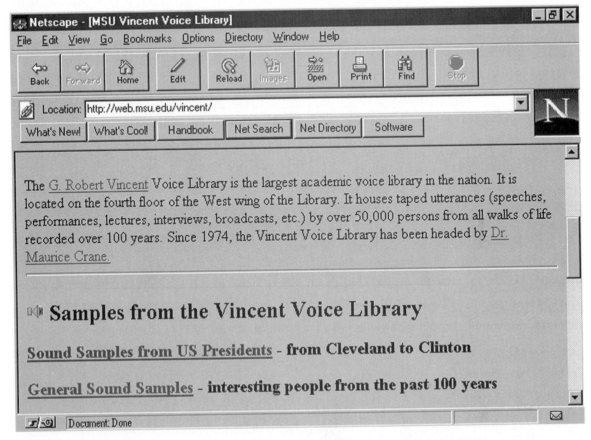

Copyright © 1996 Netscape Communications Corp. Used with permission. All Rights Reserved. This electronic file or page may not be reprinted or copied without the express written permission of Netscape. Vincent Voice Library Homepage used with permission.

never otherwise hear.[5] You might wish to search ERIC without going to the library. No problem. Just contact the AskERIC Website (http://ericir.sunsite.syr.edu/). You might wish to search CARL for materials held in that interlibrary system. No problem. Just contact the CARL Web site (http://www.state.lib.vt.us/internet/carl.htm). Not only will you be able to identify books and special collections but this source allows you to get

---

[5]A word to the wise. Listening to this collection can be both surprising and a little depressing. For instance, Theodore Roosevelt doesn't sound a bit like the actors who played him in the movies. Instead, he sounds like Maxwell Smart on the old *Get Smart* TV show.

online with searches of the *Education Index, National Newspaper Index, Legal Resources Index, Newspaper & Periodical Indexes, Transcript,* and *UnCover.* You may wish to see what is being done in psychology related to your topic. No problem. Just contact PsychREF (http://maple/lemoyne.edu/~hevern/psychref.html). If you want to see the list of publications of the American Communication Association, you need only reference their web page (http://cavern.uark.edu/comminfo/www/ACA.html). To check a large collection of communication resources, you may examine "Speech Communication World" (http://home.cc.utexad.edu/coc/speech/world/). These sources are actually just ways to use the Internet to connect with many sources identified in tables 5.4 and 5.5.

SUMMARY

Research uses past work to develop arguments. Argument is a process of advancing conclusions based on reasons and evidence. Past research guides us by: (1) providing premises for argument (a "premise" is a statement in a logical argument that is the foundation for others drawn from it); (2) giving evidence for argument claims; (3) balancing reliance on authority and empirical data. The "Einstein syndrome" occurs when misguided researchers fail to connect what has been learned from a "sudden breakthrough" and thus, do not learn from the successes of others.

Some of the most obvious things to seek in library encounters are, definitions of key concepts and variables, ways concepts and variables have been measured and studied, summary statements that people make about the subject, classic research studies on a subject (the studies that all the textbooks seem to reference), research that shows what methods to use, and research that shows what mistakes to avoid. Aside from textbooks and articles, you should examine encyclopedias, specialized dictionaries, and handbooks and annual reviews.

Students should use a research outline. To manage research materials, sound bibliographic tech-niques should be observed. First, students must master the library by learning its unique qualities. Second, tactical skills in bibliographic research should be practiced, including taking notes in brief form, practicing good note-taking skills, following proper reference form, and avoiding inadvertent plagiarism ("the act of using another person's ideas or expressions in your writing without acknowledging the source").

There are two major library research strategies. The general-to-specific approach starts with general sources to find leads to specific sources. Scholarly article titles reveal whether an article is worth reading since they have descriptive titles that often use standard phrases. The specific-to-general method begins with specific sources to obtain citations to related research and theory.

Hierarchical systems reveal where common material is found—in the same location in the library. Keyword-based systems send you to different locations in the library to find articles and papers. CD–ROMs contain indices and directories of sources. On-line database systems are used to search for books, articles, and reports. Steps in the process of an on-line search include selecting keywords from the problem statement (keywords are terms under which information about the topic may be found), developing alternative lists of descriptor terms, combining keywords, and undertaking on-line activity. An index lists locations of resource materials and articles whereas an abstract also provides a brief summary. Since no single hard copy index covers the entire wealth of our field, you may wish to check different sources to find citations to the most valuable articles.

Using the library includes managing the actual conduct of the library session. Troubleshooting in the library is necessary to avoid difficulties: (1) When a source is unavailable, you can use interlibrary loans or (less advised) triangulate information from secondary descriptions. (2) When there seems to be "no information on my topic," you can use the "known to unknown" search pattern. (3) When the journals are missing, you can check microform copies, check for name changes, or contact interlibrary loan services. (4) When the material is technical and complex, you can rely on resource tools, interpretations from books, and critiques and abstracts.

The Internet is a growing system of information available through interconnected networks of computers. It includes the World Wide Web (WWW)—an information distribution system that organizes information using hypermedia (hypermedia are information approaches in which each page of information can contain embedded references to images, sound, and other pages of information. When a user selects an item, the hypermedia system follows the associated reference). Internet elements are in two basic groups: mail-based systems and information retrieval systems. The mail-based systems include E-mail—a system for sending messages to other Internet users (the leading use of the Internet)—and newsgroups—applications of E-mail that connect you to discussion groups composed of Internet users who share a common interest (a variation is called "IRC" [Internet Relay Chat] in which participants hold "conversations" with others in very nearly "real time" exchanges, though such groups usually are not productive for research pur-

poses). The major tools for retrieving information are (1) FTP ("File Transfer Protocol")—a tool that allows Internet users to move files from one computer on the Internet to another; (2) Telnet—a software application that permits Internet users to log on to a computer at some other location and run programs on it; (3) comprehensive browsers, such as Netscape Navigator and Microsoft Explorer, that provide access to many tools and all parts of the Internet. A browser is a program that lets you search and display things on the Internet. The major browsers (Netscape Navigator and Microsoft Internet Explorer) are available to students for free. To get on the Internet you need access to some equipment, a software browser, and a phone connection, most of which are free to you as a student.

World Wide Web information is provided as a series of "pages," starting with a "home page" from each source. A comprehensive browser permits you to use commands, buttons, and toolbars to move to different locations on the Internet. Every location on the Internet has an address or URL (Uniform Resource Locator). When you browse the Internet for information you are "surfing" the net. Items on pages that appear in highlighted underlined form are called hyperlinks and allow automatic connections to other Internet sites. To save the URL of an interesting Web page, you can add the location to a bookmark file. Finding resources on the Internet is helped by using search engines that rummage through Internet sites for keywords and content areas. Major search tools tend to fall into three categories: (1) automated search systems—such as Yahoo! and AltaVista; (2) gophers—collections of menus or catalog listings on a topic (particularly useful if you cannot find what you need on the automated systems); (3) other systems that are special collections or search guides to individual topics. Electronic journals have emerged in communication-related areas and researchers must search them. Many standard sources found in libraries have become available over the Internet including popular search indices and guides. In addition, many special collections available only in some libraries have been made available over the Internet.

TERMS FOR REVIEW

argument	E-mail
premise	newsgroups
Einstein syndrome	Internet Relay Chat (IRC)
plagiarism	FTP (file transfer protocol)
keywords	Telnet
annotations	browser
subject tracings	URL (Uniform Resource Locator)
CD–ROM	hyperlink
Internet	bookmark file
World Wide Web	search engine
hypermedia	gopher

CHAPTER 6

Composing Communication Research

God is love but get it in writing.

–Gypsy Rose Lee

BEFORE WE GET STARTED . . .

Research is not like other writing. Researchers select words carefully and waste no time explaining things that can be looked up elsewhere. Students new to the craft may be surprised that research writing is so terse. To be successful scholars, you need to know how research is mapped out and composed.

CONSTRUCTION OF THE ARTICLES YOU WILL READ AND REVIEW

You may have wondered why research articles look the way they do. This section will help you understand how articles are designed so that you can use them comfortably. To aid you, this chapter includes a brief article that shows how each part of an article is handled (Boxes 6.1, 6.2, and 6.3).

construction of research articles

Title

Let's be blunt about it. Research articles have boring titles. They could have catchy, poetic titles, but indexing services might misplace them if titles did not reveal the content. Such titles as "The Effects of Source Credibility of Women on Attitude Change" may not have verve and punch, but you know what is studied.

Abstract

Many journals include abstracts. The abstract is a courtesy summary for the reader, not part of the article itself. It can help you decide whether to read the entire article. For your own term papers, you probably do not need to include an abstract, but it is required for work that is published or presented at professional meetings.

Introduction and Context of the Problem Justification

In introductions to articles and research papers the author must show why the topic is relevant to the field and indicate the article's approach. Authors mention the field's name frequently in their introductions to let both editors and readers know that the article is central to the field, rather than peripheral to it. Studying the relationship between age and self-esteem may be interesting, but it is not a communication question since no message-related behavior is involved.

   Some articles cannot be understood without some background. Thus, authors may extend introductory remarks to place the topic into perspective. Though the lines of reasoning may differ, the context of the research often is explained by a combination of three methods: quoting authoritative sources, referring to past research, and arguing directly for the need for this work. As part of the context, scholars are expected to advance clear definitions for concepts of interest. As part of the context, articles attempt to argue that research is needed—or at least invited. Three major justifications tend to be used:

- *Filling a Gap in Knowledge.* One or more variables of interest may have been examined separately, but there may be a void in the area researchers want to probe. Finding a gap in knowledge is a good foundation to argue that new research would be wise. Thus, scholars review literature to find "holes" that invite new work.

- *Solving Practical Problems.* Sometimes there is an immediate need to help overcome a tangible problem. In such efforts, literature from popular sources—such as controversial books, newspaper articles, and magazines— may be referenced. Research foundations or government agencies may identify practical issues that they wish to have addressed. Sometimes practical problems involve measurement difficulties. For many years it was difficult to study communication apprehension (of which stage fright is only one particular form) since valid measures were unavailable. James McCroskey (1978) used this problem to justify studies to validate a new measure, called the Personal Report of Communication Apprehension.

- *Extending and Improving on Past Research.* Research articles frequently end with suggestions for future inquiry. Though most follow-up work tends to be completed by the same researcher who made the initial suggestions, the recommendations are clear calls for additional research. Sometimes inquiry is invited because past methods have been flawed and improvements are needed.

Statement of the Problem

Among the most important parts of research articles is the statement of the problem. Some researchers place it in the introduction. Some place it near the end of a brief literature review. Some research skips it altogether, a choice that usually is a hallmark of unfocused study.[1] The problem statement tends to appear early in research articles because it helps readers understand the new research contribution and the author's goals. Sometimes problem statements are hidden as "purpose statements." Thus, when you read, "The purpose of this research was to discover the extent of the use of 'devil terms' in the speeches of Senator Joseph McCarthy," you should recognize that it is equivalent to a problem statement that asks "What was the extent of the use of 'devil terms' in the speeches of Senator Joseph McCarthy?" When reading articles you should look for these problem statements—wherever they are hiding—to include them in your notes.

importance of stating the problem

problems can appear as purpose statements

Review of Literature

Though not always formally labelled, every research article contains a literature review. The review of literature extends the context of the problem by providing additional discussion, definitions, and notes on methods. Three basic questions should be answered in this section:

review of literature elements

- What do we already know or do?
- How does the new research question relate to what we already know or do?
- Why select this particular method of investigation?

The literature review is usually (informally) divided into sections that serve as the researcher's justification for undertaking the study, which for quantitative articles and papers, often appear in this order:

1. Conceptual definition of the variable or issue of interest (if there are controversies about legitimate conceptual definitions, this section discusses them and explains the author's decisions about the matter)
2. Problems with identifying, observing, or measuring variables or issues (often summarized by the term "operational definitions," this discussion concerns strengths and weaknesses of ways researchers actually try to conduct studies on a variable or issue)
3. Explanation of the importance or usefulness of the variable or issue (by citing past research that used the variable or issue successfully or by pointing to its practical importance)
4. Underlying theories that explain the important roles or functions of the variable or issue (any limitations on the usefulness of specific theories are placed here)

---

[1] You need to drop the idea that research must be good if it is published. Some poor work sometimes gets published despite weaknesses. Perfect research probably has not been completed in our field—although some researchers have come very close. It is all right, therefore, for you to criticize portions of research articles for deficiencies that exist. You are not attacking the person writing the article when you do so, and you are not pretending to be superior to those authors when you evaluate research according to standards found in this book.

5. The invitation to current or future research (gaps in knowledge, solving practical problems, extending past research).

After the review of the first chief variable or issue is covered, the method is repeated with a second, and so forth until all variables or issues are covered.

For qualitative articles and papers, the review of literature usually follows these topics, though rarely with explicit subdivisions:

- Definitions of any key concepts presumed in the article (e.g., redemptive rhetoric, conversational analysis, and so on), including controversies about proper conceptual definitions and the author's decisions about them
- Explanation of underlying theoretic foundations that underlie the methods used (e.g., social interactionism, the interpretive approach, the "great man" theory of history, and so on) and any adaptations the author believes should be made in applying these systems
- Identification and justification for examining the communication domain chosen, including discussion of the potential value of such study and any other invitations to current or future research in the area
- Background for the communication form to be studied, including historical or social information.

Researchers often end literature reviews with statements of the status of the subject. Lists of chief conclusions and priorities for future studies often appear. Such summaries can be very helpful when researchers have reviewed a fairly large body of research and thinking related to a subject.

Rationale for Hypotheses

isolating hypotheses   Immediately before a statement of any hypotheses, we should expect to find a paragraph or two in which a rationale for hypotheses is provided. If our thinking about the related literature is correct, then the hypotheses are what we expect to see. If an article does not include hypotheses (such as in Box 6.1), it should have a very specific problem statement. Some authors fail to give a specific rationale for their hypotheses. But experienced researchers usually take time to show links between the literature review and hypotheses.[2] Bruce Tuckman explained (1978, p. 315):

justifications of hypotheses   Hypotheses may be justified on two grounds—logical or empirical. Logical justification requires the development of arguments based on concepts or theories related to the hypotheses, while empirical justification requires reference to other research. It is necessary to provide justification for each hypothesis to insure the reader of its reasonableness and soundness. (Justification is especially critical in the proposal.)

The hypotheses are often set off in reduced type with symbols such as H_1, H_2, H_3 to indicate different hypotheses. If a hypothesis is not clearly identified, the article just plain doesn't have one.

---

[2] Technically, failing to link the literature review to hypotheses make the hypotheses *non sequitur* ("not in sequence"/"does not follow") fallacies.

BOX 6.1
Sample Article

THE WESTERN JOURNAL OF SPEECH COMMUNICATION 46
(Summer of 1982), 291–298

Differences in Impact Between Local and ———————— Title with key
National Televised Political Candidates' Debates†   words

ALLEN LICHTENSTEIN* —— Author

Televised debates between Presidential candidates have become an
integral part of the American political scene. In 1960, 1976 and 1980 the
major candidates for President appeared before television cameras for the
"Great Debates." Those who participated did so because of their belief in
the importance of the debates for winning the election.[1] With the major
emphasis on winning and losing, however, the debates took on the
appearance of and generated the media coverage of the "Super Bowl" of
politics. According to Sears and Chaffee, "Instead of their overt content,
news reports of the debates were preoccupied with 'who won' and
generally with the competitive, horse-race aspect."[2]

    Interest in the Presidential debates has been very high. In 1960, 90% of —— Context of
American households watched at least some of the Nixon/Kennedy debates,   Problem and
and for the Ford/Carter debates in 1976, the figure was 83% for American   Review
adults.[3] Reviews of research studies of the 1960 debates by Katz and Feldman (combined)
and of the 1976 debates by Sears and Chaffee suggest that a substantial
proportion of voters formed opinions and made decisions about the election
prior to viewing the debates.[4] The debates did not, therefore, generally alter
or form preferences but, rather, reinforced existing predispositions and made
voters more sure of their choice: "Debates would be expected mainly to
reinforce both the standing party allegiances and the candidate preferences

    *Mr Lichtenstein is Assistant Professor of Speech Communication at the
University of New Mexico, Albuquerque 87131.
    [1]Herbert E. Alexander and Joel Margolis, "The Making of the Debates," in *The
Presidential Debates: Media, Electoral, and Policy Perspectives,* eds., George F.
Bishop, Robert G. Meadow and Marilyn Jackson-Beeck (New York: Praeger
Publishers, 1978), p. 29. Sidney Kraus, "Presidential Debates: Political Option or
Public Decrees?" in *The Great Debates: Carter vs Ford, 1976,* ed., Sidney Kraus
(Bloomington: Indiana University Press, 1979), p. 3.
    [2]David O. Sears and Steven H. Chaffee, "Uses and Effects of the 1976 Debates: An
Overview of Empirical Studies," in *The Great Debates: Carter vs. Ford, 1976,* p. 229.
    [3]*With the Whole Nation Watching: Report of the Twentieth Century Fund Task Force
on Television Presidential Debates* (Lexington, Massachusetts: Lexington Press, 1979),
p. 42.
    [4]Elihu Katz and Jacob J. Feldman, "The Debates in Light of Research," in *The
Great Debates, Carter vs. Ford, 1976,* p. 211: Sears and Chaffee, p. 253. Churchill
L. Roberts "From Primary to Presidency: A Panel Study of Images and Issues in the 1976
Election," *Western Journal of Speech Communication, 45* (1981), 1.

BOX 6.1
(Continued)

built up over many prior months of campaigning, primary elections and conventions."[5] These findings are consistent with other research about the impact of television on attitudes. Television is apparently far more effective in strengthening attitudes than in altering them.[6]

The lack of research on televised debates, other than those concerned with Presidential elections, increases the probability that findings may be improperly generalized. Such generalizations do not take into account important **Gap in** differences in televised debates between candidates for local offices and the **knowledge** "Great Debates" for the office of President. For example, few local cam- **identified** paigns can attract the publicity and public interest of the race for the Presidency. Because of this, local candidates may be less known to the public and their positions on various issues less clear. Then, too, Presidential candidates affect local races on the same ballot (the coattail effect), but the opposite would be a rare occurrence. Finally, there appears to be less interpersonal communication concerning local races. According to Rothschild:

> Kline (1972) was one of the first to report on key differences in communications effects as a function of the level of the election race. He presented a review and re-analysis of data from several national and local election field studies which generally examined the agenda setting function of the media. Kline concluded that there are two types of elections. Presidential elections affect people of varying involvement levels in similar ways, and voting tends to be quite stable. Party elections (i.e., below the presidential level) are quite unstable situations for the low-involvement voter. Here people rely on simple presentations and deviate from party identification as a result. Because they did not have enough information to make a rational decision, people relied on their simple recall of images, consequently, in Kline's scenario, the predominant image received the vote. This finding is important in demonstrating that, while the limited effects model holds in the high level election, the media can have considerable power in the low level race.[7]

Problem The focus of the present investigation was on the impact of local televised **Statement** debates in comparison with Presidential televised debates. Specifically, how did the two types of debates compare with regard to: (1) level of interest, (2) providing information, (3) reinforcing predispositions concerning the election, and (4) changing attitudes about the candidate for whom to vote? Also, if differences in impact existed, were they attributable to the audiences drawn to the two levels of debaters or the debaters themselves?

---

[5]Sears and Chaffee, p. 253.

[6]Joseph T. Klapper in *The Effects of Mass Communication* (New York: Free Press, 1960), p. 11, argues that "Research has pretty well established that such [persuasive] mass communication is more likely to reinforce existing opinions than to change them, and more likely to produce modifications than conversions."

[7]Michael L. Rothschild, "On the Use of Multiple Methods and Multiple Situations in Political Communications Research," in *Political Communication: Issues and Strategies for Research,* ed., Steven H. Chaffee (Beverly Hills, California: Sage Publications, 1975), p. 247.

Method

The method section of a study describes what the researchers did in enough detail so that others could repeat or replicate it. For qualitative studies—such as evaluating the speeches of Susan B. Anthony or engaging in extended naturalistic studies of police—the method section tends to be *very* brief. Often, no formal section labelled "Method" appears, though many historical-critical studies include justifications for critical standards or analysis tools. For quantitative studies, the methods may be explained in detail, complete with subheadings. We will consider these elements next.

methods described in enough detail for replication

Data or Documentary Sample

Regardless of the type of research, some actual documents or sample data are used. Researchers explain the characteristics of such materials, where they came from, and how they were selected. For content analysis of mass media communication, the materials in the sample are documents or records, including oral and video records. Both the accuracy of the records and any omissions of materials must be explained. For empirical or experimental work, samples of people (often called "subjects") are typically gathered. In addition to reporting the number of subjects, sample characteristics (e.g., age, sex), and sources (e.g., college students, adults in field settings, volunteers), any methods for random sampling should be detailed (since this method requires extra steps).

content analyses samples are documents

samples in empirical studies

Operational Definitions of Variables

Conceptual definitions—such as those found in specialized dictionaries—give you an idea of the meaning of a term. An **operational definition** of a variable is nothing like a dictionary definition. Operational definitions isolate a concept by specifying the steps researchers follow to make observations of the variables. They are descriptions that include: (1) manipulations or tasks completed to make observations, (2) special measures used for key variables, or (3) methods for assignment of subjects to different conditions based on some common characteristics. Articles are also expected to provide information on the accuracy and reliability of their operational techniques. Reports of reliability for measurements have been routinely demanded in most professional journals since the early 1980s. Thus, justifications—not just descriptions—for the choices made to make observations are a major part of the discussion of measures used.

operational definition distinguished

Procedures

Researchers describe how the study was completed—step by step. The best studies are written so clearly that you could understand what it was like to be a subject in the study. Information on instructions, debriefing, and protection of subjects should be shared.

procedures identified

Methods for Analysis of Data

Though qualitative studies rely on theoretic orientations to interpret data, empirical and experimental studies employ statistical tools to examine hypotheses. Specific names, such as "*t* tests" or "analysis of variance" are mentioned with little explanation, since they are recognized by scholars who have taken a course such as the

in quantitative studies, data analysis refers to statistics

SPECIAL DISCUSSION 6–1
Anatomy of Articles that Present New Theories

Some articles present research and some present theories and conceptual discussions of things. Just as articles that present research have a fairly well-known organizational pattern shared in common, articles that advance new theories also have some common (though different) features.

The first part of each of these theory articles begins with a review of the context of the problem. Theories of attitude change review work on predicting attitude change, argumentation theories review different ways to describe arguments, and theories on the effects of violence on television review the status of theory on violence. The conclusion of the context of the problem is a statement of the desirability of isolating a different theoretic perspective. Sometimes articles attempt to "trash" past efforts, but this strategy is not highly regarded by scholars. Showing a meaningful new contribution is enough of a justification for the new orientation.

The second major section of the theory article is expected to define all terms clearly and concisely. The discussion of definitions is detailed and filled with justifications, since definitions are based on key assumptions that new theories are expected to state explicitly.

The third section includes statements of key propositions (in predictive theories) and implications of definitions (in the case of definitional theories). These statements include defining the roles of key concepts.

Fourth, the theory article is expected to present information on the usefulness of applying the theory. Any advantages in interpreting research and explaining phenomena should be reviewed. In addition, any limitations are advanced. Finally, the implications for future work with the theory are expected to be listed and explained as part of a call to future research.

---

one you probably are completing now. If statistics are not so widely understood, the author may explain them with increasing detail. Box 6.2 shows this section from a research article.

Results

results section does not interpret findings

The results section of an article does not explain the meaning of study findings. The results are simply that—presentations of findings—without comment on their substantive importance. The results section often includes tables and sometimes graphs to report analyses. Since the results section is technical, researchers are expected to provide enough detail to help readers understand what was found. This section tends to be brief.

Discussion

discussion interprets results

Though short articles may combine the results and discussion sections (as in our example), most authors write a separate discussion section. The discussion section is the researcher's chance to argue about the meaning of results. Though researchers are

BOX 6.2
Sample Article, Part 2

METHOD

During the Fall of 1980, public television station KNME-TV in Albuquerque, New Mexico aired "The Candidates," a series of debates between candidates seeking election to a variety of local offices. These were shown during the same general time period that the Reagan/ Anderson and Reagan/Carter debates appeared on the major networks. Like the Presidential debates, "The Candidates" was sponsored by the League of Women Voters.

————— Method

————— Materials

One major difference between the Presidential debates and "The Candidates" was in the number of races covered. There is only one national election, the race for President. In contrast, on the local level were a multitude of offices whose candidates all competed for limited publicity. Thus, while "The Candidates" differed from the Presidential debates insofar as the number of races covered, this situation reflects actual differences in the different level election as described by Kline.

In order to make a comparative analysis of audience perception and impact of the local and Presidential debates, a telephone survey was undertaken. Interviews were conducted with 234 randomly selected persons from the KNME mailing list.[8] The interview, which took approximately seven minutes, consisted of 25 questions concerning "The Candidates," the Presidential debates, and, if the respondent saw both, a comparison of the two. The interviews were conducted in early January 1981 by trained volunteers.[9]

————— Sample

————— Measures

Results obtained from such a sample cannot be generalized to the general public or any other population. It is not the purpose of this study to do so. However, results showing substantial differences in audience perception and impact between Presidential and local candidate TV debates, for even one group, would be important. These results could lend support to the idea of the inability to make generalizations concerning televised political candidate debates from Presidential debate research alone. They would suggest further that the impact of any televised candidate debate is strongly influenced by the particular situation and context in which the debate is held.

Although there was considerable interest in the local debate series, the Presidential debates were far more popular (see table 1). This finding is not surprising given the publicity and news coverage for the Presidential debate series. Also, the national debates were aired over commercial networks, and "The Candidates" appeared on a local public

---

[8]Two hundred thirty-four respondents completed the interview of the initial 300 contacted, resulting in a completion rate of 78%.

[9]The training included instructions and practiced interviews. In addition, randomly selected interviews were monitored during the study to insure the accuracy and the neutrality of the procedure. The survey was conducted in January to allow enough time to elapse after the election so that the respondents' answers would reflect their reactions to the debates themselves rather than the candidates.

BOX 6.2
Sample Article, Part 2

RESULTS AND CONCLUSIONS

TABLE 1 Viewing of "The Candidates" and the Presidential Debates

Saw "The Candidates"	
one	8%
two	17%
three or more	14%
total (saw at least one)	39%
Saw The Presidential Debates	
Reagan/Anderson only	4%
Reagan/Carter only	27%
both	49%
total (saw at least one)	80%

Analysis of _____ results by percentages

television station. Even if the races were perceived as being of equal importance, the publicity and coverage difference would account for a considerable portion of the difference in viewership.[10]

The local and national races were not viewed as equally important by the public; the Presidential election was thought to be more important. The overwhelming difference is not surprising and supports Kline's conclusions.[11] Interestingly, however, 76 percent of the respondents watched the Reagan/Carter debate, and only 54 percent saw the Reagan/Anderson one. This result may be due to the greater support and interest that Jimmy Carter generated, but these figures and this explanation cast doubt on the notion that viewers tuned in the debates to learn more about the unknown candidate. If that were the case, Anderson would be expected to draw a larger audience.

Expectedly, both Presidential debates drew substantially more viewers than the entire series of local candidate debates. However, 80 percent of the people who tuned in one local debate came back to see at least one more. This may indicate that "The Candidates" was considered useful to the people who saw it, a conclusion supported by the results displayed in table 2.

The local debates were perceived as considerably more informative and influential to the viewers than the Presidential debates. Influence, however, probably took several different forms. An undecided voter could have made up his or her mind, a "leaner" would have made a definite decision, and an already decided voter could have switched or become undecided. Local debate viewers reported being more influenced in general, changing their minds more, and being made more sure of their choices.

---

[10]According to the February 1981 Nielsen NS1 report, the weekly cumulative DMA audience for KNME is 54%. This compares with 93% for KGGM, the CBS affiliate; 92% for KVAT, the ABC affiliate; and 90% for KOB, the NBC affiliate.

[11]Rothschild, p. 247.

given freedom to draw conclusions, the rules of sound reasoning must be obeyed, and the arguments must appeal to research evidence (and not go far beyond them). Structurally, the discussion section usually interprets hypothesized and unexpected results, the significance of the study, study limitations (problems that may be overcome in future research), and implications for future inquiry. Since the literature review raised invitations to new research, the discussion of results should respond to *each* issue raised early in the paper. Otherwise, the research would not have been a fitting response to research invitations. Box 6.3 shows how such a commentary is included in the discussion.

Conclusion

The conclusion usually is a statement of one or two paragraphs in which the researcher summarizes what was done in the study. The conclusion is not a stirring call to future inquiry—it simply summarizes what was accomplished.

conclusion is a summary

References

The final part of a research article is a list of references. To understand the *detail* of citation methods, it is a good idea to read the materials in the accompanying student manual and the *Publication Manual of the APA* directly. In addition, you will find practical advice on ways to improve your own writing and prepare a professional looking research paper.

references using the APA format

WRITING SCHOLARSHIP

There is no way around it. Research involves crisp and clear writing. You may expect to develop your own writing skills as a result of studying research methods. You might have to write only short papers in the class you are taking, but you certainly will be expected to *write well.* Though developing good writing skills is, and should be, a lifelong undertaking, you can take some immediate steps to improve your writing. This section provides some practical advice about planning and structuring your scholarly writing.

research demands clear writing

Using Proper Formats and Subdivisions

The flow of a paper can get lost unless you use some helpful aids. The most obvious way to enhance understanding is to use headings to highlight your main points. Like it or not, your instructors often grade your papers while facing frequent interruptions. In all but your shortest projects, headings and subheadings can help keep main ideas in the instructor's mind despite distractions (we are talking about "defensive writing" here). You should start with a major heading for each main point on your outline and add subheadings as the discussion gets involved or lengthy.

desirability of using subdivisions

Matters of Style

In this context, style does not mean a special sense of fashion or personal flair. **Style** refers to the choice and use of words. Indeed, many books that discuss good writing use the word *style* in their titles (such as *The Elements of Style* by William Strunk and E. B. White, 1979). By consulting such books, you may make rapid progress by looking at ways to make your writing clear and precise.

meaning of style

BOX 6.3
Sample Article, Part 3

Results and Discussion

TABLE 2 Impact of "The Candidates" and the Presidential Debates

	Local Debate Viewers (%)	Presidential Debate Viewers (%)
Decided voting choice before seeing debates	40	70
Learned more about candidates from seeing debates	80	55
Voting decision influenced by debates	57	29
Voting preference changed because of debates	20	9
More sure of choice because of debates	79	63
	(90)	(187)

Two possible explanations exist for the differing impact of the televised debates for different level elections. The first explanation is that different types of people are drawn to the different level debates. According to this explanation, people who watch local debates tend to be more interested in politics, more open minded, and in general, engage in more information seeking behavior.[12] Their tuning into the local debates is an example of information seeking. Thus, the greater impact of the local debates can be attributed to the specific reasons that this select group of people watch them. The second explanation, following Kline's conclusions, is that the differing nature of the campaigns and the publicity surrounding them cause the differences in impact; the type of people drawn to the programs is not the crucial factor.

These alternative explanations can be tested by comparing the influence of the two types of debates on people who saw both. If the people-centered explanation is true, then there should be no difference in the impact of the local and the Presidential debates on viewers who saw both. If the local debate had greater impact on those people who saw both types (following the general pattern for their sample), the "nature of the audience" explanation would not be supported.

Results indicated that the kind of debate televised, and not audience characteristics, determined impact. . . . A nearly identical pattern appeared for these people who saw both levels of debate as for the entire sample. Although they were more decided about the Presidential debates before viewing, they learned more from the local candidates' debates, were influenced more, changed their minds more, and were made sure of their choices more often.

The impact on the Presidential debate viewers, for this sample, shows consistency with the 1960 and 1976 findings. Seventy percent of the people decided their choice for President before watching the debates, compared with only 40% for the local candidates. Because of the greater coverage and publicity of the Presidential race, voters tended to make decisions early, possibly by January prior to the election. Televised debates appear a more important information source for local elections which lack the coverage of the national races. Results support this view: 80% of the viewers said they learned more about the candidates from seeing the local debates, whereas only 55% of the Presidential debate viewers reported such learning. This is consistent with Kline's findings about the different roles of mass media in the different level elections.[13]

---

[12]Rothschild, p. 247.

[13]Maxwell E. McCombs and L. Edwards Mullins, in "Consequences of Education: Media Exposure, Political Interest and Information Seeking Orientation," *Mass Communications Review, 1* (1973), 27–31, discuss the association of information-seeking behavior and education. Public television audiences tend to be skewed toward the higher educated. Jack Lyle, in *The People Look at Public Television* (Washington, D.C.: Corporation for Public Broadcasting, 1975), points out the upper SES and education skew for the public television audience.

**BOX 6.3
(Continued)**

Not only was "The Candidates" more informative, it was also more influential. Almost twice as many of the local debate viewers (57%) as the Presidential debate viewers (29%) felt their votes were influenced by the debates. For both groups of viewers, the major effect was to reinforce previously made decisions rather than change voting preferences. Although these results support conclusions of research of the 1960 and 1976 Presidential debates, both types of influence, change and reinforcement, were greater with the local televised debates. Twenty percent of "The Candidates" viewers changed their minds as opposed to only 9% for the Presidential debates. Seventy-nine percent were made more sure by the local debates, 63% by the national.

. . .

Respondents who saw both local and national debates were asked which they thought were more informative, interesting and influential. The results (see table 5) revealed a curious paradox: people who saw both were more influenced by the local debates . . . and perceived the local debates as more informative; however, they also saw the Presidential debates more interesting and influential.

Table 5 Perceptions of the Debates*

	Local Debates (%)	Presidential Debates (%)
More informative	40	31
More interesting	19	57
More influential	24	41
	(76)	(76)

*Questions were asked of persons who saw both local and Presidential debates.

The explanation for this paradox may very well lie in the discrepancy between an individual's own reactions and his or her perceptions of how other people react. The belief in the power of the Presidential debates is widely held. Findings of this study, consistent with the findings of research from the Presidential debates from 1960 and 1976, suggest limited informational and cognitive effects. Yet, this research is unfamiliar to the majority of the public. There persists the belief that the Presidential candidate debates are more important than the research would indicate.

Generalizations based on this study, with its unique and limited population, are as limited as generalizations from research conducted only on debates between Presidential candidates. The response of this sample to "The Candidates" does not follow the patterns revealed by studies on the Nixon/Kennedy and Carter/Ford debates. Although the limited-effects model appears to hold for the Presidential debates, it does not appear to explain the greater impact on this sample of "The Candidates." Effects are mitigated by the myriad particular circumstances of each campaign, including the level of the election. Future research needs to address the questions concerned with what types of situational campaign variables affect the impact of a televised debate, and for what groups.

Limitations and Call for future study

SPECIAL DISCUSSION 6-2
Outlines As Recipes for Success

It is nearly impossible to write good research without using an outline. You probably never needed an outline to write papers in high school, but that situation is all over now. Make it your policy to begin each assignment by composing a rough outline before doing anything else—this step may serve as the basis of your library research outline. List the major topics you are told to cover on a large sheet of paper. Leave space between headings and start filling in details of substructure for each of your outline topics. Then check the logic of your outline. Are there any unsupported statements? Are there any sections where the reasoning is weak? You usually can spot these problems on your outline and correct them before investing much time into the project.

Students often resist working from outlines because they may think that they can sit down and write a paper without one. In research work, however, they often find themselves face to face with four facts. First, without an outline describing each detail of the paper, they cannot take breaks for meals, phone calls, exercise, or emergencies. Second, without an outline it may be difficult to make changes. If a student finds that a project should be modified according to a professor's advice, it is easy to change an outline, but it is very painful to change complete pages and paragraphs that have been written. Third, without working from a full outline, it is difficult to plan time to research the topic or to fill in previously undiscovered gaps. Fourth, without a complete outline, it may be difficult to get help from a professor in the early stages of a project. Though students ask professors for advice on completing research papers, there may be little that they can do if there is no outline to review. There is no real doubt about it. Working from an outline is not a luxury—it is your recipe for success.

---

internal organizers identified

Clear writing is led by very organized thoughts. In addition to outlining, other methods can promote clear writing. Making active use of **internal organizers**— phrases that preview, summarize, and transition between main points—can underscore your content. It is helpful to preview all the subpoints before you cover any of them. A full summary of each subpoint provided at subsection endings emphasizes the order of ideas in the paper. Using summaries and previews increases chances for your ideas to be understood.

ambiguity shunned in scholarly writing

It is important to avoid ambiguity in scholarly writing. You should use terms that are direct and, whenever possible, you should rely on language that is understandable to the greatest number of intelligent people. Einstein expressed this concern best: "Ideas should be stated as simply as possible, but no simpler." You should not avoid topics that are technical—quite the contrary! But, your writing should use only those specialized terms that are essential. Furthermore, you should define every major term you use. Clear writing can often be enhanced by employing paragraph structures that have obvious topic sentences. If you use active summaries, previews, and internal organizers, avoid ambiguity, and rely on standard paragraph structures, your writing will be clear and understandable.

use summaries, previews, and topic sentences

WRITING CLASSROOM REPORTS

Communication students are often asked to write papers that refer to research. Though your instructors will give you specific details for each assignment, you should observe some general formats. This section will describe the obligations you routinely should expect to satisfy. It will cover three types of papers: the definitional criticism paper, the literature review (or explication) paper, and the research prospectus (or proposal).

need to revise written work

As a general piece of advice, remember that scholarship is not written so much as it is rewritten. Yet, to revise your writing, you often need to get distance from your own work. For all your projects, you should complete a first draft as soon as you can and then set it aside for a day or so. When you begin revising, you will find plenty of things to improve. After time, you will learn to revise your work within a few hours of completing a first draft.

Strategies for a Definitional Criticism Paper

A definitional paper takes a concept of interest to you—such as propaganda, stuttering, or comparative advertising—and considers issues that involve the proper definition of the concept. You do not just choose your favorite definition. Instead, these papers contrast different approaches to understand definitional questions.

Organizing a Definitional Review Paper

The definitional paper usually begins with an introduction that mentions the topic area and justifies it as a part of the study of communication. The introduction actively refers to the field and cites communication sources (and other related subjects) that indicate the concept is important enough to investigate. Any context needed to understand the topic is often included in the introduction, rather than as a completely separate discussion. Depending on the paper's length, the introduction ends by previewing the rest of the paper's main points.

format and design of the definitional criticism paper

The bulk of a definitional paper compares and contrasts different schools of thought for the concept of interest. The writer does not try to explain how important the variable is in everyday life but considers the proper way to define the term. Schools of thought are distinguished by different details or key starting points. Each school of thought is usually introduced with a typical quotation expressing that point of view. Then, comments are made to point out any weaknesses in the definition. Though Chapter 3 provided you with standards for definitions to satisfy, for now you should know that criticisms are made by applying specific criteria, not your personal feelings about the authors or their implied values. You should also examine problems that exist in finding useful operational definitions (measurement or methods to observe the concept in action) for your concept of interest.

contrasting different schools of thought

evaluating definitions

After discussing each definitional school of thought and its limitations, you will need to offer some sort of conclusion. Is one definition clearly superior to the others? Are all the definitions acceptable, but most applicable to different situations? Do you have an alternative definition that is superior to the others? If so, are you prepared to show how your new definition meets all the standards expected of good definitions? Any of these conclusions is acceptable but you must choose an approach and defend it.

Isolating and Categorizing Schools of Thought

sources for
definitional schools
of thought

Students sometimes doubt their ability to identify different schools of thought. The task, however, is quite simple. You simply look for definitions of the concept and then you categorize the different schools of thought. Most of the time definitions are found in specialized dictionaries and encyclopedias, or in textbooks. Once you have found books that might contain such definitions, seek your term in the book indexes. If you find it, jot down the definition on a bibliographic note card. In specialized dictionaries, more than one definition may be provided. Do not assume that the first definition is preferred. By protocol, dictionary authors list definitions in the general chronological order that can be determined, though archaic definitions are usually placed at the end of the list. Make sure to identify any critiques of definitions, since you may use these comments to help complete your own paper.

methods to identify
different schools of
thought

The easiest way to identify different schools of thought is to sort your bibliographic cards containing definitions. Take the cards that seem to be saying the same thing and put them in one stack. Those definitions that add an element or that seem to move in a unique direction can be placed in a different stack. You will soon see that you have identified the major schools of thought on an issue. You may wish to re-read definitions within each group to make sure that meaningful distinctions have not been missed. To write the paper, you will need to consider each school of thought. Sometimes students who are new to research ask instructors how many sources are to be included in such a paper. Though instructors sometimes set limits for novice researchers, the question really cannot be answered. To complete the work, all conflicting schools of thought must be included—involving only a few sources or perhaps dozens.

Strategies for the Literature Review

Perhaps the most common papers you will write in your academic career will be literature reviews. These papers attempt to tell the reader what is known about a subject and the current status of the knowledge about the matter.

Organizing a Literature Review

The literature review generally has seven sections:

review sections
1. justify subject as
communication
2. context of the
problem

1. An introduction, which justifies the study of the topic in the field and previews the rest of the paper (It is typical to indicate how the topic is related to the field and to cite sources to support one's selection of the variables of interest.)

2. The context of the problem (a section that usually but not always is included), which isolates the role of the concepts in communication studies by such methods as quoting authoritative sources, referring to past research that invites new work, or arguing directly for a need for this work

3. background
definitions of terms

3. The background definitions of terms (not as extended as in a definitional paper), which assess *major* conceptual and operational definitions, including *problems* that researchers have faced when measuring or observing the concept or variable (General expository listings of operational definitions are not very interesting in a literature review paper—your attention should focus on operational problems that limit conclusions that researchers have drawn.)

4. The relevant theory reviewed to explain how and why the variable or concept functions in communication (Theories should be stated in enough detail to show their ability to explain the role of your variable or concept in the communication process, but you need not complete a full review of the theory).

    4. review of relevant theory

5. The research survey (or literature review), which usually is the longest part of the study. Based on limits set on your review, you may complete either an exhaustive or exemplary literature review:

    5. survey of literature

    - **exhaustive literature reviews** are research surveys that include all material related to the subject
    - **exemplary literature reviews** are surveys of only the most important contributions.

    exhaustive and exemplary literature reviews

    Published articles tend to use exemplary reviews because of space limits, and you probably will be asked to complete exemplary literature reviews in your classes (but don't let yourself off the hook—you must review research extensively before completing any sort of review).

6. A list of the opportunities for future research that suggests the "heuristic" merit of research (The term *heuristic* comes from the Greek word that means "to invent;" the **heuristic** merit of research, hence, is its ability to lead scholars to new inventions, ideas, explanations, or research avenues).

    6. research opportunities or heuristic merit described

7. A conclusion, which summarizes main points and states a bottom-line conclusion.

    7. conclusion

Selecting a Summary Organization

The literature review is not a collection of "mini–book reports." Instead, it makes arguments for which the research studies serve as evidence. Studies are arranged to create a logical discussion of research findings. The most prominent summary patterns are found in Table 6.1, though they are often combined in literature reviews.

using a summary organization

Select a literature summary pattern with care. If there is not much known about a research subject, you may wish to rely on the known-to-unknown format. The most frequently used literature review strategy probably is the chronological method (remember: we are discussing *summary* patterns, not library *search* strategies). Even so, many students also find the topical or the known-to-unknown patterns very useful. The extensiveness of research and the question investigated should guide selection of the method. Remember, the review must stick to scholarly research completed on the subject. Personal applications are not relevant and should not be included.

chronological method most popular

You may be requested to write a general **explication** of a topic. The assignment requires you to complete a literature review that makes an issue clear and comprehensive. Make sure to cover all points listed in this brief description of literature reviews to be certain that you have addressed yourself to all the important issues.

explication paper indicated

Strategies for the Research Prospectus

Of all the papers you may write, the research prospectus may be the most involving since it includes the components of definitional and literature review papers along with new suggestions for research. A **research prospectus** is a complete proposal for a research activity to be completed at a future date. All the details are set out so that the study could be executed immediately after the proposal's acceptance.

research prospectus identified

TABLE 6.1 Summary Strategies for Literature Reviews

Note: *Experience suggests that you will find the first two patterns listed most useful for those situations in which there seems to be little research directly related to your specific research question.*

Summary Strategy	Description
Known to Unknown	Reviews literature by considering what (little) is known separately about each variable in the research review question and then announces what remains to be learned.
Deductive	Reviews literature by considering what is known in general categories, followed by increasingly specific categories that are related to the topic (e.g., starting with studies of communication climate, followed by related studies on communication climate in high-tech organizations, followed by perceptions of communication climate of women in high-tech organizations).
Problem-Solution	A problem and its cause are suggested, followed by a research suggestion that might solve the problem (e.g., the problem of identifying highly communication apprehensive students in the elementary schools has resulted in many children going without help in developing this social skill; thus, a research solution in the form of a quick rating scale to be completed by teachers following interviews with students is proposed as a solution).
Chronological	Studies are summarized in their order of publication from the oldest study through the most recent one. Since this organizational pattern almost invites "mini–book reports" of literature, students should be very careful about selecting this method.
Inductive	Study findings in a given area are summarized by producing general propositions (laws or rules) that are demonstrated by each subcollection of them (studies are grouped largely by their findings, rather than their input variables).
Topical	Studies are summarized by reference to content categories into which the studies fall (e.g., studies related to effects of mass media sources, public figure sources communicating directly, and interpersonal sources on formation of voter opinion are covered in three different categories).

Standard Elements

first five sections of the research prospectus unchanged

The first five portions of a research prospectus are identical to those described for other papers. Only the remaining sections diverge.

1. An introduction specifying the relevance of the general subject matter to communication and overviewing the remaining parts of the paper begins the prospectus.
2. The context and the problem statement may be separated into different categories depending on the flow of the paper.
3. The significance of the problem area is frequently indicated before methods are described, though some prefer it be placed as part of the discussion section of the paper. This significance discussion shows why the area posed by the research question is meaningful and important, rather than peripheral and trivial.
4. A full statement of definition of terms is included. Concerns for both conceptual and operational definitions are a part of this discussion. The review is meant to justify later choices for identifying or measuring variables.

5. The review of the literature argues for variables chosen, sets up hypotheses, and presents evidence to support methods proposed.

The following steps are unique to the prospectus:

6. The rationale and hypotheses are stated. These expectations are stated with a brief rationale for each. It is *not* a rationale to say "based on the literature review, the following hypothesis was advanced . . ." Explanations of the links are required.

unique parts:
· rationale and hypotheses statement

7. The method to collect data is described. Quantitative researchers describe and justify proposed sample methods, measures, and materials for study, procedures, design, and additional control steps.

· methods described

8. The proposed methods of analysis (including statistical tools) are explained and justified.

· analysis methods

9. A final section suggests conclusions that would be drawn if the hypotheses were supported and what would be concluded if the hypotheses were not supported. This section previews the discussion that would emerge if the study were completed. Some subdivide this section into discussions on study limitations, suggestions for future research, and potential importance of the research. These subdivisions are matters of preference by researchers.

· conclusions drawn if hypotheses were or were not supported

If a proposal is submitted to some group for evaluation, such as the submission of research for funding, a timetable, budget, and proposed method of presenting and publishing results are also included along with the researcher's own professional credentials.

additional elements

Mistakes Often Found in the Prospectus

Research writing requires attention to detail. Naturally, students often make some mistakes in their initial efforts. Some of the most frequent errors (translation: your instructor has seen them and does not like them) are:

mistakes found in writing the prospectus

- Selecting a problem that is too vast or too vague to investigate meaningfully (Borg, 1963, p. 38)
- Relying too heavily on secondary sources for literature reviews (Borg, 1963, p. 67)
- Concentrating research findings when reading research articles, thus overlooking valuable information on methods, measures, and so forth (Borg, 1963, p. 67)
- Failing to provide information on validity and reliability of research instruments to be used
- Reciting facts without synthesizing or integrating these facts into meaningful generalizations (Borg, 1963, p. 233)
- Excessively using secondary sources of information—frequently found in studies not dealing with recent events (Borg, 1963, p. 233)
- Failing to specify detailed plans for analysis of data
- Describing procedures incompletely
- Assuming the results of causal comparative or correlational research to be proof for a cause and effect relationship (Borg, 1963, p. 286).

> ### SPECIAL DISCUSSION 6–3
> ### A Question of Ethics
>
> The quality of research is reflected in the completeness and accuracy of the reports of those research efforts. Scholars are obligated to communicate their research work. Keeping research quiet and secret prevents others from examining it and assessing its merit. So, a refusal to present one's research—or claiming to have research that one refuses to reveal to others—may be viewed as an ethical breach.
>
> In addition, research reports are expected to be completely reported so that their lessons can be learned by others. Russell Schutt (1996, p. 449) lists what should be done in a report:
>
> - Provide an honest accounting of how the research was carried out and where the initial research design had to be changed. . . .
> - Maintain a full record of the research project so that questions can be answered if they arise. . . .
> - Avoid "lying with statistics" or using graphs that mislead. . . .
> - Acknowledge the sponsors of the research.
>
> Of course, reports need not describe irrelevant things that occurred during the research. But all important information should be included. Schutt warns:
>
> > You do not need to report every twist and turn in the conceptualization of the research problem or the conduct of the research. But be suspicious of those reports that don't seem to admit to the possibility of any room for improvement. Social science is an ongoing enterprise in which one research report makes its most valuable contribution by laying the groundwork for another, more sophisticated research project. (1996, p. 449)

SUMMARY

Research articles are organized in very specific ways. The titles of research articles have descriptive titles to aid in their indexing. The abstract summarizes an article as a courtesy for the reader. The introduction and context of the problem justification show why the general topic is relevant to the field. As part of the context discussion, scholars are expected to advance clear definitions and to argue that research is invited. The statement of the problem is included, though sometimes hidden as a "purpose statement." Though formats differ for quantitative and qualitative studies, the review of literature extends the context of the problem by answering three basic questions: What do we already know or do? How does the new research question relate to what we already know or do? Why select this particular method of investigation? The rationale for hypotheses are provided immediately before a statement of any hypotheses. The method section of a study describes what the researchers did in enough detail so that others could repeat or replicate the study. For qualitative studies, often no formal section labelled "Method" appears. For quantitative studies, the methods may be explained in detail under the headings of (1) data or documentary sample, (2) operational definitions of variables (conceptual definitions give you an idea of the meaning of a term; operational definitions isolate a concept by specifying the steps researchers follow to make observations of the variables), (3) procedures that describe how the study was completed, (4) methods for analysis of data (qualitative studies rely on theoretic orientations to interpret data, empirical and experimental studies employ statistical tools), (4) results, which simply present study findings, (5) discussion, which interprets results and reason to applications, (6) conclusion, which simply summarizes what was accomplished, and (7) references (most of which follow the APA format).

Scholarship must be written clearly. Using proper formats and subdivisions and paying attention to effective style (choice and use of words) can help you achieve clarity. In addition to outlining, you can make your writing clear by use of internal organizers (phrases that preview, summarize, and transition between main points), avoiding ambiguity, and relying on standard paragraph structures. It is important to avoid ambiguity in scholarly writing by using terms that are direct and employing language that is understandable to the greatest number of intelligent people. Furthermore, you should define every major term you use.

Writing classroom reports may involve three major forms. The definitional paper takes a concept of interest and considers issues that involve the proper definition of the concept. In addition to structuring the definitional paper, the paper involves following steps to isolate each key school of thought (usually through a process of sorting definitions into categories). The literature review paper attempts to tell the reader what is known about a subject and the current status of the knowledge about the matter.

The literature review generally has seven sections: (1) an introduction, which justifies the study of the topic in the field, (2) the context of the problem, (3) the background definitions of terms, (4) the review of relevant theory to explain the variable or concept, (5) the survey of the research (completed either as an exhaustive literature review that includes all material related to the subject or as an exemplary literature review that surveys only the most important contributions), (6) a list of opportunities for future research suggesting the heuristic merit of research (its ability to lead scholars to new inventions, ideas, explanations, or research avenues), and (7) a summary of main points.

In addition, the literature review follows clear strategies that summarize research. An explication assignment requires you to complete a literature review that makes an issue clear and comprehensive. The research prospectus is a complete proposal for a research activity to be completed in the future. The first five steps of a research prospectus are identical to those steps described for other papers. The remaining steps include: statement of the rationale and hypotheses; description of methods to collect data; justification of proposed methods of analysis; and conclusions that would be drawn if the hypotheses were supported or not supported. If a proposal is submitted to some group for evaluation, such as the submission of research for funding, a timetable, budget, and proposed method of presenting and publishing results are also included along with the researcher's own professional credentials. In addition to effective writing of the prospectus, students need to avoid making critical errors in composing the prospectus.

TERMS FOR REVIEW

operational definition style
internal organizers
exhaustive literature review
exemplary literature review

heuristic
explication
research prospectus

CHAPTER 7

The Communication Research Argument: The Reasoning and the Evidence

Science is simply common sense at its best—that is, rigidly accurate in observation, and merciless to fallacy in logic.

—Thomas Huxley

RESEARCH AS ARGUMENT
THE EVALUATION OF
RESEARCH ARGUMENTS
    Finding and Making Research
      Arguments
    Patterns of Argument Found in
      Each Section of an Article

THE EVALUATION OF
RESEARCH EVIDENCE AND
INFORMATION
    Factual Information
    Opinions

BEFORE WE GET STARTED . . .

Most people realize that research is a form of argument. But saying it and acting like it are two very different things. When students are first exposed to research methods, they rarely understand that standard tests of good reasoning and logic apply directly to our field's inquiry. This chapter will show you where different kinds of arguments appear in research, the evidence used, and how to test arguments found in research studies. It will teach you how to separate worthy from unworthy research claims.

RESEARCH AS ARGUMENT

argument defined

In this book we have defined an **argument** as a process of advancing conclusions based on reasons and evidence. Since researchers draw conclusions from evidence (some very well, some poorly), they are engaged in advancing arguments that can be tested by standards of reasoning and evidence. This does not just mean that researchers are successful at haggling. Research and scholarship are different from other social interactions and arguments. Research is argument that makes appeals to the standards of sound scholarship. R. Michael Bokeno (1987) examined the use of argument in science and concluded that it is an oversimplification to say that research is an exercise in persuasion. Instead, science requires arguments to be based on the methods of science without appealing to the prejudices or biases of the masses. In fact, good research virtually requires that you understand how to construct and evaluate sound arguments. It makes sense to look at the reasoning patterns and evidence types that researchers and scholars legitimately can use.

THE EVALUATION OF RESEARCH ARGUMENTS

Although research articles certainly are informative, they are not predominantly informative papers. Every piece of information is presented to help justify, explain, or prove a point. Hence, when we write our own research papers we must make sure that every assertion is included for a reason that advances the whole paper. Similarly, when we read other research, we need to dissect the sections of research articles so that we can evaluate the worth of the scholarship. Since scholarship must employ sound reasoning, charging that a piece of research is illogical or riddled with fallacies is a particularly devastating attack.

Finding and Making Research Arguments

Research arguments are found in each major section of a research piece. These arguments function a bit differently in each section and it helps to understand the sorts of arguments that people make in each section before considering ways to evaluate them.

The Introduction Argument

Strange as it may seem, the introduction to a research paper is an argument. Researchers must prove that the topic they have selected is relevant to the field under discussion. Researchers frequently refer to a tradition of research in the field or they cite past scholarship on one or more of the variables they wish to study. These methods help them prove that their research topic is worthy of the reader's attention. Most introductions end with a preview of the paper itself. This preview is a contract of sorts between the writer and the reader. Thus, its wording is to be considered carefully since it commits the researcher to presenting certain information from which to draw conclusions. If the paper moves in other directions, the work is not logically related to its purposes (a fallacy that logicians call *non sequitur* when conclusions are "not in sequence" with premises). Thus, when an article fails to deliver what is promised, the article may not be only disappointing, but illogical as well.

introductions prove that the topic is relevant to the field

the preview commits the researcher to present certain information to draw conclusions

The Review of Literature Argument

Research literature reviews present reasons showing that research is needed (or at least invited) and why particular methods have been selected. Literature reviews are not intended to give "general information." They are intended to make a point. As Chapter 6 indicated, such reviews develop arguments to prove:

four arguments developed in the literature review

- Why current study is invited (such as filling a gap in knowledge, solving a practical problem, or extending past research)
- What future methods should be used (including a justification for the selection of methods or measures eventually used in a study)
- What mistakes to avoid
- Why a given research area is legitimate.

Literature review arguments set up the logical flow of the rest of the study. They also establish reasons for any hypotheses that are advanced. The research argument in the literature review tends to reason from specific *examples* of past research and from *applications of theories* related to the variables.

The Method of Study Argument

Though an article's study method section may look like a simple report of tools that the researcher has selected, it is much more than a simple description. The researcher is expected to make a good faith effort to show that the methods are appropriate. Methods often involve explanations that show:

three arguments developed in the study method

- That examples of communication behavior selected are relevant and representative
- That methods of assessing and evaluating communication are sound responses to research questions
- That tools of analysis are responsive to the data.

The explanations tend to be brief, but they should be fitting responses to the problem questions that are asked. Researchers frequently use footnotes to indicate other related reasoning to support their choices. In addition, researchers frequently rely on *comparisons* of methods used in current study with methods used in past efforts. These sorts of explanations are abbreviated arguments.

The Discussion Argument

The discussion of results of any study provides the researcher with a forum to make broad general interpretations. But there are limits to the sorts of conclusions that can be drawn. Researchers are expected to make statements about:

four arguments developed in the discussion

- The answers to problem questions and hypotheses
- The implications of the research findings
- The theoretic importance of the research findings
- The limitations on study findings and invitations to future inquiry.

tools of logic may be used to test these arguments

The methods and actual information examined in the study are the premises for these conclusions. Thus, the forms of reasoning used to draw conclusions can be evaluated by using the tools of logic, in which the relationships between argument premises and conclusions can be evaluated. Sometimes scholars draw conclusions that are irrelevant to the research methods and actual findings. Sometimes, the reasoning is logically flawed. Most of the time, of course, we hope that research conclusions flow logically from the information in the study. Thus, researchers use formal lines of argument when asserting conclusions.

Patterns of Argument Found in Each Section of an Article

Different sections of research articles tend to feature some arguments more than others. It would be helpful to see where major sorts of arguments are used most prominently in research and how to test them.

Inductive Reasoning to Conclusions

Inductive reasoning is "the process by which we conclude that what is true of certain individuals is true of a class, what is true of part is true of the whole class, or what is true at certain times will be true in similar circumstances at all times" (Mill in English & English, 1958, p. 259). Hence, we start with incomplete information on an issue and try to draw some (tentative) conclusions. This reasoning form typically appears at some locations more than others. It might help to mention some major species of inductive arguments. We will not attempt to do much more than introduce these forms.

*The ubiquitous **argument from definition** is a method of reasoning in which people submit that things do or do not belong in a certain class of things (Reinard, 1991, p. 333; see also Ray & Zavos, 1966, pp. 89–93). Many times the arguments used in conclusions of articles really are just applications of definitions, though they may *sound* like explanations of facts. For instance, as part of a larger study dealing with substantive issues, Perse (1996) reported support for the hypothesis that people who are high in sensation seeking (a biologically based trait that makes people "seek novel, varied, and intense stimuli and/or experiences" [pp. 37–38]) prefer to watch "arousing television program genres" (Perse, 1996, p. 43). As another example, a student once proposed a study to explore whether stutterers had greater dysfluencies than nonstutterers. The student was unhappy to be told that the question was not really worth studying because it could not be disproven by gathering data. If completed, the study would have drawn a conclusion that is true by definition (and a trivial one, in this case): stutterers stutter. Even so, researchers can get into very heated arguments about matters that cannot be settled by reference to the facts because what is being disputed actually involves the proper meanings for words. Consider these statements that have stimulated researchers to argue actively with each other:

- *Argumentative communication among people may be transacted nonverbally* (Willard, 1981; Burleson, 1980). A definition of communication is the use of both nonverbal and verbal cues—to say that "argumentative verbal and nonverbal cues may be transacted nonverbally" is actually a definition.
- *All-news radio stations succeed because their programming is monotonous* (Woal, 1987). One definition of monotonous is "repetitive"—to say that "all-news radio stations are repetitive," that is, they repeat the news, is a definition.
- *"Only for those households with cable are children offered both variety and diversity of programming"* (Wartella, Heintz, Aidman, & Mazzarella, 1990, p. 63). The rationale section of the paper accepted a definition of *variety* as the number of different media available to children. *Diversity* was the number of different kinds of programs available to children. Thus, saying that children with cable have access to increased numbers of mass media communication sources and increased access to different program types is really a definition.

inductive reasoning defined

argument from definition defined

- *The use of a logical positivist approach to conduct research is so concerned with abstraction and quantification of data that it fails to capture "the density of meaning present in the pre-structured social world"* (Delia & Grossberg, 1977, p. 37; see response from Miller & Berger, 1978, esp. p. 47). "Density of meaning in the pre-structured social world" apparently is a label to refer to things that are not capable of abstraction and quantification. Thus, the definition really asserts that the logical positivist approach to research fails to capture things that the logical positivist approach to research fails to capture—a statement that is true by definition.

Though these statements may seem to be research matters that deal with the facts, they are really controversies about the proper meanings of words. No data one could collect could prove or disprove the statements. In fact, the statements are assertions of definitions.

tests of arguments from definition

Nevertheless, argument from definition can be used as a method of reasoning. We can test whether an argument from definition is acceptable by asking several questions:

1. Is the definition a true equivalent to the term defined?
2. Is there sound evidence for the appropriateness of "word meanings or usage" (Ray & Zavos, 1966, p. 93)?
3. If the reason for a conclusion is a definition, are conclusions properly limited to the meaning of terms in the research setting? (after Ray & Zavos, p. 93)

As you can tell, this method of arguing is one of the most frequent approaches taken by researchers. When reading research, therefore, we must be vigilant to see if an article really draws conclusions about the facts or about applications of special definitions.

argument from example and generalization defined

*The **argument from example and generalization** involves taking some particu-lar cases and arguing that what is true of the instances is generally true in the population of events. This method may be considered a form of pure inductive reasoning. As such, we find that most of the conclusions drawn in carefully controlled experiments are arguments by example and generalization. Even studies that analyze past speeches draw conclusions from specific communication instances. For instance, as part of their proof for their claim that "President Reagan lied when he suggested the invasion [of Grenada] was undertaken primarily to rescue imperiled American citizens" (p. 105), Ralph Dowling and Gabrielle Ginder (1995) presented at least five examples of claims for which he lacked evidence, at least two examples of fabricating evidence, and a host of examples of misrepresenting or misinterpreting evidence. In fact, this reasoning method is among the most popular forms of drawing conclusions in research.

tests of argument by example and generalization

Because we probably can find examples to "prove" almost anything, we need to examine such arguments very carefully. To test these arguments, we may ask:

1. Are the examples typical and representative?
2. Are enough examples cited?
3. Are the examples relevant to the conclusions drawn?

If the answer to any of these questions is unsatisfactory, the conclusions drawn from the reasoning can be limited accordingly.

   *The **argument from analogy*** is often used in the sections of a study dedicated to the rationale and to the conclusion. Analogies compare "two things known to be alike in one or more features and . . . suggests that they will be alike in other features as well" (McDonald, 1980, p. 164). There are two forms of analogies, literal and figurative. A **literal analogy** compares something to an event or object that really exists. A **figurative analogy** compares something to a hypothetical situation. Researchers argue from analogies when they claim that because past research has found a pattern of results, a new study might produce similar results, despite some admitted differences from past inquiry. Researchers also use many analogies in their interpretations of results, especially when they try to draw similarities between their research and theories that have been developed by others. Sometimes these claims are strained, and sometimes they seem to be well founded. Denise Bostdorff (1991) examined the speaking of vice presidential candidates and found strong similarities between the speaking of 1984 candidate Geraldine Ferraro and Vice President Dan Quayle. Just as Ferraro took a role similar to the traditional female role in a comedic drama, so too, was Quayle viewed as taking this kind of role. Bostdorff flatly summarized, "The campaign of Dan Quayle paralleled, in many ways, that of Ferraro" (p. 1). Analogies are frequently drawn in conclusions advanced by scholars.

   Some people think analogies are best used as illustrations, rather than proof. But research arguments make such prominent use of analogies that you should not be surprised to see them employed unashamedly. You may test whether the analogies are acceptable or not by asking some specific questions:

1. Are the cases similar in many, rather than a few, essential respects?
2. Are there so many dissimilarities that comparison is not reasonable?
3. Since literal analogies are preferred as proof, are literal analogies relied on instead of figurative analogies?

Analogies tend to occur most in the discussion of conclusions, but you can expect to see them used at many locations in research pieces.

   *The **causal argument*** reasons that "a given factor is responsible for producing certain other results" (Reinard, 1991, p. 197). Cause-and-effect reasoning appears in most historical and experimental studies, just as it should. Yet, causal arguments are often made in the conclusion and discussion sections of survey and descriptive studies—where they usually are *not* appropriate. Though experimental research uses methods to permit making cause-and-effect statements, descriptive research does not. Even in some experiments, causal claims can be inappropriate. For instance, one study (Daly, Vangelisti, & Weber, 1995) measured students' speech anxiety and then had them prepare speeches. The authors did not experimentally manipulate the students' levels of speech anxiety, and they were careful to avoid causal claims when reporting their results. Yet, in the article's discussion section the authors let their language get away from them by stating, "To summarize, public speaking anxiety affects speech performance in part through affecting the ways in which speeches are prepared" (p. 396). Since anxiety was not an experimental variable, causal conclusions about it

Margin notes:

argument from analogy defined

distinguishing literal and figurative analogies

analogies used as more than illustrations

tests of analogies

causal argument defined

were dubious. Thus, we should read research that makes cause-and-effect conclusions very carefully to see if the methods really permit drawing such conclusions.

Even studies that use appropriate methods to permit drawing cause-and-effect conclusions may present problems. To test whether cause-and-effect conclusions are used properly you should ask the following questions:

tests of causal arguments

1. Is there a direct and potent relationship between the cause and effect?
2. Can other causes actually explain the effects instead?
3. Can something else prevent the effect from occurring?
4. Is the cause capable of producing the effect all by itself (or must it be accompanied by other forces to produce the effect)?[1]

Armed with these types of questions you may evaluate whether the cause-and-effect claims are reasonably asserted.

Deductive Reasoning and the Formal Tests Available

Although much research reasoning employs inductive reasoning, not all of it does. A general principle is often applied to a related case. This method is deductive since it starts with a general rule and then states that what is true of the larger class is true of a specific event in the class. You might have heard someone say that deductive reasoning is "reasoning from general to specific" and inductive reasoning is "reasoning from specific to general." But that claim is confusing and not very helpful. Some deductive arguments seem to move from one generalization to another generalization. Others seem to move from one set of specifics to other specifics. **Deductive reasoning** is simply a form of argument in which a valid conclusion necessarily follows from premises.

deductive reasoning defined

syllogism defined

Deductive reasoning involves using syllogisms. A **syllogism** is a set of two premises that result in a conclusion. They are formal logical arguments and can be tested by rules developed by logicians. You do not have to study much formal logic to appreciate how people use syllogisms in research. Articles with a strong theoretic rationale use deductive reasoning. So do articles that appeal to some general principle to explain their research findings. Researchers use three major forms of syllogisms.

categorical syllogism identified

The **categorical syllogism** is a syllogism that starts with a categorical statement (an "allness" statement about things). Surely the most well-known syllogism is the following categorical syllogism expressed by Aristotle, the person who invented formal logic:[2]

Major Premise: All men are mortal.

Minor Premise: Socrates is a man.

Conclusion: (Therefore) Socrates is mortal.

---

[1]This distinction between types of causes involves what are called necessary and sufficient causes or conditions. A *necessary condition* is one of several contributors required to produce the effect. A *sufficient condition* is capable of producing the effect all by itself. People often say that a cause is "necessary but not sufficient" when they mean that more than one contributor to the effect must exist to produce the effect.

[2]Think about it. *Some*body had to invent logic. Aristotle did about 2,300 years ago (though his mother probably developed her own version of it sometime earlier).

SPECIAL DISCUSSION 7-1
How Can We Argue for Cause and Effect Relationships in Research?

There are many ways that an apparent causal relationship might not be a real one. A possible cause might only be accidentally related to an effect. A surface cause may have had a cause of its own that really explains effects. A cause might produce many effects, some of which may conflict with each other. So, how can you determine causes and effects? The issue comes down to one of research design.

If the proper research design is used, cause-and-effect conclusions might be tenable. Paul Lazarsfeld (1959), a pioneer in survey research, suggested three requirements of designs and research thinking. First, the cause must precede the effect in time. If attractiveness is believed to influence a source's persuasiveness, a study should first present sources of different attractiveness to subjects before determining their attitudes toward the topic under discussion. Second, the variables must be empirically (observably) correlated with each other. If no attitude change were observed in our hypothetical example, no causal claims could be made. Third, the design must make sure that the causal relationship cannot be explained by the presence or absence of another variable that causes both. For instance, there is a relationship between the rate at which newspaper subscriptions are suspended and the number of drownings. Perhaps drownings could be reduced if people did not suspend their newspaper subscriptions when they went on vacations. But a third variable, the season of the year, explains both effects. People go swimming most in the summer and they also suspend their newspaper subscriptions most often in the summer. This third variable upsets the otherwise simple relationship.

When researchers make a mistake and draw erroneous cause-and-effect conclusions, the false cause fallacy (called *post hoc*) occurs. In one study, the Smith-Corona typewriter people surveyed 400 high school and college instructors who reported that students who typed their papers usually got the highest grades (*Typing . . .* , 1976). Though it may sound as though the typing was responsible for the difference, the cause might not have been typing, but other activities of typers. It could have been that students who typed their papers were more conscientious about their writing than other students. Similarly, students who could afford typewriters probably had access to other educational resources that come with increased family incomes generally. In fact, other researchers (Marshall & Powers, 1969) found no differences in the grades of typed and untyped papers when they surveyed 420 high school teachers in a study that controlled student paper content, wording, length, and spelling.

terms in the categorical syllogism

The terms all have names to help in applying rules. The biggest term of all, "things that are mortal," is called the major term. The smallest or most specific term, "Socrates," is called the minor term. The remaining term between the major and minor terms, "men," is (appropriately) called the middle term. When proper structure is violated, the reasoning is "invalid" because the conclusion cannot follow logically from the premises.

uses of the categorical syllogism

This method is the chief tool in the literature review and the discussion section arguments. For instance, one article found that television is used by Korean immigrants to become socialized into the U.S. political system (Chaffee, Nass, & Yang, 1990). They concluded:

> When a lack of both English language skills and U.S. political understanding pose a significant constraint on reading, television news can fill the gap [to secure political understanding]. For at least a short time, television becomes the principal agent of political socialization for many immigrants. . . . [T]elevision . . . links home political understanding with host political knowledge for those who have little choice. (p. 284)

With some transposing and a little help, we may cast the argument in syllogistic form as:

MP: People who have a significant constraint on reading English use television to secure political understanding.

mp: For at least a short time, immigrants have a significant constraint on reading English.

C: For immigrants, television becomes the principal agent to secure political socialization.[3]

If the premises are true and the reasoning is valid, the conclusions are guaranteed to be true. Table 7.1 shows the major tests used to assess the validity of syllogisms. Obviously, we expect good arguments to pass these formal tests. You may use them to evaluate the merit of the reasoning researchers use in literature review arguments and conclusions.

disjunctive syllogism defined

The **disjunctive syllogism** makes an "either-or" statement in the major premise. These syllogisms are found in research arguments in which scholars try to compare the predictions of conflicting theories or expectations. For instance, there is a body of research on the impact of violent programming on television viewers. Two conflicting

---

[3]You may have noticed that it took some work to make the syllogism fit proper form. Without assistance, as worded, the syllogism might not be valid, as in: MP: Television links home political understanding with host political knowledge for those who have little choice; mp: For at least a short time, television becomes the principal agent of political socialization for many immigrants; C: (Therefore) When a lack of both English language skills and U.S. political understanding pose a significant constraint on reading, television news can fill the gap [to secure political understanding]. The argument has the middle term used in the conclusion without having been distributed in the major premise, and it uses the reworded conclusion as the major premise.

TABLE 7.1 Rules for the Syllogism

Rules	Example of Forbidden Reasoning
The Categorical Syllogism	
1. The syllogism must have a middle term which is distributed (used in an "allness" statement) at least once.	MP: All credible speakers are persuasive. mp: Attractive speakers are credible. C: Therefore, attractive speakers are persuasive.
2. No term may be distributed in the conclusion if it is not distributed in a premise.	MP: Stutterers have high communication anxiety. mp: Teenage boys have high communication anxiety. C: Therefore, teenage boys are stutterers. (This flaw is called an illicit conversion.)
3. A negative conclusion can occur only when one of the premises is negative.	
4. Both premises cannot be negative.	MP: No newspapers report lies. mp: *The New Republic* is not a newspaper. C: Therefore, (?)
5. If a conclusion describes a particular, one premise must be particular.	MP: All household pets are domestic animals. mp: No unicorns are domestic animals. C: Therefore, some unicorns are not household pets. (This example [Copi, 1968, p. 174] implies that unicorns actually exist without showing the particular in a premise.)
6. A syllogism must have exactly three terms that are used exactly twice.	
The Conditional Syllogism	
1. The minor premise must not deny the antecedent.	MP: If speakers are men, they will be credible. mp: Speakers are not men. C: Therefore, (?)
2. The minor premise must not affirm the consequent.	MP: If speakers are men, they will be credible. mp: Speakers are credible. C: Therefore, (?)
The Disjunctive Syllogism	
1. The major premise must include all alternatives.	MP: Either people write essays in favor or against their personal beliefs. mp: People write essays irrelevant to their personal beliefs. C: Therefore, (?)
2. The minor premise must deny or affirm a term in the major premise.	MP: Either people write essays in favor or against their personal beliefs. mp: People write essays neither in favor nor against their personal beliefs. C: Therefore, (?)
3. The alternatives must be mutually exclusive of each other.	MP: Either people write essays in favor or against their personal beliefs. mp: People write essays in favor and against their personal beliefs. C: Therefore, (?)

theories have been developed. One theory called *arousal* predicts that watching TV violence leads people (especially children) to be aroused or stimulated to other acts of violence. A second theory called *catharsis* holds that watching TV violence reduces people's tendencies to engage in violence. A raft of studies contrasted these two theories (see Huesmann, 1982). The rationale for the studies focused on an obvious disjunctive syllogism:

MP: Either the arousal theory is supported by research or the catharsis theory is supported by research

mp: [for example] The catharsis theory is not supported by the research

C: (Therefore) The arousal theory is supported by research.

By the way, this syllogism has been the basis of major literature reviews (e.g., Milavsky, Kessler, Stipp, & Rubens, 1982), leading to the general conclusion that its reasoning is materially true and structurally valid. You will find similar sorts of arguments at different locations in research. It is helpful to use the tests found in Table 7.1 to help evaluate the merit of such arguments.

conditional syllogism defined

The conditional syllogism makes an "if-then" statement in the major premise. When people speak of the logic of hypothesis testing, they are not kidding. The conditional syllogism is the logic that is used in the hypothesis, methods, and discussion of results sections of research articles that test hypotheses. In essence, when a researcher states a hypothesis, the major premise of the conditional syllogism is being composed. All hypotheses boil down to if-then statements, such as "If stutterers are given delayed speech feedback, then the amount of stuttering will decrease." The major premise of a conditional syllogism is simply a hypothesis. The methods section

used in the logic of hypothesis testing

of a research article is designed to describe the materials and procedures that are used to complete the minor premise. The minor premise of these syllogisms must either affirm the "if" part of the hypothesis or deny the "then" part of the hypothesis. The conclusion is simply a statement of the results that must occur if the hypothesis can reach a valid conclusion. The material for the conclusion describes the eventual findings that relate to the hypothesis. If the hypothesis, the methods, and the results all match up, then a logical argument for the hypothesis can be made. If there is an error, then the hypothesis cannot be supported.

The form of the conditional syllogism is as follows:

MP: If stutterers are given delayed speech feedback, then the amount of stuttering will decrease.

mp: Stutterers in a study were given delayed speech feedback.

C: (Therefore) the amount of stuttering decreased.

Each section of a research article serves as support for the premises and conclusions. If the truth of the premises and conclusions is accompanied by valid reasoning, then the hypothesis is supported. The rules for the valid use of the conditional syllogism are found in Table 7.1.

SPECIAL DISCUSSION 7-2
The Special Fallacies of Research

Though fallacies of research reasoning are simply extensions of the examination of fallacies generally, there also are some additional fallacies that are unique to researchers. They are ones that, if identified, may place a research effort into some doubt.

The Ecological Fallacy (Schutt, 1996, p. 139) is committed when a researcher gathers data from groups of people and draws conclusions about individuals. For instance, researchers might observe that the smallest number of newspapers are sold on college campuses with the youngest mean age. The problem would be created when a researcher then concludes that the youngest students are uninformed since they do not buy newspapers.

The Delphi Fallacy (Giere, 1979, pp. 137–138) is the use of vague predictions as research claims. The fallacy takes its name from the Oracle of Delphi which gave predictions that were so vague that they could not help but come true. Once King Croesus asked the Oracle if he should wage war on Persia. The Oracle responded, "If you wage war on Persia a mighty empire will be destroyed." So, Croesus waged war and an empire was destroyed—his own. The problem with vague predictions in research is that if they cannot be shown untrue, they are not really testable. Thus, vague predictions have no place in communication research.

The Jeanne Dixon Fallacy (Giere, 1979, pp. 139–141) involves making multiple predictions and claiming partial support. "Psychic" Jeanne Dixon became famous when she claimed to have predicted the assassination of President Kennedy (she actually only predicted that Kennedy would die in office). Publishing hundreds of predictions each year, she publicizes those that are correct calls. But if you make enough predictions, some are likely to occur by dumb luck. This research fallacy occurs when scholars advance a host of hypotheses to support a theory, find most of them disproved, but claim "partial support" on the basis of the remaining hypotheses. Many know the power of this fallacy.

> There is a story, perhaps apocryphal, about a group of confidence men. . . . They contacted a lot of people (for purposes of example, say 1,000,000), told them that they had developed a new economic model that accurately predicts stock-market fluctuations, and mentioned one or two stocks which would shortly go up. . . . In fact, they had . . . made about fifty different predictions to fifty groups of 20,000. In some cases, the stock mentioned did go up. . . . After three or four series of predictions a few thousand people had had outstanding financial advice and many were lured to sign up and pay handsomely for future advice. (Alcock, 1981, p. 96)

The Patchwork Quilt Fallacy (Giere, 1979, pp. 141–145) involves making no predictions, but offering explanations after the fact. The fallacy gets its name from a quilt composed of random pieces of cloth, forming a pattern. Yet, in research, we expect justifications for selecting evidence. Erich Von Daniken wrote a book titled *Chariots of the Gods?* in which he argued that remarkable advances in architecture and recurrent legends existed between the new and old worlds. He argued that these facts result from the earth being visited by beings from other worlds.

When dissimilarities existed, he simply ignored them. Thus, we actually have no way to test whether Von Daniken is correct or incorrect. Moreover, the pieces of his patchwork quilt were not justified as uniquely relevant to his explanation.

The Ad Hoc Rescue (Giere, 1979, pp. 145–147) involves claiming support for a theory despite failed predictions. A large religious group that sells newsletters and visits people door-to-door has predicted the end of the world for six dates in the twentieth century. Each time the world did not end, they added additional explanations including computation errors and imprecise biblical references. In the last few years they began denying ever making any predictions at all, though a written record exists to the contrary. Religious beliefs are personal matters, of course. But in research, the ad hoc rescue occurs when theory that is claimed to predict matter fails and is followed by an effort to rescue it with random excuses. In scholarship, the false prophesy of a failed theory is enough to make people reject the entire research argument.

THE EVALUATION OF RESEARCH EVIDENCE AND INFORMATION

evidence defined

In research, **evidence** is the information that scholars use to support claims. Though you can group such research evidence, there appear to be two general categories: factual information, including statistics, and opinions offered to interpret facts.

Factual Information

Solid research appeals to facts, rather than to authority or personalities. Though different sorts of facts can be used to build research arguments, **factual evidence** consists of descriptions and characterizations of things. Sometimes these "things" are events of the past (as in historical research). Other times these "things" are new samples that we gather (as in experimental research or descriptive research). The two major categories of factual information are reports and statistics.

factual evidence defined

Reports

reports defined

A **report** is an account of what took place whether by a participant or by an outside observer. In qualitative as well as quantitative research, reports are actively used. Researchers can gather these reports themselves, or they can use reports that others have previously gathered. We need to understand the types of reports researchers use in their arguments and the ways that we should join with them to test such reports.

primary and secondary sources distinguished

Reports may be subdivided into two groups. **Primary sources** provide information obtained from individuals who have firsthand experience with the events reported. **Secondary sources** provide information obtained from individuals who do not have firsthand experience with the events. Thus, primary sources provide evidence "straight from the horse's mouth." Secondary sources provide information that is one step removed from direct observation. Diaries and news accounts written by eyewitnesses to speeches are considered examples of primary evidence. Most history books, however, are considered secondary sources since their authors usually were not eyewitnesses to all the events described. As you might suspect, we have greater confidence in research reports from primary sources than from secondary sources. There are exceptions of course, and scholars (including you) must always test the credibility of reports.

primary sources generally preferred

We ask questions that test the credibility of reports to determine whether evidence offers compelling support for a researcher's claims. If the evidence and reasoning are strong, then we may be eager to accept research claims. If the evidence is weak, there may be little reason to accept the statements advanced by researchers. The three major tests of reports are

tests of reporting evidence

1. Can the reports be corroborated? Reports of events are often made even though they are not consistent with other established facts. For instance, you may have heard the oft-repeated statement that Lincoln's Gettysburg Address was not received positively by the immediate audience. Such a claim (along with the baloney that it was dashed out on the back of an envelope) is not true, no matter how many times it is repeated. The New York *Tribune* reported that the speech was interrupted by applause five times and received "long continued applause" at its conclusion (Sandburg, 1954, p. 445). Though some partisan newspapers used the occasion to continue attacks on Lincoln, the Gettysburg Address was received very positively by the immediate audience.

2. Are primary sources being used? Secondary sources often get stories wrong. You may have heard that in the 1960 presidential debates between John Kennedy and Richard Nixon, polls supposedly showed that people who watched television thought that Kennedy won whereas people who listened on the radio thought that Nixon won. It is often repeated by secondary sources and has become political folklore (e.g., Germond & Witcover, 1989, p. 54). Yet, David Vancil and Sue Pendell (1987) found that although secondary sources often reported the myth, primary sources told a different story. In fact, credible polls that distinguished between TV viewers and radio listeners could not be found, though anecdotes and nonscientific samples were reported. Even so, you are likely to hear this misinformation repeated—but always from secondary sources.

3. Is the reporter reliable? Researchers may have to rely on reporters who lack special skills or education required to grasp what they witness. Sometimes reporters cannot report competently because of factors beyond their control. For instance, scholars studying the debates in the British House of Commons have often been frustrated since reporters did not always take accurate shorthand notes of important debates. Indeed, G. Jack Gravlee (1981) found that in some of the most significant debates conducted in the House of Commons, incomplete notes taken by reporters without shorthand skills made it nearly impossible to be confident about the reports of actual speeches presented. In contemporary times, the use of audio and video recordings has finally improved the matter.

SPECIAL DISCUSSION 7-3
Urban Folklore and Fits of Fancy

We often hear reports that have the ring of truth, even though they later prove to be untrue. Some are simple rumors, but some are examples of "urban folklore." Two folklorists, Paul Dickson and Joseph C. Goulden (1983), have written extensively on the development of urban folklore. For instance, you may have heard the rumor that the City of New York hired big game hunters to shoot alligators living in the city's sewer system (apparently souvenirs from Florida flushed down toilets when they started to grow from baby alligator size). You may have heard the story about the person who visited several tanning booths in a single day and was hospitalized for third degree burns shortly thereafter. These stories are not true but they get repeated, often on national radio programs. Here is a list of damaging and *untrue* stories that Dickson and Goulden warn us to reject (pp. 15–16):

- There is prune juice in Dr. Pepper.
- Proctor and Gamble uses a logo that promotes devil worship.
- Kentucky Fried Chicken served up a rat in a bucket of chicken purchased by a customer—this customer is now suing.
- Madelyn Murray O'Hair has filed a law suit to have "In God We Trust" taken off U.S. currency.
- A dead mouse was found in a coke bottle—the person who found it sued for a million dollars and won.

During the Persian Gulf war, reports filtered out of Kuwait that Iraqi soldiers had entered hospitals, taken incubators for their own use and left babies to suffer and die. A young woman named Nayira (later identified as the Kuwaiti ambassador's daughter) tearfully testified before a committee of the U.S. House of Representatives about the events. When hospital employees were finally liberated by U.N. forces, the incubator story was exposed as a fraud.

Cornell psychologist Thomas Gilovich, writing in his book *How We Know What Isn't So,* (1991) explained that our desire to believe secondhand information has resulted in people believing the following phony stories. In each case, they are untrue:

- At the end of the last century, "an official of the U.S. Patent Office resigned his post because he thought there was nothing left to invent" (p. 104).
- "The Ten Commandments contain 297 words. The Declaration of Independence is stated in 300 [sic] words. The Gettysburg Address contains 266 words. A recent directive by the Office of Price Stabilization to regulate the price of cabbage contains 26,911 words" (pp. 104–105).
- "An American woman over 40 is as likely to be killed by a terrorist as to experience matrimony" (p. 100).
- "Bobby McFerrin, the creator of the song, 'Don't Worry, Be Happy,' committed suicide" (p. 104).
- A man "(my brother's friend, this guy, etc.) began flirting with a particularly attractive woman at a bar in the city (on a Caribbean vacation). One thing led to another and they ended up sleeping together. The next morning when he woke up, the woman was gone. He saw a note on the bed (a message on the bathroom mirror): 'Welcome to the world of AIDS' " (p. 96).

Statistical Reports

To read communication research, you will have to deal with statistics. Political polls, surveys of needs for speech therapy, and trends in the use of cable television, involve statistics that are used by all sorts of researchers in communication (not just experimental researchers).

In common usage statistics are just numbers. But a precise understanding of the meaning of statistics is essential for everyone, regardless of their avowed specialty in communication. **Statistics** are quantitative reports based on observations in a sample. When researchers gather facts, they may wish to summarize their findings with numbers. If these numbers are based on samples, we call them statistics. If every single event in a population were included in the study (difficult to pull off, unless the population is very narrowly defined), then numbers that describe the population are called **parameters.**[4] The numbers that people deal with can cause difficulty if we are not careful. Hence, it makes sense to ask some simple questions to test their proper use. At a subsequent point in this book, the forms of statistics will be mentioned in increasing detail.

statistics defined

parameters distinguished

Questions that test the credibility of statistics help researchers separate worthy statistical information from the unworthy. Though these tests sometimes involve mentioning related statistical concepts covered in Chapter 4, you will find that they turn out to be very simple notions when we put them into practice here.

tests for statistical evidence used in research

1. *Are the statistics recent?* Statistics are only as good as the time period they cover. In studies during the early 1970s statistics tended to show that men used very little touching when communicating with other men. By the later 1970s, that statistic was questioned by some surveys. Hence, in dealing with statistics, you must be careful to identify the most recent relevant statistics, not just those that are conveniently available.

2. *Was the sampling properly completed?* As the name suggests, samples do not include every person or event in the population. Instead, events are left out when samples are drawn. But since screwy samples probably can be found to prove any fool thing, researchers are supposed to draw samples that represent the populations. The most famous example of a misleading sample is the *Literary Digest* presidential poll of 1936. The *Literary Digest* was a popular magazine that was as frequent in American homes as, say, the *Reader's Digest* is today. The magazine conducted the largest public opinion survey ever. They collected over 2 million responses. The *Literary Digest* predicted that Alf Landon of Kansas would win. In reality, Landon was crushed in a landslide election for Franklin Roosevelt.

---

[4]Don't confuse the word *parameter* with a boundary or limit on some subject. The word for a boundary is *perimeter*—close in spelling, but miles away in meaning. Parameters, speaking in metaphorical terms, can refer to defining characteristics of a population of events. But the parameters we most often look at are averages and amount of variability. A boundary could be one of many parameters researchers look at (not very often, though), but most parameters are not boundaries. Got it? Don't say parameter when you mean boundary or perimeter. They do not mean the same thing at all.

Obviously, there was something wrong with the sample (see Wheeler, 1977, pp. 82–86). In the first place, magazine subscribers—not a representative group—were asked to mail postcards to the magazine to indicate their presidential preferences. In the second place, people who purchased new automobiles in the middle of the Great Depression—another unrepresentative group—were surveyed. In the third place, people with listed telephone numbers were contacted—but in the 1930s telephones were not the essential utility that they are today. In the fourth place, people were permitted to send in additional postcards during the survey. But the individual's previous "ballot" was not replaced with the new one. In the late part of the campaign, when Republican voters turned against Landon in large numbers, the survey made the shift impossible to detect. The magazine went out of business early in 1937. These days, if people have heard of the *Literary Digest* at all, they know only the embarrassment the magazine brought on itself by its poor sampling. Research statistics must be based on sound sampling to be worthwhile.

3. *Were the measures accurate?* Statistics are only as good as the data they measure. One study evaluated the social interaction and communication of mental patients taken on a camping trip by the staff of a mental hospital near Salt Lake City (Tuttle, Terry & Shinedling, 1977). Patients' interactions with others were recorded and their interaction patterns were evaluated at the beginning of the trip on Monday and on the following Friday. The staff members used Bales' Interaction Process Analysis forms (without training) and assessed all the patients. They noticed that at the end of the week, the patients' quantity and variety of communication increased. The problem probably has occurred to you. Though the raters were unfamiliar with the rating scale at the beginning of the week (and surely missed examples of communication), by the end of the week, their experience had improved their ability to identify and rate communication on the scales. Thus, the responses on the instrument were not reliable from the pretest to the post-test. If the researchers had trained raters before the camping trip, this problem might have been avoided. Yet, as it was, the differences may have had less to do with the effects of the camping trip than the unreliable use of the measure.

4. *Were the procedures and methods appropriate?* Some public relations research has been criticized for the use of procedures that are inappropriate. For instance, in one mass media blitz, Coke and Pepsi compared taste tests (Coke-Pepsi Slugfest, 1976). Coke drinkers were approached by the Pepsi people and asked to give their preferences between cola drinks from containers marked Q (Coke) or M (Pepsi). Pepsi "won." The procedures were doubtful since the labelling may have produced the reaction, not the quality of the drinks. Coca-Cola repeated the study placing Coke in *both* the M and Q containers. People still preferred the M container soda. Thus, the original Pepsi preference should be treated with suspicion. Reasonable conclusions require using statistics from studies in which the procedures and methods are appropriate.

5. *Were the statistics misleadingly presented?* Sometimes statistics can suggest things that they cannot really support. There are different ways this problem might emerge. On one hand, there might be simple errors in analysis. For instance, Nicotera and Rancer (1994) explored whether men and women differ in their

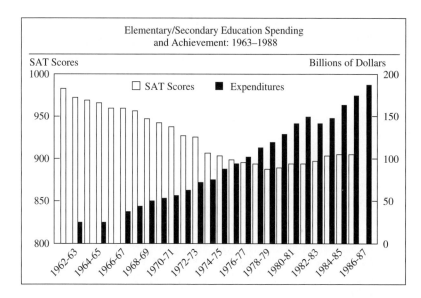

Elementary/Secondary Education Spending
and Achievement: 1963–1988

FIGURE 7.1
Misleading Graph
Relating School
Spending to SAT
Scores

Source: *ETS Policy Notes,*
Vol. 1, No. 1, July 1988.
Reproduced with
permission of the Policy
Information Center,
Educational Testing
Service.

self-perceptions and stereotyping of aggressive communication behavior. Because they used incorrect statistics, they reported differences between men and women related to one of their research questions. Following feedback from some alert readers, a subsequent correction (Errata note, 1995) was published in which the error was noted and readers were advised to revise some of the study conclusions for themselves. On the other hand, reports of data might be misleading. For instance, in 1988 an education policy maker produced a chart that apparently supported opposition to increased federal spending on U.S. education. The chart linked the amount of money spent on education to SAT scores, the latter of which had been declining. The chart suggested that SAT scores declined as funding levels increased (see Figure 7.1). But the chart was misleading. In the first place, SAT scores range from 400 to 1600, but the chart only showed the range from 800 to 1000. If appropriately drawn, the chart would have looked like Figure 7.2. In the second place, the money spent on education was a simple total of dollars, rather than constant dollars adjusted for inflation. If constant dollars had been used, the chart would have looked like Figure 7.3, revealing a very modest increase in education investments over the years. In the third place, the SAT is not a measure of achievement, but a predictive tool. The chart originally presented was quite misleading.

Opinions

Though scholars work with the facts, they often use opinion statements as evidence in their research arguments. **Opinions** are interpretations of the meaning of collections of facts. Opinions can be used to help researchers make sense of the facts that they have gathered.

opinions defined

FIGURE 7.2
SAT Scores,
1963–1986

Source: *ETS Policy Notes,*
Vol. 1, No. 1, July 1988.
Reproduced with
permission of the Policy
Information Center,
Educational Testing
Service.

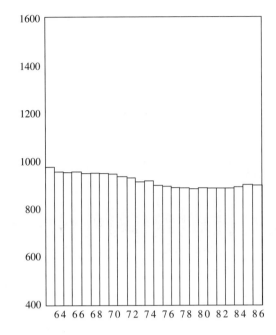

FIGURE 7.3
Elementary/Secondary
Education Spending in
Constant Dollars
(billions)

Source: *ETS Policy Notes,*
Vol. 1, No. 1, July 1988.
Reproduced with
permission of the Policy
Information Center,
Educational Testing
Service.

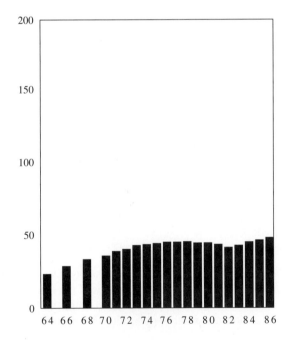

Types of Opinion Information

Researchers use opinions, regardless of whether they complete qualitative or quantitative research. Though opinions often come from lay people, in research, we seek
opinions only from people who are experts in the field of inquiry (sometimes called
expert opinions). You may see quotations from experts who have summarized a body   **expert opinions**
of literature in the field or offered a judgment about the importance of an area of study.   **distinguished**
These statements are examples of expert opinions if they are derived from scholars
who have special training and ability.

Testing the Credibility of Opinions

Researchers can ask key questions to determine when opinions deserve respect and
when they should be discounted. This list of questions can be applied to opinion
information regardless of the location of the opinion in a research article or paper.

1. *Is the opinion maker source competent?* Among other things, a trustworthy opinion
   is the result of competent examination of the facts by knowledgeable people. Often
   things that amaze lay people are shown to be explainable when examined by
   people with some competence on the issue. For instance, in the 1970s an Israeli
   man named Uri Geller claimed to have supernatural powers. He claimed that his
   mind had the power to start watches, bend keys, guess the images others are
   thinking, and make things appear and disappear. He had persuaded his manager,
   Yasha Katz, that he was a true psychic and for many years the manager expressed
   the opinion that Geller's activities were the results of actual psychic powers. Geller
   amazed many people including a host of celebrities and members of the public.
   When others trained in spotting magic tricks examined Geller's actions, however,
   each of his feats was revealed as a magic trick or sleight of hand (Randi, 1981;
   Marks & Kammann, 1981). Even Geller's manager, Yasha Katz, eventually
   confessed to participating in Geller's magic tricks (in Randi, 1981, pp. 125–126).
   Thus, we probably should learn a lesson. Opinions from sources who have special
   competence deserve respect whereas opinions from the inexpert can be misleading.
2. *Is the opinion maker biased so much that the opinion is unreliable?* Everyone is
   entitled to his or her opinion (and most are *welcome* to them!). But a source who
   has very strong biases may not have reliable opinions. Consider these examples of
   clearly biased opinions found by comedian Jay Leno in U.S. newspapers:

   > A Headline: "Attorneys don't want ban on lawyer-client sex"
   > [Leno's comment "Now there's a shock."] (p. 10)
   > Headline: "MGM bounces checks, but says finances OK"
   > [Leno's comment: "Yeah, right, tell it to my landlord."] (p. 39)
   > Headline: "Ten Commandments declared obsolete by 'News King' Turner: TV Mogul
   > Issues His Own 10 Rules"
   > [Leno's comment: "I guess if you've broken them all, they *are* obsolete."] (p. 16)

   Obviously, such opinions are difficult to swallow and the biases of the sources give
   one reason to question them.
3. *Is the opinion consistent?* Contradictory or internally inconsistent opinion statements should be criticized by readers of research since they are not compelling

interpretations of the facts. For instance, many books in business communication (Thill & Bovee, 1991, pp. 57–59) and decision making (Levine, 1988, pp. 82–85) recommend brainstorming as a deliberation tool that is allegedly superior to individual problem solving. Brainstorming involves gathering a group of people together to have a free-flowing oral sharing of ideas under strict time limits and set rules. Fortunately, other scholars have revealed such advice to be most inaccurate. Studies since 1964 have failed to support the superiority of decisions made by brainstorming. In fact, direct research indicates that brainstorming can lead people to generating fewer alternatives than if they were left alone (Lamm & Trommsdorf, 1971) and the method may be very inefficient (Graham & Dillon, 1974). The body of research has impressively shown that the conventional wisdom has been horribly overstated (Jablin, Seibold, & Sorenson, 1977; Mongeau, 1993). Thus, the consistency of claims with the facts they interpret is a vital part of assessing the worth of such opinions.

SUMMARY

Research arguments are found in each major section of a research piece. Introductions justify the selection of the topic as relevant to the field and make a commitment to research claims. Reviews of literature develop arguments that prove why current study is invited, what future methods should be used, what mistakes to avoid, and why a given research area is legitimate. The method of study argument involves the research's good faith effort to show that the methods are appropriate. The discussion argument provides the researcher with a forum to reason about the answers to problem questions, implications of the research findings, theoretic importance of the research findings, limitations on study findings, and invitations to future inquiry. Different sections of research articles feature different arguments. Inductive reasoning (the process by which we conclude that what is true of certain individuals is true of a class, what is true of part is true of the whole class, or what is true at certain times will be true in similar circumstances at all times) is found in reasoning to conclusions. There are several sorts of inductive arguments including (1) the ubiquitous argument from definition (in which people submit that things do or do not belong in a certain class); (2) the argument from example and generalization (which takes some particular cases and argues what is true of instances is generally true in the population of events); (3) the argu-

ment from analogy, which is often used in sections of the study dedicated to the rationale and to the conclusion. An analogy compares two things known to be alike in one or more features and suggests that they will be alike in other features as well (a literal analogy compares something to an event or object that really exists, whereas a figurative analogy compares something to a hypothetical situation); (4) the causal argument (which reasons that a given factor is responsible for producing certain other results).

Deductive reasoning involves inference in which a valid conclusion necessarily follows from premises. It includes some use of a syllogism (a set of two premises that result in a conclusion). The categorical syllogism starts with a categorical statement and is a chief tool in the literature review and the discussion section arguments. The disjunctive syllogism has an "either-or" statement in the major premise and is found in research arguments that try to compare the predictions of conflicting theories or expectations. The conditional syllogism has an "if-then" statement in the major premise and is used in the hypothesis, methods, and discussion of results sections of research articles. The major premise of a conditional syllogism is simply a hypothesis.

Scholars reason from evidence to advance their conclusions. Two categories of research evidence are used: factual information, including statistics, and opinions offered to interpret facts. Factual information consists of descriptions and characterizations of things. The two forms of factual information are reports and statistics. A report is an account of what took place whether by a participant by an outside observer. Primary sources of reports provide information obtained from individuals who have firsthand experience with the events reported, whereas secondary sources are from individuals who do not have firsthand experience. To test the credibility of reports, you should ask (1) Can the reports be corroborated? (2) Are primary sources used? (3) Is the reported reliable? Statistics are quantitative reports based on observations in a sample. If every single event in a population were included in the study, the numbers that describe the population would be called parameters. To test the credibility of statistics you should ask (1) Are the statistics recent? (2) Was the sampling properly completed? (3) Were the measures accurate? (4) Were the procedures and methods appropriate? (5) Were the statistics misleadingly presented?

Opinions are interpretations of facts. Expert opinions come from people who are experts in the field of inquiry. To test the credibility of opinions, you may ask (1) Is the opinion-maker competent? (2) Is the opinion-maker biased so much that the opinion is unreliable? (3) Is the opinion consistent?

TERMS FOR REVIEW

argument
inductive reasoning
argument from definition
argument from example and generalization
argument from analogy
literal analogy
figurative analogy
causal argument
deductive reasoning
syllogism
categorical syllogism

disjunctive syllogism
conditional syllogism
evidence
factual evidence
report
primary sources
secondary sources
statistics
parameters
opinions
expert opinions

SECTION III

Design of Research

8

Conducting Textual Analyses

9

Participant Observation Research

10

Design of Descriptive Empirical Research

11

Experimental Research

12

Sampling

CHAPTER 8

Conducting Textual Analyses

The interest in life does not lie in what people do, nor even in their relations to each other, but largely the power to communicate with a third party.

–Virginia Woolf

ANALYSIS OF MESSAGE QUALITIES
QUALITATIVE ANALYSIS: CRITICAL STUDIES OF TEXTS
  Neo-Aristotelian Criticism
  Burke's Dramatistic Criticism

The Never Ending Development of
  Critical Methods
QUANTITATIVE ANALYSIS
  Content Analysis
  Interaction and Relational Analyses

BEFORE WE GET STARTED . . .

Many studies examine the content and flow of messages directly. These methods for analyzing message qualities are popular in communication studies. This chapter introduces three major forms of these studies to you: qualitative work in the form of critical assessment, quantitative work using content analysis, and interaction and relational analyses.

ANALYSIS OF MESSAGE QUALITIES

Much communication research analyzes message structures. Researchers use this approach when they want to focus on message qualities that are unique, rather than generic. They often distinguish nomothetic from idiographic research. **Nomothetic research** is designed to find general law-like patterns that apply to many instances. **Idiographic research** is designed to develop a full understanding of "a particular event or individual" (English & English, 1958, p. 347). Though analyzing message qualities is often suited to nomothetic research, the method can also be appropriately

nomothetic and idiographic research distinguished

used for intensive idiographic studies of a single communication event, such as a presidential debate or a discussion between a particular pair of communicators. We will consider three general categories of communication analysis: (1) critical views; (2) formal content analysis of messages, especially of public and mass media communication; and (3) interaction and relational analyses of conversations.

QUALITATIVE ANALYSIS: CRITICAL STUDIES OF TEXTS

Rhetorical criticism is a dominant area in communication studies. By criticizing speeches, written messages, and movements our field may discover new insights or theories. The term **rhetorical criticism** means the use of standards of excellence to interpret and evaluate communication (in turn, **rhetoric** is the study of the available means of persuasion). By studying texts of speeches and other examples of messages, you can understand social and historical movements, form explanations for effective communication practices, and discover excellent communication practices.

rhetorical criticism and rhetoric defined

    In full **criticism,** however, standards of excellence are announced (which, in turn, can be argued as relevant or irrelevant) for application. To the extent that a message meets the standards, it is evaluated positively. The further away from the standard the message is, the harsher is the negative evaluation. Sometimes we use the term **impressionistic criticism** to refer to the statements of opinion (or personal impression) made by reviewers. Yet, scholarly criticism is not a matter of personal opinion—it is a direct application of standards. Readers can evaluate a critic's argument since the standards are known in advance, and we can double-check descriptions of data.

criticism

impressionistic criticism identified

    In essence, therefore, all criticism involves three steps. First, standards of excellence are presented. Second, the data (messages) are described and applied against the standards. Third, the degree to which the data meet or fall short of the standards is described. Thus, researchers make critical statements that point out how far an actual message is from the ideal. Scholars rely on systems of categories that list matters to examine so that they may determine what is good or bad, right or wrong, sound or unsound in communication.

the three steps of criticism

Neo-Aristotelian Criticism

When Aristotle developed his discussion of rhetorical communication about 2,300 years ago, he employed categories that came to be known as the **canons of rhetoric.** Over time, when people used the canons to organize their criticism, their work was called neo-Aristotelian criticism (*neo* is a word form that means "new"). Hence, Neo-Aristotelian criticism really is a new use of Aristotelian standards. Aristotle was not the only major writer in Ancient times who used the canons of rhetoric. Among others, the Romans Cicero and Quintilian also used them. Each of these authorities, however, offered very different advice. Technically, we should reserve the term *neo-Aristotelian criticism* for situations in which Aristotle's standards are used, *neo-Ciceronian* when Cicero's standards are referenced, and *neo-Quintilianic* when Quintilian's standards are employed. When selecting a standard, critics are expected to identify sources used to develop criteria for evaluation. Thus, critics must prepare by reading a lot.

canons not unique to Aristotle

critics using the canons must find a standard

The canons of rhetoric encompass the following major issues:

invention defined:

- *Invention* is the canon of rhetoric concerning the types and sources of ideas. Invention of ideas is derived from all forms of appeals used by a communicator. Most neo-Aristotelian critics subdivide invention into three categories of appeals. The first category is *ethos* sometimes called "ethical appeals."

ethos

Ethos is actually the speaker's credibility and includes the methods the speaker uses to build and use credibility in a speech. The second category is

pathos

pathos, also known as "pathetic appeals." **Pathos** is the use of emotional or motivational appeals by a speaker. Both the sources of the appeal and the audience emotions are considered by the critic. The third category is **logos,**

logos

which most critics treat as logical appeals, including the evidence and reasoning used by a speaker, though *logos* is a Greek word that has no direct translation into English (in context, this term means the rational idea behind things *and* the symbolic expression of those ideas through words).[1]

arrangement defined

- *Arrangement* is the organization of ideas in a message. In this category, critics assess the structure of the introduction, body, conclusion, previews, transitions, and organizing patterns.

style defined

- *Style* is the choice and use of words. (We sometimes see commercials claiming that using a particular brand of cologne, for instance, will give a person "style," but this meaning is not the classical sense of the term). The critic looks at the suitable vocabulary of the speaker, the tone of the words used, and the clarity of expression.

delivery defined

- *Delivery* is the use of nonverbal cues by communicators when presenting messages. The critic looks at major nonverbal categories of voice, movement, and eye contact to find clues to effective communication.

memory defined

At one time a fifth canon, memory, was included in a list of "Five Canons of Rhetoric." **Memory** was the speaker's ability to recall passages and examples for utterance. Though communicators often train their memories to avoid using notes, memory is rarely examined by critics. Hence, memory is sometimes called the "lost canon" (Hoogestraat, 1960).

applications and limits

Neo-Aristotelian critics constantly ask whether speakers made good choices of persuasive appeals from the means that were available to them. The method can often be extended to movements or campaigns that involve more than one speech. The neo-Aristotelian method has been employed successfully in much research, including now-classic studies of Lincoln's speaking at Cooper Union (Mohrmann & Leff, 1974); the analysis of Richard Nixon's November 3, 1969, address defending his Vietnam policy (Hill, 1972); and the speeches of Woodrow Wilson (Craig, 1952). The method may be difficult to apply to messages relying chiefly on extra-logical strategies. The strategy of a speaker who chants at an audience is difficult to capture within the

---

[1]These three categories have occasionally been called the "Three Musketeers of Rhetoric" because of the reference to the main characters in the novel by Alexandre Dumas. As a rather dry joke, Dumas named his three Musketeers, Athos, Porthos (ethos, pathos, get it?), and Aramis.

SPECIAL DISCUSSION 8-1
Fantasy Theme Analysis

Fantasy theme analysis is a method of analyzing collections of communication to determine underlying "world views" that people hold, judging by the messages they use (Cragan & Shields, 1981). This approach assumes that groups of people form images or "rhetorical visions" of the way the world is organized. Though the term *fantasy* is used in these discussions, the word does not necessarily refer to something that is fanciful but untrue (some "fantasies" have a factual basis). The method does not attempt to judge the quality of messages, although most scholars comment on it in passing. Thus, fantasy theme analysis draws conclusions that are more sociological than are those drawn by most other communication studies. It uses communication to find clues about the ways people think about the world.

The process of fantasy theme analysis involves three steps. Though they are not always distinct, they tend to be typical in nearly all such inquiries.

- First, researchers collect samples of all sorts of communication from groups of people who speak out on an issue.
- Second, researchers sift the messages to find recurring phrases, themes, or strategies. They look for expressions that different communicators use. They look for common themes that are used in different messages.
- Third, the researcher attempts to label the fundamental fantasy themes that indicate the "rhetorical visions" held by the collective mind of the group of people who use them. The researcher asks how people must view the world given the common patterns they use.

Fantasy theme analyses have been completed on many different areas ranging from the rise of the interdenominational Christian Church (Disciples of Christ) (Hensley, 1975) to the relationship styles of characters in romance novels (Hubbard, 1985).

categories of this approach. Despite its limits, however, this method is a useful way to organize criticism of messages.

Burke's Dramatistic Criticism

Many critics have benefitted from the thinking of poet, essayist, and critic Kenneth Burke (1945, 1950). Burke's communication notions start with the idea that people are essentially the same, with the same drives and motives. But they have grown apart from each other by society's artificial boundaries. Thus, the job of communication is to help bring people together. The key concept in this system is identification. **Identification** is the uniting of people by the use of ideas, images, and attitudes shared in common. If you identify with another person, you accept that person's words because they almost seem to be your own thoughts. Thus, Burke explained "Wherever there is persuasion, there is rhetoric. And wherever there is 'meaning' there is 'persuasion' " (1950, p. 172).

elements of the Burkean approach

concept of identification defined

You have heard Shakespeare's words, "All the world's a stage, And all the men and women merely players." Taking that notion very seriously, Burke called his system the *dramatistic pentad* and asked critics to look at communication as they would examine a play. He views communication as including five (that's where the word *pentad* comes in) categories:

the dramatistic pentad:

1. act defined

- The **act** is the symbolic action (the speech, for instance) actually exchanged. In this category, the message document is examined. The critic is expected to provide evidence of its textual authenticity and complete accuracy.

2. scene defined

- The **scene** is the setting in which the act takes place. The setting includes the entire situation in which the message is exchanged. Primary and secondary audiences, their expectations, and the effects of the message are all assessed. But the general condition of society also is a matter that influences the ability of the speech to create a sense of identification.

3. agent defined

- **Agent** refers to the actor or rhetor who performs the act. The history of the individual is searched to determine why he or she said the sorts of things that were contained in the message. Thus, this category requires critics to complete biographical criticism and determine authorship for the act. The first three elements of the pentad are matters that critics might be concerned about regardless of the critical method they use. The remaining elements are unique to the Burkean system.

4. agency defined

- **Agency** consists of the symbolic and linguistic strategies used to secure identification. Sometimes, these linguistic strategies are arguments. Sometimes they are appeals to common interest. Sometimes they are subtle uses of language such as irony or satire. The critic explains the strategies used to achieve identification by communicators. Usually speakers rely on a small number of such strategies (or "agencies") in a single message. For instance, in 1965 at a rally in Montgomery, Alabama, a young man named Stokely Carmichael (now Kwame Toure) grabbed a microphone and began to shout "Black power!" over and over. Soon some members of the audience began to join in. Before long, the entire crowd was chanting in unison "Black power, black power, black power." After the chanting, Carmichael was cheered loudly and his calls for action were received enthusiastically by the crowd. This strategy of chanting was not an argument, but the language created a sense of oneness between the audience and the speaker. The Burkean concept of agency requires critics to identify this strategy and explain how it helped the speaker and audience achieve identification with each other.

5. purpose defined

- **Purpose** of the message is the intention of the rhetor. A message's impact can be evaluated by determining whether the speaker's intentions are satisfied. But the intention of a speaker is also checked to see if the purposes are clear, relevant, and socially responsible.

Taken together, the dramatistic pentad provides a way to organize communication and to explain how people influence each other.

The flexibility of Burke's approach has been attractive to many scholars because they are not obligated to use traditional methods that focus on formal arguments and systems of appeals. The method has been used to analyze scores of key messages including the defense strategy of Clarence Darrow in the *New York vs. Gitlow* case (Sanbonmatsu, 1971), the rhetoric of the frontier women's suffrage movement in the United States (Burkholder, 1989), the confrontation of churches and their opponents in the sanctuary movement (Nelson & Flannery, 1990), the rhetoric of the 1992 presidential campaign (Stuckey & Antczak, 1994), and the rhetoric of the political correctness debate in U.S. colleges (Bello, 1996). People who use the Burkean system focus heavily on the language used by communicators. Though this attention can lead to valuable insights, the method has its limitations. First, the way a message is judged is largely based on its effects: If identification is promoted, the message is judged effective. There is no artistic standard beyond the "bottom line." Second, the method may occasionally be difficult to replicate since it is not really a fixed system. Burke's added interest in developing notions of redemptive rhetoric and his suggestion that there might be a sixth element to the pentad called "attitude" indicates that the system is so fluid that it may prove frustrating for serious scholars to pin down. Even so, the Burkean approach has aroused a great deal of respect and use among critics in communication.

The Never Ending Development of Critical Methods

The way scholars actually do criticism is not restricted to the two formal systems described here. Scholars are always developing additional methods and models. A few examples might give you an idea.

constant development of new methods

Walter R. Fisher developed one of the most influential alternative views in his **"narrative paradigm,"** which analyzes messages by looking at them as stories. In his book, *Human Communication as Narration: Toward a Philosophy of Reason, Value, and Action,* Fisher explained that people have a natural need to tell stories to each other. Through explaining stories, people develop understandings of each other. Fisher suggested some standards by which critics can evaluate the stories people use. First, Fisher believes that good stories, as with good reasons, have strong probability. Second, Fisher asks critics to evaluate the "narrative fidelity" of messages. **Narrative fidelity** is the consistency of new accounts with other stories people have heard. Since most communication makes use of story telling the method has created considerable interest.

narrative paradigm

narrative fidelity defined

Starting in the late 1970s some critics started examining communication by using the "mythic perspective." Though most of us define myth as an untrue story, those who use the **mythic perspective** do not view it that way. They prefer to define myths as something like "a story about a particular incident which is put forward as containing or suggesting some general truth" (Sykes, 1970, p. 17). These stories are the legends and folklore that we take as part of a culture. Critics try to identify the underlying stories to which speakers appeal. Then they explain how some appeals are more influential than others. Applications have been made to the broad news coverage of the Patty Hearst kidnapping of the mid-1970s (Mechling, 1979), mass media treatment of the "New Frontier" rhetoric of President John Kennedy (Rushing, 1986), the structure of Hitler's *Mein Kampf* (McGuire, 1977), and use of the "myth of white superiority" in the film *Mississippi Burning* (Brinson, 1995). Though there is controversy about whether myths should be restricted to stories that are believed to be true, the use of myth has become a popular way to look at some communication.

mythic perspectives

speeches compared with religious models

Comparisons of speeches with religious models, such as the Sermon on the Mount, have been popular in the literature of speech criticism. For instance, Malinda Snow (1975) examined Martin Luther King's letter from the Birmingham jail and found that its structure was consistent with the most complex epistles of St. Paul. Since these religious images are prominent in Western cultures, it is not surprising that such comparisons can be made.

creative analogies

Sometimes a creative analogy can be used to explain communication that defies traditional understanding. For instance, Larry S. Richardson (1970), a musician and communication scholar, examined the unusual speaking of Stokely Carmichael by comparing it with the interaction between an audience and a jazz musician who is improvising on a theme. Carmichael's deliberate repetition and frequent movement from one idea to the next without transition was explained by the same sort of dynamic that leads a jazz musician to repeat successful "hot licks" and to shift quickly to another motif when the audience begins to lose interest. By looking for creative analogies, critics can explore interesting new ways to investigate communication.

creative methods may help develop new theory

Creative methods of criticism do more than evaluate messages. They also help develop new theories. For instance, as a result of her analysis of President Bush's speaking about the Persian Gulf war, Kathleen M. German (1995) both described the importance of "directive language" in Bush's rhetoric and promoted a descriptive theory of this method. Furthermore, applying new approaches may reveal insights that can help people improve their own communication effectiveness.

QUANTITATIVE ANALYSIS

Texts and messages are often examined with quantitative methods. Though there are many such tools, we will consider the two most prominent options: (1) content analysis, and (2) interaction and relational analysis.

Content Analysis

content analysis defined

Content analysis is a systematic method to analyze the content and treatment of communication, which usually results in the development of objective and quantitative information (see Kerlinger, 1986, p. 477). For instance, if you wanted to find the number of references to sex in prime-time television programs, you might identify categories of sexual content as (a) noncriminal sex acts, (b) criminal sex acts, (c) sexual language and innuendo. Then you would count the number of references during a sample of television programming (see Sapolsky & Tabarlet, 1991).

Using Content Analysis

uses of content analysis: 1. characterize communication

Content analysis is a very flexible method that has been widely applied to text by linguists, journalists, and communication scholars, as well as professionals in psychology and sociology. Content analyses are useful to monitor the content of mass media communication. The information can be highly revealing, as were the famous studies showing an increase in violence in children's cartoons at a time when violence in other televisions programs did not increase (Gerbner, 1971), the emphasis on the "cult of femininity" (not feminism) in women's magazines (Ferguson, 1983), the generally evil portrayal of businesspeople in television entertainment programs (Therberge, 1981; cf. Thomas & LeShay, 1992), and the sexiness of women's business clothing in media presentations (White, 1995). Content analyses can be useful to characterize communication and make intriguing comparisons, such as the type of language used in closing statements at the Nuremberg Trial (Schmid & Fiedler, 1996).

Though once used almost exclusively by scholars in mass media studies, content analysis methods are now used in many other settings. In studies of organizational communication, comments by employees may be assessed by using content analysis methods. Sometimes speech therapists content analyze the conversation of aphasic clients to find clues to the type of injury the patient has. An interesting twist has been the use of content analysis of newspapers to gauge trends in society (Naisbitt & Auberdene, 1982).

2. study nontraditional settings

Performing Content Analysis

Some fairly standard elements should be included in any sound content analysis. Though many content analyses can be completed by a computer, others involve work done by hand. Should you decide to complete content analysis studies of your own, you will want to check for the availability of such computer programs to aid you. We will consider the basic steps along with an example.

content analysis steps:

First, define and limit the communication population to be studied. The communication domain must be isolated so that it is consistent with the problem question raised by the researcher. Furthermore, the population to be sampled should be defined narrowly enough to permit gathering manageable types of information. For studies on the rise of the number of sexual references in rock music lyrics, it is important to decide which types of rock are to be included (rap, heavy metal, light rock) and which sources are to be used to select such lyrical material (lists from *Billboard* and local Top 40 lists have notoriously different listings). The communication population to be studied must be carefully defined and distinguished from others.

1. define communication population to be studied

Suppose the problem statement asked what the relationship was between the sex of a person in a television ad and that person's portrayed occupation (Dominick & Rauch, 1972). A sensible communication population would be the commercials aired on the three major TV networks during prime time. Other time periods might not feature a mix of people in commercials and, hence, might not be helpful in answering the research question. Similarly, radio ads might not provide enough information about occupations of participants to permit a reasonable study.

Second, select coding units and classification systems for study. **Coding units** are categories used to count the communication forms in the examples chosen. In the example of studying jobs of men and women in TV commercials, the researcher needs a comprehensive list of occupations. Fortunately a list is readily available from the U.S. Department of Labor's *Occupational Outlook.* (This list is very detailed and some categories that never appear in TV commercials may be eliminated.) The general groupings of occupations include managerial and professional specialties; technical sales and administrative support; service occupations; precision production, craft, and repair; operators, fabricators, and laborers; and farming, forestry, and fishing. Regardless of the categories chosen, the classifications should

2. select coding units

requirements of coding

- be "exhaustive" and cover all the possibilities (to make sure, categories sometimes will include an "other" division, but the number of items that fall into that category should be fairly small);

- be mutually exclusive (that is, an event should not fall into more than one category);
- include a coding rule for placing objects in categories (criteria should be established in advance to decide what must occur for an item to be coded at all).

In formal content analysis, categories are established before collecting data.

variations in coding systems

Many different units of analysis might be coded, of course. In the example on the relationship between sex and occupation in TV ads, the unit of analysis included men or women who appeared on screen for at least three seconds and who had at least one line of dialog. There are other ways that things could be coded of course. If they wanted, the researchers could have coded the amount of time males or females were shown on the screen. They could have rated whether men or women were portrayed positively or negatively on a 7-point scale ranging from −3 (very negative) to +3 (very positive). They could have rated the number of words spoken by each character. In short, researchers have great freedom in selecting many different things that can be enumerated or counted. When examining newspapers, the number of column inches dedicated to a topic is often identified. Sometimes researchers attempt to identify themes, which are recurring similar assertions made by communicators (after Budd, Thorp, & Donohew, 1967, p. 34). For instance, Brown (1961) used content analysis to study the use of anti–Roman Catholic themes developed to oppose the presidential candidacy of John F. Kennedy. He found 18 major themes in anti-Kennedy campaign materials mailed to voters, including such outrageous assertions as the claim that Roman Catholics are assassins of presidents (supported by observing that "Lincoln, Garfield, and McKinley were assassinated by Roman Catholics"). In their analysis of Internet messages sent to NBC Nightly News, Newhagen, Cordes, and Levy (1995) coded the types of messages in many categories, including the type of audience targeted by the E-mail (macro-scopic messages written in the style of public pronouncements; mezzo-scopic messages written in the style of messages to a small group of respondents; micro-scopic messages written in the style of messages to single individual respondents). Krippendorf (1980) observed that content analysts have five kinds of units to study: (1) a physical unit (such as number of articles, inches of space, or number of pages); (2) a syntactic unit (such as number of words, phrases, or sentences); (3) a referential unit (such as presence or absence of objects); (4) a propositional unit (such as statements or argument units); and (5) a thematic unit (such as repeating patterns of ideas or treatments). In the TV ad example, the problem question could be answered best by simply tallying the number of times male and female characters in commercials were portrayed as having different occupations.

3. sample messages

Third, sample messages from the population of events. The sampling must be large enough to permit meaningful conclusions to be drawn. Furthermore, the samples are completed so that the communication can be claimed as representative of the larger population. Content analysts usually take pains to explain how they gathered their samples and when the sampled communication actually occurred. In the TV ad example, a sample was drawn for the same one-week period across the three major networks. Sometimes it is not possible to obtain every event in a sampling frame. So, researchers may select a reduced number of events. There are many ways to sample, and in content analysis there is no one best method. You can choose from several options (Budd, Thorp, & Donohew, 1967, pp. 21–23):

- Random—in which every instance in the population has an equal chance of being selected
- Stratification—in which strata are identified (such as geographic region, type of radio station format, type of ad) and a sample (usually random) within each strata is proportionately selected
- Interval—in which a sample is drawn by selecting instances of communication at specific units (such as coding every third commercial during prime time for a month)
- Cluster—in which groups of messages appear in a cluster that already exists (such as the cluster of articles from a single newspaper)
- Multistage—in which instances are selected sequentially (such as selecting commercials from one month, selecting one week from that month, selecting three hours from the days of the week, and so on)

sampling methods

Researchers are expected to sample events so that the conclusions drawn can be representative of such communication. In the above example, a sample of commercials during one week of prime-time broadcasting on the three major TV networks was sampled, producing a total of 230 women and 155 men.

Fourth, code message content to produce numbers that can be tallied and reported. Whether general themes or specific measures, frequencies are tallied. Sometimes the process can be computerized (such as content analysis of readability of textbooks), but most of the time researchers rely on other people to help. In many cases, it is a good idea to have the results recorded by coders who are not aware of the researcher's hypotheses. Regardless of the individuals involved, the messages are presented to the coders (in some written, audio, or visual form) who then record their observations on tally sheets.

4. code message content

Researchers are expected to show that the categories are used consistently and in meaningful ways (along with statistics to show the degree of consistency or **reliability** in using the categories). It is important to describe the methods used to train content analysts since incompetent coding of communication can result in meaningless data. If several coders are involved, their degree of agreement is sometimes called "intercoder reliability." In Chapter 4 we described the formula for Scott's *pi* to compute the consistency among different raters. If consistency is not very high (if coders disagree with each other too often) the inconsistency should be noted, but the data should not be included as part of the data set formally analyzed.

training and reliability indicated for coding

Fifth, analyze the data, most often by reporting simple descriptive statistics. Sometimes, however, advanced statistical tests might be applied to the data to spot key patterns and underlying factors of interest. It is typical for content analysts to report tables of results, such as the one for our example, Table 8.1. As you can see, the types of jobs people had in television commercials showed a wide range for men, and a very limited range for women. In other data in this study, women were shown indoors twice as often as they were shown outside (19% for women versus 44% for men). The simple descriptive statistics tell much of the story in these data.

5. analyze data

TABLE 8.1 Content Analysis ExampleOccupations of Men and Women in Television Commercials			
Females (Number of women = 230)	**Percent**	**Men (Number of men = 155)**	**Percent**
Housewife/mother	56	Husband/father	14
Airline cabin attendant	8		
Model	7	Professional athlete	12
Celebrity/singer/dancer	5	Celebrity	8
Cook/maid/servant	3		
Secretary/clerical worker	3		
		Construction worker	7
		Airline pilot	6
		Business person	6
		Sales representative	6
		Criminal	5
		Lawyer	3
		Mechanic	3
		Radio/TV interviewer	3
Other	18		27

Adapted from Dominick and Rauch (1972).

6. interpret results

Sixth, interpret results to illuminate the research question. Many content analyses are also completed to help evaluate whether communication patterns are as they should be. Yet, describing results can be troublesome. Wimmer and Dominick (1997) warned about one aspect of this problem:

> Researchers are often faced with a "fully/only" dilemma. Suppose, for example, that a content analysis of children's television programs reveals that 30% of the commercials in these programs were for snacks and candy. What is the researcher to conclude? Is this a high or low amount? Should the researcher report, "*Fully* 30% of the commercials fell into this category," or should he or she present this same percentage in a different light: "*Only* 30% of the commercials fell into this category"? The point is that the investigator needs some benchmark for comparison. Thirty percent may indeed be a high figure when compared to commercials for other products or those shown during adult programs. (p. 126)

Thus, as with other types of research, interpreting results is a vital but challenging process.

Limitations:

Limitations of the Approach

Naturally, there are some limits on content analysis methods. Some questions can be answered by content analyses and some questions cannot. Though these methods are useful in describing major communication trends, they are restricted to descriptions. **1. cannot draw cause-effect conclusions** Thus, the first limitation is that content analyses do not permit one to draw cause-and-effect conclusions (see Wimmer & Dominick, 1997, p. 115). One may describe the number of anti-Iraqi references in newspapers, but content analysis does

SPECIAL DISCUSSION 8-2
Conversational and Discourse Analyses

Conversational and discourse analyses are forms of content analysis in which the categories are suggested from naturally occurring conversations and their settings. These approaches, however, do not produce numerical information. The structure or organization of conversations is examined along with functions that conversations perform for communicators. A somewhat fluid distinction is often drawn between conversational analysis, which tends to analyze macroscopic message characteristics such as themes and stories and the rules they suggest, and discourse analysis, which tends to analyze microscopic message components in a pattern much like traditional linguistic analysis or translation (see Levinson, 1983).

not reveal the impact of those references on people. Of course, some content analysts make causal statements anyway. But you should recognize that such conclusions are examples of drawing conclusions from irrelevant evidence—hasty generalizations, at best.

A second limitation involves the difficulty in finding representative examples of communication (see Berg, 1989, p. 125). Searching through newspapers and watching videotapes of television programs may sound simple, but it can be very tedious. There is some controversy about whether using audio or visual records as opposed to transcripts is preferable. On one hand, transcripts frequently have errors in them (often in efforts to make the written materials easy to read). Yet, using audio or visual records may also introduce errors unless the researcher is very careful about coding material accurately. Thus, researchers need to balance these concerns. Sometimes researchers select convenient examples and, hence, miss important matters. Unfortunately, it is not easy to tell if researchers have made these mistakes just by reading their articles. Scholars can be very clever in vaguely describing the exhaustiveness of their searches. In other situations, such as content analysis of the notes left at the Vietnam War Memorial, access to such materials might be difficult or ethically controversial to obtain. Thus, access to important communication examples may on occasion be difficult.

2. difficult finding representative examples

A third limitation is that the results of one content analysis cannot be generally applied to others that use different categories (see Wimmer & Dominick, 1997, p. 115). The systems that have been used by scholars to study violence on television, for instance, have been very different—some include threats as violence, some include only overt violent acts, some include good-natured roughhousing, some include contact sports, some include psychological violence, some include references to off-screen violence, some include slapstick comedy as violence. Comparing different analyses may be very troublesome since similar units may not be used. In general, you must be prudent when trying to generalize results from one content analysis to another.

3. cannot generalize to other categories of content analysis

SPECIAL DISCUSSION 8-2
(Continued)

In conversational analysis, researchers sample and then examine historical, literary, or mass media conversations (from the laboratory or from the field). Conversational analysis then attempts to identify "turns" taken by people during the exchange. What a person actually says in conversation is called an **utterance.** Both nonverbal and verbal cues are coded from transcriptions of the conversation, complete with symbols to indicate vocal inflections and pauses. Eventually researchers attempt to extract rules for conversational structures. Anita Pomerantz (1990) explained the sorts of claims drawn from conversational analysis. The first form asserts

> that interactants are "doing" particular social actions, identities, and/or roles. For example, we may assert an utterance is "agreeing," "rejecting an invitation," "fishing for information," "being an expert," "being a teacher," etc. A second type of claim is when we offer analyses of methods that interactants use in accomplishing particular actions, roles, or identities. The third type of claim is when we propose how methods work: their sequential features and interactional consequences. I will refer to the first type of claim as a *characterization* of the action, the second type as a *proposed method*, and to the third type as its *proposed features*. (pp. 231–232)

This full array of conclusion-drawing permits one to determine communication rules.

Discourse analysis is sometimes distinguished from conversational analysis (see Levinson, 1983). In this view, discourse analysis considers naturally occurring messages to examine "sequential and hierarchical organization, system and structure" using methods that are fairly "standard in phonology and linguistics" (Stubbs, 1981, p. 107). These studies tend to get very specific in identifying ways that guide using language and symbols. For instance, Labov and Fanshel (1977) examined the discourse between psychotherapists and patients. Among other things, they found that the exchanges were distinguished by the use of indirect requests as substitutes for direct statements. Discourse analysis attempts to discover the structures that underlie messages people use.

Naturally, there are limitations in using these methods. First, conversational and discourse analyses draw conclusions from examples, though the examples may not be typical and may not show what occurs in communication generally. Furthermore, it is hard to disconfirm falsely asserted rules by using examples (Cappella, 1990). Second, methods for interpreting the conversation/discourse may be so personal that it may be difficult to replicate many such analyses. Third, much research from this tradition has produced such microscopic information about communication that conclusions often seem to be simple relabelling rather than explanations.

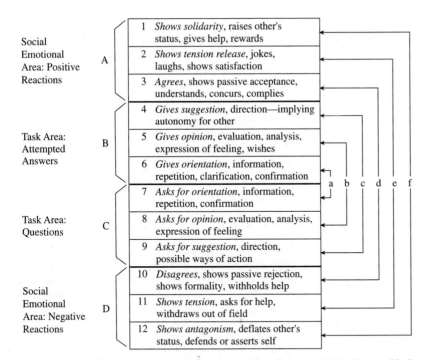

FIGURE 8.1

Bales's Interaction Process Analysis Categories

Adapted from Robert Freed Bales. "A Set of Categories for the Analysis of Small Group Interaction," *American Sociological Review,* 15 (1948): p. 59. Courtesy of American Sociological Association.

Chart I. The System of Categories Used in Observation and Their Relation to Major Frames of Reference.

Key:

a. Problems of orientation   c. Problems of control   e. Problems of tension-management

b. Problems of evaluation   d. Problems of decision   f. Problems of integration

Interaction and Relational Analyses

Scholars of interpersonal communication often look at examples of messages people have exchanged to see if they can discover something about the nature of the relationship between the people. The messages give clues regarding who is in charge and who is controlling the exchange. In a general sense, **interaction and relational analyses** are forms of content analysis designed to describe the continuing oral communication between people. These methods apply categories to conversations and discussions to find out how people affect and control each other.

interaction and relational analyses defined

Interaction Analysis

Interaction analysis focuses on ways of tracking individual acts of communicators. Scholars studying interpersonal and small group communication often have looked at such communication examples. One of the most popular early forms was Robert Bales's Interaction Process Analysis (1948; see Figure 8.1). The method involves recording a group as it deliberates and listening to each statement a person makes. Those statements, in turn, are counted in each of the categories listed on the figure.

interaction analysis distinguished

Bales himself moved to an increasingly complicated system called SYMLOG (see Bales & Cohen, 1979), and researchers in communication have also been interested in developing uses of the SYMLOG system (e.g. Cegala, Wall, & Rippey, 1987). Yet, the notion of interaction analysis can be demonstrated by looking at Bales's initial approach. Bales was able to explain that successful groups of people need to balance the task dimension of their work with the social-emotional dimension. This chart allows us to identify sorts of activities that take place from one phase of group decision making to another.

study of interacts and double interacts

B. Aubrey Fisher and his associates contributed a variation of the Interaction Process Analysis approach (Fisher & Drexel, 1983). They urged that the interaction between people, especially people taken two at a time (called *dyads*), be studied by looking at what were called "interacts" and "double interacts." The researcher looks at one person's conversation and the reaction of another—an interact. The researcher also looks at the first person's response to the other's reaction—the double interact. Though the concept was originally associated with management theorist Karl Weick (esp. 1969, p. 46), Fisher's work extended this method to discover how people develop a sense of belongingness in groups and how leaders emerge in groups (Fisher, Glover, & Ellis, 1977; Fisher & Hawes, 1971), and how people conduct themselves during formal interviews (Hawes, 1972). Taken as a whole, the method of interaction analysis has taken researchers in some interesting directions.

Relational Control Analysis

relational control analysis defined

Relational control analysis tracks message sequences to determine the relative patterns of position and control in the relationship. Rogers and Farace (1975) developed a set of methods to categorize who is "in charge" in personal exchanges. Thus, researchers check communication to see who seems to be in control of interpersonal exchanges. This method records people in conversations, usually in groups of two, but sometimes in increased numbers (DeStephen, 1982; Ellis, 1979).

categories of relational control

Statements made in these conversations are coded into categories called "one-up," "one-down," and "one-across." A one-up statement is one in which somebody is dominant over another because he or she asserts one's "definitional rights." A one-down message communicates that a person submits to the opinions or definitional rights of another. A one-across message extends the discussion without increasing assertions or accepting others' statements. The most obvious method simply counts the number of messages that fall into each category so that the general exchange can be characterized. The number of statements in each category lets you know who is in charge and, over time, what types of people are in charge.

Using Interaction and Relational Control Analyses

steps in interaction and relational control studies:
1. decide on a coding system

Using these methods involves deciding on a coding system to use, training people to code messages, gathering samples of communication, coding message content, and analyzing and interpreting message content.

First, decide on a coding system. Researchers have several choices when selecting the coding system. For interaction analyses, the classification systems developed by Bales might be contrasted with modifications developed by others. For instance, some researchers wish to focus attention on the impact of interaction in different time units (e.g., Amidon & Hough, 1967; Hawes, 1972). These researchers rely on methods that code the behavior at specific time intervals (such as 10-second intervals in the Hawes study). Other researchers have decided to look at each "speech act" during an interaction. For researchers of relational control, the coding systems can be fairly complicated. A popular check sheet was developed by Rogers and Farace (1975). Others have modified this form to improve validity. In their criticism of the coding methods, Folger and Poole (1982) suggested that coding should be checked with individual communicators' reports of whether *they* believe their own messages indicate one-up, one-down, or one-across relationships. This method is recommended to assure "representational validity." Researchers following this advice add an interview with communicators as part of their research. Whether such a step is necessary is controversial, but the use of alternative approaches must be explained and justified.

  Second, train people to code communication examples. Researchers do not do this sort of research alone. Instead, they work with other people to make sure that there is some consistency in using the categories. Thus, raters must be trained so that they know how to use coding check sheets and charts. Regardless of whether interaction analysis or relational analysis is involved, researchers are expected to explain how the training was completed. Furthermore, researchers are expected to reveal how consistently different people rated the same communication behavior.

2. train coders

  Third, sample communication transactions. Though we can attempt to get very scientific in such sampling, the reality of the matter is that sampling conversations and group discussions tends to involve a lot of compromises. A researcher must get permission to record deliberations of a group. Securing signed consent forms is typically required. Sometimes researchers ask people to come to a specially prepared room to carry on a discussion. Sometimes people are sampled in a naturally occurring environment. Researchers report the number of conversations sampled, the number of people involved, their ages, their sex, the length of the conversations, and the topics discussed. These days, researchers are expected to interview participants after the project, explain any purposes of the research, and ask for feedback. Any information from these "debriefing" sessions is made part of the final research report. The best analyses are those for which the researcher can provide some argument for the representativeness of the samples drawn.

3. gather samples

  Fourth, code the message content. Researchers find that they must spend most of their time listening to tapes (or reading transcripts) and coding messages by using the rating sheets or check sheets that have been chosen. Some analyses are simple tallies of the numbers of statements that fall into each category. Most relational control research has used this sort of method. Other times researchers can look at combinations of sequences of messages. In one outing, researchers found that marital satisfaction was most highly associated with the frequency of one-across messages between husbands and wives (Vanlear & Zeitlow, 1990). Work in interaction analysis has occasionally been fairly subtle. For instance, in a piece of classic research in small group communication, Scheidel and Crowell (1964) adapted Bales's Interaction Process Analysis by adding a few specific categories and completed what they called

4. code message content

"contiguity analysis." Contiguity analysis asks what sort of message *follows* immediately after another message type. They observed that the first reaction to a statement was another person's *repeating* the same sort of statement. Instead of group members responding to another's "asking for information" by "giving information" (which would seem logical), someone else in the group first repeated the request for information in different words. Groups seemed to do everything twice before making progress! Scheidel and Crowell suggested that group interactions might be described as a spiral in which forward progress is anchored in a backwards spiral. (Put another way, groups take two steps forward and one step backward.) Coding the message content and relationship can be as simple or as sophisticated as the imagination of the researcher.

5. analyze and interpret message content

The last step in interactional and relational analysis is interpretation. Researchers try to develop theoretic explanations for their findings. Interactional and relational analyses do not tell whether the communication is "good" or "bad," but describe how people use messages. Relationships with other variables can be drawn, but explaining *why* those patterns exist requires researchers to develop ideas and suggest models. Most often researchers explain how current theories are supported or challenged by their work. Yet, some studies lead researchers to suggest new directions for theories.

Limitations of the Approach

Limitations:
1. may not be useful to assess perception or interpretation of others

The interaction and relational analysis approach has two limitations that focus on the validity of the information measured. First, the methods may not be useful if the researcher's theoretical or explanatory basis is the perception or shared interpretation of individuals. Rather, these procedures are most appropriate when individual motivations are considered less important than other bases for understanding or explaining human behavior. (Tardy, 1988, pp. 292–293) Such a limitation may make these methods impossible for attempts to answer many mainstream research questions.

2. cannot yield cause-effect statements

Second, since the method takes actual communication and observes relationships with other variables, it cannot be used to draw conclusions about cause-and-effect relationships. Variables related to interaction or relational categories can be assessed, but the method does not allow us to determine which came first.

SUMMARY

Researchers sometimes focus on message qualities that are unique, rather than generic. Thus, researchers distinguish nomothetic research (designed to find general laws that apply to many instances) from idiographic research (designed to develop a full understanding of a particular event or individual).

Rhetorical criticism uses standards to interpret and evaluate communication (rhetoric is the study of the available means of persuasion). Impressionistic criticism refers to opinion (or personal impressions) made by reviewers. Criticism involves (1) presenting standards of excellence, (2) contrasting the messages against the standards, and (3) explaining the degree to which the messages meet or

fall short of the standards (critical statements tell how far an actual message is from the ideal). Neo-Aristotelian criticism relies on the canons of rhetoric: invention—the types and sources of ideas, including *ethos* (ethical appeal or the speaker's credibility), *pathos* (pathetic appeals or the use of emotion), and *logos* (logical appeals); arrangement (message organization); style (choice and use of words); and delivery (use of nonverbal cues). Though helpful to examine significant speeches, the method strains when applied to messages that rely chiefly on extra-logical strategies. Burke's dramatistic criticism method places the concept of identification (uniting people by the use of ideas, images, and attitudes shared in common) central to the system. The dramatistic pentad examines the act (the symbols actually exchanged), scene (the setting for the act), agent (the actor or rhetor), agency (symbolic and linguistic strategies used to secure identification), and purpose (intention of the rhetor). Though the approach is flexible, messages are judged largely by their effects and the method occasionally may be difficult to replicate. Other critical methods constantly are being developed, including, systems based on the "mythic perspective," comparisons with religious models, the narrative paradigm, or use of creative analogies.

Content analysis is a systematic method designed to analyze the content and treatment of communication. Content analysis steps include (1) defining and limiting the communication population to be studied, (2) selecting coding units and classification systems (coding units are the categories used to count the communication forms), (3) sampling messages, (4) coding message content (including determining consistency of coders and providing adequate training), (5) analysis of data, usually by reporting simple descriptive statistics, and (6) interpreting results. Limitations of the method are (1) inability to draw cause-and-effect conclusions, (2) difficulties in finding representative communication examples, and (3) generalizing from one content analysis to another.

Interaction and relational analyses are forms of content analysis designed to describe the continuous oral communication between people. Interaction analysis focuses on ways of tracking individual acts of communicators. A variation of direct coding approaches (such as Bales's Interaction Process Analysis) is the examination of "interacts" (one person's conversation and the reaction of another) and "double interacts" (which add the first person's response to the other's reaction). Relational control analysis tracks message sequences to determine the relative patterns of position and control in the relationship. Statements made in these conversations are coded into categories called "one-up" (in which somebody is dominant over another because he or she asserts one's "definitional rights"), "one-down" (in which a person submits to the opinions or definitional rights of another), and "one-across" (message extensions that extend discussion without increasing assertions or accepting others' statements). To use these methods involves (1) deciding on a coding system to use, (2) training people to code messages, (3) gathering samples of communication, (4) coding message content, and (5) analyzing and interpreting message content. These methods are limited by the fact that the methods may not be useful if the researcher's theoretical or explanatory basis is the perception or shared interpretation of individuals, and it cannot be used to draw conclusions about cause-and-effect relationships.

TERMS FOR REVIEW

nomothetic research
idiographic research
rhetorical criticism
rhetoric
impressionistic criticism
canons of rhetoric
invention
ethos
pathos
logos
arrangement
style
delivery
memory
identification
fantasy theme analysis

act
scene
agent
agency
purpose
narrative paradigm
narrative fidelity
mythic perspective
content analysis
coding units
reliability
utterance
interaction and relational analyses
interaction analysis
relational control analysis

CHAPTER 9

Participant Observation Research

The way to do research is to attack the facts at the point of greatest astonishment.

–Celia Green

THE ROLE OF PARTICIPANT OBSERVATION STUDIES IN COMMUNICATION RESEARCH
    The Purposes of Participant Observation Methods
    Suitability of Participant Observation Methods to Research Questions
FORMS OF PARTICIPANT OBSERVATION STUDIES

    The Position of the Observer
    Ethnography
THE FLUID PROCESS OF PARTICIPANT OBSERVATION STUDY
    Steps in Participant Observation
    Limitations of the Approach

BEFORE WE GET STARTED . . .

Communication researchers often become active participants in the research setting. They may join Alcoholics Anonymous to learn of the informal communication that reinforces the famous 12-step program, they may work in a car dealership to study special methods of influence, or they may live with the Tasaday "stone age" people of the Philippines to learn how legends are communicated. They "get their hands dirty" by gathering data in the natural environment rather than relying on formal questionnaires or experiments. This type of active inquiry is the subject of this chapter.

THE ROLE OF PARTICIPANT OBSERVATION STUDIES IN COMMUNICATION RESEARCH

Participant observation studies are based on a desire to focus on communication behavior that is not affected by the research process. The researcher explores communication by engaging in the natural environment. Many terms are used to describe this form of research, including fieldwork, participant observation, naturalistic study, and qualitative research. **Fieldwork** may be defined as "the study of people acting in the natural course of their daily lives. The fieldworker ventures into the worlds of others in order to learn firsthand about how they live, how they talk and behave, and what captivates and distresses them" (Emerson, 1983, p. 1). For our purposes, fieldwork and naturalistic studies are interchangeable terms. **Naturalistic studies** are nonexperimental inquiries completed as subjects are involved in the natural course of their lives. **Participant observation** is the most well-known form of fieldwork in which researchers study groups by gaining membership or close relationships with them (see Wax, 1968, p. 238). In this chapter we will not equate naturalistic studies with qualitative research (although some people do). Some fieldwork may yield quantitative data, though most of it does not. Naturalistic/fieldwork designs are used to gather information, regardless of whether it is qualitative or quantitative. This chapter's applications focus on naturalistic fieldwork with special emphasis on participant observation.

fieldwork defined

naturalistic and participant observation distinguished

The Purposes of Participant Observation Methods

Participant observation methods are characterized by the attempt to use nonintrusive ways to gather information.[1] Rather than asking individuals to complete questionnaires reporting about themselves, as they might in a survey, participant observation researchers join with groups of people to observe them from within the group. Scholars who use naturalistic methods look at such things as how people say good-bye at airports, the stories people tell each other at work, and ways newscasters choose stories to cover. Though researchers who complete laboratory experiments try to get some distance from the subjects in the research, participant observation researchers try to get "up close and personal" with the people they study, as opposed to passing out questionnaires or conducting structured interviews.

Fieldwork studies have three major purposes. First, they try to answer questions in settings where use of questionnaires and direct reports would be inappropriate or impractical. In studies of health communication, for example, it is often not possible for a nurse to conduct research by asking several hundreds of patients detailed questions about the "bedside manner" of physicians. Yet, a nurse might watch patients who try to explain their medical problems to apparently uninterested physicians. Patterns may be identified in conversations between patients and doctors. Such naturalistic studies may explore questions where tight survey or experimental methods are impossible.

purposes: 1. when questionnaires are inappropriate

Second, fieldwork is often undertaken when a setting has been so unexplored that formal hypotheses may not have been developed. Though this invitation to research is not unique to participant observation work, it is true that by immersing

2. when the setting is so new hypotheses are undeveloped

---

[1]Some writers like to emphasize three qualities that must exist in naturalistic settings. Kraut and Johnston (1979) explain that naturalistic research involves unobtrusive ways of gathering information, of natural events, in a natural setting, stimulated by naturally occurring events. Yet, some work included in the category of naturalistic studies has actually employed "unnatural" settings and artificial stimuli (e.g., Byrne, Ervin, & Lamberth, 1970). Thus, for purposes of accuracy, we will limit naturalistic studies to situations in which, at minimum, natural behavior is studied through unobtrusive means.

yourself in the field setting you might be able to acquire insight that cannot be gained as well in other ways. By looking for unexpected events, researchers can develop intriguing hypotheses to be explored in other inquiries.

3. developing grounded theory

Third, these studies are completed by researchers who wish to develop grounded theory. **Grounded theory** is a set of explanations that has immediate relevance to a specific field setting under investigation. Using this method, participant observers attempt to discover categories to describe their observations after they have entered the field. Then researchers make additional observations to refine and modify these categories. Eventually, a theory may emerge. An alternative approach called **analytic induction** involves researchers starting with some tentative hypotheses that they apply in fieldwork. If these hypotheses are inadequate they may be abandoned or reformulated. Though distinctions can be drawn between these views, many participant observer researchers find that their practical work involves some features of both.

analytic induction identified

Thus, the chief difference between participant observation methods and other studies is the method of gathering data. This approach still argues from information to conclusions. The data are empirical (empirical means "observable") and can be examined by others. Hence, solid participant observation fieldwork is at least as demanding as any other research.

such studies still empirically grounded

Suitability of Participant Observation Methods to Research Questions

research questions involve: naturally arising behavior not consistently produced in laboratories

Fieldwork and participant observation methods are invited when a researcher is interested in naturally arising behavior that has not always been shown to have regularities that can be produced in the laboratory. Sometimes researchers try to find the answers to such questions as

- When is the insanity defense accepted by juries?
- When does the use of threat by a manager increase productivity?
- When do reporters choose to stick to a newspaper story despite threats on their lives?

By working in the field, researchers might find examples of each situation. Then, by examining such occurrences, they might find explanations.

By recording conversations and exchanges, researchers can gain special insight. As three scholars of the subject explained:

> Field-workers and participant observers become engaged in the conversations, actions, and lives of the people they study. And unlike the standardized questions and procedures used by experimenters and survey researchers, the questions and actions of a field-worker may vary from one person and setting to the next. Instead of approaching each respondent with the same list of questions, a field-worker engages in conversations and observations that may last several hours or continue for several days, weeks, or months. The conversations move in directions that cannot be anticipated, so the researcher's questions cannot be duplicated from one person to the next. To the extent that the researcher participates in the lives of the people under study, each day will provide new opportunities as a result of the previous day's activities.
>
> How can field research be systematic if the procedures vary so from one person or day to the next? The systematization occurs not by having uniform procedures but by recording faithfully what is seen and heard. (Judd, Smith, & Kidder, 1991, p. 299)

SPECIAL DISCUSSION 9-1
Observational Studies

Researchers who look at naturally occurring communication, but avoid direct involvement with the phenomena, are engaged in observational studies. In such work, one may take the view of a complete observer or unobtrusive measurer.

A **complete observer** has no contact with the individuals he or she is observering. Research of this form typically occurs when scholars go to field settings, such as airports or bus stations, and watch behaviors of interest from a distance. Behavior may be recorded by photographs or by taking detailed notes. For instance, one scholar watched overweight students in a college cafeteria (Krantz, 1979). It was found that heavy people selected less food to eat when they were going to carry on a conversation with others during lunch.

Unobtrusive measurement uses artifacts that do not influence the behavior being studied. These unobtrusive methods include accretions and erosions, though some lists of these methods include other techniques as well (see Webb et al., 1981, who include archival information, private records, simple observations, and contrived observations).

Accretions are deposits of material left by some action. Sometimes layers are placed down naturally, but communicators often may deposit remnants of their own. Much work on accretion resembles archaeology. Two researchers examined the graffiti left on the walls of a juvenile corrections facility in New England (Klofas & Cutshall, 1985). The language and kinds of remarks revealed that the young people in the facilities had been socialized into a unique "incarceratory culture" in which the outside world and authority were viewed as objects to manipulate and where ordinary trust was viewed very suspiciously. Thus, by looking at deposits, some interesting clues may be found. One area of study that examines such artifacts is called **urban archaeology.** These studies survey objects created by humans that are the "leftovers" of communication activity. Searching trash cans in a neighborhood to find evidence of the rate of alcoholism is an example of the sort of work that often passes for such inquiry. Of course, such artifacts can be sketchy or misleading (one might have many liquor bottles in a trash can because of a recently held party for a large number of people, or someone might have run out of room and deposited liquor bottles in a neighbor's trash cans). Thus, researchers usually try to find several signs before interpreting results.

Though most methods described in this chapter are techniques you might spot in nearly any communication journal, some naturalistic methods are derived from special backgrounds and ways of approaching knowledge. Despite any extra baggage they may have, all these methods are undertaken when the research problem statement demands fieldwork exploration of questions for which use of standardized forms or tools would not be appropriate.

SPECIAL DISCUSSION 9-1
(Continued) ·

Erosions consist of the wear or use of objects. One of the most popularly cited erosion studies involved inquiry into attention paid to different exhibits at the Chicago Museum of Science and Industry.

> The vinyl tiles around the exhibit containing live, hatching chicks had to be replaced every six weeks or so; tiles in other areas of the museum went for years without replacement. A comparative study of the rate of the replacement around the various museum exhibits could give a rough ordering of the popularity of the exhibits. (Webb et al., 1981, p. 7)

Though such data could have more than one explanation, there was reason to believe that the chick exhibit had attracted a larger amount of traffic (and attention) than many others. By finding examples of such erosions, it is possible to gather interesting circumstantial evidence related to key questions of interest.

Unobtrusive methods may be used in many sorts of studies. For example, an experimental study in the laboratory *could* use erosion measures (such as the amount of scratch paper used in a discussion as an indicator of the amount of thoughtful activity used in the group). Yet, unobtrusive methods are most often associated with naturalistic research.

FORMS OF PARTICIPANT OBSERVATION STUDIES

The role and the approach of the researcher can be very different among participant observers. In fact, to do such inquiry, you must decide what position to take, the advantages of different levels of participation, and the wisdom of taking an ethnographic approach.

The Position of the Observer

Researchers can observe communication at a distance, or they can attempt to become involved in the communication activities themselves. The sort of involvement researchers choose affects their ability to acquire highly subjective information that might otherwise be lost. Yet, the level of participation a researcher has with groups studied can also affect that person's objectivity and the degree to which conclusions drawn may be free from undue bias. There are two general ways to enter the field.

Full Participation Observation

full participant observation defined

Full participant observation research is characterized by the investigator's gathering data while taking part in the activities of a group—and while concealing his or her research identity. In short, people are studied and they do not know it. A researcher might join an organization and follow its activities as an insider. He or she might record conversations with others in the organization. Rather than just observe a political campaign, newspaper staff, or activities in a speech clinic, the researcher might work within them. The reports might suggest interesting interpretations since the full participant may gain as intimate information as opportunity invites.

Full participation observation is not easy. In a famous participant observation study, Festinger, Rieken, and Schachter (1956) studied a woman they called Mrs. Keech who had predicted the end of the world by a mighty flood. After reading about Mrs. Keech in a newspaper, Festinger's group joined her followers to see what would happen when the world did not, in fact, come to an end. Mrs. Keech claimed to have been receiving messages from a group called the Omnipotent Guardians from the planet Clarion. They had sent her messages through a combination of telepathy, automatic writing, and crystal ball gazing to indicate that at midnight on a particular December evening the world would be destroyed, killing all humanity except for Mrs. Keech's group. They were to be rescued by flying saucers sent from Clarion to Mrs. Keech's home. During the weeks before the "end of the world," several of the group members quit their jobs and spent their savings in preparation for the end. Messages continued to arrive daily to Mrs. Keech. At meetings Festinger and his associates frequently would excuse themselves and write down their notes while in the bathroom. At one meeting, the members were asked to look into a crystal ball and report any new pieces of information. One member of Festinger's group was forced to participate, even though he was hesitant to take a vocal role in meetings. After he remained silent for a time, Mrs. Keech demanded that he report what he saw. Choosing a single word response, he truthfully announced, "Nothing." Mrs. Keech reacted theatrically, "That's not nothing. That's the void." On the final evening, members of the group waited for midnight. During the evening other instructions arrived. Cultists were told to remove their shoelaces and belt buckles since these were unsafe aboard flying saucers. When midnight passed without any end of the world in sight—and without any flying saucers visible—members of the group began questioning whether they had misunderstood the instructions. Mrs. Keech began to cry and whimpered that none of the group believed in her. A few of the group comforted her and reasserted their belief in her. Some members reread past messages and many others sat silently with stony expressions on their faces. Finally in the wee hours of the morning, Mrs. Keech returned to the group with a new "automatically written" message from the Omnipotent Guardians. Because of the faith of the group, the Earth had been spared. The cult members were exuberant and during the weeks that followed actually attempted to secure additional converts. One can find both insight and some entertainment in such a participant observation study. To Festinger's group of scholars, the experience permitted them to provide a field study examination of the theory of cognitive dissonance that they were trying to develop at the time—a theory that later became a major force in communication and social psychology.

Though the ability to get involved in groups that otherwise would not welcome a researcher permits gathering data, the method creates ethical difficulties. The invasion of privacy of others is an obvious objection that may not have a satisfactory defense. In addition, concealing the researcher's identity has been charged with introducing "false and hypocritical interpersonal relationships between the actual participants and the participant observers" (Fox, 1969, p. 513).

case study of a full participant observation inquiry

ethical problems with the full participant approach

FIGURE 9.1
Ideal Typical
Continuum of
Fieldworker Roles

Figure from STRATEGIES
OF SOCIAL RESEARCH,
Third Edition by Herman
W. Smith, copyright ©
1991 by Holt, Rinehart
and Winston, Inc.,
reproduced by permission
of the publisher.

Complete Participant	Participant-as-Observer	Observer-as-Participant	Complete Observer

Subjective Sympathetic Involved Deceptive	Role Continuum	Objective Unsympathetic Detached Candid

Participant as Observer

participant as observer method defined

Most participant observation research follows the **participant as observer** method in which the group to be studied is made aware of the researcher's role. Upon agreeing to permit the researcher's participation, other group members typically become resources who explain and help interpret that group's actions. In one such study, Martin S. Weinberg (1965) visited three nudist camps to study nonverbal behavior of participants. In each case, he first identified himself as a researcher and requested permission to attend the camps as a nudist during the summer months. When attending the camps Weinberg identified himself as a researcher to the nudists. He reported that the nudists seemed uninfluenced by his presence, and they were willing to discuss matters with him. He had two potential hypotheses to guide his work, each one of which was opposite of the other. Perhaps people in nudist camps might be as unrestrained in their language and gestures as in their clothing. Or, perhaps since displays of the body are obvious, nudists might compensate by increased restraint in their language and gestures. He found strong support for his second hypothesis. He noticed that "verbal modesty" was common—there were few dirty jokes told, and sexual innuendo in conversation was frowned upon. Staring and body contact were discouraged. Similarly, use of alcohol was strictly forbidden. When Weinberg later interviewed 101 nudists in the Chicago area, he found that they were harsh in their judgments of others who violated their very strict norms. Furthermore, nudists lived a lifestyle in which nudity and sexuality were largely unrelated matters. As this example illustrates, the participant as observer does not hide his or her identity (or much of anything else). Instead, the observer becomes an active participant and develops increased appreciation for the actions and communication of the group.

Balancing Involvement

The two approaches involve some trade-offs. Figure 9.1 shows the relationship between the researcher's approach and the types of claims drawn. When the researcher tends toward complete participation, interpretations become subjective, the researcher shares sympathy and concern for the communicators studied, plays an active role in the communication to be studied, and usually goes into the research setting in disguise to get close to the data. On the other hand, researchers who tend toward complete observational research are objective, unsympathetic, detached, and usually candid about the sorts of research completed. Since the fieldwork of the participant observer tends to emphasize the involvement in the setting, his or her work may be tipped more toward one side of the continuum than the other. Participant observers must weigh the advantages and disadvantages of each approach to balance some of the benefits of one position against the costs that go with the levels of involvement.

Ethnography

Ethnography is research in which the investigator participates, overtly or covertly, in people's lives for an extended period of time, collecting whatever data are available to describe behavior. As can be seen, ethnography is a broad term that includes a great deal, including most participant observation research (though participant observation work need not occur over very long time periods). The sorts of studies completed by Margaret Mead while living with the Samoan people or the natives of New Guinea are archetypes of ethnography (even though it appears that in some cases she may have been hoaxed by some native groups). By living with a group for an extended time, even with periodical breaks along the way, it is possible to acquire knowledge that is unexpected and often exciting. Ethnography has been used quite a bit in communication and educational studies. For instance, by working (for free during the study) at a harness racetrack for seven months, James Helmer (1993) found that the stories people told each other helped people draw distinctions between different sorts of people in the horse-racing world. Stories drew strong distinctions between (1) track administrators, who were characterized as bureaucrats, and horsemen and -women, who were identified as sporting people; (2) "chemists," who doped horses, and honest horsemen and -women, who practice fair play; (3) men whose orders were followed and women whose opinions were not seriously considered. Interestingly enough, Helmer also supplemented his ethnography with traditional interviews in other parts of his study.

> **ethnography defined**
>
> **most participant observation as a special case of ethnography**

It is sometimes confusing to hear ethnography mentioned because so many researchers have used the term in very different senses (see Agar, 1988). The word **ethnomethodology** is sometimes used as though it were interchangeable with ethnography, when, in fact, it is a distinct specialty. The "new ethnography" (Berg, 1989, pp. 51–52) is the study of the mundane and ordinary activities of everyday life, concentrating on the methods used by people to report their common sense practical actions to others in acceptable rational terms. Ethnomethodology attempts to impose a rational scheme onto essentially practical activities (practical reasoning). When it works properly, we can find patterns to explain the implicit rules or guidelines that people use to make sense of exchanges with each other. Although ethnomethodology occasionally has been criticized for being "almost willfully obscure" (McNeill, 1990, p. 94), it has grown in popularity among students of communication since it focuses on how people use messages to perceive the world as they do.

> **ethnomethodology distinguished from ethnography**

THE FLUID PROCESS OF PARTICIPANT OBSERVATION STUDY

As with other research approaches, participant observation studies follow some fairly consistent methods. Furthermore, they have some limitations of which reseachers must be aware.

SPECIAL DISCUSSION 9-2
Other Qualitative-Naturalistic Methods

Though the typical naturalistic methods used in communication research are common enough, other tools sometimes appear. Some of the most frequently heard methods are the following:

- "A 'life-history' or 'life story' is the autobiography of a person which has been obtained though interview and guided conversation" (McNeill, 1990, p. 85). The term "oral history" is often used as a synonym for the life history study. This method does not result in composing an autobiography, but it uses life histories (usually witnesses to major communication events) to gather information on significant times or events. Such studies are useful since collecting many of such studies allows us to reconstruct a sense of a time period and the practice of communication across time.
- Time-budgeting studies are inquiries in which "the researcher asks the subjects of the research to keep a detailed diary over a given period" (McNeill, 1990, p. 88). Time-budgeting studies are often used in organizational communication and communication education to help determine whether professionals are using their time in ways that are most constructive and expected given their job descriptions. The maps constructed by time-budgeting studies can help identify areas of dominant focus and areas where readjustments might be advised.
- Community studies "involve a researcher or a team of researchers in studying a whole community of people, usually in a small town or village, or possibly part of a larger town" (McNeill, 1990, p. 90). Unlike ordinary ethnographic research, many methods are used, including such tools as direct observation, use of informants, and informal and formal interviews with individuals.

Steps in Participant Observation

Participant observation studies are completed by steps that often overlap and cycle back and forth. The entire method has a fluid quality about it, though a protocol has established some clear phases in this type of research.

Selecting Settings and Cases

Steps: 1. selecting settings and cases

Researchers often choose research settings and fields that appeal to their personal interests. Thus, one researcher may focus on observing people at airports, another may attempt to spy on private conversations, and still another might try to have long visits with subjects. There is some disagreement about whether it is most desirable to study unusual and exotic settings or to stick to the ordinary and mundane. Those who urge study of exotic practices believe that looking at unusual activities may reveal things that challenge conventional wisdom. Those who want researchers to emphasize ordinary behavior hold that regularities in communication can be identified most efficiently by looking at typical rather than aberrant behaviors.

controversy over study of exotic or ordinary behavior

Getting into the Setting

Participant observers must take time to define their levels of activity. A passive observer may have difficulty getting a group's permission to observe key behavior. Yet, a researcher who does not reveal his or her own purposes to the individuals under study may face some dangers. Laud Humphreys (1970) studied the practice of casual homosexual sexual encounters. Without identifying himself as a researcher, and without choosing to participate, Humphreys agreed to serve as a "lookout" at a public restroom where men had brief homosexual affairs. He was presumed to be a voyeur or "watch queen." He found that many of the men were married and led otherwise heterosexual lives. Such research, though, proved dangerous. Humphreys was arrested once and was beaten up by a gang of kids another time.

2. getting into the setting

The ethical difficulties of concealing one's identity can be great. One research team (Berg, Ksander, Loughlin, & Johnson, 1983) studied a group of teenagers' criminal activities. Along the way, they acquired information about plans for car robberies, burglaries, assaults, shoplifting, and drug deals. These clearly illegal and violent activities were never reported to police, nor were victims warned. Did the researchers owe society or the victims anything? They apparently did not think so—nor was their own property stolen, nor were they assaulted. The authors possessed a Federal Certificate of Confidentiality, which guaranteed that individuals involved in research studies would not have their records subpoenaed, and which required that confidential materials not be revealed. The ethics involved in learning more than one wishes to know constitute a major challenge in much, but not all, naturalistic study.

ethical challenges in research

Sampling Within the Case: Selecting the Types of Behaviors to Monitor

Based on their knowledge and theoretic interests, researchers gather data that they believe will be most meaningful. Though some researchers keep their early observations relatively unstructured, all seem to give attention to information about the physical setting, relationships among people, information that is overheard, and locating guides who can help explain the new surroundings (Berg, 1989, p. 68). Researchers usually begin by noting nearly everything that they can identify as a potentially useful piece of information. Most, however, choose behaviors to track based on a combination of personal interest and the level of talk they notice other participants giving the concepts. When examining behavior, many participant observers ask themselves the following key questions to isolate and describe key behavior (Nachmias & Nachmias, 1987, p. 301, after Lofland & Lofland, 1984):

3. selecting types of behaviors to monitor

1. What type of behavior is it?
2. What is its structure?
3. How frequent is it?
4. What are its causes?
5. What are its processes?
6. What are its consequences?
7. What are people's strategies?

By a combination of direct observation and asking questions, meaningful communication processes and variables can be identified.

Keeping Records and Observations

**4. keeping records
and observations**

While attempting not to distract participants from their ordinary actions, researchers maintain records of the things they have recalled and observed. These pieces of information are the hard data to be analyzed later. Often the setting requires that they keep records "on the run." Researchers try to record words and phrases they hear, the sequences of events, and their impressions. Though some researchers seem to invest a small lifetime into making observations, others set time limits on their entry into a setting. They frequently leave the setting and attempt to give themselves some room to "clear their minds" and organize their thoughts. The quality of a participant observation study is only as good as the records kept by researchers. Hence, the following questions are often raised to decide whether reports are sound ones (after Lofland & Lofland, 1984, p. 51):

Question	Evaluation of Answer
1. Is the report firsthand?	Hearsay may be very inaccurate.
2. Where was the observer?	The observer should be in a position to see or hear what is described.
3. Did the participant have a reason to give false or biased information?	Information from biased sources is unreliable. Participants who cannot tell the truth cannot give solid information to draw conclusions.
4. Is the report internally consistent?	Equivocal information prevents drawing clear conclusions.
5. Can the report be validated by other independent reports?	Reliance on isolated reports from participants may be unreliable.

As with all other kinds of data, researchers must show the validity of the information they use to make meaningful interpretations.

Interpretive Analysis of Data

**5. interpretive
analysis**

The results of participant observation studies involve descriptions of communication settings. Scholars often rely on references to transcendent perspectives (such as phenomenology or symbolic interactionism) to explain their results. Other times they may look at the language of communicators to find the underlying structures or "grammars." Researchers may look at the so-called "surface devices" that people use to express themselves. Or they may search for evidence of "deep devices" that underlie language use. In reality, there is no real limit on the imagination of researchers in finding creative ways to assess their results.

**interpretive
approach
distinguished**

One of the most popular methods has been the development of the "interpretive approach" (Denzin, 1983). The **interpretive analysis of data** identifies communicators' interactions to determine such things as the situations in which people find themselves, the structures within which they work, and the practical features of their world. Researchers frequently hang around communicators and listen to the stories they tell and their use of language. One such study was completed by Trujillo and Dionisopoulos (1987) on "Cop Talk." By accompanying police officers on calls for four months, they found that police used a vocabulary that emphasized their own sense of drama or excitement about their jobs.

The drama of police work is also a social construction, enacted in the everyday communicative performances of the officers. The job of law enforcement, thus, may involve forms, tickets, false alarms, but the experience of being a cop involves motorcycle maggots, crushed esophaguses, and grilled assholes. And so as they call the public names, talk tough at the station, and share stories about what went down, cops create and maintain the organizational drama of police work. (p. 207)

By looking at the language and stories of communicators, you can interpret the function of messages to structure reality in specific social settings.

Exiting the Field Setting

Though it may seem obvious, participant observers need to set a time at which they exit the setting (at least as researchers). Yet, many participant observation researchers develop personal attachments to other participants and have a difficult time leaving. Moreover, if researchers "go native" and never leave the setting, they may lose their ability to make scholarly contributions. Participant observation researchers are usually expected to make arrangements in advance to terminate the research process. Researchers who end the experience unexpectedly and abruptly may create additional troubles. Participants may feel used and irritated. If the researcher wishes to renew contact at another time, he or she might find the participants to be reluctant. Thus, the timing and manner of exiting the research setting should be scheduled at the time the research is begun. Though many fieldworkers ignore this part of the project, they soon learn how important it is.

6. exiting the field setting

Limitations of the Approach

Though participant observation methods have many benefits, there are limits on the approach.[2] First, these methods are very time consuming and expensive. The amount of labor and required finances make them impractical for many research outings.

limitations:
1. time-consuming and expensive

Second, and perhaps most obvious, is the fact that such work tends to rest on unreliable measurement. Since researchers rarely have the privilege of using standardized research tools, inquiries may suffer from measurement deficiencies. Furthermore, lessons learned in one naturalistic study may be highly unstable since observation methods may have unknown reliability.

2. unreliable measurement

Third, the participant observers can become overidentified with a group. By becoming an active participant, a researcher may develop biases and sympathies that color the fairness and accuracy of reports or interpretations. A researcher may begin subconsciously to report what he or she expected or what may put the studied group in the best light. Moreover, though they may try to avoid influencing the group, the behavior of participant observers might alter actions seen in the natural setting. The prudent researcher must be careful of such tendencies. You should know that some scholars believe that such notions as "reliable measurement" and "researcher bias" come from a set of assumptions that are not really relevant to ethnography. Perhaps. But you should expect to see these questions asked when such research is presented.

3. overidentification with a group leading to researcher bias

---

[2]The first three limits are drawn from the discussion by Berg (1989, pp. 83–84).

4. cannot reach comprehensive conclusions alone

Fourth, naturalistic studies cannot reach comprehensive conclusions without combining many different sorts of data. There is a tendency to draw fascinating conclusions from sketchy evidence. Yet, in participant observation work, conclusions probably cannot be argued successfully unless many different sorts of information are available.

SUMMARY

Participant observation studies are based on a desire to examine communication behavior that is not affected by the research process. Fieldwork is the study of people acting in the natural course of their daily lives. For our purposes, fieldwork and naturalistic studies are interchangeable terms. Participant observers study groups by gaining membership or close relationships with them. Fieldwork studies have three major purposes: (1) answering questions in settings where use of questionnaires and direct reports would be inappropriate or impractical, (2) examining a setting that has been so unexplored that formal hypotheses may not have been developed, (3) developing grounded theory. Such research argues from empirical facts to conclusions.

One can enter the field in two ways. Full participant observation research is characterized by the investigator's gathering data while taking part in the activities of a group—and while concealing his or her research identity. This method creates obvious ethical difficulties. The researcher may not satisfactorily be able to defend the privacy of others. In addition, concealing the researcher's identity can introduce potentially harmful interpersonal relationships. Most participant observation research follows the participant-as-observer method in which the group to be studied is made aware of the researcher's role. The different approaches involve some trade-offs. As the researcher tends toward becoming a complete participant, interpretations become sub-

jective, the researcher shares sympathy and concern for the communicators studied, plays an active role in the communication studied, and usually goes into the research setting in disguise. Ethnography is research in which the investigator participates, overtly or covertly, in people's lives for an extended period of time, collecting whatever data are available to describe behavior. Ethnography is a broad term that includes a great deal including most participant observation research (though participant observation work need not occur over very long time periods). Ethnomethodology or the "new ethnography" is the study of the mundane and ordinary activities of everyday life, concentrating on the methods used by people to report their common sense practical actions to others in acceptable rational terms.

The fluid steps of participant observation include: (1) selecting settings and cases; (2) getting into the setting; (3) sampling within the case by selecting the types of behaviors to monitor; (4) keeping records and observations; (5) the interpretive analysis of data; and (6) exiting the field setting. Limitations on the use of the approach include: (1) these methods are very time consuming and expensive; (2) such work tends to rest on unreliable measurement; (3) researchers can become over-identified with a group and develop biases and sympathies that color the fairness and accuracy of reports or interpretations; (4) such studies cannot reach comprehensive conclusions alone.

TERMS FOR REVIEW

fieldwork
naturalistic studies
participant observation
grounded theory
analytic induction
complete observer
unobtrusive measurement
accretions

urban archaeology
erosions
full participant observation
participant as observer research
ethnography
ethnomethodology
interpretive analysis of data

CHAPTER 10

Design of Descriptive Empirical Research

A science is any discipline in which the fool of this generation can go beyond the point reached by the genius of the last generation.

–Max Gluckman

BEFORE WE GET STARTED . . .

Descriptive empirical research in communication tends to rely on quantitative methods, though empirical observations are also involved in other types of studies. The tools discussed in this chapter involve collecting data and summarizing them in numbers. Hence, this chapter deals with the very basic issue of how descriptive empirical research is completed. It will introduce you to the forms of such research and give you some details about survey research.

INVITATIONS TO EMPIRICAL RESEARCH IN COMMUNICATION

empirical defined

The study of communication often relies on empirical research. The term **empirical** actually means "observable" and thus applies to nearly all communication research that tests statements against data. Empirical descriptive research involves gathering fresh data to test statements. Empirical descriptive research is most invited when problem questions ask about current descriptions of things and explore explanations that characterize things as they are now. J. Jeffrey Auer explained that such questions may have three emphases (1959, p. 147):

1. *Ascertaining norms:* Where are we? What is?
2. *Establishing goals:* Where should we be? What is best?
3. *Developing methods:* How do we advance from norm to goal? What is best to do?

Surveys, content analyses, and observational studies can help researchers understand what is occurring. Surveying attitudes and opinions can show sentiments about directions to move. Scholars who attempt to develop new research methods and measurement tools can promote other studies to help solve practical problems.

experiments show causal relationships

experiment defined

Some questions ask about cause-and-effect relationships between variables. Although historical research can answer such questions if we have enough time, the only way to get contemporaneous evidence of cause-and-effect relationships is through experimentation. An **experiment** introduces a variable and determines its effects while controlling all other variables. Achieving such control is difficult, but if successful, experiments provide direct immediate evidence of cause-and-effect relationships. This chapter focuses attention on nonexperimental methods, and the next chapter explores experimental research.

SURVEY RESEARCH

survey research defined

The term "survey" means the process of looking at something in its entirety. It scrutinizes the complete scope of something. In quantitative research, a **survey** is an empirical study that uses questionnaires or interviews to discover descriptive characteristics of phenomena. We often think of surveys as polls, questionnaire studies, and interviews in which large groups of people are asked their views. Yet, relatively small groups of people such as employees of a company or a plant can be surveyed. Their responses may be used to identify employee sentiment. Or their responses could form the basis of a network analysis.

surveys are used in all branches of communication

Surveys are used across communication studies. In fact, students often find that after graduating they are asked to construct questionnaires in their jobs. Professionals also use this method actively. In speech and hearing science, Lewis (1990) surveyed family histories of children who had phonological disorders to discover the presence of dyslexia, learning disabilities, and speech disorders across generations. Rescourla (1989) used the survey method to validate two new measurement instruments to diagnose delayed language development in preschool children. In mass communication, Barnett and his associates (1989) surveyed students from rural areas in northern Belize (formerly British Honduras), and found strong associations between students' English-speaking ability and the amount of American television they watched. In

SPECIAL DISCUSSION 10–1
Forms of Descriptive Studies

Though surveys are the dominant form of descriptive studies, there are several different forms of such studies (after Auer, chap. 6).

Studies of Behavior: Facts and Opinions. These studies are designed to determine the current status of conditions or attitudes. In addition to surveys by questionnaires and interviews, researchers may make direct observations of communicators. Sometimes the observation can rely on special technologies, such as special screening rooms equipped with "wiggle-meters" (that measure how attentive people are by tracking how often they shift weight [wiggle] during a broadcast).

Studies of Status and Development. Intensive detailed study of individual cases and events often reveals information that can be used to develop other hypotheses or to answer practical questions, including case studies or genetic studies (for example, inquiries into the "growth and development among individuals and groups" [Auer, 1959, pp. 151–152]). These studies are usually long-term inquiries that trace the genesis and change of a group of people throughout a life cycle.

Methodological Studies. These studies deal with the development and validation of new tools and measuring instruments. Some studies examine the integrity of different research approaches generally, such as Burgoon, Hall, and Pfau's (1991) check on the validity of persuasion studies that employ only one persuasive message topic (they found no major statistical or logical difficulty when different studies had provided replications across topics). Another type of methodological study develops research instruments, such as Weber and Patterson's (1996) validation of a new scale to communication-based emotional support.

communication theory, Troester and Mester (1990, p. 424) surveyed chairs of communication departments and found that although "student interest in [the area of] peace communication is waning," faculty members believed it to be appropriate for study. As you can see, survey research can add intriguing information to our store of knowledge. The four general forms of survey studies are questionnaire studies, interview studies, focus group studies, and network analysis.

THE QUESTIONNAIRE SURVEY

Completing a questionnaire survey involves six steps. At each point along the way, researchers explain and justify their choices.

Selecting Questions and Providing Instructions

Questionnaires are survey forms in which individuals respond to written items. Questionnaires ask people to report their understanding of things, often including their own behavior. Developing the questions is often difficult for students. In general there are three ways to develop survey items. Early in your own research you might want to

questionnaires defined

three ways to develop survey questions

resources for questions

rely on the first two, and as you become more experienced you can learn to use the third option.

1. Find standard forms in resource works. Collections of measures can be found in such sources as *Communication Research Measures: A Sourcebook,* edited by Rubin, Palmgreen, and Sypher (1994); *Measurement of Communication Behavior,* by Emmert and Barker (1989); *Measures of Personality and Social Psychological Attitudes,* by Robinson, Shaver, and Wrightsman (1991); and *A Handbook for the Study of Human Communication,* by Tardy (1988). In addition, *Mental Measurements Yearbook* is a multivolume set including references to hundreds of measures, though most of them must be purchased from private companies. These resources can help you find ways to measure communication concepts.
2. Select measurement forms that have been used in research articles you have read. Researchers often provide copies of their items in research articles. If not, they will often cite sources from which their measures were drawn.
3. Develop them yourself by (a) reading on the subject, (b) composing a rough draft of items based on your reading of statements on the issue, (c) putting them into a suitable format (such as those found in this chapter), and (d) evaluating them against the standards discussed in this chapter.

Researchers face several tactical challenges when phrasing questions and preparing survey forms. People must cooperate in completing questionnaires. Moreover, respondents must report the way they honestly perceive things. This reporting can be difficult since respondents sometimes do not know how they perceive things. Other times, respondents may feel pressure to respond in ways they believe the researcher wants. Naturally, these matters are not to be taken lightly. Thus, researchers try to use methods that avoid contaminating data.

In general, preparing questionnaires and interview schedules requires researchers to observe three criteria (Tuckman, 1978, p. 197):

1. To what extent might a question influence respondents to show themselves in a good light?
2. To what extent might a question influence respondents to be unduly helpful by attempting to anticipate what researchers want to hear or find out?
3. To what extent might a question be asking for information about respondents that they are not certain, and perhaps not likely, to know about themselves?

There are several options for designing survey items. Table 10.1 shows the sorts of questionnaire forms that communication researchers typically use.

Researchers must also decide on a format for their questions. Alternatives include the following:

- *Direct or indirect questions* (Tuckman, 1978, p. 198). Though direct questions ask for obvious reports, indirect questions ask respondents to react in ways that imply information. Instead of asking whether people enjoy programs on public television, a researcher might ask subjects to describe the quality of programs on public television. Speech and hearing therapists may ask clients to describe their communication problems, rather than asking them

TABLE 10.1 Types of Questions

TYPE and DESCRIPTION	EXAMPLE	USEFUL WHEN
Open-ended questions: Questions to which people respond in their own words	12. What fringe benefits offered by this company are most important to you? _____ _____ _____	1. Respondents may not have information on the topic 2. Respondents are motivated to communicate and spend time on the project
Closed-ended questions: Questions to which people respond in fixed categories of answers	12. The fringe benefits at this company are: (check one) [ ] superior [ ] excellent [ ] good [ ] fair [ ] poor	1. Possible answers are limited in number 2. Respondents are known to possess information on the topic 3. Terms are commonly understood by respondents
Paired-comparison questions: Questions that ask respondents to make a judgment between alternatives taken two at a time	12. If you had to choose between the following two options, which one would you prefer in your career? [ ] enjoyable work [ ] high income 13. If you had to choose between the following two options, which one would you prefer in your professional career? [ ] good people to work with [ ] high income	1. Items to be rated are very close in desirability and simple ranking is difficult 2. Options are fairly limited in number 3. It is practical to contrast all options against each other
Contingency questions: Questions "asked only of *some* respondents, determined by their responses to some other question" (Babbie, 1995, p. G2)	12. Have you given a speech in the last three months? [ ] Yes (If yes, please go to question 13) [ ] No (If no, please go to question 20)	1. Situations in which responses from only certain subjects are desired 2. Questions apply only to some sorts of people
Ranking questions: Closed-ended questions that ask respondents to rank a set of options	12. Which sources of news do you rely on most? (rank your first choice number 1, your second choice number 2, and so forth until you have ranked all five sources) _____ television _____ newspapers _____ radio _____ magazines _____ friends	1. A small number of items are to be ranked 2. All categories to be ranked are applicable to all subjects 3. When priority information is desired, rather than information about degree of differences in evaluations

TABLE 10.1 *—Continued*		

TYPE and DESCRIPTION	EXAMPLE	USEFUL WHEN
Inventory Questions: Closed-ended questions that ask respondents to list all responses that apply to them	12. How did you hear about the speech and hearing clinic services? (check all that apply) [ ] newspapers [ ] school officials [ ] health professionals [ ] friends [ ] radio [ ] television [ ] yellow pages listing	1. Respondents differ in their backgrounds in items on the inventory 2. Categories are fairly well known 3. Categories are not mutually exclusive of others
Matrix questions: Closed-ended questions that ask respondents to use the same categories to supply information	For each of the following statements, circle SA if you strongly agree with the statement, A if you agree with the statement, N if you neither agree nor disagree with the statement, D if you disagree with the statement, and DS if you disagree strongly with the statement. 12. Management is competent SA A N D DS 13. Management is inept SA A N D DS 14. Management is trustworthy SA A N D DS 15. Management is honest SA A N D DS	1. Standard methods such as Likert scaling are invited 2. Many reliable statements are known to measure the domain of interest 3. Items reasonably can be added together to create a logical scale
Multiple-choice questions: Closed-ended questions that ask respondents to select a category response from a range of possible responses	12. How long have you been a major in your current field? [ ] 0 - 1 semesters [ ] 2 - 3 semesters [ ] 3 - 4 semesters [ ] 5 - 6 semesters [ ] over 6 semesters	1. It is desirable to group responses into meaningful underlying units 2. Exclusive categories can be found

to identify the disorder they believe they have. Though it usually requires more indirect questions than direct questions to obtain information, these questions can often yield honest responses when topics involve sensitive matters or issues people may try to answer in ways that put them in the best light.

- *Specific or general questions.* Specific questions focus on individual activities, whereas general questions ask about global evaluations. In organizational communication, employees are often asked about their satisfaction with the physical work environment. They may be asked specific questions regarding how satisfied they are with the temperature of the work environment, the cleanliness of the workplace, and the ease of operating equipment. General questions may ask about their overall view of the work environment, for example, "How satisfied are you with the company's physical work environment?'' Though specific questions are used extensively by researchers to get precise information, in some cases individuals may grow unusually "cautious or guarded and give less-than-honest answers. Nonspecific questions may lead circuitously to the desired information but with less alarm by the respondent" (Tuckman, 1978, p. 198).

- *Questions versus statements* (Tuckman, 1978, p. 199). Some questionnaire items ask questions. Others make statements and ask subjects to indicate how much they agree or disagree with them. Both methods are useful. Yet, researchers typically select one mode or the other to minimize the number of different instructions that respondents must follow.

Of course, researchers often combine forms on a single questionnaire. Thus, questionnaires may include a broad repertoire of response modes.

Phrasing items on a questionnaire is a major challenge. Through tricky phrasing, a researcher can "rig" a survey to produce results that he or she wants. Thus, one must carefully look at survey items to make sure that they are worded appropriately. Table 10.2 lists generally accepted requirements for wording items. These requirements are standards that you may use to double-check questionnaires you compose or read. — **phrasing items on questionnaires**

Questionnaire instructions are designed to enlist involvement of respondents and to explain how they are to answer questions. The instructions must be clear and should explain to people how they are to complete the questionnaire. As a matter of routine, many researchers find it useful to provide a category where the respondent can indicate "no response" or "not applicable." This strategy is useful since researchers can separate incomplete responses from thoughtful refusals to respond. Table 10.3 shows some typical instruction methods for some major response formats. Although instructions usually take a fairly standard form, experienced researchers learn the wisdom of running a pilot study on the instructions and survey items. Such a study helps find problems and eliminate potential confusion before completing the full inquiry. — **use of questionnaire instructions**

Formatting

The actual composition of the survey tends to be fairly direct. Most survey forms begin with a brief statement of introduction to announce the survey, request participation, assure confidentiality (if appropriate), and indicate how to return the survey form. A letter of introduction is included with mailed survey forms, though sometimes such letters are used in other settings as well. — **format issues: introduction**

The meat of the survey form usually includes the questions or statements to which respondents must react. In practice, most questionnaires place demographic questions (sex, age, academic major, etc.) first. Yet, some argue that demographics should be placed last to avoid boring people with dull background questions at the outset (Babbie, 1992, p. 157). Next, questions that rely on the same sort of response mode are grouped together, preceded by instructions for completing the items. Some researchers recommend that questions that deal with the same issue should be grouped together. Yet this ordering can sometimes create bias in response. People may try to respond in ways that are consistent with early statements on the survey. For instance, suppose subjects are asked to evaluate the quality of teaching in communication — **order of questions** / **grouping of items**

TABLE 10.2 Problems in Wording Questions

DIFFICULTY	EXAMPLE	COMMENT AND SUGGESTIONS
Double-barreled questions	Do you favor expanded bus and fixed rail mass transit systems?	If you want only one option, you must answer "no" to this question. Instead, two questions should be used; one for each alternative.
Loaded language	Do you favor reduced military expenditures in light of the reduced world threat from the former Soviet Union?	The justification for the position is advanced along with the question itself. Questions should leave out the arguments for one side or another.
Improper grammar	Do you know any one of U.S. taxpayers who are willing to pay for increases in public higher education?	Some questionnaire respondents will detect the incorrect grammar and will be distracted from the content. The question should read, "Do you know any one of U.S. taxpayers who *is* . . ."
Incompleteness	Do you believe that more money should be spent on public higher education?	More than what? Technically, this wording is a fragment, rather than a complete interrogative sentence.
Vagueness	What do you think of your local Cable TV company?	Such a question makes it impossible to get at specific, interpretable information. Researchers should ask questions to gather information they wish to have.
Ambiguous terms	Do you believe that women get their due at your company?	The term "get their due" is subject to many different interpretations. If the researcher wants specific information, unambiguous language must be used.
Lengthy items	When engaged in special project teams, do members of management rely on responsive listening techniques prior to giving reactions to suggestions made by subordinates?	Questions should be asked as briefly as possible, but no briefer.
Complex questions	Should serious communication students be required to take a foreign language?	If one disagrees with requiring communication students to take a foreign language, the question still would be answered "yes." The question only asks about "serious" students—an extra weasel word that restricts the question to a small group.
Averaging or reconstructive questions	In the average week, how many hours of television news do you watch?	It may be difficult for a person to come up with an average. Instead one should ask about a limited time period, such as a week.
Leading questions	Do you agree with most Americans who believe that the quality of public argument is poor?	Such a question creates pressure to go along with the wishes of the questioner. Such prompts as "wouldn't you agree with me that . . ." similarly are dangerous examples of leading questions.
Abbreviations	"Should the city council approve the construction of an interactive CATV system?" (Wimmer & Dominick, 1983, p. 113)	Abbreviations and acronyms may not be universally understood. It is best to preface this question with a brief explanation of the meaning of the abbreviated term.

TABLE 10.2 —*Continued*

DIFFICULTY	EXAMPLE	COMMENT AND SUGGESTIONS
Imprecise questions	Does your cable TV company leave something to be desired?	Such imprecise language guarantees useless data. Whether a person is satisfied or dissatisfied with a local cable TV company, the answer would be "yes" since there is *always* something more that one could desire.
Misspelling	Should children with cleft palates increase there time spent on drills?	Questionnaires are communication encounters. Misspellings show contempt for readers who notice them.
Awkward construction	How many students do you have broken down by sex?	Drinking is more of a problem with us.
Items with only one logical answer	Can television programs promote acquisition of language skills among immigrants?	Anything is possible in the future. Thus, questions that ask if something "can" or "might" occur have only one logical answer.
Presumptive questions	How severe is your child's stuttering?	Assuming information in a question makes it impossible to answer fairly. This example is much like the famous "wife beating" question. One might ask a man, "Have you stopped beating your wife?" If he answers yes or no, you've got him cornered.
Elevated vocabulary	Is the personal life of a presidential candidate germane to your choice of a candidate?	Simple words should be used where possible. Surprisingly, many people do not know that germane means relevant. Though one should not "dummy down" to respondents, simple language should be used as much as possible.
Imprecise agents of action	Should we adopt a guaranteed income to replace welfare?	Who is "we?" Items should specify the active agency, as in the question, "Should the federal government adopt a guaranteed income to replace welfare?"
False bipolar	Do you like coffee with or without caffeine?	Such a question misleads since it assumes that the respondent likes coffee at all.

classes. At a later point in the survey they may be asked to state what they believe are the most important needs at their school. It is quite likely that they will mention the quality of teaching—perhaps more than they would have otherwise. There is no simple way around this difficulty.

> The safest solution is sensitivity to the problem. Though you cannot avoid the effect of question order, you should attempt to estimate what the effect will be. Thus, you will be able to interpret results in a meaningful fashion. If the order of questions seems an especially important issue in a given study, you might construct more than one version of the questionnaire containing the different possible ordering of questions. You would then be able to determine the effects. At the very least, you should pretest your questionnaire in the different forms. (Babbie, 1992, p. 157)

TABLE 10.3 Sample Instructions

Example 1

Please help us by rating a number of behaviors related to your communication on the job. Using the scales provided, please indicate your degree of performing each behavior on the job and your confidence in your ability to perform the behavior. Just circle the number that best reflects your response to each item. If the statement does not apply to you, circle NA.

	My performance of this skill on my job	My confidence in my ability to perform this behavior successfully
	very rarely very regularly	very low very high
Encouraging others to communicate problems before they turn into major issues	1 2 3 4 5 NA	1 2 3 4 5 NA
Using communication patterns that promote a supportive climate	1 2 3 4 5 NA	1 2 3 4 5 NA

Example 2

Please use the scales below to indicate your evaluation of the underlined term. For each scale, place a check mark on the position that best reflects your feelings. If you believe that a term applies extremely to the concept, check the positions closest to the adjective as in the following example:

            bad   _X_:____:____:____:____:____   good

or   bad   ____:____:____:____:____:_X_   good

If you believe that the term applies quite a bit to the concept, check the positions indicated as follows:

            bad   ____:_X_:____:____:____:____   good

or   bad   ____:____:____:____:_X_:____   good

If you believe that the term applies slightly to the concept, check the positions indicated as follows:

            bad   ____:____:_X_:____:____:____   good

or   bad   ____:____:____:_X_:____:____   good

If you are undecided or if you believe the scale does not apply to the concept, check the central position. Check only one position for each scale. Please work quickly. We are most interested in your first impressions.

Management of this TV Station

    positive ____:____:____:____:____:____ negative

    unfair ____:____:____:____:____:____ fair

    friendly ____:____:____:____:____:____ unfriendly

Example 3

Please look at the items below. Place a check mark next to all statements that apply to you.

If a suggestion box program were adopted at this speech clinic,

_____ I would be willing to participate if cash awards were given for outstanding suggestions.

_____ I would be willing to participate if noncash awards were given for outstanding suggestions.

_____ I would be willing to participate if additional vacation time were awarded for outstanding suggestions.

_____ I would be willing to participate if no awards were given for outstanding suggestions.

Though similar classes of questions may be grouped together, it does not follow that all the items within each category should be grouped together. For instance, if you wished to evaluate the credibility of management at a company, you might group all these ratings together. But since there are at least two dimensions of credibility, character and competence, it makes some sense to mix the order of such credibility items within the same section of the survey form.

      Determining the appropriate length for a survey form is a continuing struggle for researchers. In general, brief surveys are preferred to lengthy ones. But sometimes researchers may be stuck with long questionnaires. If you use standard measures of some personality traits, you may have to include many questions. In addition, when developing measures of your own, you may wish to use at least three scale items for each concept. It is difficult to determine the reliability of a single question or item. Hence, if you use three items to measure a concept (such as example 2 on Table 10.3), you have some insurance. If one of the items proves unacceptable, you will still have two items left to complete analyses. If you use only a single item, however, and it proves unacceptable, you might wind up with a fistful of air. Even so, you should be careful about using very lengthy questionnaires and avoid the temptation to "throw in" scales to measure other, unrelated matters. If you use a lengthy survey, it is a good idea to prepare several questionnaire forms that put the scales groups in different orders to control for subject fatigue.

(margin note: scale items can be placed in random order)

(margin note: length of questionnaires)

(margin note: use of at least three items to measure a concept)

Determining Reliability and Validity

Researchers must evaluate questionnaires to determine whether they are valid measures of the concepts under question. **Validity** is the degree to which a measure actually measures what is claimed. To show that a set of questions is valid, we first must show that it is stable. This requirement, called **reliability,** is the consistency of a measure with itself. In Chapter 4 you found specific methods to determine validity and reliability.

(margin note: validity defined)

(margin note: reliability defined)

      In addition to formal methods to establish validity, researchers often include other controls in their surveys. Sometimes they try to detect when people are not responding consistently or accurately. Three types of controls are check questions, test-taking measures, and alternating polarity of items. A **check question** involves asking the same question twice at different locations in the questionnaire, usually once positively worded and once negatively worded, such as

(margin note: additional controls)

(margin note: 1. check questions)

| The physical working conditions are good. | SA A N D DS |
| The physical working conditions are poor. | SA A N D DS |

If people pay attention, they should answer the items consistently. If they answer in very different ways, then they are not really alert when completing the survey. Check questions help identify people who are not responding consistently so that they can be discarded from the final sample. A second control method is the use of measures of test-taking behavior. Scales have been developed to reveal whether an individual is responding in unrealistic ways to survey items. Table 10.4 shows some of these popular measures. A survey researcher can sprinkle these types of measures throughout a questionnaire. Then, scoring these subscales will reveal biases among respondents.

(margin note: 2. measures of test-taking behavior)

TABLE 10.4 Measures of Test-Taking Behavior

Type and Description	Example	Comment
Social Desirability Scale A measure of the degree to which people attempt to describe themselves in ways that they think are acceptable, desirable, or approved by others (Crowne & Marlowe, 1960)	Circle T if the statement is true for you and circle F if the statement is false for you. T F 3.* It is sometimes hard for me to go on with my work if I am not encouraged. T F 4. I have never intensely disliked anyone. T F 5.* On occasion I have had doubts about my ability to succeed in life. * Credit for socially desirable response scored if person answers false.	• The scale consists of 33 items, but researchers sometimes choose a subset, such as the examples provided here to identify any responses that indicate answering in socially desirable ways. • If people score high on these items (the mean for nondepressed people is approximately 14 [Tanaka-Matsumi & Kameoka, 1986]), they are answering in ways to put themselves in the best light, rather than giving candid reactions. Many researchers delete such respondents from their final samples and others prefer to study this effect directly. • Some researchers view this scale as measuring a general tendency to seek approval (Strickland, 1977) or, at least, to avoid disapproval (Millham & Jacobson, 1978).
MMPI Lie (L) Scale A scale to identify respondents who are attempting to avoid being candid and honest in their responses (not a general personality disposition toward dishonesty) (Meehl & Hathaway, 1946)	Circle T if the statement is true for you and circle F if the statement is false for you.* T F At times I feel like swearing. T F I get angry sometimes. T F Sometimes when I am not feeling well I am cross. *Any answer of "false" is scored as a lie.	• The scale consists of 15 items interspersed in the Minnesota Multiphasic Personality Inventory (the most popular general personality test in the world). • Scoring high on these items (mean = 4.2 for males and 4.8 for females [Swenson, Pearson & Osbourne, 1973]) often requires a minimum score of 8. Such respondents can be deleted from the sample. • Some believe that the lie scale can be faked by testwise respondents (Dahlstrom, Welsh, & Dahlstrom, 1972).
Infrequency Index A measure of the inconsistency of response, indicative of a person giving random responses (Jackson, 1973)	Circle T if the statement is true for you and circle F if the statement is false for you.* T F Sometimes I get hungry or thirsty. T F** I make all my own clothes and shoes. T F I can run a mile in under three minutes. *Credit for infrequency response if a person answers false. **Credit for infrequency if a person answers true.	• The full scale includes 20 items systematically dispersed through the Jackson Personality Inventory. • For each item there is only one correct answer. Thus, individuals who respond incorrectly are not responding consistently to items on the research instrument. • Though the infrequency index is useful to identify those who are answering questions in random ways, attentive respondents sometimes are surprised at being asked such stupid questions.

A third method of control is the use of **polarity rotation** of items. This process means (1) avoiding phrasing all items positively and (2) avoiding placing all positive adjectives on the same side of the measurement items. Researchers are often concerned about **response set,** which is a tendency for subjects to follow predictable patterns of responding to test items. If a person gets in the habit of responding positively to items on a survey form, he or she may not be attentive to the content. Furthermore, at one time research reported (probably apocryphal) that when right-handed people got tired they tended to check positions toward the right side of questionnaires, whereas when left-handed people got tired they tended to check positions toward the left side of questionnaires. A way to break these habits is by changing the wording of questions and shifting polarity of items. Every so often researchers might ask questions that are worded negatively. If bipolar adjective scales are used, the locations of positively and negatively oriented adjectives might be switched to break up the pattern.

3. polarity rotation and control for response set

Sampling Subjects

Researchers carefully select groups of respondents by defining the universe they wish to sample. After identifying important population characteristics, researchers must define the sampling units. They decide whether to sample reports, actual behavior, or examples of communication. In each case, they try to secure a sample that is representative of the population. Often this requirement means that a random sample is drawn, but other times researchers must use a nonrandom sample. Regardless of the methods they use, researchers are expected to describe and justify their sampling methods and their choice of a sample size.

samples are drawn to be representative

Administering the Questionnaire

In questionnaire studies, people are given survey instruments along with instructions and left to provide their answers in writing. In experimental studies, the questionnaires may be accompanied by some sort of variable the researcher introduces, but in typical survey research, the respondent is pretty much left alone. Questionnaires can be administered through the mail, by fax, or even in classrooms. In each case, the researcher is guided by limits of subject willingness and the expense of such methods. People do not participate in survey research just because they are asked. Some people will not participate—for any number of reasons. Researchers face sampling biases when people choose not to respond to a survey. For mailed questionnaires, one popular guideline is that "a response rate of at least 50 percent is *adequate* for analysis and reporting. A response rate of at least 60 percent is *good*. And a response rate of 70 percent is *very good*" (Babbie, 1992, p. 267). Though these guidelines are just suggestions, they highlight the sorts of choices that researchers often make and possible ways to evaluate their efforts. After collecting questionnaires, it is typical for researchers to explain—in person or in writing—what the study was about and to offer additional feedback to subjects who wish it. This "debriefing" is not just a nicety—it is required in all ethical research.

administering the questionnaire

response rates

Analyzing and Interpreting Results

Survey research establishes information about relationships, but not about causal relationships (we need experiments or long-term historical studies to make those sorts of claims). In particular, researchers use statistical tools to analyze the data. They can

surveys cannot establish causal relationships directly

SPECIAL DISCUSSION 10–2
A Question of Ethics: Confidentiality and Anonymity

Asking people questions and watching their communication behavior frequently means probing into their lives. Even if they consent to it, ethical questions about privacy are raised unless care is taken to assure anonymity where possible and confidentiality generally.

Anonymity is the "protection of research participants by separating specific identities from the information given" (Frankfort-Nachmias & Nachmias, 1996, p. 585). Most research data can be collected without requiring subjects to identify themselves. Responses can remain nameless and neither researchers nor any others can identify whose responses are involved. Unfortunately, in some research (especially ethnographic research) the names of people are revealed to researchers and anonymity is impossible. At least researchers can guarantee a high degree of confidentiality.

Confidentiality is the "protection of the identity of research participants" (Frankfort-Nachmias & Nachmias, 1996, p. 587). Though researchers may know the identities of the people they interview or ask to complete questionnaires, the requirement of confidentiality requires that they not reveal those identities to others outside the research team. If confidentiality cannot be maintained, it must be communicated to participants before they participate in the study. To help assure confidentiality researchers may delete all names and identifiers from data revealed about individuals, report only broad categories of responses, use macroaggregation (constructing "average persons" from the data), and add errors to the original data to detour others from identifying participants (after Riecken & Boruch, 1979, pp. 258–259).

---

use simple descriptive statistics to show averages and spread of data. They can also use additional statistics to measure associations and to identify significant relationships.

Regardless of the extent of statistical analyses, questionnaire studies—and interview survey studies for that matter—interpret results to reveal answers to problem statements and hypotheses that focus on descriptions of current affairs and relationships. In each case, the emphasis is on describing patterns, rather than asserting cause-and-effect relations.

THE INTERVIEW SURVEY

reasons for interview studies:
1. reducing refusal rate
2. recording information missed in questionnaires

Though questionnaires can be handy, researchers sometimes find interview methods most useful for a couple of reasons. First, though it is easy for many people to ignore a cold questionnaire, it may be difficult for them to ignore a live person who asks questions. Of course, the interviewer may arouse some suspicions, but it is part of the job to involve respondents in the task. Second, the interviewer may record information (such as a respondent's manner and nonverbal actions) that might be lost with the questionnaire method. Of course, there is some art involved in completing interview studies. Thus, when you read studies that use the interview method, you can imagine the give and take involved in the interviews and the sorts of pressures the researcher and respondent felt.

Selecting Questions

First and foremost, interviews are ways for researchers to get answers to questions. The same question formats used in questionnaires may be employed in interviews. Indeed, most major polling organizations use formats that make their interviews sound like oral questionnaires. These interviews are called **structured interviews** since they use specific lists of questions. In contrast, **unstructured interviews** permit respondents to indicate their reactions to general issues without guidance from highly detailed questions. Furthermore, unstructured interviews allow interviewers to participate in extended exploration and follow up on new matters introduced by the respondent.

structured and unstructured interviews distinguished

Interviewers sometimes use special strategies to organize their questions. Unlike questionnaires that may place demographic questions at the end of the survey, interviewers place these items first to help respondents get comfortable with the interview process. Five major strategies can be used for both initial and follow-up questions during interviews. Table 10.5 shows these strategies along with examples and explanations of applications. Good advice on the phrasing of interview questions has been around for some time. As far back as 1940, the Gallup organization, which runs the Gallup polls, advanced these six recommendations for interviewers (Gallup & Rae, 1940, p. 101):

strategies for organizing questions

1. The question should be brief and to the point. Long conditional or dependent clauses tend to confuse people.
2. The words and phrases should be simple and in common day-to-day use among all groups in the community.
3. The question should not include words which have strong emotional content.
4. The question must avoid all possible bias or suggestion in favor of or against a particular point of view.
5. The question should include all the important alternatives which may emerge on a given issue.
6. When the individual is being asked to choose between different alternatives, this choice of alternatives must be given as early in the interview as possible.

Training and Controlling Behavior of Interviewers

Interview data can be strongly affected by the interviewer. Thus, if several people conduct interviews, researchers must train them to avoid actions that might bias results. Interviewers are trained to use the same introductions, the same answers to respondent questions, and the same manner of asking questions. Typically, the trainer instructs interviewers on ways to provide common instructions and ways to deal with typical problems that they might face in the field.

training interviewers as a necessity

Sometimes the very selection of interviewers can bias results. For instance, following the Watts riots of August 1965, H. Edward Ransford completed some survey work in the area (1968). When Ransford and other white interviewers conducted door-to-door surveys in south-central Los Angeles, results indicated great sadness

selection of interviewers can bias results

TABLE 10.5 Major Interview Question Strategies

Type and Description	Example	Comment
I. STRATEGIES FOR INITIAL QUESTIONING		
A. Funnel Questions: A strategy that starts with an open-ended question and follows up with increasingly narrow questions	Q: How do you feel about the newspapers in your city? Q: How would you rate coverage of business news by the newspapers in your city? Q: How would you rate coverage of the stock market by the newspapers in your city?	This question format is useful when: • Respondents must be screened to determine whether a question area applies to them; • Respondents may need to think about the general issue before answering thoughtfully; • Respondents "know the topic, feel free to talk about it, and want to express their feelings . . . open questions are easier to answer, pose less threat to interviewees, and get interviewees talking" (Cash & Stewart, 1988, p. 75).
B. Inverted Funnel Questions: A strategy that starts with a very specific question and expands by asking increasingly general questions	Q: What is your favorite TV show? Q: Do you like other shows that have the same format? Q: What types of TV shows do you like?	This question format is useful when: • The larger issue is so broad that vague answers might be given if the final question were asked at first; • Respondents need specific referents to answer logically; • Respondents need encouragement to talk.
II. STRATEGIES FOR FOLLOW-UP QUESTIONING		
A. Mirror Questions: Questions repeating previous responses to gain additional information	Q: What types of news programs do you watch on television? A: Non tabloid shows. Q: Non tabloid shows?	This type of question is useful when the interviewer: • Does not understand what the respondent means or simply wants to double check; • Wishes to get further explanation without making judgmental statements.
B. Probing Questions: Questions that directly ask for elaboration and explanation	Q: Why did you seek speech therapy for your son? A: He was having problems with other kids at school. Q: In what way? Could you explain that?	This type of question is useful when: • Specific areas require definition; • It is important to elicit examples.
C. Climate Questions: Questions asking respondents to explain how they feel about the interview	Q: You seem to become uncomfortable when I ask about the reasons you wanted speech therapy for your son. Is there some problem with talking about this matter?	This type of question is useful when: • The respondent is acting in ways that indicate an unwillingness to be candid; • The interviewer senses difficulty in completing the interview with the subject.

about the riots among the predominantly African American community. Yet, when Ransford hired African American interviewers, he found very different results. Respondents told African American interviewers that they thought the riots were proud symbols of anger and perhaps even inevitable. Furthermore, the African American interviewers found that the likelihood of a person's participation in the riots was linked to isolation from whites and a deep sense of powerlessness. In contrast, the McCone Commission, which investigated the riots on behalf of the City of Los Angeles, employed white interviewers to complete its work. That commission concluded that the riot was an aberration and was regretted in the African American community. Their major recommendations included hiring increased numbers of African American police officers and installing two-way radios in ambulances. Obviously, the interviewers can make a difference in the data collected.

Determining Reliability and Validity

In structured interviews the methods to determine reliability and validity are identical to those for questionnaires. Interviewers are also expected to make notes on the nature of the interview so that responses can be put in context. If a respondent seems distracted, the interviewer is expected to provide such a report on the interview form. If a respondent indicates difficulty in understanding questions, such information should be recorded. Check questions frequently are added to interviews to make sure that consistent responses are received. Thus, signs of reliability may be found from several different sources.

interviewers look for additional clues of reliable and valid responses

When an interview goes properly, validity claims often are quite strong. Since interviews permit use of follow-up questions, researchers can often tell whether the respondents are reacting to the questions as the researcher intended. In fact, interpreting items may be quite clear. The interviewer attempts to figure out what the subject is "driving at" in addition to getting simple answers to questions. Thus, validity claims are a natural counterpart of sound interview methods.

Sampling Subjects

As with questionnaire studies, interviewees should be selected to represent the population. Interviewers must isolate populations, decide on methods to sample events, and select an appropriate number. To secure a useful sample, individuals must be contacted to get their permission to be interviewed. Thus, interviewers must take time to promote participation before the sample can be taken. Face-to-face interviews may have a higher completion rate than questionnaires since most people have difficulty refusing to talk to another person. For interview studies, response rates in the neighborhood of 70% or more are quite common (McNeill, 1990, p. 40). Thus, collecting a sample may be as involving for interviews as it is for questionnaire methods.

sampling in interviews

Analyzing and Interpreting Results

Interview studies typically employ statistical tools to analyze results. Since some information—such as comments and explanations made by respondents—may be qualitative data, researchers might use special tools for these data. Sometimes

interpretation

SPECIAL DISCUSSION 10–3
Credibility of Questionnaire and Interview Data

Some researchers question whether we can trust information from questionnaires and interviews (Nisbett & Wilson, 1977a, 1977b; Wilson & Nisbett, 1978). There are two general concerns. First, they doubt that respondents are aware enough to give useful reactions. Sometimes people may not know how they feel about topics. Though there have been responses to such attacks (e.g., White, 1980), there is little doubt that it is not sensible to ask people questions that they cannot answer. Researchers have tried to deal with these matters by including questions that test whether respondents are responding accurately and with awareness. Martin Orne (1970) recommended that accuracy of respondent reports should be checked by the use of "sacrifice groups." These groups are interrupted during the interview or questionnaire process to see if they really understand what is meant by specific questions. Since these respondents have been distracted somewhat, they are "sacrificed" and their responses are used only to validate the survey question content.

A second problem involves subjects' *recall* of information. Researchers often ask people to remember such things as an argument with a parent or a recent conversation with a friend (e.g. Motley & Reeder, 1995). But people often recall things inaccurately. Researchers sometimes have dealt with the difficulty by asking more than one person to describe the same event—such as a conversation—and obtaining a common description. Another method involves using carefully designed **funnel questions** that start very broadly and then move to increasingly specific details. This method appears to enhance the accuracy of recalled information from respondents (Adair & Spinner, 1981). Sometimes simply instructing the respondents to respond honestly and accurately can enhance accuracy (Bowers, 1967).

content analyses or special statistics are employed. Regardless of the methods, however, the researcher tries to interpret results to reveal relationships among variables.

interviews can probe for reasons behind the answers

Unlike many questionnaire studies, interviews can produce interpretations for the reasons behind answers. By reporting on the results of follow-up questions and funnel question patterns, interviewers often gain insight to explain previously unknown reasons. Of course, the interviewer may report what he or she expects to see rather than the facts of the matter. But interviews can also yield information that might otherwise "fall between the cracks" of formal questions. It should be emphasized that research using interviews is not somehow superior to questionnaire research. In many ways, questionnaires provide controls on investigator behavior that interviews do not. Whether a particular study should use questionnaires or interviews must be decided by considering the purpose of the research and the degree of maturity of the research area.

THE FOCUS GROUP SURVEY

A **focus group** is "an interview style designed for small groups. . . . To be more specific, focus group interviews are either guided or unguided discussion addressing a particular topic of interest or relevance to the group and the researcher" (Berg, 1995, p. 68). Rather than interviewing one person at a time, a carefully selected collection of people is interviewed together in a session led by a moderator or facilitator. By asking key questions, the moderator finds the sentiments of the group and the reasons for their views. Unlike many group discussions, focus groups feature controlled group discussion in which information is gathered to meet the researcher's needs. There are four general purposes of focus groups (Wimmer & Dominick, 1997, p. 97):

- to gather preliminary information for a research project,
- to help develop questionnaire items for survey research,
- to understand reasons behind a particular phenomenon, or
- to test preliminary ideas or plans.

This method can be very helpful in both field and applied settings, and the most prominent uses have been in mass media, advertising, political campaigns, and communication and the law. In fact, any time researchers are interested in knowing *why* people feel as they do, rather than the proportions that feel a certain way, focus groups may be appropriate. This distinctive purpose is very important:

> If quantification is important, it is wise to supplement the focus group with other research tools that permit more specific questions to be addressed to a more representative sample. Many people unfamiliar with focus group research incorrectly assume that the method will answer questions of "how many" or "how much." In fact, focus group research is intended to gather qualitative data to answer questions such as "why" and "how." (Wimmer & Dominick, 1997, p. 98)

The method of focus group interviews was developed during World War II when efforts were make to assess the effectiveness of morale-boosting radio programs (Libresco, 1983; Merton, 1987, p. 552). After the war most work with focus groups was completed by advertising and marketing researchers (Hayes & Tathum, 1989). Yet, since the 1980s focus groups have become popular in other research fields including family studies (Lengua et al., 1992), health education (Basch, 1987, 1989), intercultural studies (Pramualratana, Havanon, & Knodel, 1985) and, of course, communication (Foss & Alexander, 1996).

The Focus Group Method

Focus group studies usually involve five general steps (after Dominick & Wimmer, 1997, pp. 99–100, 455–456).

1. *Assembling the Groups.* Focus groups are not random samples of individuals, though focus groups may be randomly assigned to different conditions where they may be exposed to different messages. Focus group participants are screened to obtain a particular sample of interest. For instance, researchers might want to sample only people over 45 years old to react to a Metamucil commercial. Others might wish to create a "shadow jury" composed of people who have the same backgrounds, ages, occupations, and religions as actual jurors in a court trial. In

focus group defined

focus group purposes

background of the focus group method

application of focus groups

steps for focus groups

1. assembling groups

such cases as these, collecting samples is based on careful screening of individuals often by use of a series of questions to make sure that the participants are "qualified" to be in a study.

size ranges from 6 to 12

There is some controversy about the ideal size for a focus group. Some recommend between 6 to 10 participants (Morgan, 1989, p. 43). Others recommend as many as 12 (Lengua et al., 1992, p. 163). Regardless of the size, the groups are composed of people who are targeted because they possess characteristics of interest to the researchers. Sometimes researchers may use only one focus group, but most of the time at least two focus groups are obtained. The participants typically are paid for their time, and most of the time participants are requested to sign forms in which they promise to keep the focus group discussions confidential.

more than one group typically used

2. preparing study mechanics

2. *Preparing Study Mechanics.* The physical surroundings of the focus group are fairly standard. Group participants may be recruited (often by a field service that specializes in securing focus group members) in shopping malls, by telephone, or even by referrals. Once they agree, they may be asked to attend a focus group session, sometimes immediately but often some days later. The session may be at special facilities or perhaps at a conference room in a hotel or motel. In some settings observers watch the group from behind a one-way mirror. On other occasions, observers may listen to the discussion from another room. The focus group exchanges are recorded on audio- or videotape. A variation of the traditional focus group involves what is called the **telefocus session** in which focus group sessions are completed by teleconferencing methods over the telephone.

the telefocus session identified

3. preparing session materials and questions

3. *Preparing Focus Group Session Materials and Questions.* Experienced focus group leaders prepare a "moderator's guide" that describes the events to occur during the session, their order, and the questions that are to be asked (though the moderator is invited to ask additional unscripted follow-up questions). Many focus group facilitators like to have the participants complete a questionnaire before the formal focus group begins. This step makes sure that the participants are thinking about the topic as the discussion starts. This step also may ask respondents to take a stand on particular issues. By doing so, respondents may be increasingly willing to speak up even if their opinions are in the minority. A set of questions, usually of the open-ended format are designed to get information from group participants. For instance, in a shadow jury, participants may be asked to watch the trial each day and then indicate what evidence they found most memorable, which lawyers they liked or disliked (and why), and things they did not understand. They might be asked to watch a "rough draft" of an opening statement so that they might give their reactions to it. Regardless of the application, initial questions to be asked of the focus group are prepared in advance.

a presession questionnaire may increase willingness to speak

4. conducting the session

4. *Conducting the Session.* The moderator usually introduces the broad topic to the group, and the focus group participants often are presented with some type of stimulus message to get the discussion going. Focus group members may be shown a TV commercial or they might listen to a radio version of a political campaign message. Then members are asked to begin considering questions related to the topic. The group members are encouraged to respond to others in the group and to link new ideas to others they have heard.

Facilitators are not restricted to the questions that are prepared as part of the "moderator's guide." Instead, the facilitator is free to explore comments and issues raised by members of the group. Of course, this exploration requires as much art as preparation on the part of the moderator, Yet, by asking follow-up questions and tracing new ideas, the moderator helps the group complete a thorough analysis of the topic. **questions not restricted to moderator's guide**

Sometimes moderators have to deal with different sorts of group members including **challenges to deal with people**

shy people who must be encouraged to speak up;

know-it-all people who must be prevented from dominating the group;

over-talkers who must be encouraged to be brief;

obnoxious people who must be cut off and perhaps removed from the group. (Wimmer & Dominick, 1997, p. 460)

A skillful facilitator is vital in dealing with such different people. Above all else, the moderator must help the members of the focus group work well together despite any differences they may bring with them.

Sometimes focus group deliberations can be completed in one meeting, such as the focus groups collected at shopping malls to react to products and services. Many times, however, focus groups involve many meetings over a period of weeks. Thus, the pacing of sessions becomes an issue of interest. Rather than hold a few lengthy sessions, most moderators prefer to host many short sessions. **single or multiple meetings**

5. *Analyzing Data and Preparing a Summary Report.* The moderator or research team is responsible for documenting the results of the focus group. The report given to the sponsor may be brief or lengthy depending on the agreement that is made. In most cases, the facilitator draws conclusions about the trends observed in the group, paying particular attention to the reasons group members had for their opinions. In some cases, the report consists of a detailed content analysis of the comments made by the group members. When an outside sponsor is involved, the sponsor is permitted to take possession of any recordings of the focus groups. **5. analyzing data and reporting**

Focus Group Advantages

Focus groups have become popular not just in marketing and the law, but in general social science research as well. The reasons for this popularity are not hard to understand. **advantages:**

First, focus groups are very flexible. The ability to ask additional questions beyond those in the moderator's guide make the method helpful to probe unexpected issues. Rather than restricting the moderator, focus groups often are designed to give the facilitator the freedom to move into areas that were uncharted by the original researchers. **1. flexible**

Second, focus groups are very helpful in pilot studies. By giving a focus group copies of survey forms or questionnaires, it is possible to get feedback regarding areas of possible misunderstanding. Researchers can often avoid research disasters by using focus groups to catch mistakes before they actually happen. In addition, when an area has not yet been explored, focus groups appear to be useful ways to discover what variables and settings are most worth identifying and studying (Morgan, 1989). **2. useful in pilot studies**

**3. may promote
honest idea sharing**

Third, many focus groups promote frank and honest sharing of ideas that might not occur in other settings. Not only does probing for reasons behind answers promote insight, but people are often willing to "open up" when they are in groups. They may be stimulated by comments from other group members to share their frank opinions in ways that would be lost in other interviews or questionnaires. Unfortunately, it also is

**but fewer original
ideas**

the case that research has revealed that group interviews produce fewer original ideas than individual interviews (Fern, 1982).

Focus Group Disadvantages

disadvantages:

For all their benefits, focus groups have some drawbacks. In each case, however, the drawbacks limit their applications, rather than negate the method as a whole.

**1. cannot generalize
to population**

First, one cannot generalize results from one focus group to an entire population. Since focus groups are not people selected at random, it may be that results gathered from this setting are not shared to the same degree in the population as a whole. In addition, since every group is not asked the same exact questions (though a set of starting questions is help in common), the sessions themselves are not identical. This limitation aside, however, focus groups are not undertaken for purposes of generalizing samples to entire populations. They are completed to help make improvements in future research and to discover the reasons behind opinions people have. Thus, researchers who wish to generalize results of focus groups must complete additional survey research as well.

**2. only as good as
the moderator**

Second, the focus group is only as good as the ability of the moderator. An unskilled moderator may act in ways that bias the group. Especially in lengthy focus groups, the moderator may unintentionally reveal his or her own biases on the topic. By the tone of questions or the use of nonverbal cues, the facilitator may encourage some kinds of responses and inhibit others. In addition, the moderator must be able to control members who might attempt to dominate the group. Unless the moderator is in control of the group, the group may not be productive.

**3. reasons may
become increasingly
extreme**

Third, as a result of group discussion, many sets of reasons and comments tend to become more and more extreme. In one study (Sussman et al., 1991), focus group responses were compared to questionnaire responses. Those deliberating in focus groups became more extreme and less moderate as a result of their deliberations. Thus, the effect of additional group participation may lead to extreme shifts of opinion that may mislead researchers about true feelings.

NETWORK ANALYSIS

Network analyses are most often used in studies of organizational communication, though studies of interpersonal and group networks have also been popular. The flow of communication through a company or organization may be traced to gain insights about the ways people use information. We will consider the approach of network analysis, the method, and its limitations.

The Approach of Network Analysis

**network analysis
defined**

Network analysis is a method that obtains individuals' reports of their communication activities with others for the purpose of observing and describing the flow of information in a particular organizational system. In a network, some people are "in the loop" of information and others are "out of the loop." Network analysis identifies such patterns so that the situation might be described and improved. Network analysis often results in a complicated chart showing the actual flow of messages.

There are three general purposes of network analyses. First, it is used to construct maps of the interaction among people in organizations. Whereas business scholars ask, "Who has the power in the organization?" communication scholars using network analysis ask, "Who has the information?" Granted, information is a major source of power, but communication scholars focus primary attention on the nature of the message and information flow. A second purpose of network analysis involves diagnosing problems in communication flow. Often there are failures in the flow of messages (we hesitate to call them communication breakdowns because that term is technically contradictory), and people who are supposed to get information do not. By finding the roadblocks, researchers can identify these sources of difficulty so that action can be taken. In one factory in the Midwest where the author completed an applied project, changes in company procedures on sick leave and lateness policy were communicated to employees in writing on a bulletin board located outside the break room (a room with vending machines and a microwave oven). Since many employees did not read very well, checking the written messages was a chore for them—a chore they usually ignored during their short breaks. The block in the flow of information was identified, and the plant manager adopted a system to make important announcements orally to the incoming shift, rather than relying on the bulletin board alone. A third purpose of network analysis is to identify the roles played by different group members. Informal methods of communication exist in organizations. Network analysis can help identify these "grapevines." Sometimes small groups or cliques talk almost exclusively with each other. Yet, some people serve as bridges or "liaisons" between these groups, keeping up communication between them. With a knowledge of such informal communication channels, organizations may look at ways to spread critical information and methods for spotting problems before they turn into major crunches.

purposes:
1. constructing a map of interactions

2. diagnosing problems in communication flow

3. identifying roles played by different group members

The Method of Network Analysis

Network analysis involves gathering data to construct a communication map or diagram. Choosing important categories may be a challenge for researchers. Networks are not "things" that can be touched. They are patterns of communication that people use as they work with each other. Thus, networks are abstract matters that are "constructed" by people to organize information about the structure of communication. One researcher explained

choosing categories challenging

> All communication networks are constructed out of two elements: a set of communicators and one or more relations among the communicators. The relations define the nature of the connections among the communicators. Many forms of relations can be used to study societal networks. For example, a kinship relationship could be "is the partner of," "is the sister of," or "is married to." An authority relationship could be of the form "reports to" or "supervises;" a resource relation might be "shares workers with" (Monge & Miller, 1985). Communication networks are constructed out of communication relations, which describe the nature of information flow among people. Typical communication relations are "shares information with," "talks to," "receives reports from," and "discusses new ideas with." (Monge, 1987, p. 243)

steps: 1. selecting communication variables

Finding the structure of communication flow requires carrying out four steps. First, network analysts select communication variables of interest consistent with the problem question that guides all inquiry. Such elements often are the frequency people communicate with each other, the importance (or perceived importance) of the information, the direction of the communication flow, and types of communication exchanged.

2. securing individual reports

Second, the researcher secures individual reports from all members of the group. Questionnaires are often constructed for group members to identify their communication with others. Sometimes actual uses of messages can be traced (such as numbers of telephone calls placed to a given location, or numbers of memos sent *to* a person as a ratio of the number of memos sent *from* a person). Thus, network analyses may use observational or self-report data.

3. constructing network map

Third, researchers construct network maps to track information flow. Developing the network patterns can be complex since the flow of information among many people can become nested and quite involved. Even so, as Figure 10.1 shows, some general patterns may emerge. Each pattern has some predictable communication effects. For instance, the chain pattern tends to be efficient when direct orders are to be given along a strict command structure, but the overall member satisfaction can be low since often only a limited picture of the entire project is possible for most group members. On the other hand, the all channel pattern permits individuals to coordinate their activities with others, but if there is a struggle for leadership or power within the group, or if any network members are hostile to any others, the all channel model may not be particularly useful.

FIGURE 10.1
Types of
Communication
Networks

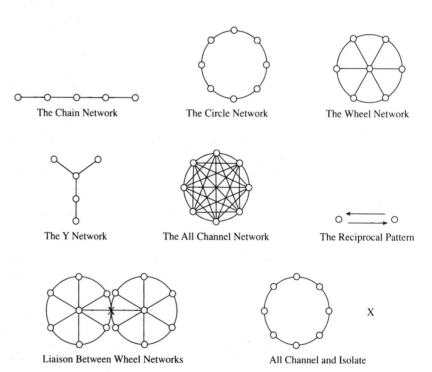

The Chain Network   The Circle Network   The Wheel Network

The Y Network   The All Channel Network   The Reciprocal Pattern

Liaison Between Wheel Networks   All Channel and Isolate

The reciprocal, liaison, and isolate patterns are interesting. A reciprocal pattern is one in which individuals share a nearly identical network pattern among themselves. People who are personally close or who have similar sorts of positions that include a lot of teamwork are examples of such a pattern. The liaison person links people of different networks. In Figure 10.1 the liaison between two groups (identified by the X) is performed by one person who—officially or unofficially—is a member of both groups. The isolate is an individual who is not actively involved in any established communication network. This person usually is bypassed and occasionally may not even be aware that he or she is an isolate in the eyes of others. These individuals are out of the communication flow and, thus, may not hold potential for making productive contributions until their involvement levels are altered. These patterns may be interpreted and the description used to help make improvements.

interpreting network patterns: reciprocal, liaison,

isolate

A final step in network analysis involves interpreting results by comparing the network with a desired standard, such as an organizational chart. Checking whether people who *should* be communicating with each other really *are* allows evaluation of the flow of information. By contrasting the network against the organizational chart, the logic of the organization's structure can be verified—or questioned. By finding that people who are not expected to communicate actively with each other actually are involved in extensive conversation, it is possible to identify where informal channels emerge. These channels may be nurtured and attempts to explain them explored.

comparing the network with a desired standard

Limitations of the Approach

Though most often used in studies of organizations and bureaucracies, network analyses have looked at communication within families, job networking groups, social networks, organizational networks, and links among people of different organizations. Even so, there also are two major limitations to network studies. First, network analysis emphasizes structural information rather than content information. Though we can identify who is talking with whom, it is difficult to know the content of the information. People could be socializing, or they could be working on common projects. We may not know. Some researchers attempt to get additional information about the dominant sort of information exchanged, but structure of communication flow is dominant in network analysis. Second, network analysis allows researchers to identify relationships among communicators, but the technique does not permit the researcher to make claims about the reasons for the relationships. We cannot know for sure why a person was bypassed in the network, though the network may show that bypassing has occurred. We cannot identify why someone became a liaison between groups, but we can identify relationships to be explored with other research methods.

limitations

1. emphasis on structural information rather than content

2. reasons for the relationships not known

SUMMARY

The term *empirical* actually means "observable." Descriptive empirical research involves gathering data to test statements. It is most invited when problem questions ask about current descriptions of things and explore explanations that characterize things as they are now. Surveys cannot answer questions about cause-and-effect relationships, though experiments can (an experiment introduces a variable and determines its effects while controlling all other variables). A survey is an empirical study that uses questionnaires or interviews to discover descriptive characteristics of phenomena.

Questionnaires are survey forms in which individuals respond to items they have read. There are six steps in completing a questionnaire survey: (1) selecting questions and instructions (including developing questions, facing tactical issues in phrasing questions, and preparing survey forms); (2) formatting questionnaires to promote response; (3) determining reliability (the consistency of a measure) and validity (the degree to which a measure actually measures what is claimed) including other controls such as check questions, which ask the same question twice (once phrased positively and once phrased negatively) at different locations, measures of test-taking behavior, and polarity rotation of items (to avoid response set, or the tendency for subjects to follow predictable patterns of responding to test items); (4) sampling; (5) administering the questionnaire; (6) analyzing and interpreting results.

Interview methods are used to increase willingness to participate and to gather information that might be lost in the questionnaire method. The steps of interview studies include: (1) selecting questions (structured interviews use specific lists of questions; unstructured interviews permit respondents to indicate their reactions to general issues without guidance from highly detailed questions); (2) training and controlling the behavior of interviewers; (3) determining reliability and validity; (4) sampling subjects; (5) analyzing and interpreting results.

A focus group is an interview style designed for small groups. To be specific, focus group interviews are either guided or unguided discussion addressing a particular topic of interest or relevance to the group and the researcher. There are four general purposes of focus groups: (1) to gather preliminary information for a research project; (2) to help develop questionnaire items for survey research; (3) to understand reasons behind a particular phenomenon; (4) to test preliminary ideas or plans. Focus group studies usually involve five general steps: (1) assembling the groups (participants—usually 6 to 12 people—are screened to obtain a particular sample of interest); (2) preparing study mechanics including settings and recording devices (a variation is called the telefocus session in which focus group sessions are completed by teleconferencing methods over the telephone); (3) preparing focus group session materials and questions including a "moderator's guide" that describes the events to occur during the session, their order, and the questions that are to be asked (participants often complete a questionnaire before the formal focus group begins to assure that participants are thinking about the topic and to stimulate respondents to speak up even if their opinions are in the minority); (4) conducting the session, including introducing the topic, presenting some type of stimulus message, answering questions related to the topic, and responding to others in the group (the moderator is free to explore comments and issues raised by members of the group and also must deal with problem people in the group); (5) analyzing data and preparing a summary report that may be a facilitator's summary or a detailed content analysis of the comments made by the group members. Focus groups have three primary advantages: (1) Focus groups are very flexible and give the facilitator the freedom to move into areas that were uncharted by the original researchers. (2) Focus groups are very helpful in pilot studies. (3) Focus groups promote frank and honest sharing of ideas that might not occur in other settings. Focus groups have three disadvantages: (1) One cannot generalize results from one focus group to an entire population. (2) Focus groups are only as good as the ability of the moderator. (3) As a result of group discussion, many sets of reasons and comments tend to become more and more extreme.

Network analysis is a method that obtains individuals' reports of their communication activities with others for the purpose of observing and describing the flow of information in a particular organizational system. There are three general purposes for network analyses: (1) to construct a map of the interaction among people in an organization; (2) to diagnose problems in communication flow; (3) to identify the roles played by different group members. Informal channels of communication exist in organizations. Network analysis involves four steps: (1) selecting communication variables consistent with the problem question; (2) securing individual reports from members of the group; (3) constructing network maps and tracking information flow; (4) interpreting results by comparing the network with a desired standard, such as an organizational chart. There are two major limitations on network studies: (1) They emphasize structural information rather than content information; (2) They allow researchers to identify relationships among communicators, but not the reasons for the relationships.

TERMS FOR REVIEW

empirical
experiment
survey
questionnaires
validity
reliability
check questions
polarity rotation
response set

anonymity
confidentiality
structured interviews
unstructured interviews
funnel questions
focus group
telefocus session
network analysis

CHAPTER 11

Experimental Research

Experiment is the consummation of the marriage of reason and experience, and although it is not in itself the life of the mind, it is the most passionate and fruitful expression of our intellectual life and loves.

–Abraham Kaplan

BEFORE WE GET STARTED . . .

Though descriptive empirical studies can reveal many relationships, some questions require experiments to answer. This chapter defines experiments, explains how they are designed, and discusses sources of invalidity and strategies to deal with special problems. It also explains the research abbreviations that experimenters use to examine hypotheses.

THE NOTION OF AN EXPERIMENT

Most people think that an experiment is just another name for a carefully completed study. But experiments involve much more than being careful. It is helpful to understand the logic of an experiment, the concept of control, and the sorts of research questions that are suitable for experimental research.

SPECIAL DISCUSSION 11–1
A Question of Ethics: Deception in Research Designs

Deception in an experiment occurs when "the research participants have been either: (1) uninformed that an experiment was being conducted or (2) intentionally misled about the nature of the study in which they are participating" (Greenberg & Folger, 1988, p. 40). Despite heated debate about the issue among psychologists, as recently as 1983 deception was found in 49.7% of the experiments published in the *Journal of Personality and Social Psychology* and 81.2% of the experiments published in the *Journal of Experimental Social Psychology* (Adair, Dushenko, & Lindsay, 1985). Deception may occur in three major ways.

1. *Concealing the true purpose of the experiment.* Though researchers are not expected to reveal their research hypotheses to subjects in experiments, it does not follow that researchers have a right to lie to subjects. Indeed, a

---

An **experiment** is the study of the effects of variables manipulated by a researcher in a situation where all other influences are controlled, and completed for the purpose of establishing causal relationships. It might help to break that definition down into its parts. First, experiments study "the effects of variables manipulated by a researcher." Unlike survey researchers, experimenters introduce variables (called "manipulating variables") that were not present to begin with. Then, they can assess the impact of these variables. Survey studies just try to identify associations among variables, but experiments add experimental variables to the existing setting to see what effects might be found. The second part of the definition states that "all other influences are controlled." This requirement is the hard part. Most of the topics covered in this chapter involve ways to exercise experimental control. The third part of this definition states that we complete experiments "for the purpose of establishing causal relationships." Though the method of history can permit researchers to draw long-term cause-and-effect relationships, only experiments can provide immediate evidence. If we can control other sources of variation and introduce one new experimental variable, then any effects must be caused by the experimental variable.

As mentioned, exercising control is not easy. When introducing variables, a careless researcher might manipulate other variables by accident. For instance, in a study on the impact of evidence on persuasion, researchers could manipulate message length or language as well. Thus, the evidence manipulation may be mixed up with other sources of variation. This situation is called **confounding** and occurs when variation from one source is mixed (or confused) with variation from another source so that it is impossible to know whether effects are due to the impact of either variable separately or some combination of the two. Such confounding can mislead researchers. A hypothesis should deal with only one experimental variable, but the actual experiment might involve a complex of independent variables. Confounding hides another variable in the hypothesis and makes inference impossible.

experiment defined

1. manipulating variables

2. control of variables

3. attempt to find causal relationships

confounding defined

respect for others requires that researchers follow the same standards as the rest of society—standards that view lying as wrong (Warwick, 1975; Goldstein, 1981). Kelman (1967) sadly observed that in some experimental settings "the usual criteria for ethical interpersonal conduct become irrelevant" (p. 5). Yet, even Kelman admitted that sometimes deceiving subjects could be justified to secure scientific knowledge (see also Baron, 1981). Most researchers can avoid this form of deception by telling subjects what the study is about in very broad language—without revealing the independent and dependent variables. Instead of saying "This project is a study examining the amount of evidence used in speeches on attitude change," you could say "This project is a study of the ways people respond to different sorts of persuasive messages."

2. *Concealing the purpose of the participants' own actions.* This problem is created when subjects are told that their behavior is designed for one purpose when, in fact, it is not. For instance, Festinger and Carlsmith (1959) completed a classic study in which "subjects expressed their attitudes about an experimental task under the pretext of informing a waiting participant about the task they just completed" (Greenberg & Folger, 1988, p. 42). Such behavior may raise a problem regarding deception.

3. *Concealing experiences that researchers have planned for subjects.* This form of deception occurs when the researchers keep the subjects ignorant of the things that will happen to them in the course of the experiment.

The second and third sources of deception are not easily handled. Aside from the ethics of lying to subjects, there also is a matter of informed consent. If subjects do not know the true reasons they are asked to perform behavior or if subjects do not know what researchers have planned for them, they cannot really give their informed consent to participate. Without knowing what is in store for them, they do not really have a free choice about whether to participate in the research.

Granted, most subjects do not view experimental deception as a problem (Clark & Word, 1974; Ring, Wallston, & Corey, 1973), but the ethical issues raised do not disappear just because no one complains. One suggested alternative involves asking subjects to role play their behavior. Instead of telling a person that he or she is writing an essay to be used by representatives of the U.S. State Department for a pamphlet they are preparing (Elms & Janis, 1965), subjects may be asked to write essays "as if" they were to be used in such a setting. Though this role-playing strategy avoids many ethical difficulties (Bok, 1974; Darroch & Steiner, 1970; Kelman, 1967), the ability to generalize such results remains controversial (see Freedman, 1969; Ginsburg, 1979).

The Maxmincon Principle

Experimenters must stay in command of all sources of variation. Fred Kerlinger phrased this need as the **maxmincon principle.** It is a reminder to experimenters to follow procedures of carefully designed experimentation.

> *Maximize systematic variance, control extraneous systematic variance, and minimize error variance.* In other words, we must *control variance.*
>
> According to this principle, by constructing an efficient research design the investigator attempts (1) to maximize the variance of the variable or variables of his [or her] substantive research hypothesis, (2) to control the variance of extraneous or "unwanted" variables that may have an effect on his [or her] experimental outcomes, and (3) to minimize the error or random variance, including so-called errors of measurement. (Kerlinger, 1986, p. 284)

the maxmincon principle

The principle advises researchers to plan studies so that the impact of variables of interest will be recognizable while all others are held constant. Studies designed with this principle in mind tend to be rigorous, and the results are unambiguous. Thus, you should look for evidence that researchers attempted to exercise control over all sorts of variation in their experiments. A sloppy experiment will not control extraneous variance; a solid experiment will.

Questions and Hypotheses in Experimental Designs

Experiments are designed to answer research questions that deal with cause-and-effect relationships. But there is a slight catch. The causes must be matters that can be manipulated by the researcher. Thus, you cannot complete an experiment to show that being a woman causes a person to be more persuaded by a fear appeal than does being a man. One cannot reasonably manipulate the sex of subjects—we have to take people pretty much as they are. You can conclude that the sex of the receiver is *related* to the persuasiveness of fear appeals, but there is no way to say that the sex of the receiver *caused* the effect (as opposed to differences in self-esteem or levels of submissiveness). On the other hand, it is possible to find out if messages that use internal organizers (previews and summaries) cause more attitude change than messages that omit them. Messages can be prepared by the experimenter with and without internal organizers and then presented to randomly selected audiences. Thus, experiments are limited to dealing with causal relationships stemming from **experimental independent variables.**

experimental designs permit drawing causal claims about variables that can be manipulated

experimental independent variables

Hypotheses in experiments are phrased to explore such causal relationships. Typical experimental hypotheses in our field have included:

experimental hypotheses probe causal relationships

- During early adolescence (12 to 15 years), the presence of a label [a label on a recording warning of potentially offensive material] should, other things being equal, make a given song or album less attractive rather than more so. (Christenson, 1992, p. 107)
- Mirroring behavior [mimicking the nonverbal behavior of another person] that is attributed as deliberate will be read as sending greater relational messages of similarity and interest than will behaviors seen to [be] intentional. (Manusov, 1992, p. 73)

- As the level of sexual imagery in rock music videos increases, subjects will find both the visual and music content more appealing. (Hansen & Hansen, 1990, p. 213)

In each case, the hypothesis suggested a cause-and-effect relationship that was manipulated successfully in experimental research.[1]

The Concept of Control

control defined

Control refers to methods researchers use to remove or hold constant the effects of nuisance variables. The effort to improve control increases the ability of researchers to make clear statements that experimental variables are responsible for observed effects. To make sure that all elements in an experiment are controlled except for the new variable introduced by the experimenter, several major approaches are used: elimination, holding constant, matching, blocking, randomization, and statistical control (after Kerlinger, 1986, pp. 287–289).

- **Elimination and removal.** We are rarely able to study the impact of one variable by itself. Other "nuisance" or "intervening" variables often get in the way. Careful researchers try to control these influences. The most obvious way to control for a nuisance variable is to remove it from the experimental setting. For instance, researchers often control extraneous variables such as temperature and illumination problems by collecting data in classroom "laboratory" settings where these sources of distraction may be eliminated completely.
- **Holding constant.** Technically, all control methods involve taking nuisance variables and holding them constant. When we eliminate variables, the nuisance variables are held constant at "zero influence." Sometimes researchers control for other variables by limiting the range of intervening variables so that they are equal across studies. There are three major ways to hold variables constant in experiments. First, limiting the population may control a nuisance variable. For instance, in very early self-disclosure research, results showed wild variation when men and women were paired with each other. To control for the sex composition of pairs, researchers soon learned to limit their studies only to populations of people of the same sex self-disclosing to each other. Second, using subjects as their own controls may control for the impact of nuisance variables. People may be sampled before and after some experimental treatment to identify their average amount of improvement despite any differences they may have had at the outset. Third, **counterbalancing** rotates the sequence in which experimental treatments are introduced to subjects in an effort to control for extraneous variables, such as fatigue or cumulative learning effects. With this method, the fatigue effects do not go away, but the variation produced is distributed across the experiment equally—hence, the term *counterbalanced.*

counterbalancing defined

---

[1]The third hypothesis was supported and the first two were not.

- **Matching.** The method of matching involves pairing subjects on some variable on which they share equal levels and then assigning one of them to an experimental group and the other to a control condition. Researchers sometimes use this method to control for initial differences people bring to a study. For instance, people might be matched because they share the same age, sex, job classification, intelligence level, or the like. In a study of attention to content of commercials by children, it might be important to control for the sex of the child, since girls tend to develop verbal abilities earlier than boys. Thus, a researcher might identify the number of boys and girls in a sample and then assign half of the girls to one experimental condition and half to a control group. Similarly half the boys might be assigned to each group in the experiment. Researchers can match individuals or groups of people (the most frequent use of matching). Even so, you should know that some researchers consider many applications of matching doubtful since they can introduce distortions. You can "overmatch" subjects so that they no longer represent the population. Furthermore, when matching on several nuisance variables, you may begin to lose subjects. As Fred Kerlinger explained: "If one decides to match intelligence, sex, and social class, one may be fairly successful in matching the first two variables but not in finding pairs that are fairly equal on all three variables. Add a fourth variable and the problem becomes difficult, often impossible to solve" (1986, p. 289).

  matching defined

  matching individuals or groups

  limits on matching

- **Blocking.** Blocking adds a nuisance variable into the design as another independent variable of interest.[2] In a study of the impact of a female source's physical attractiveness on the persuasiveness of a message, the sex of the respondents might make a big difference in the results obtained. Thus, one might include the sex of the respondents in the study as another variable. Blocking permits one to draw conclusions about the impact of each independent variable separately or as part of an interaction. Of course, adding variables to a study requires that researchers have fairly sizable samples to permit the subdivisions. If such samples are available, however, this method may be among the most desirable options for control.

  blocking defined

- **Randomization.** Randomization, a basic requirement for sound experimental control and subsequent inferential statistical analyses, involves assigning subjects so that each event is equally likely to belong to any experimental or control condition. In short, randomization involves using the rules of chance to balance groups of subjects. Respondents may be selected at random from the population, and they may also be assigned at random to experimental or control conditions. The ways in which groups of people can differ from each

  randomization defined

  random selection and assignment

---

[2]Some writers prefer to reserve the term "blocking" for situations in which the additional variable factor is on a nominal scale, such as the sex of respondents (Campbell & Stanley, 1970). When the additional variable is on a ranking scale, they suggest using the term "stratifying" rather than "blocking." If the additional variable is measured on an interval or ratio scale (such as dividing groups into high, moderate, and low self-esteem groups), they recommend using the term "leveling."

other is almost infinite. Yet, randomization increases the likelihood that groups of people in different conditions will be comparable in ways that researchers might otherwise never imagine. Fred Kerlinger explained the importance of randomization:

> The *principle of randomization* may be stated thus: Since, in random procedures every member of a population has an equal chance of being selected, members with certain distinguishing characteristics—male or female, high or low intelligence, conservative or liberal, and so on and on—will, if selected, probably be offset in the long run by the selection of other members of the population with counterbalancing quantities or qualities of the characteristics. . . . (1986, p. 115)
>
> Another way to phrase it is: if randomization has been accomplished, then the experimental groups can be considered statistically equal in all possible ways. This does not mean, of course, that the groups are equal in all the possible variables. We already know that by chance the groups can be unequal, but the probability of their being equal is greater, with proper randomization, than the probability of their not being equal. For this reason control of the extraneous variance by randomization is a powerful method of control. All other methods leave many possibilities of inequality. . . . A precept that springs from this equalizing power of randomization, then, is: Whenever it is possible to do so, randomly assign subjects to experimental groups and conditions, and randomly assign conditions and other factors to experimental groups. (1986, p. 288)

It should be noted that individual differences do not go away when randomization is used. Instead, these sources of variation appear as random variation or background noise across conditions.[3] Thus, randomization controls a host of sources of variation so that they do not influence one experimental condition more than any other.

analysis of covariance and partial correlation as methods of statistical control

- **Statistical control.** If you can measure a nuisance variable, it is possible to use statistical tools to hold it constant. **Analysis of covariance** and **partial correlation** are two common methods of statistical control. They compute the variation associated with each nuisance variable and then separate it from the remaining total variation in the experiment. Analysis of covariance is used when the independent variables are broken down into nominal categories (such as experimental group vs. control group). The nuisance variable is called a *covariate* and is used as the basis for adjusting output variable scores. When studies investigate correlations among variables, partial correlations are used to explore the relationship between two variables while holding a third one constant.

Though all methods of control are related to some statistical model (blocking and analysis of covariance methods are equivalent, for instance) the major tactical differences described here should help you understand the options available to researchers.

---

[3]Actually, randomization causes assignable variation from nuisance variables to be confounded (or confused) with random variation.

**SPECIAL DISCUSSION 11–2
Additional Control Issues**

Experiments require control over all sources of variation. The major sources of invalidity deal with failures to exhibit such strong control. Some other common sources of error in experiments are the following (after Isaac & Michael, 1981, pp. 85–89):

- *The **halo effect.*** Sometimes strong positive or negative impressions of a source of communication may affect all ratings that follow. Researchers may find that their credibility creates pressure in the minds of subjects to respond positively or negatively, regardless of experimental treatments used.
- *The **placebo effect.*** In medical research, a placebo is a stimulus containing no medicine or no experimental treatment at all. In nonmedical work, subjects may show changes even in the absence of treatments, in reaction to the mental suggestion that they may have been given some stimulus. Thus, researchers attempt to use control groups and to exercise control over methods of providing treatments to groups.
- *The **John Henry effect.*** Named after the folklore hero who died trying to outwork a machine, this effect describes the actions of people who try to perform extra hard when they participate in an experiment. Thus, their behavior may not be consistent with their normal activity.
- *The pitfall of "do nothing" control groups.* "Control groups ordinarily should experience *all things* in common with the treatment group *except* the critical factor, per se. Control groups that 'do nothing' are apt to differ from the treatment groups in more ways than just the isolated treatment variable." (Isaac & Michael, 1981, p. 88).

EXPERIMENTAL VALIDITY AND INVALIDITY

Experiments can blow up in a researcher's face. When experiments fall apart, they have fallen prey to sources of invalidity. Sources of **experimental invalidity** are errors that prevent researchers from drawing unequivocal conclusions. There are two families of invalidity in experiments: internal invalidity and external invalidity.

experimental invalidity defined

Internal Invalidity

Internal invalidity is the presence of contamination that prevents the experimenter from concluding that a study's experimental variable is responsible for the observed effects. Table 11.1 lists the major sources of internal invalidity in experiments. To argue for cause-and-effect relationships, these sources of invalidity must be controlled or removed. If a researcher completes an experiment that controls for seven out of the eight sources of internal invalidity, the experiment still cannot lead to an unequivocal statement of experimental effect. That is, if all sources of internal invalidity are not controlled, it is not possible to claim that any observed effects were caused by the

internal invalidity defined

TABLE 11.1 Sources of Internal Invalidity

History: Events not controlled by the researcher that occur during the experiment between any pretest and posttest

Selection: Sampling biases in selecting or assigning subjects to experimental or control conditions (in essence rigging the study by taking samples capriciously)

Maturation: Changes that naturally occur over time (including fatigue or suspicion), even if subjects are left alone

Testing: Alterations that occur when subjects are tested and made testwise or anxious in ways that affect them when they are given a second test

Instrumentation: Changes in the use of measuring instruments from the pretest to the post-test, including changes in raters or interviewers who collect the data in different conditions

Statistical Regression: Shift produced when subjects are selected due to some very high or very low scores on some test (such as selecting a group of people who score high in communication apprehension for participation in some experimental treatment) and then changes on that measurement are tracked in the experiment; statistical regression holds that people will "regress toward the mean" even if they simply are left alone

Experimental Mortality: Biases introduced when subjects differentially (nonrandomly) drop out of the experiment (for instance, subjects may drop out of a weight reduction program if they receive disappointing results—thus, the remaining subjects will show inflated levels of improvement)

Interaction of Elements: Effects created by the interaction of selection biases with differential levels of maturation, history, or any other source of variation

independent variable in the experiment. Instead, researchers have to add equivocating terms (if's and maybe's) as they draw their conclusions.

External Invalidity

external invalidity defined

External invalidity refers to the degree to which experimental results may not be generalized to other similar circumstances. In a strict sense, study findings can be generalized only to the sample groups from which they were drawn. Yet, researchers often carefully sample so that some generalization of results may be possible. Regrettably, experiments sometimes are completed in ways that make it difficult, if not impossible, to generalize results to larger populations without severe limitations. These sources of external invalidity do not mean that the experimental variable did not produce the alleged effects—internal invalidity assesses *that* issue. Instead, external invalidity sets *limits* the sorts of populations to which results may be generalized. The major sources of external invalidity are listed in Table 11.2.

Ideally, an experiment should have both internal and external validity. But researchers actually give greatest attention to internal validity issues. The concern is natural. If a study does not have internal validity, its findings cannot be generalized. Even so, researchers often comment about external invalidity when reporting their work. Research articles usually include some statements that limit research findings and call for replications to test generalizability of results to other population groups.

TABLE 11.2 Sources of External Invalidity

Interaction of Testing and the Experimental Variable: Also called pretest sensitization, this defect is created when the pretesting makes subjects either more or less sensitive to the experimental variable

Interaction of Selection and the Experimental Variable: Effects created by sampling groups in such a way that they are not representative of the population, since they are more or less sensitive to the experimental variable than other subsamples from the same population (such as sampling college students in communication studies even though they may be more or less sensitive to the independent variable than the general population of people)

Reactive Arrangements: Elements in the experimental setting that make subjects react differentially to the experimental arrangements rather than to the experimental variable alone (such matters as awareness of participation in an experiment may alter normal reactions of people)

Multiple Treatment Interference: Depending on the design, if subjects are exposed to repeated additional experimental treatments they may react in ways that are not generalizable to subjects who are uncontaminated by such additional independent variables.

SPECIFIC EXPERIMENTAL DESIGNS

Experimental designs tend to follow a protocol of notation, methods, and applications. Terms tend to be mentioned without explanation in research articles. This section will help you decipher these terms.

Notation for Experimental Designs

To show what goes on in a research design, a notation system has been developed, much like notation used to sketch out a football play. Three terms are prominent. The first of these terms is

notation:

$$O.$$

O is an abbreviation for an *observation* a researcher makes of the study's dependent variable. If several observations are made, researchers sometimes add subscript numbers to keep things straight, such as

observation

$$O_1 \qquad O_2 \qquad O_3 \qquad O_4.$$

These are translated, "observation one," "observation two," "observation three," and "observation four."[4] Regardless of the ways in which a researcher measures the observations, the observations are made to help the researcher identify the effects that are found in the study.

A second term in experimental design is

$$X.$$

---

[4]Some might read these terms as "O sub-one," "O sub-two," and so forth, but this technical affectation can be a barrier to understanding. It is best to use plain language whenever you can.

experimental
variable

This abbreviation stands for the *experimental variable* used by researchers. When there is more than one experimental variable, some researchers add subscript numbers to help keep exact conditions clear. For our introductory treatment, however, we will not clutter up our notation with such subscripts.

A final term is

R.

randomization

This letter stands for *randomization*. Those experiments that include randomization (either random assignment or random sampling) include this notation prominently. For control of systematic biases, randomization is the most effective means that may be used. Thus, it plays a strong role in sound experimentation.

Pre-Experimental Designs

Some designs have good intentions but do not really exercise the sort of control necessary for a solid experiment. They are considered here because they reflect the thinking that leads to full experiments and because they are often used by researchers who feel the need to make compromises.

- *One-Shot Case Study.* In this type of study, an experimental treatment is introduced and researchers look at effects on some output (dependent) variable. Unfortunately, as Figure 11.1 shows, this design does not really control for any source of experimental invalidity. You may have seen case studies used as teaching aids in classes you have taken. Often researchers complete case studies so that they can develop hypotheses for formal testing at a later time.
- *One Group Pretest–Posttest.* As an improvement, researchers sometimes have added a pretest. Thus, subjects in an experiment can serve as their own controls. This method is a step in the right direction—and the method frequently has been used in evaluation studies—but the design does not really control for enough sources of invalidity to permit drawing clear conclusions of experimental effects.
- *Static Group Comparisons.* This design attempts to use a control group but the two groups are not known to be comparable. A researcher may sample students in a sophomore class at 10:00 A.M. and expose them to an experimental message. The researcher also might sample students in a graduate class at 7:00 P.M. for a control group. These groups are "in tact" and cannot be presumed to be comparable at the outset. These differences can throw a monkey wrench into the entire design. Sometimes researchers will complete random sampling of a smaller subgroup from each in tact group. Yet, to assure comparability, researchers should also randomly assign subjects to experimental or control conditions.

True Experimental Designs

The three true experimental designs that follow serve as the basis for increasingly complicated factorial designs used in formal experiments.

Pretest–Posttest Control Group Design

Surely the most popular design for communication experiments, the **pretest–posttest control group design** is composed of an experimental group and a control group.

	Sources of Invalidity											
	Internal								External			
	History	Maturation	Testing	Instrumentation	Regression	Selection	Mortality	Interaction of Selection and Maturation, etc.	Interaction of Testing and X	Interaction of Selection and X	Reactive Arrangements	Multiple-X Interference
Pre-Experimental Designs:												
1. One-Shot Case Study X O	−	−				−	−				−	
2. One-Group Pretest-Posttest Design O X O	−	−	−	−	?	+	+	−	−	−	?	
3. Static-Group Comparison X O / O	+	?	+	+	+	−	−	−		−		
True Experimental Designs:												
4. Pretest-Posttest Control Group Design R O X O / R O O	+	+	+	+	+	+	+	+	−	?	?	
5. Solomon Four-Group Design R O X O / R O O / R X O / R O	+	+	+	+	+	+	+	+	+	?	?	
6. Posttest Only Control Group Design R X O / R O	+	+	+	+	+	+	+	+	+	?	?	

Note: In the tables, a minus indicates a definite weakness, a plus indicates that the factor is controlled, a question mark indicates a possible source of concern, and a blank indicates that the factor is not relevant.

It is with extreme reluctance that these summary tables are presented because they are apt to be "too helpful," and to be depended upon in place of the more complex and qualified presentation in the text. No + or − indicator should be respected unless the reader comprehends why it is placed there. In particular it is against the spirit of this presentation to create uncomprehended fears of, or confidence in, specific designs.

FIGURE 11.1
Experimental Design Validity Factors
Source: Campbell, Donald T. and Julian C. Stanley. *Experimental and Quasi-Experimental Designs for Research.* Copyright © 1963 by Houghton Mifflin Company. Used with permission.

Subjects in the experimental group are pretested. They are then exposed to the experimental variable and posttested. Subjects in the control group are treated the same way except, of course, they are not presented with the experimental variable.

You might suppose that researchers simply subtract pretests from posttests to see the amount of change observed. Despite the common sense that may be involved, there are statistical problems with analyzing "change scores." First, change scores may not have distributions that make them easy to interpret with standard statistical tools. Second, by definition, change scores have lower reliability than the original measures (Allen & Yen, 1979). Thus, prudent researchers usually try to use alternatives to change scores. Most often, researchers use a method of statistical control in

change scores are not advised

which the posttest scores of experimental and control groups are compared with the pretest scores used as a covariate.

As you can see in Figure 11.1, this design controls for all sources of internal invalidity. But the story is different when we consider external validity. Sometimes pretesting people can affect the way they respond to experimental variables. Rather than responding freshly to experimental variables, people may try to recall what they did on the pretest and respond in the same way (perhaps to avoid being "wishy washy"). Thus, the pretest may "sensitize" people and cause them to respond in somewhat inhibited ways. The internal validity of the experiment is just fine, of course, since the experimental variable is the cause of observed effects. But the results of the experiment can only be generalized directly to populations of people who also have been sensitized by a pretest. To overcome the problems with pretest sensitization, two other designs have been suggested (these designs will be mentioned next).

pretest sensitization described (margin note)

Solomon Four Groups Design

You can add control groups to examine pretesting effects directly. The **Solomon four groups design** actually uses three control groups. To check for pretest sensitization, we can compare the groups that have received a pretest with the groups that have not. If pretesting inhibited responses, the design will reveal it.[5] The problem with this design, however, is that it requires doubling the sample. Thus, it may be expensive.

Posttest Only Control Group Design

Another way to avoid pretest sensitization is to delete the pretest entirely. If the researcher does not need to pretest subjects, the **posttest only control group design** is preferred. Take a look at the static group comparison design. Do you see the difference between it and the post-test only control group design? The difference is randomization. With this extra step, the experimental and control groups are made comparable. The result is dramatic. Rather than facing the limitations of the static group comparison, the post-test only control group design introduces control over the major sources of experimental invalidity found in Table 11.1.

Factorial Designs

So far we have dealt with situations in which single experimental groups are compared to control groups. Yet, these days, you will not see as many single variable experiments as once filled our journals. When more than one independent variable is used in an experiment, it is called a **factorial design.**

Uses of Factorial Designs in Research

When variables are broken down into levels (such as high self-esteem vs. low self-esteem, high readability vs. low readability, or high dysfluency vs. low dysfluency) they are called variable factors or just **factors.** These levels of variables are used

factors defined (margin note)

---

[5]If pretest sensitization is found, all is not lost. If the experimental variable produced a significant effect, pretest sensitization was not enough to prevent experimental effects. In such cases, the impact of pretest sensitization is minor when compared to the experimental variable.

SPECIAL DISCUSSION 11–3
Single Subject Experiments

Much research in speech and hearing science has involved the **single subject design** (Herson & Barlow, 1976; Kratochwill, 1978), though the design has long been used in manufacturing under the rubric of the "component search" or "comparative experiments." Therapists attempting to find the best treatment for a patient often use the single subject design. The researcher starts by getting baseline information as a control. These observations are often abbreviated with the letter *A.* Then the new treatment—perhaps a drug or a particular type of therapy—is introduced and effects measured. The new treatment may be identified as a "B" condition (standing for a "better" option, perhaps). Then researchers withdraw the treatment and see what happens. If a new treatment is effective, one would expect to see improvements with its presence and worsening with its withdrawal. To control for potential cyclical effects that have nothing to do with treatments, the order of interventions may be altered, as in the design:

A B A B B A.

To see if differences exist, researchers compare all of the "A" conditions with all of the "B" conditions. The formula for combinations can be used to assess how often such improvement patterns could be expected to occur by chance alone.

   The approach can be—and has been—extended to studies involving two, three, or more treatment options. Though of great value in therapeutic and medical settings, the use of a single subject design has limitations including (1) it is most applicable to questions of individual difference, rather than patterns across people; (2) its limited generalizability prevents examining hypotheses of social significance to most communication researchers; (3) it limits the sorts of statistical tools that might be used to help analyze results.

[handwritten margin notes: A = baseline control; B = w/new tx. Order of intervention is varied. Advantage: Many tx options can be looked at. Weakness: answers ?s of individual diffs rather than patterns. Limited generalizability. Limits statistical tools used to analyze results.]

in factorial designs to introduce independent variables. The categories of each factor are called **levels.** It is important not to confuse levels of a factor with a factor itself. If a researcher compares men and women's interest in headline news stories, "men" and "women" are not two variables. Instead, "men" and "women" are simply the levels of the variable factor "sex of respondent." When factors are used, researchers are actually creating nominal categories for the independent variables involved. As an abbreviation of sorts, researchers often list the number of levels of their variables when describing the designs. Thus, if a study involves two independent variables, each of which with two levels, the design may be called a "two-by-two factorial design." If one independent variable has three levels, it may be called a "two-by-three factorial design," and so forth.

   Researchers employ factorial designs when they have multiple independent variables. But such a statement does not tell the full story. One could complete a series of single variable designs with different input variables. Yet, factorial designs allow researchers to put input variables together to see if there are special combinations of

levels defined

abbreviation for design structure by levels

factorial designs reveal interaction effects

A. Posttest Only Control Group Design with a Single Independent Variable

R   X   O
R   O

B. Factorial Design with Two Independent Variables Using a Posttest Only Control
Group Design

Independent Variable 1

		Low	High
Independent Variable 2	Low	R X O R O	R X O R O
	High	R X O R O	R X O R O

C. Factorial Design with Two Independent Variables Using a Posttest Only Control
Group Design with Offset Control Groups

Independent Variable 1

		Low	High
Independent Variable 2	Low	R X O	R X O
	High	R X O	R X O

Control: R O

D. Factorial Design with Two Independent Variables Using a Posttest Only Control
Group Design with Inclusive Control Groups

Independent Variable 1

		Without X	With X
Independent Variable 2	Without X	R O	R X O
	With X	R X O	R X O

variables that produce unique effects. Thus, these designs examine *interactions* among independent variables that might be missed if researchers did a bunch of single variable designs.

factorial designs allow analysis of more than one independent variable

Factorial designs really are extensions of experimental designs that we have previously described. An experiment with a single independent variable may be illustrated simply as Figure 11.2A shows. In a factorial design, researchers adapt this design to fit their needs. Suppose that a researcher wishes to complete a study with two independent variables in a factorial design. Each variable might be broken down into two levels—a high level and a low level, for instance. If the researcher wishes to use

specific designs may be placed in cells of the factorial design

a posttest only method, then each cell of the factorial design contains a little post-test only control group design as shown in Figure 11.2B. In each case, the X actually is a combination of levels of each independent variable. After a time a researcher might notice that all of the control groups are treated pretty much the same. Thus, he or she might try to economize on data collection by gathering one control group sample

A. Example of a Main Effect with a Single Independent Variable

FIGURE 11.3
Main Effects

Numbers in cells
are averages of
scores on the
dependent variable.

B. Example of Main Effects with Two Independent Variables

rather than four. When this method is followed, the common control group may be placed outside the design for later comparisons. This technique is known as a factorial design with an offset control group and is illustrated in Figure 11.2C. Yet another variation builds the control group directly into the design. If both independent variables are true experimental variables, it may be possible to have a condition in the design in which the independent variables are absent. Figure 11.2D shows this adaptation. As you can see, a factorial model is not really a different method from the designs previously described, but an extension of them.

use of offset control groups

Interpreting Factorial Results

Experimenters use factorial designs to find evidence of the impact of independent variables together and separately.

   Main effects are dependent-variable effects that result from independent variables separately. In factorial designs these main effects are identified by looking at differences between levels of each independent variable across levels of the other variables in the study. Sometimes diagrams can help identify these effects. In Figure 11.3A we can see the impact of one independent variable on a dependent variable. The main effect is indicated by the presence of a sloping line (upward in our example). The levels of the independent variable are indicated in the horizontal axis of the diagram. If there were no main effect, you would see a line that ran exactly parallel to the horizontal axis. Since the line shows clear slope, the presence of a main effect is evident.

   When a second independent variable is added, it is necessary to draw two lines to represent each level of the second independent variable. Figure 11.3B shows how

main effects defined

FIGURE 11.4
Interaction Effects

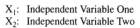

A. Example of an Ordinal Interaction Effect

B. Example of a Disordinal or Crossed Interaction Effect

 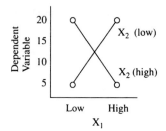

this process works. The lines are some distance apart from each other, indicating a main effect for the second independent variable. If there were no main effect, we would not see any distance between the lines at all.

interaction effects defined

Interaction effects are dependent-variable effects that result from independent variables taken together. These interaction effects involve variation arising from special combinations of levels of independent variables. Factorial designs allow researchers to identify them directly. Figure 11.4 shows two major types of interactions that might occur in research. It is important to distinguish between the types of interactions that exist because they affect the kinds of conclusions you can draw.

distinguishing interactions: 1. ordinal interactions

When drawing pictures of effects, interactions are indicated by lines that are *not* parallel to each other. In example 11.4A the lines drawn are not parallel, but they do not cross each other. This sort of pattern is called an **ordinal interaction.** Across the board, the high level for each independent variable produced higher scores on the dependent measure than the low levels did. Two main effects seemed to emerge. But put together, the high levels of each independent variable produced the same effect—but more so! Thus, the interaction is in the same direction as the main effects, but with a bonus effect thrown in. In our particular example, when variable two is at its low level, changing the level of variable one produces no appreciable effect. But when variable two is at its high level, changing the level of variable one results in great increases in the dependent variable. Thus, if the researchers wanted to produce high scores on the dependent variables, they would recommend setting both independent variables at their high levels—any other combination would not be quite so good.

When researchers are faced with an ordinal interaction it is permissible to interpret main effects for the variables involved in the interaction without fear of misrepresenting the facts. The interaction means that the real story lies in the special combinations of both variables.

A second sort of interaction effect has different lessons for researchers. A **disordinal interaction** occurs when the lines drawn for each independent variable cross each other. Because of this pattern, the effect sometimes is called a "crossed interaction" for short.[6] Figure 11.4B shows such a crossed interaction. Unlike ordinal interactions, when crossed interactions are found, researchers are forbidden from interpreting the main effects for the variables involved since such interpretations would be misleading. Furthermore, if researchers plan to make recommendations or take action based on the experiment, they know that they must respond by looking at two variables at once. Thus, the type of interaction sets limits on the sorts of conclusions that researchers can draw.

2. disordinal interactions

not permitted to interpret main effects for variables in disordinal interactions

We have limited this introductory discussion to situations in which one or two independent variables are involved. But the number of variables in an interaction can include three, four, five, or potentially any number of independent variables. In such cases, separate diagrams are drawn for each level of the additional independent variables added. The number of diagrams can grow quite large. The problem is not really so troublesome, however. Experienced researchers know that whereas main effects and two-variable interaction effects are quite common, three-variable interactions are not as common, four-variable interactions seldom occur, and higher order interactions are quite rare (they can occur once in a while, however, and researchers carefully examine them).

SOME ELEMENTS FOUND IN GOOD EXPERIMENTS

Sound experiments tend to include additional features that distinguish them from others. Some of these considerations will be considered next.

The Pilot Test

Sometimes what seems to be a beautiful experiment can blow up in a researcher's face. Many prudent experimenters complete dry runs or pilot studies to find existing problems. Though not all experiments are complicated enough to require a pilot study, in general, the more experienced researchers are, the more likely they are to complete one prior to full scale experimentation. These pilot studies usually involve small samples of people (sometimes as small as 10 or 20 people) who take part in an experiment. They are interviewed, often as part of a focus group, to find out if they had

usefulness of pilot studies in experiments

---

[6]Researchers sometimes just eyeball the averages of groups to determine what types of interactions occur. When drawing graphs to illustrate the relationships, researchers usually draw two graphs to switch the independent variable that is represented by lines and the independent variable that is indicated on the horizontal axis. The fact is that many times lines will cross under one set of circumstances, but not with the other. Nevertheless, if either graph produces a crossing, a disordinal interaction is concluded.

Sometimes it is not possible for researchers to conduct experiments in which they have full control over all the variables in the design. Under such circumstances, they can employ an alternative called "quasi-experimental research" (Campbell & Stanley, 1963, pp. 34–63). In essence, quasi-experimental studies involve completion of experimental work where random assignment and control are not possible. Obviously, the sorts of conclusions that can be drawn are limited since no cause-and-effect statements can be demonstrated. But the method may be useful especially if the researcher is exploring a research field for potential hypotheses for subsequent study, or if the researcher is not particularly interested in generalizing to larger populations than the sample group.

Three major forms of quasi-experimental designs are shown here (after Campbell & Stanley, 1963, p. 40).

Time Series Designs. A time series design measures subjects across different times. In the simplest form of this design, several observations are made before an experimental intervention and several are made afterward. The design may be represented as follows:

$$O_1 \; O_2 \; O_3 \; X \; O_4 \; O_5 \; O_6$$

This design is often used in research that tries to find cyclical trends or the decay of information retention. It controls for all sources of internal invalidity, with the possible exception of instrumentation depending on the procedures used by the researcher. Sometimes the researcher tries to add control to this design but doing so requires the addition of another group that may not be equivalent to the first.

Separate Sample Posttest Designs. Subjects might be sampled as part of another group of subjects that are close, but not assured to be equivalent to the experimental group. For instance, a group of employees who complete a communication skills training seminar might be compared to a group of employees who are from the same pool, but who have not had their training. One group would receive the experimental treatment (X) and the other would not. The basic form of these designs is illustrated as follows:

$$\frac{O \times O}{O \quad O.}$$

This design resembles the static group comparison design, except that it includes a pretest. Yet, in this design the researcher tries to make groups comparable—or at least as comparable as possible without randomization. This design controls for all sources of internal invalidity except for interaction of selection with other sources of internal invalidity and (possibly, depending on the design) the regression effect.

Counterbalanced Designs. Counterbalanced designs introduce several different experimental treatments that are presented to the subjects in different orders or sequences. Though not restricted to quasi-experimentation as a method of control, the formal counterbalanced design allows for control of all sources of internal invalidity except for interaction of selection with other sources of internal invalidity.

difficulty with experimental materials or responding to measures. In addition, researchers often discover additional variables that—if left uncontrolled—could jeopardize the quality of study conclusions. After the pilot study, some modifications of the experiment can be made and additional controls can be added. Researchers cannot know in advance everything that might interfere with a successful experiment. Thus, pilot studies reveal valuable information that helps guide worthwhile experiments.

Manipulation Checks

It is one thing to introduce an independent variable, but quite another to make sure that it actually "took" in an experiment. To make sure that independent variables actually operated in a study, researchers often include manipulation checks. A **manipulation check** is a researcher's measurement of a secondary variable to determine that an experimental variable actually was operating in a study. For instance, if people in an experiment were asked to read a message with prominent use of previews, the researcher might wish to check that people really paid attention to the message. Thus, a researcher might add a brief true-false test asking subjects about information in the message. Depending on the needs of the researcher, the degree to which people perceived the message to have contained previews might also be tested. Solid experiments rarely ask readers to assume that all variables in the study actually were operating. Instead, good experiments often include manipulation checks to assure the presence of independent variables.

manipulation check defined

Care in Interpretation

Experimental research can be exciting, and researchers sometimes get carried away when interpreting their results. Yet, solid experiments avoid misstatements. Three principles guide the interpretations of careful experimenters.

1. *Resist the Tendency to Infer Long-Term Effects from Short-Term Experiments.* Occasionally an experiment will be completed over an extended time period, but most experiments are short-term affairs. Nevertheless, researchers can get carried away and draw conclusions about long-term effects even though they collected only short-term data. For instance, many researchers have examined the persuasive effects of evidence. Early on it was found that evidence presented by a highly credible speaker did not seem as persuasive as evidence presented by a moderately or lowly credible speaker. This result was based on short-term findings. When long-term effects (at least two weeks) were examined, however, evidence proved to be persuasive for all speakers (McCroskey, 1967; Reynolds & Burgoon, 1983, p. 93). Thus, researchers must be very careful when drawing conclusions, because short-term and long-term results can differ greatly. Prudent researchers are careful to avoid the tendency to draw general or long-term conclusions based on short-term experiments.

2. *Search for Nonlinear Relationships.* Experiments often compare two levels of a variable, often a "high" and a "low" level, and draw conclusions in an unqualified fashion. Unfortunately, many relationships between independent and dependent variables are not simple straight-line relationships, but curved. That is, sometimes

a low level of an experimental variable produces a low effect, a moderate level produces a high effect, and a high level produces a slightly lower effect. If experimenters compare only two conditions, they will miss any curved relationships (since you cannot draw anything but a straight line between two plotted points). Prudent researchers do two things to avoid this difficulty. First, they carefully qualify their conclusions by noting that curved relationships have not been studied. Second, they follow initial experiments with other studies that include more than two levels of independent variables.

3. *Use Multiple Dependent Variables.* Experimental variables rarely produce effects on only one output variable. Yet some studies limit themselves to only one dependent measure. The experienced researcher knows how important it is to check for effects on additional related output measures. Hence, in studies on the impact of physical attractiveness of sources, researchers tend to look at a collection of influence variables, such as interpersonal attraction, source credibility, and liking for the source. The underlying patterns behind research findings may be explored. Inexperienced researchers may look only at effects on one pet output variable, whereas experienced researchers tend to employ a collection of relevant dependent measures so that interpretations of results can be increasingly sophisticated.

SUMMARY

An experiment is the study of the effects of variables manipulated by a researcher in a situation where all other influences are controlled, completed for the purpose of establishing causal relationships. Sound experiments follow the maxmincon principle (maximize systematic variance, control extraneous systematic variance, and minimize error variance). Experiments are designed to answer research questions that deal with cause-and-effect relationships. But independent variables must be capable of manipulation. Confounding occurs when variation from one source is mixed (or confused) with variation from another source so that it is impossible to know whether effects are due to the impact of either variable separately or some combination of the two. Control refers to methods researchers use to remove or hold constant the effects of nuisance variables. Several major control approaches include (1) elimination and removal, in which a nuisance variable is removed from the experimental setting; (2) holding constant—by the methods of limiting the population, using subjects as their own controls, or counterbalancing, which rotates the sequence in which experimental treatments are introduced to subjects;

(3) matching, in which subjects are paired on some variable on which they share equal levels and then assigned to experimental or control conditions; (4) blocking, in which a nuisance variable is added into the design as another independent variable of interest; (5) randomization, in which subjects are assigned so that each event is equally likely to belong to any experimental or control condition; and (6) statistical control, in which statistical tools are used to hold nuisance variables constant.

Experimental invalidity prevents researchers from drawing alleged conclusions from the premises advanced. Internal invalidity is the presence of contamination that prevents the experimenter from concluding that a study's experimental variable is responsible for the observed effects. External invalidity refers to the degree to which experimental results cannot be generalized to other similar circumstances.

Experimental designs follow strict protocols. A notation system has been developed that includes O (an observation made by a researcher), X (the experimental variable), and R (randomization). Pre-experimental designs do not really exercise the sort of control necessary for a solid experiment. In the one-shot case study, an experimental treatment is introduced and researchers look at effects on some output (dependent) variable. The one group pretest–post-test design adds a pretest. Static group comparisons attempt to use a control group as a baseline to compare with an experimental group. Yet, these designs do not meet the requirements of internal validity. True experimental designs control sources of internal invalidity. The pretest–posttest control group design involves a pretest of experimental and control subjects. Though change scores may be considered, there are difficulties with the distribution and reliability of change scores that make them inferior to other measures. This design fails to control for the potential of pretest sensitization (an aspect of external invalidity). To control for pretest sensitization, one may use the Solomon four groups design (which tests for the impact of pretesting) or the posttest only control group design (which omits the pretest). When more than one independent variable is used in an experiment, it is called a factorial design. When a variable is broken down into levels, the levels are called variable factors. The categories of each factor are called levels. Main effects are dependent-variable effects that result from independent variables separately. Interaction effects are dependent-variable effects that result from independent variables taken together (indicated by graphs of effects that show nonparallel lines). An ordinal interaction is an interaction in the same direction as the main effects. A disordinal interaction is an interaction that is not in the same direction as the main effects (indicated by graphs of effects that show nonparallel lines that cross).

Sound experiments tend to include additional features. First, they often include pilot studies to verify procedures and identify areas for improvements in experiments. Second, they often include manipulation checks (a researcher's measurement of a secondary variable to determine that an experimental variable actually was operating in a study). Third, they show care in interpretation including: resisting the tendency to infer long-term effects from short-term experiments; searching for nonlinear relationships; recognizing the desirability of examining multiple dependent variables.

TERMS FOR REVIEW

experiment
confounding
maxmincon principle
experimental independent variable
control
elimination and removal
holding constant
counterbalancing
matching
blocking
randomization
statistical control
analysis of covariance
partial correlation
experimental invalidity
internal invalidity

external invalidity
one-shot case study
one group pretest– posttest
static group comparison
pretest–posttest control group design
Solomon four groups design
posttest–only control group design
factorial design
single subject design
factors
levels
main effects
interaction effects
ordinal interactions
disordinal interactions
manipulation check

CHAPTER 12

Sampling

You don't have to eat the whole cow to know the steak is tough.

–Samuel Johnson

**THE ROLE OF SAMPLING IN
QUANTITATIVE RESEARCH**
    Relating Sampling to Other Concepts
    Defining the Population
    Eliminating Bias
ESSENTIALS OF SAMPLING
    Representative Sampling: The Goal of
      Effective Sampling
    Sample Size
    Statistical Effects of Small Samples

FORMS OF SAMPLING
    Random Sampling
    Nonrandom Sampling
**DEALING WITH SAMPLING
PROBLEMS**
    Subject Refusal to Participate
    Evidence of Randomization in
      Research Articles

BEFORE WE GET STARTED . . .

Whether we complete descriptive empirical studies or experiments, we must collect data. Indeed, collecting data in empirical research means sampling populations of events. This chapter introduces you to the terms and methods used for sampling. In addition, it addresses some special issues that must be faced in selecting sample sizes and constructing so-called "confidence intervals." By the end of this chapter you will have some guidelines to use when making your own inquiries and reading those of others.

THE ROLE OF SAMPLING IN QUANTITATIVE RESEARCH

You do not have to gather data on every single event in a population to draw accurate conclusions. Careful sampling can often accurately identify population characteristics even with very small numbers of events. To understand the role of sampling in empirical research you need to understand how it fits into other concepts, its relationship to populations, and its purposes.

Relating Sampling to Other Concepts

Sampling involves selecting events from a population. Researchers rarely sample all possible events, but they rely on a portion of all data to draw conclusions. Since a study's conclusions can be only as good as the data on which they are based, the sample must be gathered thoughtfully and with some solid reasoning behind choices. Anything less amounts to non sequitur thinking that threatens a study. It is helpful to define our terms to avoid this error.

    A **population** is the universe of events from which the sample is drawn. Figure 12.1 shows the relationship between a sample and population. As you can see, a sample is simply a selection of events from the population (the term *events* is used to permit including samples of people, messages, behavior, or things). Researchers can sample toward the center of the population, or they might accidentally sample at the periphery of the population. The actual individual events are called pieces of **data.**

    A number computed from a sample is called a **statistic,** sometimes also called "sample statistics" or "test statistics." Grammatically, a single number (in this sense) is called a statistic and more than one number is called a group of statistics. You may have seen the term *statistics* used to refer to the study of quantitative information. In this latter sense, *statistics* is a singular term even though it ends with an *s*. Thus, you have to be careful when reading studies. If researchers refer to computed "test statistics" then you know that conclusions based on samples (and many events in the population) were omitted. If researchers talk about selecting statistics to analyze data, they mean the specific formulae they used in their studies. Almost always, communication researchers compute statistics because they gather samples to help analyze results.

    Suppose you were able to sample every single event in the population—leaving out none. These numbers would be called parameters, not statistics. A **parameter** is a number computed from a population. In practice, researchers rarely compute parameters. Instead they often inherit parameters from some other source. For instance, the federal government has told automobile manufacturers the maximum emissions permitted for cars sold in the United States. Similarly, customers often tell manufacturers what specifications must be satisfied for a product to be accepted. In each case these parameters are defined in advance as descriptions of the population.

sampling defined

population defined

data defined

statistic defined

"statistics" also refers to study of quantitative information

parameter defined

parameters rarely computed by researchers

FIGURE 12.1
The Relationship
Between a Sample and
Population

Population

Numbers from populations are called **parameters**.

Sample

Numbers from samples are called **statistics**.

Defining the Population

**populations defined
by researchers**

To draw samples from populations, researchers must first define the population. Suppose that you were interested in studying the degree to which senior citizens in the United States rely on televised news in preference to newspaper accounts. All senior citizens in the United States would be the population, and you would want to make sure that any samples carefully represented them. Though the population may be defined quite broadly—including all people or all television programs in the world, for instance—they may also be defined quite narrowly, such as including only students at large Western universities or only prime-time television programs from the three leading networks. The point is that populations are *defined* by the researcher as having certain characteristics.

**populations may be
defined narrowly**

Eliminating Bias

bias defined

Bias in sampling is a tendency for the sample to err so that it fails to represent the population. Obviously, researchers work to eliminate or minimize bias. You may be mystified when you hear of the accuracy of some political polls or television rating services. They are usually able to give highly accurate reflections of the population based on what seem to be very small samples, often as few as 1,200 people. Such accuracy does not happen by accident. Controlling bias is critical and is handled by direct action.

ESSENTIALS OF SAMPLING

The basic concepts discussed here provide a framework for understanding sampling. This section also introduces ways to draw representative samples with appropriate sample sizes.

Representative Sampling: The Goal of Effective Sampling

**representative
sample defined**

A good sample must represent the population and be big enough to permit reasonable analysis of data. These matters are related, of course. Yet for researchers, the fundamental test of whether a sample is good is the degree to which it is representative. A **representative sample** is one that accurately reflects characteristics of the population from which it is drawn. Of course, unless researchers have the knowledge of gods, they will never know if samples are really representative. So, researchers take steps to prevent knowingly biasing samples. That way, they may presume that a sample is representative unless contrary evidence emerges.

Sample Size

Collecting a representative sample involves having one large enough to make reasonable interpretations. Still, a large sample size is not enough to prove that a sample is representative of the population. Gathering a reasonably sized sample is just one step in collecting a representative sample. Research students often ask, "How big should a sample be?" To answer this question, they must decide on the amount of sampling error they are willing to accept and consider the demands created by research tools employed.

TABLE 12.1 Sample Size Requirements for Different Research Traditions

Condition	Sample Size Requirements
Pilot Studies	At least 10 events in a study (Isaac & Michael, 1981, p. 93)
Studies of Physiological Measures	At least 8 events randomly selected (if individual response ratings are involved, the sample must be increased to ordinary sample sizes for experiments)
Validation or Cross Validation Studies	At least 200 events if standard methods of validation are used (such as multiple correlation or factor analysis); with other tools "N should be at least about 60, and preferably 100 or more, for this purpose" [Tatsuoka, 1969, p. 27]
Studies that Use Multiple Correlation Methods	15 subjects for every predictor or independent variable (Stevens, 1986, p. 58)
Studies that Use Factor Analysis	At least 10 events for each variable item to be included in the factor analysis (Nunnally, 1978, p. 421)

Sampling Error

You have probably heard news reports that describe political polls. They often tell what percentage of the voters favor each candidate. They also often report a certain "margin of error" for the poll. This margin of error is the amount of sampling error associated with the sample. The term **sampling error** refers to the degree to which a sample differs from population characteristics on some measure. In general, as the sample size gets to be a larger and larger proportion of the population, the amount of sampling error is reduced. If you sample the entire population, there is no sampling error at all! Thus, a general piece of advice is to collect as big a sample as you can afford. But you often have to make some practical choices.

sampling error defined

Sampling Guidelines

Sample sizes should be suitable to the research questions and study designs. Thus, in pilot studies, small samples may be used. In speech and hearing science, samples of 8 to 15 subjects may be used in experiments in which physiological reactions are involved (and where few additional variables may need to be randomized). For studies attempting to validate new measurement instruments, researchers may be told to use quite a large sample, at least 200 events. To use some statistical tools, such as multiple correlation or factor analysis, researchers need a minimum number of events for every variable to be studied. Table 12.1 shows some of the popular guidelines suggested by students of research methods.

sample sizes should be suitable to research questions and design

Guidelines Based on Sampling Error

If samples have been drawn at random, it is possible for researchers to report **confidence intervals** indicating the probability that sample statistics "capture" population parameters, within certain margins for error. This section explains how these margins for error are used and calculated by researchers.

confidence intervals identified

**confidence intervals
for proportional data**

For instance, take the case of a poll you might complete with a sample of 100 people selected at random. Suppose you found that 60% reported anxiety about taking a communication course, and 40% did not. You might wonder how far from the true population proportions your sample data are—after all, a sample of 100 does not sound all that big. To plug numbers into the formula in Table 12.2, you need only remember that proportions are numbers expressed with decimal points included (in other words, the proportion of anxious people is .6, not 60%). Then, you can fill in the blanks. As Table 12.2 shows, the formula reveals a "margin of error" in estimating how far from the true proportion of high-anxiety people in the population our sample may be 95% of the time. Put another way, this formula states that we are 95% confident that the sample proportion is equal to the population proportion, plus or minus 9.6%. We could also say that we are 95% confident that the true population proportion of people anxious about taking a communication class is somewhere between 50.4% and 69.6%. Of course, in our example, there is a 5% chance that our sample is *way off*—not even close to the range we have reported. At least people know the odds and can make sensible choices about interpreting study results.

**confidence intervals
for averages**

**standard deviation
identified**

Not all data deal with proportions or percentages, of course. For studies that deal with means and averages, confidence intervals can also be constructed. To estimate these intervals you need to have some measure of the amount of variation that exists in the population.[1] The standard deviation is a statistic that is most often used. Though it will be explained in Chapter 13, for now let us just define **standard deviation** as a number that tells how far from the average the data are (on the average). The standard deviation is often abbreviated by the lower-case letter s. Suppose you want to know the margin for error you would have if you surveyed 100 people and found that the average number of hours they watched TV per week was 23. Table 12.2B shows this example. With a computed standard deviation of 8 hours, you can construct a 95% confidence interval around the average. As the formula reveals, with such a sample size you can be 95% confident that the sample average is equal to the population average, plus or minus 1.57 hours. You can also say you are 95% confident that the true population average number of hours people watch TV per week is between 21.43 hours and 24.57 hours.

With a little transposing of terms, you can use the formulae to help you choose the sample size for a study with different confidence intervals and margins for error. Table 12.3A shows what sample sizes might be required for different situations involving the use of proportional data. On occasion, researchers do not have measures (or even estimates) of variability but have to make some choices anyway. Fortunately there are some guidelines. Table 12.3B shows such a table for a 95% confidence interval and a margin for error expressed as a 5% range of variation, provided you know the size of the population. In national polling additional adaptations must be made. Assuming very large variability in the population, increased sample sizes have been suggested to control for the additional background variation that usually exists

---

[1] This measure should be the variation known to exist in the population. But if the researcher does not have this information, the amount of variation in the sample may be substituted since the major measures of sample variability (standard deviation and variance) are unbiased estimators of population variability.

TABLE 12.2 Confidence Intervals (C.I.) for Proportions and Means

Type of Measure	Formulae and Examples

A. For proportions (decimal point data) organized into two groups (such as *yes* or *no*)

90% C.I. = observed proportion ± 1.645   * $\sqrt{\dfrac{p * (1-p)}{\text{sample size}}}$

95% C.I. = observed proportion ± 1.96   * $\sqrt{\dfrac{p * (1-p)}{\text{sample size}}}$

99% C.I. = observed proportion ± 2.58   * $\sqrt{\dfrac{p * (1-p)}{\text{sample size}}}$

where p = proportion of responses for one category

EXAMPLE: With a sample of 100 people selected at random, if 60% favored were anxious about taking a communication class, how far from the population proportion would the sample proportion be 95% of the time?

95% C.I. = observed proportion ± 1.96   * $\sqrt{\dfrac{p * (1-p)}{\text{sample size}}}$

       =   .60   ± 1.96   * $\sqrt{\dfrac{.6 * (1-.6)}{100}}$

       =   .60   ± 1.96   * $\sqrt{\dfrac{.24}{100}}$

       =   .60   ± 1.96   * $\sqrt{.0024}$

       =   .60   ± 1.96   *   .049

95% C.I. =   .60   ± .096

B. For means

90% C.I. = observed mean ± 1.645   * $(s / \sqrt{\text{sample size}})$

95% C.I. = observed mean ± 1.96   * $(s / \sqrt{\text{sample size}})$

99% C.I. = observed mean ± 2.58   * $(s / \sqrt{\text{sample size}})$

where s = an estimate of variability in the population called the "standard deviation" (See Chapter 18 for computation of s.)

EXAMPLE: With a sample of 100 people selected at random, if the average number of hours of TV watched per week were 23 hours with a standard deviation observed (trust us!) of 8 hours, how far would the population mean be from the sample proportion 95% of the time?

95% C.I. = observed mean ± 1.96   * $(s / \sqrt{\text{sample size}})$

       = 23 hours ± 1.96   * $(8 / \sqrt{100}\;)$

       = 23 hours ± 1.96   * $(8 / \;\;10\;\;\;)$

       = 23 hours ± 1.96   *   .8

95% C.I. = 23 hours ± 1.57 hours

TABLE 12.3 Sample Sizes Required for Proportional Data

A. For Proportional Data and an Estimate of Variability
Situation: This table presumes a single (dichotomous) stratification variable, conservative proportions of .5 and .5 (for maximum heterogeneity and to assume maximum internal sampling error), an unlimited population size, and truly random sampling.

		With margin for error of			
		.10	.05	.025	.01
Confidence Interval	90%	68	272	1089	6806
	95%	96	384	1537	9604
	99%	166	666	2663	16641

B. For Proportional Data from a Population of Known Size and No Estimate of Population Variability
SITUATION: This table presumes random samples of proportions drawn from populations of a known size so as to be within 5% of the Population Proportion at a 95% Confidence Interval (after Krejcie & Morgan, 1970).

Population Size	Sample Size
under 10	N A
10	10
15	14
20	19
30	28
40	36
50	44
75	63
100	80
250	152
500	217
1000	278
5000	357
10000	370
50000	381
100000	384

(Yamane, 1967). Such tables indicate that a national poll would require only 100 respondents for a 10% margin of error. To reduce error to 5% you would need a sample of 400. To reduce error to 3% (typical among national polls) a sample of 1,111 would be needed. To trim the margin for error to one percent would require a sample of 10,000! As you can see, reducing margins of error or increasing confidence requires increasing sample sizes.

Statistical Effects of Small Samples

In general, small samples increase sampling error. Yet, another aspect of small samples may not have occurred to you. Because of the ways statistics are computed and distributions entered, it is difficult for researchers to find evidence of relationships when sample sizes are small. It is easiest to spot differences when large samples are used because the relationships tend to stand out from the background noise and variability. When small samples are used, only very big effects stand out. Thus, the impact of small samples creates a double whammy for the researcher. Not only may the sample be thrown off, but a small sample may inhibit the chances of relationships being identified by most statistical tools.

> **small samples invite sampling bias and make it difficult to find relationships**

But isn't there a point at which a small sample turns into a large one? In reality, most statisticians have observed that samples of 30 or more events tend to produce nearly identical distributions. Without getting into the detailed background of this statement, we will mention that different distributions used in statistical analysis tend to diverge from each other when the samples drop below 30 events. In fact, Leonard Kazmier (1988, p. 132) recommended that any actual sample size should be at least 30 events when estimating averages since the standard formulae for data analysis presume normal distributions. When sample sizes grow above 30, the distributions that researchers and statisticians use to help make decisions become fairly comparable to each other. So, big samples start somewhere near 30 events—but there is a catch. The events themselves in the sample must be drawn at random. To balance out other sampling concerns, researchers may need increased sample sizes.

> **sample sizes of 30 or more invite reasonable use of statistical tools**

FORMS OF SAMPLING

When sampling events from a population, researchers make critical choices. To give you an idea of those choices, we will consider categories of sampling that presume randomization and those that do not involve randomization.

Random Sampling

Sometimes called "probability sampling" techniques, the use of randomization plays an important part in research. To understand random sampling, it is helpful to grasp key terms and to understand its key role.

Random sampling is selection of data such that each event in the population has an equal chance of being selected.[2] Random sampling is presumed for nearly all statistical tools that may be applied to data. You can use distributions of randomly occurring events to figure the odds that a sample truly reflects what goes on in the population. When students hear of random sampling they often mistakenly imagine that it is a hit or miss activity ("random" sounds a lot like "accidental"). The truth is that randomization is time-consuming and many researchers try to take shortcuts. But

> **random sampling defined**

> **randomness not accidental**

---

[2] In a mathematic sense, randomization means that the probability of any event following any other is equal to zero. But the mathematic definition presumes an infinite population. Thus, for practical purposes, a quasi-random method might be involved. To say that the chance for sampling is equal is close enough for us.

SPECIAL DISCUSSION 12–1
The Use of Volunteers

You probably have been in classes in which you participated in a study by completing a questionnaire or interview. In a technical sense, then, you were volunteering your participation. But you were asked to participate. You did not ask the researcher to permit you to be a part of the sample group. Yet some research actually relies on subjects who are volunteers for such research. Sometimes researchers place ads in newspapers asking people to participate in research and they get a fair number of volunteers—especially if they offer to pay subjects. A question that faces researchers, however, is whether the volunteers give reactions that are typical of the population.

Many people are greatly concerned that volunteers differ from other members of the population. After all, people volunteer for a reason. If their reasons are not shared by the entire population, there is little reason to believe that the results from the volunteers are representative. Some scholars have noticed that volunteers tend to differ from the rest of the general population because they generally have increased needs for social approval, increased socioeconomic status, increased intelligence, and reduced conformity to authority figures (Rosenthal & Rosnow, 1969). The *Journal of Volunteerism* is a journal dedicated to identifying ways in which volunteers behave, both in and out of research settings. Though the reasons volunteers choose to engage in research may be randomly distributed (Kruglanski, 1973)—and hence not a systematic source of variation in research—in many research settings there is no doubt that the use of volunteers can introduce great bias in studies. Thus, prudent researchers tend to be wary of relying exclusively on volunteers as the chief evidence sources to draw meaningful conclusions.

---

the shortcuts throw off the whole sample and make it impossible to enter distributions accurately to decide whether research findings represent anything other than sampling error.

Obtaining a random draw of events is not a haphazard matter. One might imagine sampling a bunch of people at a nearby shopping mall. These places frequently are the stomping grounds for researchers who wish to find out people's reactions to commercials, promotional campaigns, and marketing strategies (you may have been approached at a mall by a person carrying a clipboard who asked you to answer questions or participate in a focus group meeting). Yet, sampling people at a mall is usually not random. People conducting surveys are usually told to gather data from the first set of people they can find who fall into a target population (sometimes limited to women under 30, people with children, or senior citizens). People arriving at the mall at a later time do not have the same chance to be sampled as those in the first grouping. Though researchers may claim to have been relatively unbiased in selecting individuals, they cannot claim that the study was truly random.

To improve their studies, some researchers attempt to sample according to a schedule. They might select the first five people to enter the main entrance of the shopping mall each hour. Or, they might approach every tenth person entering the mall. Though this is a step in the right direction, it is still not random since there is bias in favor of those who arrive promptly at the beginning of the hour. Thus, this method cannot claim all the advantages of random sampling. It is best described as **systematic or periodic sampling** since it selects respondents according to a predetermined schedule other than a random sequence. You should be warned that many researchers actually use some form of systematic sampling and call it "random sampling" in passing.

systematic or periodic sampling distinguished from random sampling

Random sampling methods attempt to remove the human element from biasing the study. In the simplest sense, obtaining a random draw of events can be accomplished by taking care to insure that each event has an equal chance of selection. For instance, if you wished to expose a random sample of students to speech from a severe stutterer, you might write class members' names on pieces of paper and put them in a hat. After tossing the pieces of paper around for a while, you might sample by pulling names from the hat. If you are successful, you might gather a fairly random sample. But if the population is fairly large, it may not be practical to draw names from your hat.

There is a superior way. Suppose you wanted to sample a group of voters in your city. No problem. Voters must register and their names and addresses are matters of public record. You might assign each voter a number and then turn to a table of random numbers to select voters whose numbers have "randomly" come up. These tools of randomization help you effectively eliminate your own biases in data collection. Random sampling permits you to feel confident that the sample is as representative of the population—as free of bias—as possible. Randomization increases the chances that differences from one person to another in a sample will be random rather than systematic. Thus, random sampling allows you to control a host of background differences in sample groups that otherwise might foul up a study's meaningfulness.

using random numbers

There is more than one way to use random sampling. Since researchers often abbreviate their descriptions of methods, it is valuable to understand the labels used for these random sampling tools. There are three major random sampling varieties: simple random sampling, stratified random sampling, and cluster sampling.

methods of random sampling:

Simple Random Sampling

Selecting simple random samples involves identifying every event in the population and then drawing a sample by such methods as pulling names out of a hat or fishbowl. Most commonly, a method involving use of a table of random numbers is employed (see Special Discussion 12–2). Simple random sampling is useful in experiments in which assignment of subjects to experimental and control conditions can be done at random. This method is also useful when research problems do not require that samples be divided into subgroups (such as male-female; Republican-Democrat; stutterer-nonstutterer). This method has several advantages. First, sampling error can be computed for statistics computed from such a sample. Second, simple randomization can be used by researchers as a means to control for individual differences among

1. simple random sampling

uses

advantages

SPECIAL DISCUSSION 12–2
How to Use a Table of Random Numbers

Random number tables are often used to help researchers draw random samples and to assign subjects to various conditions at random. Table 12.A contains a list of two-digit random numbers, but you should know that they actually came out of a computer as single digits (the publisher arranged them into two digit numbers for convenience—thus, a good-sized table can be used by researchers for nearly any number of digits desired). Though there are several options, here is a way to use a random number table to select a sample:

1. Give every event in the population a number. To keep it simple, suppose we wanted to draw a sample of 30 college debaters from three universities with a total of 90 debaters. The possible range of numbers would be 01 through 90—thus, a two-digit table would do nicely (if we had to deal with three-digit numbers, we might add in a third column of numbers).
2. Enter the number table at random. Don't just close your eyes and point your finger somewhere on the page (right-handed people tend to let their hands drop toward the right side of the page, and lefties tend to drop their hands toward the left side of the page; the corners might as well not be on the page, given their chance of being selected!). As an alternative, you could cut cards (let aces equal 1 and face cards equal 0) or throw dice to find the column number and the row number to start with. But who carries around playing cards or dice? As another alternative, you can use one of the following techniques (adapted from Leedy, 1989, pp. 154–155).

- Ask people to give you their social security numbers. Let the first two digits identify the table column to start with; let the last two digits be the row.
- Check the daily stock quotations to find the last two digits for the Dow Jones Industrial Average high and low (to represent the starting column and row).
- One of the easiest methods involves pulling a dollar bill from your pocket and checking the serial number. Suppose yours is L 38 7321 14 G. The first two-digit number is 38 and the final two-digit number is 14. To decide which number is the row and which one is the column reference, you can flip a coin. If the coin is heads, the first number will be the column. If the toss is tails, the last number will be the column. Say the coin came up tails. You would turn to the random number table and find the point where column 14 and row 38 intersect. On our table, the number at this intersection is 42 (find it for yourself!). If the row or column numbers are greater than the number of rows or columns on your table, just add the numbers together and use the sum as your new starting number.

3. Now, we need to know whether you will read the numbers by going across the page to the right, to the left, up, or down (don't mess with diagonals; it's too confusing). Take out a coin and flip it twice:

TABLE 12.A   A Random Number Table

60 36 59 46 53	35 07 53 39 49	42 61 42 92 97	01 91 82 83 16
83 79 94 24 02	56 62 33 44 42	34 99 44 13 74	70 07 11 47 36
32 96 00 74 05	36 40 98 32 32	99 38 54 16 00	11 13 30 75 86
19 32 25 38 45	57 62 05 26 06	66 49 76 86 46	78 13 86 65 59
11 22 09 47 47	07 39 93 74 08	48 50 92 39 29	27 48 24 54 76
31 75 15 72 60	68 98 00 53 39	15 47 04 83 55	88 65 12 25 96
88 49 29 93 82	14 45 40 45 04	20 09 49 89 77	74 84 39 34 13
30 93 44 77 44	07 48 18 38 28	73 78 80 65 33	28 59 72 04 05
22 88 84 88 93	27 49 99 87 48	60 53 04 51 28	74 02 28 46 17
78 21 21 69 93	35 90 29 13 86	44 37 21 54 86	65 74 11 40 14
41 84 98 45 47	46 85 05 23 26	34 67 75 83 00	74 91 06 43 45
46 35 23 30 49	69 24 89 34 60	45 30 50 75 21	61 31 83 18 55
11 08 79 62 94	14 01 33 17 92	59 74 76 72 77	76 50 33 45 13
52 70 10 83 37	56 30 38 73 15	16 52 06 96 76	11 65 49 98 93
57 27 53 68 98	81 30 44 85 85	68 65 22 73 76	92 85 25 58 66
20 85 77 31 56	70 28 42 43 26	79 37 59 52 20	01 15 96 32 67
15 63 38 49 24	90 41 59 36 14	33 52 12 66 65	55 82 34 76 41
92 69 44 82 97	39 90 40 21 15	59 58 94 90 67	66 82 14 15 75
77 61 31 90 19	88 15 20 00 80	20 55 49 14 09	96 27 74 82 57
38 68 83 24 86	45 13 46 35 45	59 40 48 20 59	43 94 75 16 80
25 16 30 18 89	70 01 41 50 21	41 29 06 73 12	71 85 71 59 57
65 25 10 76 29	37 23 93 32 95	05 87 00 11 19	92 78 42 63n40
36 81 54 36 25	18 63 73 75 09	82 44 49 90 05	04 92 17 37 01
64 39 71 16 92	05 32 78 21 62	20 24 78 17 59	45 19 72 53 32
04 51 52 56 24	95 09 66 79 46	48 46 08 55 58	15 19 11 87n82
83 76 16 08 73	43 25 38 41 45	60 83 32 59 83	01 29 14 13 49
10 38 70 63 45	80 85 40 92 79	43 52 90 63 18	38 38 47 47 61
51 32 19 22 46	80 08 87 70 74	88 72 25 67 36	66 16 44 94 31
72 47 20 00 08	80 89 01 80 02	94 81 33 19 00	54 15 58 34 36
05 46 65 53 06	93 12 81 84 64	74 45 79 05 61	72 84 81 18 34
39 52 87 24 84	82 47 42 55 93	48 54 53 52 47	18 61 91 36 74
81 61 61 87 11	53 34 24 42 76	75 12 21 17 24	74 62 77 37 07
07 58 61 61 20	82 64 12 28 20	92 90 41 31 41	32 39 21 97 63
90 76 70 42 35	13 57 41 72 00	69 90 26 37 42	78 46 42 25 01
40 18 82 81 93	29 59 38 86 27	94 97 21 15 98	62 09 53 67 87
34 41 48 21 57	86 88 75 50 87	19 15 20 00 23	12 30 28 07 83
63 43 97 53 63	44 98 91 68 22	36 02 40 08 67	76 37 84 16 05
67 04 90 90 70	93 39 94 55 47	94 45 87 42 84	05 04 14 98 07
79 49 50 41 46	52 16 29 02 86	54 15 83 42 43	46 97 83 54 82
91 70 43 05 52	04 73 72 10 31	75 05 19 30 29	47 66 56 43 82

Source: *A Million Random Digits with 100,000 Normal Deviates* (New York: Free Press, 1955), with permission of the RAND Corporation.

- Two heads mean you read to the right.
- Two tails mean you read to the left.
- Heads followed by tails means you read up the column.
- Tails followed by heads means you read down the column.
  Say your flips give you two heads, so you read to the right.

4. Since you want to sample 30 debaters, you simply take the individuals whose numbers "come up." In your case, you select person 42, person 84, person 05, person 04, person 98 (ignore it since it does not exist in this population), person 07, and so forth until you have your sample. If the same number is repeated, you simply ignore it the second time.

There is another way to obtain random numbers, of course. These days, many inexpensive hand calculators have random number keys on them. If you purchase such a calculator, you need only press a button to generate random numbers.

subjects in the sample. Third, the representativeness of the sample is virtually assured since random sampling means that any differences between population and sample characteristics are at random. On the other hand, simple random sampling is difficult to use in many field settings because a list of all the events in the population may not exist. Furthermore, this sampling method may be time-consuming since the steps involved in identifying and choosing events can be somewhat complicated.

disadvantages

Stratified Random Sampling

This variation of random sampling defines samples based on the known proportions within the population and follows with random sampling within each group. In **stratified random sampling,** population characteristics (called stratification variables) are identified, such as the number of men and women in the population (49% and 51% respectively). Then, after deciding on the sample size to be drawn, a random sample is taken from each level of the population stratification variable. For example, out of a sample of 200, 98 men would be selected at random and 102 women would be sampled at random. This method is used by most political polling companies and popularly reported surveys. Stratified random sampling is invited where dividing the sample according to some stratification variable is an important part of the study. In addition to the weaknesses of any form of random sampling, this method involves some unique costs. Since studies using this method tend to have fairly large sample sizes, stratified random sampling often involves increased expense for the researcher. Furthermore, many times the weights that should be associated with each stratification variable are not known. Thus, the method may not be practical to explore many research questions.

2. stratified random sampling defined

uses

advantages

disadvantages

Cluster Sampling

Though one must know a great deal about a population before doing stratified random sampling, cluster sampling requires much less initial knowledge. **Cluster sampling** involves selecting events "in two or more stages, with the first stage being the random selection of naturally occurring clusters, and the last stage being the random selection of elements within clusters" (Schutt, 1996, p. 571). You might decide to identify a group of neighborhoods, businesses, organizations, or cities, for instance (they may be much easier to identify than individuals). Then the researcher takes a random sample from within each cluster. Sometimes clusters are subdivided further before random samples are drawn (in which case, the sampling is called "multistage cluster sampling"). For instance, researchers might identify large groupings such as newspapers and then lists of large city and small town newspapers might be prepared. Then random samples might be taken of newspapers in each category. Many large-scale status surveys use this method where it is easiest to find clusters of organizations rather than individuals. The method has been particularly useful when geographically based samples have been involved. This method carries the disadvantages found in any form of random sampling. In addition, the method requires larger samples than simple random sampling.

3. cluster sampling defined

uses

advantages

disadvantages

Nonrandom Sampling

Despite its advantages, sometimes random sampling simply is not possible. It would not be possible for you to do an experiment in which you randomly assign a group of people to have cleft palates and another group of people not to have cleft palates. In this situation you pretty much have to take people as they are available to you. It would be unthinkable to create people with cleft palates for the purpose of maintaining the purity of a random sample. Yet, people with cleft palates may also have some other sorts of individual characteristics that are not shared to the same degree by the general population. They tend to show slightly higher levels of communication apprehension than others. They may also tend to experience lower levels of self-esteem than members of the general population. So, a researcher has a choice: give up, or go with the available data but qualify your conclusions carefully. The second option is obviously superior. You may remember John Paul Jones's famous advice: "Do the best you can with the means available to you." Sometimes random sampling is not feasible. So, you must do the best you can with the available methods of nonrandom sampling.

randomization is not always possible

There are several different forms of nonrandom sampling. The four most prominent forms are accidental or convenience sampling, quota sampling, purposive or known group sampling, and snowball sampling.

forms of nonrandom sampling

Accidental or Convenience Sampling

Sometimes called "availability sampling," **accidental or convenience sampling** involves selecting events that are most readily available. For instance, researchers often sample college students in their experiments. They often persuade their colleagues to make their classes available to them. One class may receive an experimental treatment and the other class may receive the control treatment. No attempt is made to randomize the groups. Thus, no steps are taken to assure that they really are comparable groups. This method is often used for TV "call in" polls that

accidental or convenience sampling defined

uses

invite viewers to participate for a modest toll charge. Such polls usually are identified as "nonscientific surveys" of opinion, and rightfully so. Though this sampling technique may be found in many studies, these samples are most useful in case studies and in pilot studies that are designed to help the researcher identify problems and get feedback about research materials.

Quota Sampling

quota sampling defined

uses

This method defines samples based on the known proportions within the population and nonrandom sampling is completed in each group. Except for the absence of randomization, **quota sampling** is very similar to stratified random sampling. In each form, population characteristics are identified, such as the number of men and women in the population. After deciding on the sample size to be drawn, a "quota" for each category is identified. Then, an accidental or convenience sample is taken from each level of the population stratification variable. This approach is often used in studies where researchers want to make sure that important parts of the population are not omitted in the sampling. Of course, many times quotas are filled by researchers' sampling friends and family members. Other individuals may be excluded because sampling them is inconvenient.

Purposive or Known Group Sampling

purposive or known group sampling defined

uses

This sampling method selects events from groups that are known to possess a particular characteristic under investigation. If you wanted to study the persuasive strategies used by union organizers, it would make sense to sample the behavior only of union organizers. If you wanted to study the ways people with high intelligence communicate in their families, you might decide to sample members in the local chapter of Mensa (the organization for people with high IQ scores). In each case, random sampling would not be appropriate since you may not be interested in securing a cross section of the population. Thus, purposive or known group sampling is particularly useful for experiments or surveys where a criterion for admission to the sample clearly exist. Sometimes studies that try to validate new measurement tools use purposive sampling. In Chapter 4 you learned about the predictive validity method for determining the validity of a measure. This validation approach employs known group sampling. In addition, many intensive case studies of organizational leaders, communities, or associations make productive use of purposive or known group sampling. Purposive or known group sampling is convenient and economical when key population characteristics can be identified clearly. But sometimes the key characteristic is difficult to see in a group. Sometimes the key element is subjective, as with such variables as source attractiveness or communicator competence. In these cases, the results of known group sampling may not be trustworthy. In addition, since groups of people are identified, the observations may not be independent of each other (e.g., the local Mensa chapter would consist of people with high IQ scores who also like each other's company, probably because they share some other interests in common).

Snowball Sampling

snowball sampling defined

Snowball sampling selects events based on referrals from initial informants. A population is defined, usually composed of people who engage in deviant or illegal behavior, such as street gang members, prostitutes, or criminals. Then, contact is made with a person in this grouping and an interview may be conducted. After trust is built with this person, the researcher asks for referrals to other individuals in the population group. These people are also asked for referrals and the sample "snowballs" in size. This method is highly useful for studies of behavior that involve deviant or illegal activities. For instance, Bryan (1965) used this sampling approach to study the ways call girls are recruited and trained. Sometimes this method is employed when the study group is a subculture and where random sampling is not an option. Snowball sampling is useful when it is not really possible to identify all members of the population at the outset. Yet, when researchers use snowball sampling they do not really know whether enough referrals exist to penetrate into the group under investigation. The referrals might be to people who are on the periphery of the group, rather than at its heart. Unfortunately, the researcher might never know. Furthermore, since referrals are based on the acquaintances of initial contacts, the people in the sample cannot be considered independent. Even so, snowball sampling permits research in areas that might never be investigated otherwise.

uses

Advantages and Disadvantages of Nonrandom Sampling

Naturally, strengths and weaknesses are associated with all methods of nonrandom sampling. Some of each probably have occurred to you. A first strength of such methods is that they often are invited by field and quasi-experimental research. Researchers may want to sample naturally occurring events—such as nonverbal displays of affection people show when saying good-bye at airports. In such settings, simple random sampling is not possible.[3] A second strength is that nonrandom sampling methods often allow the researcher to get samples that would be otherwise unavailable. If you wanted to study the communication strategies employed by drug dealers to sell their products, you could not very easily put an ad in the newspaper asking drug dealers to call you for an appointment to be interviewed. You probably would hear only from police officers and narcotics agents. If the activity involves issues that are intimate, private, or deviant, nonrandom sampling may be the only way to gather any information.

strengths of nonrandom sampling

Despite any advantages involved in nonrandom samples, they have severe limitations. Most of these matters are technical issues and involve the rigor that can be claimed for a study. First, nonrandom samples tend to show great biases. Respondents cannot be presumed to be a random draw from the population because they are not selected in ways that provide each event in the population with an equal chance of selection. Thus, without randomization, the sample may have clear biases. Sometimes researchers can take steps to describe these biases, but there are so many potential sources of bias that this strategy can only be partially successful. Second, since there

general disadvantages of nonrandom samples

---

[3] Of course, some efforts to include randomization might be added to this example. One might sample randomly selected months and randomly selected airports, during randomly selected time periods. Then a smaller random sample might be selected from this large grouping by numbering all the people saying good-bye and randomly selecting a group of people to serve as the final sample.

is no distribution for nonprobability samples, no sampling error computation is possible. Hence, it is not possible to compute a confidence interval and estimate how closely our data probably are to population parameters. This limitation means that the researcher cannot use standard tools to determine the accuracy with which the sample captures population parameters. Third, the use of nonrandom samples severely limits conclusions that researchers can draw. The impact of experimental variables can be very different from one selected subgroup to another. Though nonrandom sampling provides analyses that apply to the single subgroup sampled, other subgroups cannot be generalized at all. In fact, the use of nonrandom sampling means that the conclusions a researcher can draw are limited to those suggesting relationships, but they exclude conclusions based on convincing evidence.

DEALING WITH SAMPLING PROBLEMS

Research books often describe sampling as though problems are rarities. The dismal truth is that the research craft is riddled with choices and compromises. Some of these matters are addressed here.

Subject Refusal to Participate

systematic reasons for refusal to participate as sampling error

It will come as no surprise to you that people often do not want to participate in surveys. But if too many people refuse to be part of a sample, then randomization is jeopardized. People have reasons for refusing. If these reasons are systematically shared by the portion of the population that declines to become involved, then the remaining sample may not be truly random. Thus, researchers must report such information in their studies and qualify their results accordingly.

1. initial refusal; 2. incomplete responding

Respondents may refuse to participate in two ways. They can decline initially to accept a questionnaire, answer any questions, or mail in a survey. Or, they provide incomplete responses. In each case, the researcher is expected to describe how many subjects refused to participate and any differences they may have had from others who agreed to participate. A little refusal here and there may not be a big deal, but large scale refusal suggests that something may be terribly wrong with the study research question or its procedures. David J. Fox explained:

systematic attrition is meaningful to the researcher

> When attrition reaches 25 percent or higher, even assuming that there are no statistically significant differences between accepting and data-producing samples, the researcher and reader must be concerned with the phenomena of nonparticipation. There is extensive evidence in the literature that . . . those who answer initially hold different opinions from those who do not. As we analyze data for any one study this means that we must continually evaluate the data, particularly any data of particular significance, to determine if the nonresponders could have affected the response pattern. For example, assume we find that 70 percent of the selected sample of 100 actually produced data. In studying data for a particular question, we find that of the 70 respondents, 52 answered "yes" and 18 answered "no." We can have good confidence in these data, for even if the 30 nonrespondents had the same opinion, and it was "no," the majority would still be on the "yes" opinion. However, if the 70 respondents split 39 to 31 on another question, we could have little confidence in these data, for if a majority of the nonrespondents held to either point of view they could alter the result. (1969, pp. 345–346)

Ethical research requires that human subjects' participation in research be voluntary. In fact, guidelines for research established by the federal government and a host of professional organizations include some requirement for informed consent. Russell Schutt (1996) summarized these statements, "Participation in research should be voluntary and therefore subjects must give their informed consent to participate in the research" (p. 59). Informed consent may be defined as "the procedure in which individuals choose whether to participate in an investigation after being informed of the facts that would be likely to influence their decision" (Diener & Crandall, 1978, p. 34).

The principle of informed consent requires that individuals be permitted to withdraw from an experiment or study. So, what about college classes in which students are required to participate in research? By procedures established by most college "Human Subjects Committees," students who wish to withdraw from a survey or experiment may be provided with an alternative research activity (such as summarizing a research article on the topic) that would not be objectionable to them.

Informed consent is often secured by asking subjects (or their parents if the subject is a child) to complete a form on which they are given full information about any risks involved in study participation, the voluntariness of participation, the purposes of the research including benefits to be derived, study procedures, steps to assure confidentiality, and an offer to answer any questions about the study (Greenberg & Folger, 1988, p. 25). Subjects sign the form giving their approval to participate. You may have noted that there is no requirement to reveal "in analytical detail . . . the intent of the research" (Rivlin & Timpane, 1978, p. 78). The general purposes are enough. Other elements must be present for informed consent to occur. First, the person giving consent must be competent (that is, the person must be mature and rational) to do so. Second, the respondent must comprehend the information on the consent form. Third, the consent must be voluntary.

Though work with children regularly requires prior completion of informed consent forms, there are times when informed consent may not be required. The Department of Health and Human Services authorized exemptions from the requirement of informed consent if all of the following circumstances are satisfied (Greenberg & Folger, 1988, p. 29):

1. The research exposes subjects to no more than minimal risk.
2. The absence of informed consent instructions will not adversely affect subjects' well being.
3. It would be impractical for the research to be conducted without the waiver.
4. Pertinent information not provided in advance will be disclosed after participation.

Thus, when all these conditions are met, local review boards are permitted to waive informed consent requirements. Of course, there is controversy regarding whether using formal informed consent forms is either needed (implied consent is often viewed as enough) or desirable (informed consent may reduce participation rates [Singer, 1983; Sobal, 1984]) in some survey research outings.

Researchers need to examine potential sources of nonresponse to limit conclusions and to discover additional variables for future study.

Evidence of Randomization in Research Articles

researchers show randomization by either describing methods or referencing random number tables

Researchers who use randomization tend to describe it in great detail. Research articles usually either explain how randomization was handled, or they make some reference to a table of random numbers. If researchers do not rely on either method, then we cannot—and probably should not—assume that randomization was used. Randomization is a pain in the neck and researchers who do it properly often complain about it.

To some extent, the credibility of the research project may be tested by looking at the degree to which the researcher offers evidence of randomization. Highly skilled researchers spell out their methods in enough detail for the study to be replicated.

SUMMARY

Sampling involves selecting events from a population. A population is the universe of events from which the sample is drawn. The actual individual events are called pieces of data. A number computed from a sample is called a statistic, sometimes also called "sample statistics" or "test statistics." A parameter is the label for a number computed from a population. To draw samples from populations, researchers must first define the population. Bias in sampling is a tendency for the sample to err so that it fails to represent the population. Obviously, researchers work to eliminate or minimize bias.

A good sample must be representative of the population and big enough to permit reasonable analysis of data. A representative sample is one that accurately reflects characteristics of the population from which it was drawn. Part of a representative sample involves having a large enough sample to make reasonable interpretations. Sampling error refers to the degree to which a sample differs from population characteristics on some measure. In general, as the sample size gets to be an increased proportion of the population, the amount of sampling error is reduced. Sample sizes should be suitable to the research questions and study designs. If samples have been drawn at random, it is possible to report confidence intervals indicating the probability that sample statistics "capture" population parameters, within certain margins for error. Small samples often invite sampling bias. In addition, because of the ways statistics are computed and

distributions entered, it is very difficult for researchers to find evidence of relationships when sample sizes get small. Yet, statisticians have observed that samples of 30 or more events tend to produce nearly identical distributions.

Sometimes called "probability sampling" techniques, the use of randomization plays an important part in research. Random sampling is selection of data such that each event in the population has an equal chance of selection. Obtaining a random draw of events is not a haphazard matter. Systematic or periodic sampling is not true random sampling because it selects respondents according to a predetermined schedule rather than a random sequence. To select a sample, events may be assigned numbers and chosen by reference to a table of random numbers. Random sampling permits you to feel confident that the sample is representative of the population and that differences from one person to another in a sample will be random rather than systematic. Thus, random sampling allows control of a host of background differences in sample groups. In addition to simple random sampling, other random sampling methods may be used. Stratified random sampling defines samples based on the known proportions within the population and follows it with random sampling within each group. Stratified random sampling is invited where dividing the sample according to some stratification variable is an important part of the study. This method tends to require increased sample sizes that involve increased expenses for the researcher. Furthermore, the method may not be practical to explore many research questions because the weights associated with each stratification variable may not be known. Cluster sampling involves selecting events in two or more stages, with the first stage being the random selection of naturally occurring clusters, and the last stage being the random selection of elements within clusters. The method has been particularly useful when geographically based samples have been involved. Yet, cluster sampling typically requires larger samples than simple random sampling.

Sometimes random sampling is not possible. There are four general categories of nonrandom sampling. First, accidental or convenience sampling involves selecting events that are most readily available. These samples are most useful in case studies and in pilot studies that are designed to help the researcher identify problems and get feedback about research materials. Second, quota sampling defines samples based on the known proportions within the population and nonrandom sampling is completed in each group. This approach is often used in studies where researchers want to make sure that important parts of the population are not omitted in the sampling. Yet, quotas are filled by researchers' sampling friends and family members and the samples are not representative. Third, purposive or known group sampling selects events from groups that are known to possess a particular characteristic under investigation. Purposive or known group sampling is useful for experiments or surveys where a criterion for admission to the sample clearly exist,

or when new measures are validated by use of predictive validity methods. Though this method is convenient and economical when key population characteristics can be identified clearly, sometimes the key characteristic is difficult to see in a group or the key characteristic may be subjective. In addition, since groups of people are identified, the observations may not be independent. Fourth, snowball sampling selects events based on referrals from initial informants. This method is highly useful for studies of behavior that involve deviant or illegal activities, even though researchers using snowball sampling do not really know whether enough referrals exist to penetrate into the group under investigation. Furthermore, the people in the sample cannot be considered independent. These nonrandom methods often allow the researcher to get samples that might otherwise be unavailable and are often invited by field and quasi-experimental research. They have severe limitations, however: (1) they tend to show great biases; (2) since there is no distribution for nonprobability samples, no sampling error computation is possible; (3) their use severely limits conclusions that may be drawn by researchers.

Researchers must often face problems of sampling and sampling error. First, subjects may refuse to participate (either because they initially decline or because they provide incomplete responses). Second, researchers must provide evidence of randomization (either by explaining how they handled randomization, or by referencing a table of random numbers).

TERMS FOR REVIEW

sampling
population
data
statistic
parameter
bias
representative sample
sampling error
confidence intervals

standard deviation random sampling
stratified random sampling
cluster sampling
systematic or periodic sampling
accidental or convenience sampling
quota sampling
purposive or known group sampling
snowball sampling

Statistical Analysis of Data

CHAPTER 13

Descriptive Statistics

To understand God's thoughts, we must study statistics, for these are the measure of His purpose.

–Florence Nightingale

STATISTICS IN COMMUNICATION RESEARCH
    Measures of Central Tendency
    Measures of Variability or Dispersion
DISTRIBUTIONS
    Non-normal and Skewed Distributions

Standard Normal Distribution
MEASURES OF ASSOCIATION
    Interpreting Correlations
    Major Forms of Correlations

BEFORE WE GET STARTED . . .

Many students think that *research methods* is another term for statistics. But as you have seen, statistics are just tools used by scholars to understand information. In this chapter you will learn the language of descriptive statistics and the basic methods used to help characterize quantitative data. You will find that statistical analyses involve a lot of common sense. You do not have to remember your high school math to understand statistics. Instead, this chapter does not presume that you have any background in the subject.

STATISTICS IN COMMUNICATION RESEARCH

importance of statistical understanding

These days you cannot read the literature of the communication field without some basic knowledge of statistical tools. Thus, you must understand how to use different families of statistics because they are all around you. Furthermore, a knowledge of statistical tools allows you to think critically about research and to assess the worth of different studies.

There are two general types of statistics. **Descriptive statistics** consist of numbers that are designed to characterize information. Averages, variability, and correlations are examples of descriptions. The second type is called **inferential statistics** and refers to tools that help researchers draw conclusions about the probable populations from which samples do or do not belong. This chapter discusses descriptive statistics and the next two chapters cover major inferential statistical tools.

descriptive and inferential statistics distinguished

It is helpful to realize that statisticians use the Greek alphabet to represent population parameters (remember that parameters are numbers that characterize populations) and when they discuss conceptual formulae. To balance things out, statisticians use the Roman alphabet (the one used in English) to symbolize sample statistics. This distinction will help you keep things straight.

Measures of Central Tendency

Measures of **central tendency** tell what is going on within sample groups or populations *on the average*. You may hear people talk about the "average" rainfall, "average" levels of communication apprehension, or "average" numbers of hours people watch TV. But researchers tend to use specific terms to describe averages. Let's take an example. Suppose that you gave a sample of eight classmates a 10-point rating scale to find out how much they liked the instruction of the research methods class they were taking (10 would be the most exciting course ever, and 1 would be the worst course ever). Suppose you received the following data:

measures of central tendency identified

$$3\ 4\ 5\ 6\ 6\ 7\ 8\ 9.$$

There are several ways to describe the central tendency of these data. The **arithmetic mean** is the number most people call "the average." It adds a set of scores (represented as Xs in formulae) and divides by the number of scores. Other types of means are used in different situations,[1] but if you hear someone refer to "the mean," the word *the* is a definite article indicating the arithmetic mean. The population mean is computed by using this formula:

arithmetic mean identified

$$\mu = \frac{\Sigma X}{N}.$$

The symbol μ is the Greek letter mu ("mew") and represents the population mean. The capital N stands for the number of events in the population. The Σ is called "sigma" and is a math symbol instructing us to "sum" or add up everything that follows. For the sample mean, the formula is:

$$\overline{X} = \frac{\Sigma X}{n}.$$

---

[1]For instance, the "geometric mean" is used to average ratios or proportions. If money deposited in a savings account grew from $100 to $300 in 5 years, the average percentage increase would *not* be computed by dividing the 200% increase by 5 (because of the presence of compounded interest). The *geometric mean* would be used. To find average miles per gallon for a car that was driven for 10 miles at 35 miles per hour, 5 miles at 20 miles per hour, and 8 miles at 40 miles per hour, the *harmonic mean* would be used.

The sample mean is represented by $\bar{X}$, which is read "X bar." The lowercase "n" is used to indicate the number of events in the sample. If we plug in the numbers from our sample into the formula, we find that the mean is 6. The formulae for sample and population means are very similar. In fact, the sample mean is said to be an **unbiased estimator** of the population mean. This statement asserts that a representative sample mean is likely to approximate the population mean. Certainly, it is *more likely* to equal the population mean than any other measure we can find. Hence, if researchers do not have the population mean for a formula that requires it, the sample mean may be substituted. Though the mean is a very useful number, it can be thrown off by a small number of extreme scores. So, other methods of central tendency may be examined.

unbiased estimators

The **median** is a score that appears in the middle of an ordered list of scores. As such, the median separates one half of the data from the other half. For our data, we have eight scores that have been listed from lowest to highest. So, there is no score in the "middle." What are we supposed to do? To identify the median, we "split the difference" between the two scores surrounding the middle. In our case, the two scores that surround the middle are 6 and 6. Hence, splitting the difference between these two numbers yields a score of 6.

the median identified

The **mode** is the most commonly occurring score. In this example, the score 6 appears most often. Sometimes data have more than one mode. When data have two modes, they are called **bimodal.** But if data have many modes, the mode may not be a meaningful way to depict central tendency.

mode defined

bimodal distributions

Measures of Variability or Dispersion

In addition to characterizing the averages of scores, researchers may want to determine how close the data are to the mean. This matter can be important. Suppose you were on a bowling team and one of your players got ill and you needed a substitute. If you had a choice between Pat (whose last three games were 155, 175, and 210) and Merle (whose last three games were 172, 180, and 188), which substitute bowler would you ask first? Each bowler has exactly the same average! Yet, most people would ask Merle first. Consistency with the average matters. Measures of dispersion or variability tell how far from the average the data tend to be.

Range

the range identified

The **range** is the difference between the highest and lowest scores. In our example, Pat has a range of 55 pins, and Merle's range is only 16. Sometimes researchers further divide the range into quartiles to describe additional divisions. The range is often used to summarize data, but since the range does not deal with the spread of scores around a measure of central tendency, researchers may not be able to compare ranges very usefully. Furthermore, the range is greatly affected by extreme scores.

Variance

variance identified

The **variance** is a measure of the average of squared differences of scores from the mean. As a matter of notation, the symbol s^2 represents the variance of a sample. The symbol σ^2 (sigma squared—that's lowercase sigma) represents the variance of the population. But these definitions do not give you much of a feeling for these highly useful measures of variability.

It often is helpful to read statistical formulae by using shorthand symbols. By learning a few details, the summary formulae can be very useful. Let's look at the formula for sample variance:

$$s^2 = \frac{\Sigma(X - \overline{X})^2}{n - 1}.$$

To read such a formula, we start with items inside the parentheses. In this case, we are told to take an X score, subtract the sample mean ($\overline{X}$) from it, and square the difference. Because of the presence of the sigma sign, we know that we are going to continue this process for all the other X scores as well.

The sigma sign (Σ) tells us to sum—or add up—the values we have computed. This sigma sign is shown here in its abbreviated form, but you should know that it actually has subscripts and superscripts that may be used. For instance, the following form is fairly standard:

$$\sum_{i=1}^{n, 1} X_i.$$

This statement still means that we sum the X scores that follow, but there is additional detail. The "i=1" statement below the sigma sign means that we are to start our summation with the first instance. The "n, 1" above the sigma means that we are to continue through the total number of events in the data set by intervals of one. Suppose we wanted to add up the even numbered events out of our first 20 events. The sigma would indicate:

$$\sum_{i=2}^{20, 2} X_i.$$

You will notice that the X score has a "i" to indicate that is represents instances of X scores that are to be included in the summation. If you see a sigma sign without the additional symbols, it is a shorthand for summing up scores starting with the first instance, and moving through all of them by intervals of one. The subscripts are often deleted, in which case it is to be assumed that the formula is to include each instance of a score.

Other symbols are frequently used in statistical discussions, including

* multiplied by

/ divided by

> greater than

< less or fewer than

≥ equal to or greater than

≤ equal to or less (or fewer) than

≠ not equal to

In each case, these symbols can help summarize a great deal of information to be followed in making statistical calculations.

Let's use some common sense. You want to find a number that tells the average distance of data from the mean. For now, pretend you have a data set that includes the entire population of events. If you want to tell people how far from the mean your data happen to be, you should find out how far each data point is from the mean; then you can average the distances. Do it one step at a time; it is important to understand the common sense of this statistic.

You could start by subtracting the mean (μ) from each score (X). If you used the data discussed earlier in the chapter, it would appear as

X	μ	(X – μ)
3 –	6	–3
4 –	6	–2
5 –	6	–1
6 –	6	0
6 –	6	0
7 –	6	1
8 –	6	2
9 –	6	3

Now, we just need to average these differences, right? Try it!

It doesn't work, does it? When you add up all the difference scores, the plus and minus signs cancel out the differences. When you add up the positive and negative numbers, you get 0. It happens every time you subtract a mean from the data you used to compute that mean. So, you need to get rid of the negative numbers on a temporary basis. You could accomplish this objective by squaring the differences (multiplying each difference score by itself). Then you could average these "squared differences" and finish up by "unsquaring" the average so that you get back to the kinds of cardinal numbers you started with. Try it.

X	μ	(X – μ)	(X – μ)^2
3 –	6	–3	9
4 –	6	–2	4
5 –	6	–1	1
6 –	6	0	0
6 –	6	0	0
7 –	6	1	1
8 –	6	2	4
9 –	6	3	9
			sum = 28

Sometimes this sum is called the "sum of squares" (short for the "sum of squared differences of scores from their mean"). Now, you take the average of this sum. Twenty-eight divided by 8 is 3.5. This number is called the variance. Thus, the variance really is just the average of squared differences of scores from the mean. It is all common sense, but the plus and minus signs caused you to take an additional step or two.

When the pieces are put together, the formula for variance may be symbolized as follows:

$$\sigma^2 = \frac{\Sigma(X - \mu)^2}{N}.$$

This formula reads, "sigma squared (the population variance) equals the sum of the squared differences of the population mean subtracted from each of the scores, and divided by the number of scores in the population."

You have been pretending to have the entire population of events. Suppose you only had a sample from the population. Then things change a little. You see, the mean of the sample ($\overline{X}$) is an unbiased estimator of the population mean (μ). But it is only an estimator. It probably is close, but it is not exact. Thus, if you acted as if the sample mean perfectly identified the population mean, you would not only fool yourself, but you would "low ball" the amount of variation that truly exists in the population. Furthermore, your sample variance (s^2) would become a biased estimator of the population variance (σ^2). That won't do.

Permit an explanation (see also Aczel, 1989, pp. 171–175). You could have computed variation many ways. You might have subtracted each score from every other score. But you did not. You used a fixed point—the sample mean—around which to make comparisons. Selecting that starting point meant that the range of variability of the individual scores was artificially restricted to average out to the sample mean. The degrees of freedom of the first data-points in the sample to take on any values were unrestricted. But by the time the last data-point was reached, the only way the mean could be as reported is if the last data-point had no degree of freedom in taking a value. Think of it this way. Suppose you offered to three friends their choice of candy bars: Milky Way, Three Musketeers, and Snickers. The first friend you ask has a choice (she chooses Snickers). The second person also has a choice (he chooses Milky Way). But by the time you get to your third friend, there is no choice left at all. Similarly, when you have an arbitrary point around which to make comparisons of events in a sample, the freedom of the events to take on values is restricted by the time you get to the last data-point. If you had the entire population, you could live with it, since there would be no error in estimating the population mean. But every time you compute a *sample* variance, you "lose a degree of freedom" equal to the number of sample means you computed to make comparisons. Thus, statisticians say that every time one "estimates a parameter from a sample" (a sample mean is an unbiased estimator of the population mean, remember?), a degree of freedom is lost. It always works that way—every time you estimate a population mean, you lose a degree of freedom.[2]

losing a degree of freedom every time you estimate a parameter from samples

To estimate a population mean legitimately from a sample mean, you have to "pay the kitty" for the privilege. To use the sample mean in the formula for the variance, you must "ante up" by altering the way you compute the variance: divide the sum of squared differences of scores from the sample mean by the number of events *minus one for the mean you estimated from the sample*. Thus, the formula for sample variance is

$$s^2 = \frac{\Sigma(X - \overline{X})^2}{n - 1} .$$

[2]It works with all parameters estimated from samples. For instance, in multiple correlation, a degree of freedom is lost each time a beta weight is computed.

The sample variance in this case would be a little different since the divisor of this formula is n−1 (8−1). Thus, if we divided 28 by 7, we would get a variance (s^2) of 4.

The variance is—with some adjusting for using sample means—the average squared difference of scores from the mean. But these numbers are difficult to interpret. To return to cardinal numbers, researchers need to remove the effect of squared differences on averaging. This step leads to the last part of our common sense way of measuring variability.

Standard Deviation

standard deviation distinguished

The **standard deviation** shows how far the average score deviates from the mean. Since the variance is the average of squared deviations of differences of scores from the mean, if we want to get to "unsquared" differences (the cardinal numbers with which we started), we simply take the square root of the variance, using these formulae:[3]

Sample Standard Deviation   *Population Standard Deviation*

$$ s = \sqrt{\frac{\Sigma(X - \overline{X})^2}{n-1}} \qquad \sigma = \sqrt{\frac{\Sigma(X - \mu)^2}{N}} $$

The standard deviation is, in essence, an average of "unsquared" deviations of scores from their own mean. It tells the average difference of scores from the mean. In the example, the variance (s^2) was 4. Thus, the sample standard deviation would be the square root of 4. Hence the sample standard deviation (s) is 2. Since the population variance(σ^2) is 3.5, the population standard deviation (σ) is 1.87.

standard deviations permit use of the standard normal curve

Another quality makes standard deviations so valuable to researchers. These numbers make it possible for researchers to use the standard normal curve to help make decisions. To grasp this matter, you must understand the notion of distributions.

DISTRIBUTIONS

Data tend to form distributions that have different appearances. A knowledge of the patterns they form can help researchers understand what the data really are saying. This section looks at two types of distributions: data distributions and the standard normal curve.

Non-normal and Skewed Distributions

The location of the median, mean, and mode can indicate quite a bit about the nature of underlying data patterns. Several different patterns might be found in the data. In each, the data are "talking" to the researcher; he or she just has to know how to listen.

Types of Skew

skewness identified

An off-center distribution is **skewed.** Contrary to popular belief, skewness does not tell where data are. Instead, it indicates where the long tail away from the "hump" of the

---

[3]These formulae are the correct ones for standard deviation of samples and populations. Without naming names, it is the case that for nearly a quarter of a century some books in communication research methods have confused the formulae for sigma and s with each other.

data is located. There are formulae to compute skewness, but for this discussion it is most important just to understand the basic ideas. If the distribution is perfectly centered and symmetrical, there is no skew at all (and formulae report skewness coefficients of 0). The tails on each side of the mean would start at the same location and be equally as long. If skewness is negative, the long tail is "below" the mean (our "ground zero"). Then, you could say that the distribution is "skewed to the left" or has "negative skew." Figure 13.1A shows such a pattern. If the skewness is positive, then the long tail is "above" the "ground zero" mean. As Figure 13.1B shows, positive skew means that the distribution is "skewed to the right." In the sample of class ratings, the distribution is not skewed one way any more than the other. A bimodal distribution, such as that found in Figure 13.1C, exaggerates skew because the hump in data is found at two different locations.

negative or leftward skew

rightward or positive skew

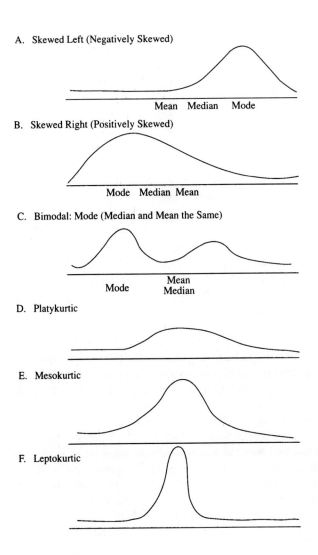

FIGURE 13.1
Distribution Forms

Peakedness of Distributions

kurtosis identified

In addition to measuring "centeredness," there are ways to find out how peaked a distribution is. The measure of peakedness is called **kurtosis.** Since the formula is a bit cumbersome, we will not present it here. But here is the basic idea. In a perfect normal distribution, the distribution is as high as 3 standard deviations is wide. If the peak is higher than 3 standard deviations is wide, then the kurtosis is greater than 3. If the peak is shorter than 3 standard deviations is wide, kurtosis is lower than 3. This explanation does not give credit to the computation methods for kurtosis. Furthermore, you should know that many popular computer programs now subtract 3 from the kurtosis formula. So, you must be careful when looking at kurtosis numbers to make sure you do not misinterpret them.

distributions:

platykurtic
mesokurtic

leptokurtic

Figure 13.1D shows a distribution that has a kurtosis lower than 3. It is very flat and its profile looks somewhat like a plateau. This distribution is called, by coincidence, **platykurtic.** Figure 13.1E shows a distribution that has a peak that is neither very high nor very low (kurtosis of 3). This distribution is called **mesokurtic.** The last figure (13.1F) shows an extremely peaked distribution, which seems to leap upward. This pattern is called **leptokurtic.** By looking at both skewness and kurtosis, the researcher can get a good picture of the data.

Standard Normal Distribution

One of the basic tools used by researchers is called the **standard normal curve.** Because this distribution is the basis for many other distributions and statistics, we should understand something about it.

The Gaussian Curve

probability distributions and data distributions distinguished

The standard normal curve is a mathematic ideal. It is a **probability distribution** that tells the expected value that would be obtained by sampling at random. Data you collect (**data distributions**) can form normal curves, but they cannot be the standard normal curve unless they meet the exact definitions for this kind of distribution. In the early part of the 19th century, mathematician Carl Friedrich Gauss (1777–1855) and the Marquis de Laplace (1749–1827) developed the language of the standard normal curve (Pearson, 1924). Though at the time, Gauss was trying to find clues to the normal deviations in orbits and polar "wobbles" of planets, he also found that many types of ordinary data tended to cluster around their averages with fewer and fewer pieces of data at the extremes. As you can see in Figure 13.2, the standard normal curve is perfectly centered and peaked. The median, mean, and mode are all at the same place on the distribution. The skewness is 0 since the distribution is completely centered. The kurtosis of the standard normal curve is 3. You can also see that the tails of the standard normal curve never really touch bottom—they go out forever.

naming the standard deviation on the standard normal curve

Starting at the top of the curve, Gauss observed the point where the slope changed direction. To identify this location on the curve, he dropped a line down to the baseline. Then he noticed that there was a second point where the slope changed direction again. He dropped another line to mark the spot and soon he observed that the intervals between his lines were identical whether he followed the curve above the mean or below the mean. He called these points deviations of slope on the standard normal curve or "standard deviations" for short.

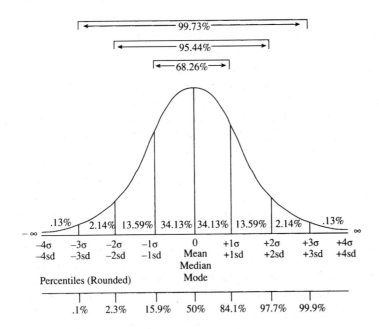

FIGURE 13.2
Standard Normal
Curve

John C. Reinard.
*Foundations of Argument:
Effective Communication
for Critical Thinking.*
Copyright © 1991.
Dubuque, IA: Wm. C.
Brown Communications
Inc. Used with permission.

The mean, median, and mode are symbolized by the Greek letter mu (μ). The standard deviation is symbolized by the Greek lowercase letter sigma (σ). Figuring that numbers might be needed, statisticians defined the center of the distribution as ground zero, or just 0. Each standard deviation is set to be 1 unit wide. Hence σ is defined to be equal to 1. A standard deviation below ground zero has a negative sign in front of it and a standard deviation above ground zero has a positive number. Researchers often collect data that have normal distributions. But if they do not have a mean of 0, a standard deviation of 1, a skewness of 0, a kurtosis of 3, and tails that stretch to infinity, they do not have standard normal curves. Yet, we can compare actual data to a standard normal curve to help identify long range expectations and to make sound decisions. The section that follows shows how researchers use this curve.

**requirements of a
standard normal
curve**

Interpreting Areas under the Normal Curve

Gauss reported the density function for the standard normal curve, which indicates what percentage of the total area under the standard normal curve extends *from ground zero out* to a point of interest. As you can see, approximately two-thirds of the distribution exists from 1σ below the mean to 1σ above the mean (though the amount actually is 68.26 percent). Over 95% (actually 95.44%) of the curve extends from −2σ to +2σ. All but .27% (that's "point 27 percent" not "27 percent") exists from −3σ to +3σ. The density function has been summarized on tables that are widely available (see Appendix A). These tables have many uses. For instance, suppose you had an instructor who wished to "grade on the curve." Though few instructors really use a strict curve, the method submits that if you assume that grades have a generally normal distribution (and experience shows that grades generally do), then you should be able

FIGURE 13.3
Standard Normal
Curve Used in
Grading on the
Curve

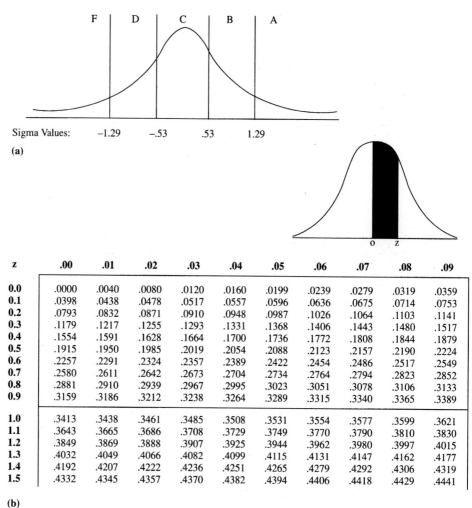

(a)

z	.00	.01	.02	.03	.04	.05	.06	.07	.08	.09
0.0	.0000	.0040	.0080	.0120	.0160	.0199	.0239	.0279	.0319	.0359
0.1	.0398	.0438	.0478	.0517	.0557	.0596	.0636	.0675	.0714	.0753
0.2	.0793	.0832	.0871	.0910	.0948	.0987	.1026	.1064	.1103	.1141
0.3	.1179	.1217	.1255	.1293	.1331	.1368	.1406	.1443	.1480	.1517
0.4	.1554	.1591	.1628	.1664	.1700	.1736	.1772	.1808	.1844	.1879
0.5	.1915	.1950	.1985	.2019	.2054	.2088	.2123	.2157	.2190	.2224
0.6	.2257	.2291	.2324	.2357	.2389	.2422	.2454	.2486	.2517	.2549
0.7	.2580	.2611	.2642	.2673	.2704	.2734	.2764	.2794	.2823	.2852
0.8	.2881	.2910	.2939	.2967	.2995	.3023	.3051	.3078	.3106	.3133
0.9	.3159	.3186	.3212	.3238	.3264	.3289	.3315	.3340	.3365	.3389
1.0	.3413	.3438	.3461	.3485	.3508	.3531	.3554	.3577	.3599	.3621
1.1	.3643	.3665	.3686	.3708	.3729	.3749	.3770	.3790	.3810	.3830
1.2	.3849	.3869	.3888	.3907	.3925	.3944	.3962	.3980	.3997	.4015
1.3	.4032	.4049	.4066	.4082	.4099	.4115	.4131	.4147	.4162	.4177
1.4	.4192	.4207	.4222	.4236	.4251	.4265	.4279	.4292	.4306	.4319
1.5	.4332	.4345	.4357	.4370	.4382	.4394	.4406	.4418	.4429	.4441

(b)

to slice off the top 10% of students to receive grades of A and the bottom 10% to receive grades of F. The next 20% in from each extreme would receive grades of B and D, and the remaining 40% would receive grades of C. Figure 13.3 shows how normally distributed scores are arranged when a teacher grades on the curve. The C range is in the middle of the distribution and approximately 40% of the curve extends from ground zero up to .53σ and down to −.53σ.

using the table for the standard normal curve

You may wish to look at Appendix A to see what is going on here. We have reproduced a portion of it in Figure 13.3. Here is how to use this table. The term z identifies the number of sigmas or standard deviations of interest. Read the column marked z until you find 0.5. That step brings you to the first decimal point. Now read across the top row to find the column identified .03. This column picks up the second decimal point: 0.53. Where this column and row intersect, you see the number .2019.

This number means that 20.19% of the total area under the standard normal curve exists from ground zero out to .53 sigmas. The shaded area in the picture at the top of the table illustrates this relationship. This distribution is symmetrical. So, to figure out how much area exists from .53 sigmas *below* the mean up to .53 sigmas *above* the mean, simply double the area (.2019 * 2 = .4038). Thus, the amount of area from −.53σ to +.53σ is approximately 40%. To pick up an additional 20% of the grades around *C,* you would have to go out to 1.29σ in each direction. The 10% of the total area left over on each side of the distribution would be identified as *A* and *F* ranges.

using the standard normal curve to identify unusual occurrences

As you can see, the standard normal curve can help identify long-run expectations you might have for samples you draw. These distributions are used as probability distributions to help you understand when unusual patterns exist in the data—so that you can make appropriate decisions.

Using z Scores

Researchers usually are not lucky enough to collect data that have a mean of zero and a standard deviation of 1. Yet, they can still use the standard normal curve to make decisions by changing data into "z scores." Because z scores allow us to use the "standard normal" curve to help make decisions, these scores sometimes are called "standard scores." **Z scores** permit us to represent data scores as units under the standard normal curve. Thus, we can use z scores to compare general patterns of scores to others. The formula for z is

z scores identified

$$z = \frac{X - \mu}{\sigma}.$$

The "X" is a score of interest to the researcher. For example, much communication research examines the role of receiver intelligence on reactions to messages. Scores on the popular Stanford-Binet IQ test are normally distributed with a population mean (μ) of 100 and a population standard deviation (σ) of 15. Suppose you scored 115 on an IQ test. Assuming for the sake of argument that IQ tests measure something, how many people would your scores exceed? We might insert numbers as follows:

$$z = \frac{X - \mu}{\sigma}$$

$$= \frac{115 - 100}{15}$$

$$= \frac{15}{15}$$

$$= 1.00.$$

So, how many scores would yours exceed? You need only look at the table. In Figure 13.3 find the column for z and identify the row corresponding to 1.0. To find the second decimal point value, continue across the top of the table to the column marked ".00". The intersection of this column and this row reveals the number .3413, indicating that 34.13% of the area lies between the mean and a z value of 1.00.

How do we find out how many scores are below yours? You might suppose that you just double the value of .3413. DON'T DO IT! The 115 score is above average, right? So you have a higher score than all the people who were "below average."

Since 50% of the area is below the mean (and 50% above the mean), you know that your score is automatically better than the 50% of the below average scores. In addition, the z table shows that your score is greater than 34.13 of the scores that were average and above. Thus, your IQ score is greater than 50% + 34.13%, for a total of 84.13%. Your score is greater than those of approximately 84% of other IQ scores.

z scores when population mean and standard deviation estimated from samples

Suppose you do not have the population mean (μ) or the population standard deviation (σ)? No problem. The sample mean ($\overline{X}$) is an "unbiased estimator" of the population mean (μ). The sample standard deviation (s) is an "unbiased estimator" (provided the right formula was used for the sample standard deviation) of the population standard deviation (σ). So, you can substitute the sample means and standard deviations for population means and standard deviations to compute our answers. Let's return to the example of a teacher grading on the curve. Suppose the mean on the test is 50, your test score is 61, and the standard deviation is 10. What grade would you get, given the dividing points used in the example? We complete the following formula:

$$z = \frac{X - \overline{X}}{s}$$
$$= \frac{61 - 50}{10}$$
$$= \frac{11}{10}$$
$$= 1.10$$

Look up this value in Figure 13.3, and notice that you would get a *B* on this exam. If we wanted to know how many people got lower scores than you did, you could look at the z table. As the area under the normal curve shows, 36.43% of the scores on the normal distribution exist between the mean and 1.10 z scores. Thus, your test score is higher than the 50% of students who were below average, plus 36.43%, for a total of 86.43%.

uses of the standard normal curve

Despite its usefulness, you might wonder why so much fuss is made about the standard normal curve. Researchers often use the standard normal curve to describe the presumed way variables occur. They may gather samples and use the standard normal curve to learn how likely such samples could be found at random from an underlying distribution in which only ordinary and random variation exists. Suppose, for instance, that you gather some sample data whose typical z score is 2.6 or greater. By looking at the standard normal curve, you know that such data could be found very rarely if the distribution is normal and centered at its assumed mean. What would you do? We *could* conclude that you sampled data that just happened to come from the upper end of the underlying distribution. *Or,* you might conclude that the underlying distribution from which the sample was drawn is not really as ordinary as assumed. You might conclude—by looking at the odds of getting samples such as yours at random—that your data have been systematically influenced to make them different from the assumed "ordinary" distribution. By using the standard normal curve (and its variations) you can "play the odds" to see how likely new sample results could have occurred at random. This thinking is the basis for significance testing, which is described in the next chapter.

MEASURES OF ASSOCIATION

One major way to describe data statistically uses measures of association or correlation.[4] A **correlation** is just a measure of the coincidence of variables. Most people use the word *coincidence* to mean an "accidental" or "bogus" relationship. But in reality, a coincidence means simply that two variables "coincide" with each other. Correlations show the degree to which variables "coincide" with each other by use of formulae that show the amount of coincidence.

correlation defined

For correlations, you must have data on two measures (though some correlations allow the use of more than two variables) from each event in the sample. For instance, your income and the number of magazines to which you subscribe can be correlated. You could check the association between the severity of articulation disorders among children and their school grades. Each situation requires that events in the sample include scores that can be plotted and analyzed to reveal associations. This section considers the ways that correlations are interpreted and two major methods used to determine correlations.

Interpreting Correlations

Correlation coefficients can have a range of values from −1.00 to 1.00, but you probably will not see many 1.00 correlations in research. Instead, you will see numbers behind decimal points. The closer the number is to 1 (regardless of the sign before it), the stronger is the correlation. Two types of relationships can be revealed. The first is called a **direct relationship,** which indicates that as one variable increases, the other variable also increases. Similarly, as one variable decreases, so does the other. Figure 13.4A shows the general pattern (called a scatterplot) that is indicated by direct relationships. As an aid to interpretation, researchers often add a line of "best fit" through the data. This line sometimes is called a "line of regression," because Karl Pearson, who refined correlation formulae, used data that investigated the "regression effect" when he drew the first line—and the name stuck. Both diagrams reveal high direct correlations since the line of "best fit" shows that as the variable on the horizontal axis increases, so does the variable on the vertical axis. The second illustration shows a perfect 1.00 correlation since all the data are exactly on the line. Though often misunderstood, the correlation is not the steepness of the line's slope—the slope is called "covariance." Instead, correlation size is shown by the closeness of the data to the line of best fit. If you look at Figure 13.4C, you will see scatterplots showing no relationship. If one of the variables is held constant (and not a variable at all), a correlation of zero also will be found. As you can tell, if a chart is drawn according to standard protocols, zero correlations are reflected in plots that form perfect circles (or lines that are perfectly horizontal or perfectly vertical, in the case of situations in which one "variable" has only one value in the data).

direct relationships identified

line of best fit or regression noted

An **inverse relationship** is one in which an increase in one variable corresponds to a decrease in the other. These correlations are identified by the use of negative signs,

inverse relationships identified

---

[4]Some writers reserve the term "association" for measures on the nominal or ordinal levels of measurement.

FIGURE 13.4
Forms of Correlations

A. Direct or Positive Relationships

High Direct Relationship

Perfect Direct Relationship
(Unity)

B. Inverse or Negative Relationships

High Inverse Relationship

Perfect Inverse Relationship
(Unity)

C. No Relationships

Nearly No Relationship

Perfect Zero Relationship

D. Curvilinear Relationships

but you should interpret negative signs as subtractions or "take away." A correlation of −.82 is a strong one. The negative sign does not mean that this correlation is "less than" a positive correlation of .15. The minus sign only indicates that as one variable increases, the other declines (see Figure 13.4B). There are many such examples in communication research. As the amount of conflict within a group increases, the amount of ambiguity the members feel about the issues declines. The higher one's intelligence, the fewer hours of television one might watch. Such patterns occur frequently in communication research and can be very interesting. To understand how to judge the size of different correlations, statistician Robert Koenker developed this general guide (1961, p. 52):

.80 to 1.00	highly dependable relationship	**guidelines to**
.60 to .79	moderate to marked relationship	**interpret correlations**
.40 to .59	fair degree of relationship	
.20 to .39	slight relationship	
.00 to .19	negligible or chance relationship.	

There are some common sense exceptions to these guidelines, of course. If you examine questions searching for the last few contributors to effects, you might interpret a small coefficient more favorably than you would otherwise.

Let's see how the method works. Many communication students eventually pursue careers in law and they usually take the Law School Aptitude Test (LSAT). This test seems bothersome to most students, but the test scores correlate .50 with first-year grades in law school. When a student's undergraduate grades are added to the mix, the combination correlates .70 with first-year law school grades (Anastasi, 1968, pp. 431– 432). Thus, it seems that the test alone is a "fair" predictor of first-year law school grades, and when undergraduate grades are included, the combination becomes a "marked" predictor of success in law school.

Some students look at correlation coefficients as percentages. They think that a .80 correlation explains 80% of the effect. NOT TRUE! A correlation uses its own metric to identify correspondence between scores. To find out the percentage impact one variable has on another, you can simply square the correlation coefficient. This number is called a **coefficient of determination** and shows the percentage of variation in one variable that can be explained by a knowledge of the other variable alone. Hence a correlation of .80 means that 64% ($.80^2 = .64$) of the variation in one variable can be explained by the other one alone. In the example of LSAT scores, the combination of first-year test scores and undergraduate grades explains 49% of total variability—slightly under half. This relation surely is better than intuition alone, but the coefficient of determination also reveals that there is plenty of room for improvement.

not confusing correlations for percentages

coefficient of determination

Sometimes the data show different patterns, as indicated in Figure 13.4D. These relationships are curvilinear since the best fit of a line to the data is not a straight line. These curves invite the use of special correlations that can identify the magnitude of the curved effect (such as the correlation ratio, eta [η]). Furthermore, they tell the researcher that there is an optimal low point or high point that will be missed if the researcher is not careful.

curvilinear relationships

Major Forms of Correlations

There are many correlation formulae that have been developed for different sorts of data. Table 13.1 lists these major forms. As you can see, they differ most in the sorts of data they allow researchers to examine for relationships. Thus, the levels of measurement for the independent and dependent variables are listed. If you need to use any of these tools, you can find them explained in many comprehensive statistics books (e.g., Glass & Hopkins, 1984; Aczel, 1989). For the purposes of this book, only the two most commonly used tools will be described.

forms of correlations

TABLE 13.1 Forms of Association and Correlation Measures

Measures Designed for Two Variables

Levels of Measurement for:

One Variable	Other Variable	Correlation Method
N O M I N A L	Nominal	Tetrachoric Correlation (for two false dichotomies)
	Nominal	Yule's Q (for use if both variables have only two categories)
	Nominal	Phi Coefficient (computed from chi square based on two variables with only two categories)
	Nominal	Asymmetric lambda (computed from number of events in mode category and distinction made between independent and dependent variable)
	Nominal	Symmetric lambda (computed from number of events in mode category)
	Nominal	Contingency Coefficient (for two or more categories in each variable; coefficient upper limit affected by category numbers)
	Nominal	Cramer's V (for two or more categories in each variable)
	Interval or Ratio	Biserial r (for false dichotomy in nominal variable)
	Interval or Ratio	Point Biserial r (for true dichotomy in nominal variable)
O R D I N A L	Ordinal	Spearman Rank Order Correlation
	Ordinal	Goodman and Kruskal's gamma (for use with any sized tables)
	Ordinal	Kendall's tau a, tau b, Kim's d (for use when many tied ranks are present)
	Ordinal	Kendall's tau c (for use when variables have different numbers of categories)
	Ordinal	Somers' d (for use when distinction made between independent and dependent variable)
	Interval or Ratio	Jaspen's coefficient of multiserial correlation (used when assuming that the ordinal variable is derived from a normally distributed interval variable)
	Interval or Ratio	Mayer and Robinson's M_{yu} (for assumption that the ordinal variable is composed of ordered levels of an underlying variable)
I N T E R V A L (or Ratio)	Interval or Ratio	Pearson Product Moment Correlation (for linear relationships)
		Eta (a.k.a. correlation ratio) (for nonlinear relationships)

MEASURES DESIGNED FOR MORE THAN TWO VARIABLES

Correlation Method	Application
Kendall's Coefficient of Concordance	correlation of more than two sets of rankings
Partial Correlation	correlation of an interval level dependent variable with one predictor variable while holding a third variable constant (the proportion of variance that is not associated with a third controlled variable)
Part Correlation (semipartial correlation)	correlation equalling the unique contribution made by a predictor variable (the variation between the predictor variable and other potential predictors is eliminated)
Multiple Linear Correlation (Multiple Regression Analysis)	correlation of a single interval level criterion variable with multiple predictor variables
Canonical Correlation	correlation of a set of multiple predictor variables with a set of criterion variables
Multiple Discriminant Analysis	correlational method used to predict group membership categories (measured on the nominal level) from a set of interval level variables
Multivariate Multiple Regression Analysis	an extension of multiple linear correlation for situations in which more than one criterion variable is treated as a common set

SPECIAL DISCUSSION 13–2
Correlation and Causality

Though causal relationships should produce high correlations, a correlation cannot show causation by itself. To show cause-and-effect relationships directly, researchers must use the experimental method (or use the method of history if they can wait long enough). Researchers who think correlations show cause-and-effect relationships can make some silly mistakes. Li (1975) reported a study of factors predicting birth rates among Taiwanese. The researchers observed that birth rate decreased as the number of small appliances one owned increased. Thus, it seemed that one could control population growth by sending toasters, hair dryers, and the like to Taiwan. Of course, owning small appliances does not cause one to have a small family. But it might work the other way around—if you don't have children you have more money to purchase small appliances. Thus, the researchers made a double error. Not only did they assume a causal relationship, but they claimed a mistaken direction for the difference.

Glass and Hopkins explained the reasons that it is unwise to assume a causal relationship based on correlational information:

> First, even when one can presume that a causal relationship does exist between two variables being correlated, r_{xy} can tell nothing by itself about whether X causes Y or Y causes X. Second, often variables other than the two under consideration could be responsible for the observed association. Third, the relationships that exist among variables in behavioral and social science are almost always too complex to be explained in terms of a single cause. (1984, p. 104)

Experienced researchers resist the temptation to view correlations as identical to causal relationships.

Pearson Product Moment Correlation

Developed by Karl Pearson, the **Pearson product moment correlation** method is suitable for situations in which the independent and dependent variables (identified as X and Y respectively in most notation) are *interval* or *ratio* level measures. Table 13.2 shows how to use the Pearson product moment formula. We compute the covariance and divide it by the product of the standard deviations of each variable. The "covariance" often is abbreviated s_{xy}, even though that symbol makes it look like some kind of standard deviation (s), which it is not.

Pearson product moment correlation

Spearman Rank Order Correlation

Sometimes researchers have measures on the ordinal level. For instance, a manager might decide to explore whether there is a relationship between the number of successful salespeople and the number of hours they have spent in communication skills training classes. The scores on each variable might be expressed by ranks. For instance, the manager might rank nine salespeople from best (1) to worst (9). Then,

TABLE 13.2 Computing the Pearson Product Moment Correlation

Consider a study relating the average amount of time spent watching sporting events on TV each week and the average number of bags of potato chips purchased per month.

One simply computes the differences between each score and its own mean. The result is multiplied by the difference of the other score subtracted from its mean. Then, the sum of these products is divided by the number of samples minus one.

$$\frac{\Sigma[(X - \bar{X}) * (Y - \bar{Y})]}{n - 1}$$

This term is called the covariance.

To compute the Pearson Product Moment correlation for raw scores, the following formula may be used:

$$r = \frac{\text{Covariance }(X,Y) \text{ or } s_{xy}}{s_x * s_y}.$$

For our example, we could compute these matters as follows:

Family	Hours Watching Sports on TV X	(X − X̄)	Bags of Potato Chips Purchased Monthly Y	(Y − Ȳ)	(X−X̄) * (Y−Ȳ)
Jones	3	−3	2	−4	12
Smith	4	−2	5	−1	2
Chan	6	0	6	0	0
King	9	3	4	−2	−6
Manson	5	−1	8	2	−2
Addams	7	1	7	1	1
Simpson	8	2	7	1	2
Mann	6	0	9	3	0
	X̄ = 6		X̄ = 6		sum = 9
	S = 2		S = 2.27		

The covariance is the sum of these differences multiplied by each other, divided by the number of scores minus one:

$$\text{covariance }(X,Y) = \frac{\Sigma(X-\bar{X})*(Y-\bar{Y})}{n - 1}.$$

In our instance, this formula becomes

$$\text{covariance }(X,Y) = \frac{9}{8-1} = 1.29.$$

The overall correlation becomes:

$$r = \frac{\text{Covariance }(X,Y) \text{ or } s_{xy}}{s_x * s_y}.$$

$$= \frac{1.29}{2 * 2.27}$$

$$= .28, \text{ indicating a "slight" relationship.}$$

TABLE 13.3 Computing the Spearman Rank Order Correlation

Example Without Tied Ranks
Here are data for a study relating the rankings of salespeople and rankings of the amount of communication skills training received.

Person	Ranking of Sales Person Ability X	Ranking of Amount of Communication Training Y
Manny	1	1
Moe	2	4
Jack	3	3
Larry	4	7
Curly	5	2
Patty	6	5
Maxine	7	6
Laverne	8	8
Gallagher	9	9

Differences between ranks are computed and these differences are squared, creating a term abbreviated as D^2. Then these squared difference scores are added up. Here is how it works in our example.

Person	Ranking of Sales Person Ability X	Ranking of Amount of Communication Training Y	Differences D	D^2
Manny	1	1	$(1 - 1) = 0$	0
Moe	2	4	$(2 - 4) = -2$	4
Jack	3	3	$(3 - 3) = 0$	0
Larry	4	7	$(4 - 7) = -3$	9
Curly	5	2	$(5 - 2) = 3$	9
Patty	6	5	$(6 - 5) = 1$	1
Maxine	7	6	$(7 - 6) = 1$	1
Laverne	8	8	$(8 - 8) = 0$	0
Gallagher	9	9	$(9 - 9) = 0$	0
			sum of differences =	24

The formula for the Spearman rank order correlation is

$$r_s = 1 - \frac{6 * \Sigma D^2}{n * (n^2 - 1)}$$

In this formula, n is the number of events for which there are paired ranks. Employing our data, substitute the following numbers:

$$= 1 - \frac{6 * 24}{9 * (81 - 1)}$$

$$= 1 - \frac{144}{9 * (80)}$$

$$= 1 - \frac{144}{720}$$

$$= 1 - .20$$

$$= .80$$

which is a "highly dependable" relationship.

TABLE 13.3 (Continued)

Example with Tied Ranks
Here are data for a study relating the rankings of salespeople and rankings of the amount of communication skills training received in which some people had the same number of hours of training.

Person	Ranking of Sales Person Ability X	Ranking of Amount of Communication Training Y
Manny	1	tied
Moe	2	for
Jack	3	first
Larry	4	7
Curly	5	5
Patty	6	6
Maxine	7	4
Laverne	8	tied for
Gallagher	9	eighth

To deal with tied ranks, one simply splits the difference among the tied ranks and assigns those values to all the tied ranks. Since three people are tied for first place (though they normally would receive ranks 1, 2, and 3), we give them the average of the three ranks (2 is the average of ranks 1, 2, and 3). The tie between rank 8 and 9 is settled by giving each person an average rank of 8.5. Thus, we complete the computations as follows:

Person	Ranking of Sales Person Ability X	Ranking of Amount of Communication Training Y	Differences D	D²
Manny	1	2	(1 − 2) = −1	1
Moe	2	2	(2 − 2) = 0	0
Jack	3	2	(3 − 2) = 1	1
Larry	4	7	(4 − 7) = −3	9
Curly	5	5	(5 − 5) = 0	0
Patty	6	6	(6 − 6) = 0	0
Maxine	7	4	(7 − 4) = 3	9
Laverne	8	8.5	(8 − 8.5) = −.5	.25
Gallagher	9	8.5	(9 − 8.5) = .5	.25
			sum of differences =	20.5

Thus,

$$r_s = 1 - \frac{6 * \Sigma D^2}{n * (n^2 - 1)}$$

$$= 1 - \frac{6 * 20.5}{9 * (81 - 1)}$$

$$= 1 - \frac{123}{9 * (80)}$$

$$= 1 - .17$$

$$= .83, \text{ which is a "highly dependable" relationship.}$$

they might be ranked according to the amount of communication skills training they have received. Though the Pearson product moment correlation method may be adapted if there are no ties among the rankings, the **Spearman rank order correlation** formula is suitable across settings. Table 13.3 shows how this formula can be used with both untied and tied ranks.

Spearman rank order correlation

This method is usually abbreviated as r_s, though other notation often is used (some statistics books use rho [ρ] as the abbreviation for the Spearman rank order correlation). The Spearman rank order correlation coefficient is often used even when original data are measured on an interval scale but the researcher suspects that the underlying distributions are not normal. It may be interpreted as any other correlation, including computation of coefficients of determination.

SUMMARY

Descriptive statistics are numbers that characterize information. Inferential statistics are tools that help researchers draw conclusions about the probable populations from which samples do or do not belong. Statisticians use the Greek alphabet to represent population parameters and the Roman alphabet when describing samples.

Measures of central tendency tell what is going on within sample groups or populations on the average. The arithmetic mean adds a set of scores and divides by the number of scores. The sample mean is an unbiased estimator of the population mean. The median is a score that appears in the middle of an ordered list of scores and separates one half of the data from the other half. The mode is the most commonly occurring score. When data have two modes, they are called "bimodal." But if data have many modes, the mode may not meaningfully depict central tendency.

Measures of variability or dispersion tell how close to the mean the data are. The range is the difference between the highest and lowest score in a data set. The variance is a measure of the average of squared differences of scores from the mean (we use the symbol s^2 to represent the variance of a sample and σ^2 to represent the variance of the population. The formulae for sample variance and standard deviation are different so that unbiased estimators of population variance and standard deviation may be created. The standard deviation shows how far the average score deviates from the mean.

Distributions of data often tend to be symmetrical around their averages, but sometimes it does not work that way. A distribution that is off-center is skewed. The measure of peakedness is called kurtosis. A very flat distribution is called platykurtic. A distribution with a peak that is neither very high nor very low is called mesokurtic. An extremely peaked distribution is called leptokurtic. The standard normal curve is a bell-shaped probability distribution that tells the expected value that would be obtained by sampling at random. Data distributions can form normal curves, but they cannot be "the standard normal curve" unless they meet the exact requirements for this special distribution (perfect centeredness and peakedness; median, mean, and mode equal to 0; standard deviation of 1). The areas under the standard normal curve are identified to reveal probabilities of drawing samples from one location on the distribution to another. Z scores permit representing scores from data as units under the standard normal curve. By looking at the standard normal curve, we can estimate whether such data could be found very frequently or very rarely if the distribution is normal and centered at its assumed mean.

A correlation is a measure of the coincidence of variables. Direct relationships mean that as one variable increases, the other variable also increases. An inverse relationship indicates that an increase in one variable corresponds to a decrease in the other (identified by negative signs). Correlation coefficients are not percentages. To know the percentage impact one variable has on another, the square of the correlation coefficient (called a coefficient of determination) should be computed. Sometimes relationships show curvilinear patterns since the best fit of a line to the data is not a straight line. The Pearson product moment correlation is suitable for situations in which *both* the independent and dependent variables (identified as X and Y respectively in most notation) are *interval* or *ratio* level measures. The Spearman rank order correlation is suitable when variables are measured on the ordinal level.

TERMS FOR REVIEW

descriptive statistics
inferential statistics
central tendency
arithmetic mean
unbiased estimator
median
mode
bimodal
range
variance
standard deviation
skewness
kurtosis

platykurtic
mesokurtic
leptokurtic
probability distribution
data distribution
standard normal distribution
z scores
correlation
direct relationship
inverse relationship
coefficient of determination
Pearson product moment correlation
Spearman rank order correlation

CHAPTER 14

Introductory Inferential Statistics I: Hypothesis Testing with Two Means

Statistics is a language that, through its own special symbols and grammar, takes the intangible facts of life and translates them into comprehensible meaning.

–Paul D. Leedy

BEFORE WE GET STARTED . . .

Inferential statistics help researchers figure out how likely their sample results may occur by chance. They play the odds by entering a distribution, such as the standard normal curve, to make comparisons. This chapter introduces some major tools researchers use with inferential statistics. This introduction stresses the logic behind using statistics to test hypotheses, with emphasis on making comparisons between means. The next chapter carries this notion further by looking at applications other than contrasting two means.

USING PROBABILITY DISTRIBUTIONS TO PLAY THE ODDS

To understand the process of statistical inference, we need to cover some basic ideas about ways that people can play the odds to figure out what to expect under normal circumstances. The following section examines what a probability distribution is and the ways in which it can be used.

Using the Statistics of Probability and Inference

The so-called law of averages implies to many of us that anything that can happen will (the Chicago Cubs may win the World Series, for instance—it could happen). But in the ordinary course of events, some things happen more often than others. So, it would be wise to figure the odds before concluding that you have found something striking or unusual in your research. Suppose you had a coin and tossed heads five times in a row. You might think that this pattern is very unusual among fair coins. So, is it a fair coin? If you want a certain answer, you are out of luck. But if you want to see how *probable* such a pattern is, you can get some answers. **Probability** refers to the tendency or likelihood with which an event occurs in a population. You could figure the odds of getting five heads when tossing a fair coin five times. Here's how. The chance of getting heads on a single toss of a fair coin is fifty-fifty (excluding any chance of the coin landing on its edge).[1] Thus, the probability of getting heads is .5 (point five). What is the probability of getting heads if you toss a coin once, *and* heads again on the second toss, *and* heads again in the third toss, *and* heads again on the fourth toss, *and* heads again on the fifth toss? Compute it as

probability defined

$$.5 * .5 * .5 * .5 * .5.$$

The probability of getting all heads in five tosses of a fair coin is .03125. Hence, the odds are only about three chances out of a hundred that you could get your observed pattern from a fair coin. So, what do we decide? It is always *possible* that the tosses reflect something that *can happen* approximately three times out of a hundred among fair coins—in which case, the run of heads would mean that only dumb luck or random occurrence is at work. But, the odds of getting your run of heads by dumb luck from random tosses of a fair coin is so *improbable* that the smart money would bet the coin probably is *not* fair. You could decide that your coin is *unlikely* to be fair since your sample findings could be observed very, very rarely among fair coins.

This example illustrates the basic idea behind playing the odds to see if observed relationships are unlikely to occur by chance. Statisticians have investigated probability theory in some detail and have found ways to identify the odds of getting different sorts of results for various sorts of data (see Chung, 1975; Feller, 1968, 1971). Without getting into the fine details, this chapter will discuss how to use probability distributions, the roots of statistical inference methods.

---

[1] Do not use the word *percent* when you speak about probability—it drives statisticians nuts. In probability, we keep the decimal point. So, the probability of throwing heads is "point five," not "fifty percent."

Using Probability Distributions

Distributions such as the standard normal curve can be useful to determine the probability of underlying patterns. They can describe what you might expect to see ordinarily. These distributions serve as **probability distributions** since they represent the theoretical patterns of expected sample data. This standard normal curve is very much like most data we have in much research. Despite limitations, we can often use the standard normal curve to help us figure the odds of different outcomes.

    For instance, suppose that you and some of your friends buy some quarter-pound hamburgers from a fast food restaurant. You may have been told by the nutrition information posted at the restaurant that the mean weight of the burgers after cooking is .2 of a pound with a standard deviation of .04 of a pound. Since the burgers you have been eating seem to be well below the average, you and your friends suspect that you are not getting your money's worth. If the restaurant is living up to its word, then you would expect the size of the burgers to vary at random around a mean of .2 pounds with a standard deviation of .04 of a pound. How could you figure out whether to complain? You start by looking at the standard normal curve. You could say that if you regularly start finding hamburgers that weigh in at the bottom 5% of the area under the normal distribution of burgers, you will suspect that the current distribution of burgers is not what is alleged by the restaurant—and you could complain.

    You need to look at the standard normal curve table (Appendix A) to find the z value that covers 45% of the area from ground zero, and leaves out the last 5% of the area. Figure 14.1 includes a portion of the z table. As you can see, when we compute z values to the second decimal point as this table does, there is no location that indicates *exactly 45%* of the area from the mean to that location. But there are two numbers that surround exactly 45%. A z of 1.64 covers 44.95% of the area, and a z of

probability distributions identified

using the standard normal curve to identify areas of unusual activity

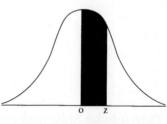

FIGURE 14.1
Section from the z Table

z	.00	.01	.02	.03	.04	.05	.06	.07	.08	.09
1.6	.4452	.4463	.4474	.4484	.4495	.4505	.4515	.4525	.4535	.4545
1.7	.4554	.4564	.4573	.4582	.4591	.4599	.4608	.4616	.4625	.4633
1.8	.4641	.4649	.4656	.4664	.4671	.4678	.4686	.4693	.4699	.4706
1.9	.4713	.4719	.4726	.4732	.4738	.4744	.4750	.4756	.4761	.4767
2.0	.4772	.4778	.4783	.4788	.4793	.4798	.4803	.4808	.4812	.4817
2.1	.4821	.4826	.4830	.4834	.4838	.4842	.4846	.4850	.4854	.4857
2.2	.4861	.4864	.4868	.4871	.4875	.4878	.4881	.4884	.4887	.4890
2.3	.4893	.4896	.4898	.4901	.4904	.4906	.4909	.4911	.4913	.4916

1.65 covers 45.05%. So, if we carry out our z value one more decimal point, we can split the difference. They call this process "interpolating" a table. Thus, a z value of 1.645 corresponds to the location on the curve that includes 45% of the area from ground zero.

using z scores   To figure out how small the hamburgers are when they fall into the bottom 5% of a normal y distribution, use the z score formula:

$$z = \frac{X - \mu}{\sigma}$$

To identify the minimum size of hamburgers to complain about, we can solve the formula for X as follows:

$$X = \mu + (z * \sigma)$$

The z value may be positive or negative. In our example, we suspect that the hamburgers weigh *less* than promised. Thus, our z value has a negative sign in front of it. Putting the data into the formula, you have

$$X = .2 \text{ pounds} + (-1.645 * .04 \text{ pounds})$$

$$X = .2 \text{ pounds} - .0658 \text{ pounds}$$

$$X = .13 \text{ pounds}.$$

Thus, any burger weighing .13 pounds or under falls into the bottom 5%. If you regularly find burgers this little, you can complain because it appears that the assumed population could produce such burgers no more than 5% of the time. Suppose your friends buy three quarter-pound burgers and weigh them. The first one is .12 pounds, the second one is .20 pounds, and the last one is .13 pounds. It would appear that two burgers are very unlikely to be found if the restaurant truly is meeting its promised standard. The two friends who got the undersized burgers might feel justified in asking for explanations. As you can see, the use of probability notions and distributions can help us play the odds very effectively.

REASONING IN STATISTICAL HYPOTHESIS TESTING

To test a statistical hypothesis, researchers need to have a formula and a distribution of the odds of finding different sorts of results.

Determining Statistical Hypotheses

statistical hypotheses test the improbability that research hypotheses are untrue   When you use tests of statistical significance, you *do not* find direct evidence that proves that your research hypothesis is so. Instead, you gather evidence that tests whether it is improbable to assume that your research hypothesis is untrue. This statement seems strange at first, but it is the way we handle such matters.

hypothesis identified   To understand this idea, you need to recall the difference between the sorts of hypotheses used in research. A research **hypothesis** (H_1) is "an expectation about events based on generalizations of the assumed relationship between variables" (Tuckman, 1978, p. 27). It is the prediction that researchers hope to examine. Arguing for this hypothesis requires the use of a null hypothesis that is capable of being judged improbable by use of statistical methods. A **null hypothesis** (H_0) states that there is no relationship between variables. This null hypothesis actually is tested directly by statistical tools:

- If the null hypothesis is rejected, then the research hypothesis may be tenable and the researchers conclude that a relationship exists among variables.
- If the null hypothesis is not rejected (logically you cannot claim to "accept" a null hypothesis), then researchers make no claim that a relationship exists among variables.

Suppose we found a sample in which people who watch lots of television report being more fearful of violence than people who watch little TV. Does this sample prove that the amount of TV viewed is positively related to levels of fearfulness? The data are consistent with such a view, but how do you know for sure? Maybe you just got a weird sample—it happens sometimes even with randomization. Perhaps you have proof or perhaps you don't. The fact is, when you look for positive proof, there is little way to find out if you are right, unless you are willing to wait a very long time for history to decide the matter.

So instead, for the sake of argument, you assume that there are no relationships among variables—and that the sample reflects only differences due to the vagaries of random sampling. In short, you temporarily assume the null hypothesis (H_0) is true. *Then,* you look at the data and ask: "How likely is it that we could find results such as we observed in our samples if no relationships existed?"

- If finding results such as yours is *quite probable* when sampling from a population in which no relationships existed, you agree to continue assuming that any differences are just random.
- If it is very *improbable* that you could find results such as yours by sampling from a population in which no relationships exist, you reject the assumption that any differences are just random.

This reasoning is a very clever way to help us decide whether to reject null hypotheses.[2] In short, we assume that nothing much is going on, and then we gather data that makes continuing that assumption unreasonable or improbable. Put another way, researchers collect data that shows that "nothing" probably "is *not*" what's going on.

Decisions in Testing Statistical Hypotheses

To make decisions based on probability, rather than intuition, researchers rely on probability distributions that presume no relationships. Then, researchers make decisions about their samples based on those distributions.

null hypothesis identified as used in testing: application to conclusions drawn

using probabilities to decide to reject the null hypothesis

---

[2] This reasoning method was not invented by statisticians. Thomas Aquinas used this method to argue for the existence of God. In *He Who Is,* Aquinas asked, "What would the world look like if God did not exist?" Then he concluded that the world was inconsistent with those explanations, leading to support for his claims. The application to scientific inquiry predates Aquinas. Aristotle explained how researchers reject chance as an explanation, "If then, it is agreed that things are either the result of coincidence or for an end, and these cannot be the result of coincidence or spontaneity it follows that they must be for an end" (*Physics*).

SPECIAL DISCUSSION 14–1
Use of Computer Programs to Analyze Statistics

Though it is important to understand the logic of statistical analysis of data, most of the drudgery has been removed by the development of computer software to analyze data. Each of the major programs has its own commands and procedures, but they usually are easy to learn and can make data analysis fast work. Versions of software listed here are available for all operating systems, including PC and Macintosh systems. Some of the most popular statistical programs are:

SPSS. (originally called *Statistical Package for the Social Sciences*). This software is the most popular statistical software in the world. At most colleges, copies are available to students since the schools have paid a "site license" fee to authorize widespread distribution of the program (check it out at your school).

DATADESK. This package includes descriptive statistics designed for Macintosh users.

SAS. This very comprehensive system permits data analysis and intermediate and advanced statistical analyses.

BMDP. (originally the "Biomed Programs" designed at UCLA). This set of separate program modules allows data analyses for nearly all types of statistical hypotheses.

STATGRAPHICS. A very user-friendly set of programs, this software emphasizes graphic representations of data suitable for all types of statistical analysis.

SYSTAT. A comprehensive data analysis package particularly suited to the professional statistician. A student version is called MYSTAT.

Finding Unusual Occurrences

Researchers often look at distributions and isolate unusual patterns, or unlikely events. In communication research it is typical to state that a pattern or event is unusual or improbable if it could be found at random only 5% of the time. This statement corresponds to a probability of .05 for finding such results by chance alone. Finding such results will lead us to conclude that our sample probably *does not* come from a population of events in which no relationships exist among variables (this fact is the reason for calling these tools "inferential statistics").

Returning to the fast food example, suppose you decided to do a "serious" study by randomly sampling 36 quarter-pound burgers. You could use the standard normal curve by slicing off a point of the distribution that separates the bottom 5% of the burgers from the rest. So, you could divide up the normal curve as shown by Figure 14.2. The last 5% shaded in Figure 14.2 is called the **critical region,** since if your test statistic falls in that zone, you can claim to have found a "significant difference." A **significant difference or relationship** is one that is beyond what might be expected to occur by chance alone. Results that place you in the critical region will cause you to reject the null hypothesis. If our results do not place us in the critical

(margin notes)
unusual events usually identified if probability of occurrence by chance is <0.5

critical region identified significant difference identified

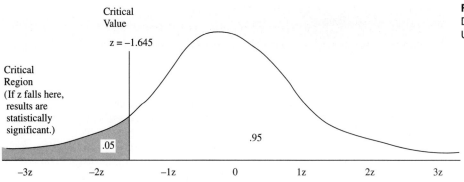

FIGURE 14.2
Distribution of the z
Used in the Testing

region, we will not reject the null hypothesis. The line that divides the critical region from the rest of the distribution is called the **critical value.** Researchers want to find statistics that are equal to or beyond this number on the distribution. Test statistics that do not reach this point lead the researcher *not* to reject the null hypothesis. In Figure 14.2, the critical region is shaded. The critical value is −1.645 (the negative sign is not subtraction; it means that the hamburgers in our sample are suspected of weighing *less* than the presumed population mean promised by the restaurant).

critical value
identified

You might compute a mean of .18 pounds for the sample of 36 quarter-pound burgers. You could enter the z distribution to compare the means of your two groups using the z formula:

$$z = \frac{\overline{X} - \mu}{\sigma}.$$

But there is a slight problem. The new formula compares a couple of *means,* but divides these differences by a σ based on *raw scores.* That's like playing basketball on a football field. You have to put the measures on the same playing field if you want to divide like terms. The difference between means should be divided by a standard deviation of means. You could go out and complete a big study to find out the size of the standard deviation of a bunch of means—but who's got time for that? There is another way around it. The central limit theorem (see Special Discussion 14−2) shows that the standard deviation of a sampling distribution of means can be found by dividing the standard deviation of raw scores by the square root of the number of events to compute the standard deviation. By the way, you should know that the standard deviation of a distribution of means often is called the **standard error of the mean.** Yet, you *should not* think "standard error" refers to mistakes. Whenever a standard deviation is based on measures other than raw scores, it is called the *standard error* of something, for example, standard error of the variance (for distributions of variances), standard error of the range (for distributions of ranges), and standard error of estimate (for distributions of predicted values). When you apply the standard deviation of the means as the key term, the resulting z formula takes this form

adaptations to
standard deviation
required to use z
when comparing
means

standard error of the
mean identified

$$z = \frac{\overline{X} - \mu}{\sigma_{\overline{x}}} \quad \text{or} \quad z = \frac{\overline{X} - \mu}{\sigma / \sqrt{n}}.$$

SPECIAL DISCUSSION 14-2
The Central Limit Theorem

Data distributions in communication studies sometimes show abnormalities. Curiously, though, a distribution of means does not work that way. This surprising finding is called the central limit theorem and states that a sampling distribution of means tends toward normal distribution with increased sample size regardless of the shape of the parent population. If you reached into a population and got a sample of 2 events and computed a mean for it, and then did it again, and again, and again (say 30 or 40 times), you could construct a histogram of these means. The distribution would tend to look pretty much like the underlying data—flaws and all. Suppose, instead, you reached into a population and repeatedly sampled 20 events and computed means. The distribution would tend toward a normal distribution. The bigger the sample gets, the more normal the distribution of means gets. This pattern is beyond common sense, but it is a regular characteristic of distributions of means.

Because of the central limit theorem, studies comparing means can safely presume underlying normal distributions. Furthermore, the average of a distribution of means ought to come closer to identifying the population mean than any other estimation. As such, the central limit theorem is the backbone of the so-called "law of large numbers." A useful application of the central limit theorem is its expression of the relationship between the standard deviations of means and of raw scores (see proof for this statement in Glass & Hopkins, 1984, pp. 188–191):

$$\sigma_{\bar{x}} = \frac{\sigma}{\sqrt{n}}.$$

This statement is used in formulae employed in tests that compare means.

Now, you can compute the z value to see if the resulting number places us in the bottom five percent of the area. If so, you can conclude that the new sample probably is *not* from the population guaranteed by the restaurant.

Run the numbers, you will find:

$$z = \frac{\bar{X} - \mu}{\sigma / \sqrt{n}}$$

$$= \frac{.18 - .20}{.04 / \sqrt{36}}$$

$$= \frac{-.02}{.04 / 6}$$

$$= \frac{-.02}{.0067}$$

$$= -2.99.$$

TABLE 14.1 Decision Table

Decision Based on Statistical Results		Actual Situation (unknown)	
		H_0 is false	H_0 is true
	Reject H_0	Correct decision	Type I error
	Do not Reject H_0	Type II error	Correct decision

This z value places your results into the area at the bottom 5% of the hamburgers. Thus, it would seem that differences between your sample of burgers and what is promised could be found no more than 5% of the time if the burgers really were cooked as promised by the restaurant. Thus, reasonable people might conclude that currently sold burgers probably are lighter than promised.

Choice and Errors in Testing Statistical Hypotheses

Researchers look at test statistics—such as z in our examples so far—and decide whether to reject the null hypothesis. This fact creates some interesting possibilities for the researcher, which are illustrated in Table 14.1. Each row indicates the decision the researcher makes based on available sample statistics—either to reject or not to reject the null hypothesis. The columns show the reality of the matter. Of course, if you knew this reality, you would not have to complete a study. But at the time the research is completed, the researcher has only the sample data to go on.

using the decision table to identify errors and risks in hypothesis testing

     Suppose that you gather data that leads you to reject the null hypothesis (the first row). If the null hypothesis truly is false, you have made a correct decision. It also is possible for researchers to reject the null hypothesis when, in reality, the null hypothesis is true.

     A **Type I error** occurs when sampling error gives the researcher samples that represent unusual (but randomly occurring) events—and the researcher incorrectly rejects the null hypothesis. At the time a study is completed, you do not know whether this mistake has been made, but you can tell the *chances* that this error might be made. The probability of incorrectly rejecting the null hypothesis is called **alpha risk** (α risk). Alpha risk is announced by the researcher at the beginning of a study for all the world to see. The alpha level determines how much area under a distribution is in the critical region. For alpha risk of .05, 5% of the distribution is in the critical region. For alpha risk of .01, only 1% of the distribution is established as the critical region.

Type I error identified

alpha risk identified

     It also is possible that you could fail to reject the null hypothesis (fail to claim that a nonrandom relationship exists). As the second row in Table 14.2 shows, a researcher who fails to reject the null hypothesis when in fact there is a relationship in

Type II error identified

beta risk identified

power identified

the population, commits a **Type II error,**[3] which means that researchers have failed to detect a relationship that is present. Though we cannot tell in advance if a Type II error has been made, the chances of such an error can be identified. This probability is called **beta risk** (β risk) and usually is associated with a study's use samples that may not be large enough to permit existent relationships to cast a shadow. **Power** of a statistical test is the probability of rejecting the null hypothesis correctly.

The Process of Examining Statistical Hypotheses

steps in testing statistical hypotheses

There are four major steps in testing statistical hypotheses. These steps will be considered in the order that researchers follow them.

1. *Determining a Decision Rule for Rejecting Null Hypothesis.* Before researchers collect data, they must decide the levels of alpha risk and beta risk. As a matter of convention—and *only* as a matter of convention—researchers usually set alpha risk at .05, often just announcing "alpha was set at .05" in their description of the statistical analyses. This statement sets a decision rule:

   - if observed results could have been found by chance no more than 5 times out of 100, researchers will claim to have found real (nonrandom) differences;
   - if observed results could have been found by chance *more* than 5 times out of 100, researchers will *not* claim to have found real (nonrandom) relationships.

statistical significance does not mean importance

Applying these decision rules, when differences are claimed, researchers report finding "statistically significant" differences. The term **statistical significance** does not mean that an important relationship has been found, but just that such results are not likely to be due to chance alone.

controlling alpha risk and beta risk

There are implications for selecting risk levels. By choosing an alpha risk of .05 researchers are telling others that 5 times out of 100, they *will* claim differences when it really is just sampling error playing a joke on them. This ratio works out to 1 test out of every 20 turning out to be "significant" by sampling error alone. Thus, researchers may replicate their studies to see if a pattern of results is stable. Beta risk is addressed by researchers' attempts to reduce background variation and by drawing sufficiently large samples.

test statistic identified

2. *Computing the Test Statistic.* A **test statistic** is a number computed from a statistical formula to test the statistical hypothesis. So far, we have used the z statistic, but other formulae are also used.

3. *Finding the Critical Value.* To find the critical region, the researcher must find the portion of the distribution corresponding to alpha risk. For most distributions, tables are available showing the critical value at which this critical region begins. When using a directional hypothesis, we are interested in only one side of the distribution. Any other location on the distribution (even if the extreme opposite tail) would not support the research hypothesis. Figure 14.3 shows how this critical

---

[3] The reason for these Type I and Type II labels stems from Aristotle's remark, "To say about that which is true, that it is false, is false. To say about that which is untrue, that it is true, is false. The first is an error of the first type. The second is an error of the second type."

A. Left-Tailed Test

B. Right-Tailed Test

C. Two-Tailed Test

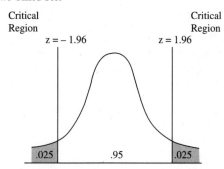

FIGURE 14.3
Using Distributions for One-Tailed vs. Two-Tailed Tests

region is distinguished in one-tailed and two-tailed tests when using the standard normal curve. Figure 14.3A shows a left-tailed test and figure 14.3B shows a right-tailed test. These tests are called **one-tailed tests** since the critical region lies on only one side of a two-tailed distribution. The relevant side of the distribution is determined by the way the research hypothesis is stated. A directional hypothesis might state

    H_1: The current average amount of time children watch television is greater than the average amount of time children watched television in 1985.

Expressed symbolically, this hypothesis states:

    H_1: μ current $>$ μ amount in 1985.

The direction sign lets us know that we have a right-tailed test. To support this hypothesis, the difference must be significant *and* in the predicted direction.

    A nondirectional hypothesis predicts *some* difference regardless of the direction. As Figure 14.3C shows, the alpha risk must be divided equally for both sides of the distribution. For this reason, these tests are called **two-tailed tests** since the last 2.5% on the left tail and the last 2.5% on the right tail of the distribution are

one-tailed tests distinguished

using distributions for two-tailed tests

SPECIAL DISCUSSION 14–3
Assumptions Underlying Parametric Tests

To use parametric statistical significance tests, researchers assume four things about the populations from which the samples were drawn:

1. Randomization in selecting events and/or assigning events drawn from populations
2. Measurement of the dependent variable on an interval or ratio level
3. Underlying normal distribution of events in a population
4. Homogeneous variances of the groups compared (This homogeneity requirement means that any differences in variances should be within the limits of sampling error.)

What happens if we do not meet these assumptions? The first two assumptions are quite firm. The remaining assumptions are the ones that you may wonder about.

Research indicates that the impact of non-normal distributions rarely is significant. Studies (Boneau, 1960; Hsu & Feldt, 1969) show that if sample sizes are 5 or below, the combination of a normal and skewed distribution and a rectangular and a skewed distribution can result in studies rejecting more null hypotheses than the announced alpha. Yet, when sample sizes are at least 15 events in each group, statisticians have found that the actual proportion of Type I errors is within 1% of the announced alpha risk—close enough to make this assumption relatively unimportant for significance testing.

If the variances are not homogenous, effects on Type I errors are insignificant if researchers keep sample sizes equal—or at least within a 4 to 5 ratio of each other (Glass, Peckham, & Sanders, 1972). If sample sizes are not equal, the true Type I error will be *less* than the announced alpha risk if the large variance comes from the large sample. If the large variance comes from the small sample, the true Type I error will be *greater* than the announced alpha risk. The bottom line is that the last two assumptions of parametric tests are not practical concerns in studies with roughly equal sample sizes.

The effects of unequal variances may reveal other interesting things for researchers. Unequal variances can stem from two families of causes: **ceiling or floor effects** in the data or **subjects by treatments interactions.** Ceiling or floor effects occur when scores are so high (or so low) in samples, that the data are "crunched up" (or down) near the end of the measurement range. Thus, variances for these samples are artificially reduced since they do not have the full room to spread. If ceiling or floor effects exist (measured by correlating cell means and variances with each other), the amount of explained variation made by the researcher is understated. Thus, these effects understate the size of relationships observed. The second family of unequal variances is caused by subjects by treatments interaction, which means that at least one additional variable uncontrolled by the researcher has introduced systematic variation influencing subjects in some conditions more than others. Thus, subjects by treatments interactions mean that researchers' studies have blown up in their faces. The researchers must reconsider their designs to find the additional variables that must be included in the study as it is reconsidered. Obviously, researchers who find unequal variances would prefer ceiling or floor effects as the explanation—otherwise they know that they have missed including at least one other significant moderating variable.

isolated as the critical regions that add up to the total alpha risk of .05. As you can see, for the directional hypothesis, the critical region begins closer to the center of the distribution than it does for nondirectional hypotheses. Thus, it should be easiest to find significant differences if researchers know enough to make directional predictions.

4. *Rejecting or Failing to Reject the Null Hypothesis.* If a test statistic falls in the critical region, the null hypothesis is rejected. Sometimes researchers try to get fancy about this rather simple and mechanical step. For instance, after setting alpha risk at .05, they might observe that their test statistic placed them in the last 1% of the distribution, and they will report a significant difference at the .01 level. This step—though common—is unnecessary since the null hypothesis died as soon as the critical region was entered. It cannot be killed again after it has been rejected.

COMPARISONS OF TWO MEANS: THE *t* TEST

Among the tools to examine how often observed results could have been found by chance alone are **parametric tests,** which make assumptions about populations from which the data were drawn. This section considers a family of parametric tests called the *t* test.

    The *t* test is used to compare observed means with those normally expected from a distribution of means. In short, the *t* test compares means to each other to check for statistical significance. This test was developed by William S. Gossett who was a chemist for Guiness Stout Malt Liquor (the same people who publish the famous book of world records). He had to control the quality of the production, but he was not permitted to take large samples. So, he designed a distribution to describe what happens to distributions of means as sample sizes get smaller and smaller. Gossett also developed a formula to permit researchers to compare one mean to another. Because he was concerned with comparing *two* means, he called this test the *t* test, and the distribution of means the *t* distribution. It is easy to remember: It is called the *t* test because it means "*t* for two and two for *t.*"[4] When Gossett made his discovery in 1908, Guiness had a policy forbidding employees to publish under their own names. So, he used the pen-name "Student"—and to this day, the method is often called the "Student's *t* test" (Student, 1908).

parametric tests
isolated

t test identified

developing the t test

Forms of the *t* Test

Four major applications of the *t* test are illustrated here with a formula for each and an example of its use in a little communication study.

One Sample t *Test*

This "classic" form of the *t* test involves examining when a new sample mean differs from a known population mean (μ) under conditions when the population standard deviation is unavailable. This application uses the following formula:

$$t = \frac{\overline{X} - \mu}{s / \sqrt{n}} .$$

---

[4] The song "Tea for Two" had nothing to do with Gossett's labelling. The song was written for a 1926 musical called "No, No, Nanette."

You may notice that this formula looks somewhat familiar. It is. In our example of testing for light weight hamburgers, we used the standard normal curve (z) to help compare a mean to a standard. Aside from the use of a different distribution, the only difference between that formula and this one is that we use the *sample* standard deviation (s) instead of sigma (σ). Thus, *t* really is a logical extension of the standard normal curve.

computing degrees of freedom (number of events minus number of new parameters estimated from samples)

On the *t* table (Appendix B) there are many rows, corresponding to different "degrees of freedom" (found in the first column). Degrees of freedom are the number of events in a study minus the number of population parameters estimated from samples. Thus, for all *t* tests, one need only look at the formula to determine degrees of freedom. For the one sample *t* test, you can see that only *one* new sample mean is computed. Thus, degrees of freedom here are the number of events in the study minus one.

Table 14.2 shows an example in which the null hypothesis is rejected after using the one sample *t* test. This method is useful to learn if samples adequately identify the population means. In addition, if researchers find differences between population and sample means, they may conclude that the new sample probably does not come from the same population—or that the population is no longer described accurately by the presumed parameters. In short, the population may have changed from its previous form, perhaps inviting corrective action.

t Test for Independent Samples

This method probably is the most frequently used *t* test in communication research. We often wish to compare two sample groups to each other (one of which often is a control or current condition). These samples are independent because the events are not matched in advance, and there is no sort of before-and-after scoring of the samples.

The conceptual test statistic for this *t* test is

$$t = \frac{\overline{X}_1 - \overline{X}_2}{s_{\text{diff}}} .$$

differences from one sample *t* test

The formula still looks like the previous formula, doesn't it? The population mean has been replaced by another sample (often a control group mean). Otherwise the only difference is that the standard deviation of means has been replaced by the standard deviation of the differences between means (s_{diff}). The term s_{diff} sometimes is called the "standard error of the difference" although, as you know, it has nothing whatsoever to do with making mistakes. To compute the standard deviation of the differences between means, a couple of steps should be explained.

standard error of the difference

You will remember that a standard deviation of means can be computed by taking the standard deviation of raw scores used to compute a mean and dividing it by the square root of the number of events, such as

$$s_{\overline{x}} = \frac{s}{\sqrt{n}} .$$

But when you have two samples, you have more than one standard deviation and more than one sample size. What can you do? You could start by averaging together

TABLE 14.2 The One Sample t test

EXAMPLE Twenty-five people are sampled from a Communication Research Methods class to find their level of "math anxiety" on a standardized measure, which has a known population mean of 50 for college students. The communication students produced a mean of 58 and a standard deviation of 20. Do the communication students have a higher level of math anxiety than the known population of college students?
With alpha risk set at .05, test the null hypothesis that the mean of the new sample is not different from the population mean of 50.

H_0: μ indicated by new sample = 50

The degrees of freedom for this test are: $n - 1$; 24 in this case.
Critical t value (for a one-tailed test) = 1.71.

COMPUTING THE TEST STATISTIC

$$t = \frac{\overline{X} - \mu}{s / \sqrt{n}}$$

$$t = \frac{58 - 50}{20 / \sqrt{25}}$$

$$t = \frac{8}{20 / 5}$$

$$t = \frac{8}{4}$$

$$t = 2$$

Since the t statistic ($t = 2$) was greater than the critical value (1.71), the null hypothesis was rejected. Thus, communication students were found to have significantly higher levels of math anxiety than the general population of students.

Effect size computation:

$$r = \sqrt{\frac{t^2}{t^2 + \text{degrees of freedom}}}$$

$$r = \sqrt{\frac{4}{4 + 27}}$$

$$r = \sqrt{.13}$$

$$r = .36, \text{ a slight relationship}$$

pooled standard deviation

the standard deviations from each group to get a pooled standard deviation (abbreviated s_p for short). Yet, mathematically, you cannot average the standard deviations, since that arrangement would presume an ordered effect that does not apply here—instead, we must average the variances (s^2) and then take the square root of that average, such as

$$s_p = \sqrt{\text{average of variances}} = \sqrt{[(s^2 + s^2)/2]}.$$

This formula can be used if samples sizes are equal in both groups. If the sample sizes are not the same, a slightly longer formula is used:

$$s_p = \sqrt{\frac{(n - 1) s^2 + (n - 1) s^2}{(n - 1) + (n - 1)}}.$$

Regardless of computation, the logic is the same. We have a pooled standard deviation created from both samples.

According to the original formula, you might expect to divide this pooled standard deviation by the number of events in the sample. But since you have two samples, you must make an adjustment. Instead of *dividing* the pooled standard deviation of the sample groups by $\sqrt{n}$, we could accomplish the same thing by *multiplying* by the pooled standard deviation as follows:

$$s_p * \sqrt{\frac{1}{n} + \frac{1}{n}}.$$

This pattern yields a test statistic formula, found in Table 14.3. This example illustrates the case with unequal sample sizes—you may use the described shortcut if you have equal sample sizes in the compared groups.

degrees of freedom for *t* test for independent samples

For the *t* test for independent samples, degrees of freedom are the number of events in the total of the samples minus 2 (the number of new means that have been computed to estimate population parameters).

t *Test for Dependent Samples*

Sometimes also called the "*t* test for correlated groups," this application may be used in situations where subjects are matched or sampled twice. For instance, to find the impact of coupon advertising on grocery purchases, you could ask a sample of people to report the average amount spent on certain groceries during a month. Then, after exposing those same people to a newspaper advertising campaign using discount coupons for targeted products, you could ask those people to report the amount spent on the targeted groceries they purchased in the *following* month. You could look at the differences in the amount spent on coupon advertised items in the months before and after the newspaper ads appeared. To employ this form, you use the following *t* test statistic:

adaptations for the *t* test for dependent samples

$$t = \frac{\overline{X}_{\text{diff}}}{s_D / \sqrt{n}}.$$

In this formula, $\overline{X}_{\text{diff}}$ is the mean difference between two measures of the same individuals. The standard deviation in the denominator of this formula (s_D) is the simple standard deviation of the difference scores.

TABLE 14.3 *t* Test for Independent Samples

EXAMPLE A random sample of 7 students read a message that featured colored printing of the headline title. A sample of 9 students in a control condition read the same message with a standard black headline. Comprehension of the information was rated on a 10-item true-false test. The mean comprehension score for the experimental condition was 8 (standard deviation of 1; variance = 1). The mean comprehension score for the control group was 6 (standard deviation of 2; variance = 4).

With alpha risk set at .05, test the null hypothesis that the mean of the color headline group is significantly different from the mean of the noncolor headline group:

H_0: color headline = standard headline

The degrees of freedom for this test are: n − 2 or 14.
Critical *t* value (for a one-tailed test) = 1.76.

COMPUTING THE TEST STATISTIC

$$t = \frac{\overline{X} - \overline{X}}{s_p * \sqrt{\frac{1}{n} + \frac{1}{n}}}$$

$$s_p = \sqrt{\frac{(n-1) s^2 + (n-1) s^2}{(n-1) + (n-1)}}$$

$$t = \frac{8 - 6}{1.65 * \sqrt{\frac{1}{7} + \frac{1}{9}}}$$

$$s_p = \sqrt{\frac{(6) 1 + (8) 4}{(6) + (8)}}$$

$$t = \frac{2}{1.65 * \sqrt{.14 + .11}}$$

$$s_p = \sqrt{\frac{6 + 32}{14}}$$

$$t = \frac{2}{1.65 * \sqrt{.25}}$$

$$s_p = \sqrt{\frac{38}{14}}$$

$$t = \frac{2}{1.65 * .5}$$

$$s_p = \sqrt{2.71}$$

$$t = \frac{2}{.83}$$

$$s_p = 1.65$$

$$t = 2.41$$

Since the *t* statistic (*t* = 2.41) was greater than the critical value (1.76), the null hypothesis was rejected.

Effect size computation:

$$r = \sqrt{\frac{t^2}{t^2 + \text{degrees of freedom}}}$$

$$r = \sqrt{\frac{5.81}{5.81 * 14}}$$

$$r = \sqrt{.29}$$

$$r = .54, \text{ a fair relationship}$$

TABLE 14.4 *t* Test for Dependent Samples

EXAMPLE A sample of 10 employees was tested for listening ability before and after attending a seminar in effective listening. Did the employees show significant improvements (increases in scores)? With alpha risk set at .05, test the null hypothesis that there was no significant improvement:

H_0: difference = 0

The degrees of freedom for this test are: $n - 1$; 9 in this case.

Critical *t* value (for a one-tailed test) = 1.83.

COMPUTING THE TEST STATISTIC (unequal sample sizes)
The data are as follows:

Person	Post-test Score	Pretest Score	Difference
Larry	5	4	1
Moe	5	5	0
Curly	4	4	0
Manny	7	5	2
Moe	5	6	−1
Patty	6	4	2
Maxine	7	6	1
Laverne	8	6	2
Jerry	9	7	2
Dino	8	7	1
			$\bar{X}_{diff} = 1$
			$s_D = 1.05$

Test Statistic

$$t = \frac{\bar{X}_{diff}}{s_D / \sqrt{n}}$$

$$t = \frac{1}{1.05/\sqrt{10}}$$

$$t = \frac{1}{1.05 / 3.16}$$

$$t = \frac{1}{.32}$$

$$t = 3.13$$

Effect Size Computation:

$$r = \sqrt{\frac{t^2}{t^2 + \text{degrees of freedom}}}$$

$$r = \sqrt{\frac{3.13^2}{3.13^2 + 9}}$$

$$r = \sqrt{\frac{9.8}{9.8 + 9}}$$

$$r = \sqrt{.52}$$

$$r = .72, \text{ a marked relationship}$$

Since the *t* statistic (*t* = 3.13) was greater than the critical value (1.83), the null hypothesis was rejected. Thus, there was a significant difference between the pretest and post-test scores.

Degrees of freedom for this form of the t test are found by taking the total number of events in the sample (*not* the total number of scores), and subtracting one for the new mean that is computed in the formula (X_{diff}). As Table 14.4 shows, this method is a simple way to look at "before and after" changes, and it also is sensitive to differences that might get lost if data were clumped into groupings as in the t test for independent samples.

t Test for the Difference Between Zero and an Observed Correlation

Though the t test has been described for comparisons among means, it can also be used to test whether a correlation is significantly different from zero (no correlation at all). This application allows you to discover if a correlation is greater than one would expect to occur by chance alone. For instance, consider the correlation that was computed in Table 13.2. This sample of 8 families revealed a correlation of .28 between hours of sports watched on TV and the number of bags of potato chips purchased by each family. To see if this correlation is significantly different from zero, you would use the following t test:

$$t = \frac{r\sqrt{n-2}}{\sqrt{1-r^2}}.$$

testing a correlation's significance

For our example, you could test this correlation with alpha risk at .05 for a one-tailed test. If you substitute the observed correlation (r) and the sample size (8) into the formula, the t test is

$$t = \frac{.28\sqrt{8-2}}{\sqrt{1-.08}} = .77.$$

Degrees of freedom for this test are the number of events minus two (one degree of freedom is lost for each of the variables being correlated). In this case, the critical t value was 1.895. Since the t statistic did not meet or exceed the critical value, you cannot reject the null hypothesis. Thus, you conclude that the correlation is not significantly different from zero.

degrees of freedom for t tests of correlations

Determining Effect Sizes

Tests of statistical significance allow the researcher to rule out chance as the probable explanation of results. But significance testing does not reveal how big or small the nonchance relationships are. So, a researcher is also expected (and required in professional journals) to report the magnitude of effects. One useful way to do so involves taking information from a t test and determining what kind of correlation is indicated between the variables. Then, a large effect can be identified and distinguished from a small effect.

other formulae required for effect size computation

For the t test, the following formula will reveal this effect size:

$$r = \sqrt{\frac{t^2}{t^2 + \text{degrees of freedom}}}.$$

This tool allows researchers to take the observed t value from the test statistic and to compute a number that can be interpreted as any other correlation.

SUMMARY

Probability refers to the tendency or likelihood with which an event occurs in a population. This notion is a foundation of statistical inference in which we attempt to see if observed relationships are unlikely to occur by chance. Distributions such as the standard normal curve can be useful. These distributions serve as probability distributions since they represent the theoretical patterns of expected sample data. The z distribution can be used to make statistical inferences.

When researchers use tests of statistical significance, they *do not* find direct evidence that proves that their research hypotheses are so. Instead, they gather evidence that tests whether assuming that their research hypotheses are *untrue* is improbable. The null hypothesis, which states that there is no relationship between variables, is the one actually tested statistically. If the null hypothesis is rejected, then the research hypothesis may be tenable and researchers conclude that a relationship exists among variables; if the null hypothesis is not rejected (logically we cannot claim to "accept" a null hypothesis), then researchers make no claim that a relationship exists among variables.

Researchers look at distributions and isolate unusual patterns or events. In communication research it is typical to state that a pattern or event is unusual or improbable if it could be found at random only 5% of the time. One location of distributions is called the critical region since if the test statistic falls in that zone, you can claim to have found a "significant difference." A significant difference or relationship is one that is beyond what might be expected to occur by chance alone. The line that divides the critical region from the rest of the distribution is called the critical value. The standard deviation of a distribution of means is often called the standard error of the mean and is used in formulae that compare means.

The ability of a statistical test to reject the null hypothesis correctly is called statistical power. Type I error involves incorrectly rejecting the null hypothesis (the probability of committing a Type I error is called alpha risk). Type II error means that researchers have failed to detect a relationship that is present (the probability of committing a Type II error is called beta risk). There are four major steps in testing statistical hypotheses: (1) determining a decision rule for rejecting null hypothesis (researchers usually set alpha risk at .05); the term *statistical significance* does not mean that an important relationship has been found, but that such results are not likely to be due to chance alone; (2) computing the test statistic (a test statistic is a number computed from a statistical formula to test the statistical hypothesis); (3) finding the critical value (when using a directional hypothesis only one side of the distribution is involved; one-tailed tests are identified as those in which the critical region lies on only one side of a two-tailed distribution; nondirectional hypotheses predict some difference regardless of the direction, requiring that critical regions be divided equally for both sides of the distribution); (4) rejecting or failing to reject the null hypothesis (if a test statistic falls in the critical region, the null hypothesis is rejected).

Parametric tests make assumptions about populations from which the data were drawn. In addition to the z distribution, this chapter considers another parametric test called the *t* test, which is primarily designed to compare two means. The one sample *t* test involves examining when a new sample mean differs from a known population mean under conditions when the population standard deviation is unavailable. For all *t* tests, degrees of freedom are the number of events in a study minus the number of population parameters estimated from samples. The *t* test for independent samples compares two sample groups to each other (which are independent because the events are not matched in advance, and there is no before-and-after scoring of the samples). The *t* test for dependent samples is used when subjects are matched or sampled twice. The *t* test of correlations examines whether an observed correlation is significantly different from zero. Following finding a significant difference, researchers may determine effect sizes by use of equivalent methods to compute correlations.

TERMS FOR REVIEW

probability distributions
hypothesis
null hypothesis
critical region
critical value
significance
standard error of the mean
significance
probability

Type I Error
alpha risk
Type II error
beta risk
power
test statistic
one-tailed tests
two-tailed tests
parametric tests
ceiling or floor effects

CHAPTER 15

Introductory Inferential Statistics II: Beyond Two Means

Statistics are numbers used as arguments.

–Leonard Louis Levinson

SELECTING AN APPROPRIATE STATISTICAL TEST
COMPARING MORE THAN TWO MEANS: ANALYSIS OF VARIANCE
  One-Way Analysis of Variance
  What to Do After Finding Statistical
    Significance
  Factorial Analysis of Variance

BASIC NONPARAMETRIC TESTING
  The Nature of Nonparametric Tests:
    The Randomization Assumption
  Tests for Nominal Level Dependent
    Variables

BEFORE WE GET STARTED . . .

This chapter extends consideration of hypothesis testing to two of the most frequently used tools found in research: analysis of variance, and the nonparametric statistic chi-square. Since the logic of other tools is consistent with those covered here, you should have little difficulty understanding other advanced applications you might encounter in your own work.

SELECTING AN APPROPRIATE STATISTICAL TEST

To explore statistical significance, the researchers need a test statistic or formula to help them enter a distribution and play the odds. Table 15.1 presents the major tests to be used to see whether significant differences exist between groups. Methods that adapt these statistics to control for additional variables (such as analysis of covariance or analysis of variance with repeated measures) are not listed here since they are extensions of the tools listed.

    The statistics are listed by the type of data used for the dependent variable and the number of groups in the independent variable compared in a study. To select a tool

TABLE 15.1 Selecting a Statistic to Test for Differences

	Measurement Level of Dependent Variable		
	Nominal Level	**Oridinal Level**	**Interval or Ratio**
Number of Sample Groups Compared			
1 (sample compared to a theoretically presumed population value)	one sample chi square (goodness of fit test) binomial z test (for data that have only two possible values)	Kolmogorov-Smirnov one sample test	z test (if n ≥ 30 and σ known) one sample *t* test
2 independent samples	chi square test of independence z test (difference between proportions) Fisher exact test (for expected frequencies <5)	Wilcoxon rank sum test Mann-Whitney *U* test (good for large samples) Kolmogorov-Smirnov two sample test (for small samples) Wald-Wolfowitz runs test (detects any differences in central tendency *or* skew; assumes initially continuous output measures)	*t* test for independent groups
2 dependent samples	McNemar test for significance of changes (for dependent sample pairs)	Sign test (for matched sample pairs; does not show magnitude of differences) Wilcoxin matched pairs signed ranks test (for matched sample pairs)	Randomization test for matched pairs (for small n) *t* test for matched dependent sample pairs *t* test for paired samples
more than 2	chi square test of independence Cochran's Q test (for matched or paired samples)	Kruskal-Wallis H test Median test (weak compared to Kruskal-Wallis) Friedman two-way analysis of variance	Analysis of variance Factorial analysis of variance (for two or more independent variables)

to test for differences between groups, you start by finding the *column* that identifies the level of measurement for the dependent variable. Next you identify how many new sample groups are to be compared in the study and find the appropriate *row*. If the subjects in the study are pairs of sample data (such as pretests and post-tests of the same subjects), or if subjects have been matched on some variable into pairs for comparison, special sets of tools are available. For ordinary independent samples, the appropriate tools are also listed. Though many test statistics are listed, you will find that only one test will really be suitable for your particular needs in a given study.

using the table to select tests of statistical significance

Because covering the details of all these tests and their computations are beyond the scope of this introductory book, you are encouraged to check specific statistics books to find details about many of the formulae listed (some of the most readable of these books are Aczel, 1989; Wagner, 1992; Glass & Hopkins, 1984; Ott & Hildebrand, 1983; Champion, 1970). The rest of our discussion will illustrate some *most commonly used* tests found in communication research.

COMPARING MORE THAN TWO MEANS: ANALYSIS OF VARIANCE

ANOVA applied to more than two group means

the notion of the *F* statistic

When you have more than two groups, the *t* test is inappropriate. Thus, the statistic called analysis of variance (ANOVA) is invited.[1] Analysis of variance involves use of the *F* distribution to compare results to those normally expected from a distribution of ratio variances. In essence, the *F* distribution—named in honor of Sir Ronald Fisher—is a distribution of variances that have been divided into each other. We can use this distribution to test for differences among sample means. To compare means, researchers may compute a variance (s^2) using sample means as the data—just as if they were ordinary scores. Then, this variance may be compared to the kind of background variation that already exists within each group. This idea is the backbone of the conceptual formula:

$$F = \frac{\text{between groups variance}}{\text{within groups variance}} .$$

the logic of the *F* statistic: variances of means get big if the means differ from each other

This formula is not a computational guide. But the idea is simple enough. The "between groups" variance is computed using sample group means as the scores of interest (a variance of means $s_{\bar{x}}^2$). This difference is divided by a measure of background variation called "within groups" variance. Within groups variance is simply the average of the variances within each of the sample groups in the study. This measure is known to us as the "pooled variance" (s_p^2). The pooled variance is nothing more than the squared *pooled standard deviation* that we computed for the *t* test for independent samples (Chapter 14).

if the variances of means are real, they will be greater than background noise

The idea behind analysis of variance is simple. If there are no differences among group means, then the variance computed from them will be very small. In fact, if the means are all the same, a variance computed from them will be zero. But if there *are* differences among means, then the variance computed from the means will get bigger and bigger. If the differences are beyond chance, then this variance of means will be greater than the average amount of background noise within groups. That's what the *F* statistic does—divides a variance of means by background noise.

When using analysis of variance there are two sets of degrees of freedom, a set for the numerator of the fraction and a set for the denominator of the fraction. Indeed, if you look at the *F* Table in Appendix C, you will notice that the upper left corner of the table shows the fraction from our conceptual formula. Thus, to find the degrees of

---

[1] You might wonder what would happen if we used both *F* tests and *t* tests to compare two means. The answer is that under these circumstances, $F = t^2$.

freedom for the numerator, you move *left to right* to the appropriate column. In general, the degrees of freedom for the numerator are the number of means compared minus 1 (1 lost for the new mean parameter that must be computed to arrive at a variance from the sample means). To find the denominator degrees of freedom, you move *down* the table to the appropriate row. The degrees of freedom for the numerator are the number of events in the study minus 1 for each of the means computed within each of the sample groups (to compute an estimate of within groups variance).

degrees of freedom for ANOVA

One-Way Analysis of Variance

To compare several means for one independent variable you use "one-way" analysis of variance. The number of levels for the independent variable is often included in labelling of such studies. For instance, a researcher may describe a "one-by-three analysis of variance." The term is shorthand for a **one-way analysis of variance** with three levels for the independent variable. This section describes what goes on with one-way analysis of variance, use of follow-up tests to find relationships, and how researchers may use the method to look for nonlinear relationships.

one-way analysis of variance and nomenclature

Let's suppose that 3 groups of 10 people each were exposed to a message from a lowly, a moderately, and a highly credible source. Their attitudes might be illustrated on a 1 to 20 attitude scale as follows:

description of one way ANOVA

Lowly Credible	**Moderately Credible**	**Highly Credible**
$\overline{X} = 5$	$\overline{X} = 10$	$\overline{X} = 15$
$s^2 = 15$	$s^2 = 25$	$s^2 = 35$.

The null hypothesis to be tested directly is:

$$H_0: \mu_1 = \mu_2 = \mu_3 .$$

You can compute a variance of the three means by entering the means as data into the formula for s^2 (see Chapter 13). If you do so, the answer is 25. Since the groups have equal sample sizes, to obtain the pooled variance s_p^2, you can just average the variances within groups. In this case—as you can see—the average of background variances is 25.

To compute F for these data, you actually use a formula that allows you to compare variances of means with averages of background variance. This appropriate adjustment leads to the following formula:

$$F = \frac{n * s_{\overline{x}}^2}{s_p^2}$$

formula for F

$$= \frac{10 * 25}{25}$$

$$= \frac{250}{25}$$

$$= 10 .$$

To figure out what this test statistic means, we check how likely these results are to occur by chance alone. The degrees of freedom for this test are

using the F table to interpret results

FIGURE 15.1
Examining the *F*
Distribution for a
One-Way Analysis of
Variance Example

Portion of the *F* Table

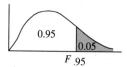

95th Percentile Values
for the *F* Distribution
(d.f.$_1$ degrees of freedom in numerator)
(d.f.$_2$ degrees of freedom in denominator)

Between Groups Degrees of Freedom
Within Groups Degrees of Freedom

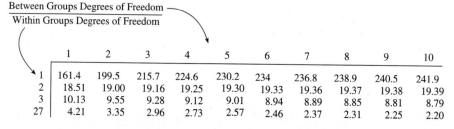

	1	2	3	4	5	6	7	8	9	10
1	161.4	199.5	215.7	224.6	230.2	234	236.8	238.9	240.5	241.9
2	18.51	19.00	19.16	19.25	19.30	19.33	19.36	19.37	19.38	19.39
3	10.13	9.55	9.28	9.12	9.01	8.94	8.89	8.85	8.81	8.79
27	4.21	3.35	2.96	2.73	2.57	2.46	2.37	2.31	2.25	2.20

F Distribution and Example Test Statistic

2 for the numerator (number of group means minus one; 3 − 1 = 2); thus, we find
ourselves on column two of the chart.
27 for the denominator (the number of events in the sample groups minus the number of
means that were computed within each group to compute the variance; 10 + 10 + 10 − 1
− 1 − 1). Thus, we would go to row 27 on the *F* table.

To test for significance with alpha risk at .05, we would use the portion of the *F* Table
found in Figure 15.1. The intersection of column 2 and row 27 gives a critical *F* value
of 3.35 for alpha risk at .05. Since variances always are positive numbers, only one side
of the *F* distribution is used to test hypotheses. As Figure 15.1 also shows, the critical
value at which the critical region begins is 3.35. To reject the null hypothesis, the test
statistic must fall somewhere in the critical region—the test statistic must be equal to
or greater than 3.35. Since the test statistic is 10, you can reject the null hypothesis.

**adjustments for
unequal sample sizes**

In the example, we had equal sample sizes. If there were *unequal* sample sizes,
then you would compute the numerator of these fractions differently. The contribution
to the total between groups variance must be weighted by the different sample sizes.
The grand mean of all group means also must be computed from the total sample,
rather than as a simple average of cell means. Otherwise the process is pretty much the
same (using the long formula for the pooled variance). The example shown in
Table 15.2 shows how to compute and summarize ANOVA with unequal sample sizes.
Of course, these formulae can be used for equal samples sizes as well, though the extra
steps involved are unnecessary.

TABLE 15.2 One-Way Analysis of Variance Including Unequal Sample Sizes

Example Researchers wanted to test whether the groups of children, adults, or senior citizens were more persuaded by "negative campaign" ads. So, they contacted three groups of people and showed them a typical negative political ad. Their reactions were assessed on an attitude scale ranging from 3 (negative attitude) to 21 (positive attitude). The following list shows the cell means, variances, and sample sizes:

Children	*Adults*	*Senior Citizens*
$\overline{X} = 14$	$\overline{X} = 9$	$\overline{X} = 12$
$s^2 = 18$	$s^2 = 18$	$s^2 = 15$
$n = 15$	$n = 10$	$n = 20$

The first thing to do is compute the grand mean from *all* the data (you cannot just average the averages since there are unequal cell sizes). You compute it by multiplying each cell group mean by the number of events in each cell. Then you add up all these numbers and divide by the total number of events in the study. In this case, the computation of the grand mean is

$$\overline{\overline{X}} = \frac{(n * \overline{X_1}) + (n * \overline{X_2}) + (n * \overline{X_3})}{n_1 + n_2 + n_3}.$$

In this example the following numbers may be substituted:

$$\overline{\overline{X}} = \frac{(15 * 14) + (10 * 9) + (20 * 12)}{15 + 10 + 20}$$

$$\overline{\overline{X}} = \frac{540}{45}$$

$$\overline{\overline{X}} = 12.$$

To compute between groups variance, subtract each cell mean from this grand mean, square the difference, and multiply by the number of events in the cell. After completing this process for each cell, add up the totals. Then, divide this number by the degrees of freedom (number of groups minus one). Complete this process as follows:

$$\text{Between Groups Variance} = \frac{\sum n_i (\overline{X_i} - \overline{\overline{X}})^2}{\text{degrees of freedom} = \text{groups} - 1}$$

$$= \frac{[15 * (14 - 12)^2] + [10 * (9 - 12)^2] + [20 * (12 - 12)^2]}{3 - 1}$$

$$= \frac{150}{2}$$

$$= 75.$$

To compute within groups variance, use the long form of the formula for the pooled variance estimate:

$$s_p^2 = \frac{(n - 1)s^2 + (n - 1)s^2 \ldots x}{(n - 1) + (n - 1) \ldots x}.$$

This pooled variance simply averages background variation after giving weights for different sample sizes. With these data, the numbers become

$$s_p^2 = \frac{(14 * 18) + (9 * 15) + (19 * 15)}{14 + 9 + 19}$$

$$= \frac{672}{42}$$

$$= 16.$$

TABLE 15.2 —*Continued*

The degrees of freedom for this within groups variance (the pooled variance) are 42. To find out if there is a difference among the means of these groups, the between groups variance is divided by the within groups variance as summarized in the ANOVA below.

ANOVA TABLE

SOURCE	df	MEAN SQUARE	F
Between Groups	2	75	4.69
Within Groups	42	16	

Since the critical value for 2 and 42 degrees of freedom is 3.22, the observed *F* value falls into the critical region with alpha risk of .05. Thus, researchers would reject the null hypothesis and claim significance differences between the groups.

What to Do After Finding Statistical Significance

Analysis of variance is not the end of the road. Additional follow-up work must be completed after finding a significant *F* ratio.

Multiple Comparison Tests

multiple comparison tests isolated

Our simple example produced evidence showing a significant difference among the group means. But *where* were the differences? Was one group different from the other two? Were all three significantly different from each other? To tease out these differences you can use some follow-up methods called **multiple comparison tests.** These methods generally are computed so that alpha risk is stretched out across comparisons.

Tukey's HSD for pairwise comparisons

Scheffe's critical S for compound comparisons

Table 15.3 shows several major forms of multiple comparison tests and their uses. For the most part, in communication studies, researchers tend to use two tools: Tukey's HSD and Scheffe's S. Though they can be applied to the same data, the methods actually have different functions. The **Tukey's HSD** (abbreviation for John Tukey's Honestly Significant Difference test) is used to make all possible comparisons of means, when the means are taken two at a time. It is the most powerful of the multiple comparison tests for making pairwise comparisons. For complex comparisons, such as comparing two cells against four others, **Scheffe's critical S** method is the most powerful tool. Each of these methods has its own method of computation and researchers should report the test statistics in their results. As Table 15.3 shows, however, there are other tools that are suitable for different sorts of situations.

Of course, if only two levels are used in the analysis of variance, the *F* test is a direct comparison of the two conditions. Thus, no additional multiple comparison test is necessary to examine differences.

Determining Effect Sizes

Though analysis of variance permits researchers to identify non-chance differences, the size of those differences is not directly observed. Thus, differences could be big ones, little ones, or somewhere in between. The researcher needs to supplement the

TABLE 15.3 Major Multiple Comparison Methods		
Method	**Application**	**Comment**
Dunn's	Used when making comparisons that have been planned or hypothesized in advance; the number is restricted to a small number of comparisons by the number of hypotheses.	Most powerful multiple comparison test (aside from running t's or F's).
Dunnett's d'	Used to compare a control group against multiple treatment groups in the study.	Pairwise comparisons only.
Newman-Keuls	Used when it is desired to have a different critical value for comparisons of individual means with each other (in descending order).	First comparisons very powerful, others less so; the method does not control for experimentwise alpha risk; requires equal sample sizes.
Duncan Multiple Range Test	Used when desired to have a different critical value for comparisons of mean arranged in descending order.	Controversial since predicated on debatable notion that as number of conditions increases the probability of finding differences increases; first comparisons very powerful, others less so; the method does not control for experimentwise alpha risk; requires equal sample sizes.
Tukey's HSD	For pairwise comparisons; thus used as a follow-up test only.	Spreads out alpha risk for all possible comparisons; requires the use of equal sample sizes (for unequal sample sizes, use Spjøtvoll and Stoline's modification of HSD.)
Scheffe's S	Most useful for compound comparisons (e.g., two cells vs. four cells).	Most powerful for compound comparisons; but least powerful when applied to pairwise comparisons.

measure of statistical significance with a measure of effect size. Though more than one tool is available,[2] perhaps the most readily interpretable are eta (η) and eta squared (η^2). Eta, known as the "correlation ratio," is directly interpreted as any correlation. An added advantage of the correlation ratio is that it can identify the size of nonlinear as well as linear effects. Thus, the overall correlation can be identified, regardless of its form.

effect size computation by eta or eta squared

The formula for eta is

$$\eta = \sqrt{\frac{\text{between groups variance} * \text{degrees of freedom}}{\text{total of all mean squares multiplied by their degrees of freedom}}}.$$

---

[2] Two other methods are the intraclass correlation ($\hat{\rho}_I$, which applies to the "random effects" model of analysis of variance) and omega squared ($\hat{\omega}^2$, which is suitable to the "fixed effects" model of analysis of variance). These methods adjust for expected within groups sums of squares and mean squares respectively (Kirk, 1982, pp. 161–163). To keep it simple, we describe eta in this chapter.

In our example using equal sample sizes, the numbers work out as follows:

$$\eta = \sqrt{\frac{(10 * 25)}{25 * 27}}$$

$$= \sqrt{\frac{250}{675}}$$

$$= \sqrt{.37}$$

$$= .61.$$

Thus, a correlation of .61—a "moderate to marked relationship"—appears to exist between the independent and dependent variables in this study. To report the percentage impact of one variable based on a knowledge of the other alone, eta squared (η^2) may be employed. In this example, η^2 is .37.

Looking for Nonlinear Relationships

So far, you have learned how to look for simple differences among the means of several groups. Yet, sometimes the underlying independent variable has levels that are arranged in some sort of continuum. This arrangement allows researchers to identify trends in the dependent variable.[3] For instance, suppose the independent variable involved low, moderate, and high amounts of information possessed by employees. The amount of employee satisfaction is the dependent measure. Given that you have three groups, you can use analysis of variance to detect any differences. You can also adapt analysis of variance to help reveal the exact contour of the relationship.

trend analysis identified

After identifying a significant difference, researchers can use a method called **trend analysis.** Trend analysis isolates the nature of linear and nonlinear trends in effects identified as significant by analysis of variance. Without getting into computational details, it is useful to show you what a set of results might look like for hypothetical data from the example. Suppose that the means for the three levels are as follows:

Amounts of Communication

Low	*Moderate*	*High*
$\overline{X} = 5$	$\overline{X} = 15$	$\overline{X} = 10$
$s^2 = 15$	$s^2 = 25$	$s^2 = 35$
$n = 10$	$n = 10$	$n = 10$

the method of trend analysis

Obviously, these data look a great deal like our previous example, but the three means now seem to rise and fall as we move from low to high amounts of communication received by employees. If you drew a line to connect the means, it would show a curve. To identify this trend in the data you can use "trend analysis." The overall observed F value remains 10 (with 2 and 27 degrees of freedom), since the means are

---

[3] Statisticians prefer that the spacing between the levels of the independent variable be equal. Provided that the levels are rationally chosen to cover the range of interest to the researcher, there is little difficulty created by this requirement.

SPECIAL DISCUSSION 15–1
Interval Estimation Methods

The tools of statistical significance testing we have been describing are called *point estimation methods.* This term derives from the estimating of a single value or point for a population based on the samples. When testing for significance, we hope (and have reason to do so) that our sample mean will lie very close to the population mean. Despite the usefulness of this method, it is not the only way to view things.

Another group of statisticians prefers to rely on interval estimates— that is, they like to report a range of values that they believe will capture population parameters. Though it may seem that both these methods are valuable, some writers have used the logic of interval estimation as a basis for attacking standard methods of significance testing, such as are described in this introductory treatment.

Those who prefer to use interval estimation methods suggest that instead of computing whether there are differences between means of samples (point estimates), we should construct confidence intervals around means and contrast them. Thus, the probable range of population values could be identified. The most extreme members of this camp have also been known to write disapproving essays about what they view as faults with significance testing statistics.

There is no reason that researchers could not do *both,* of course, but they generally do not. Mathematically, the methods of interval estimation and point estimate tests of statistical significance are equivalent. Thus, the interval estimation method also permits one to identify the presence of significant differences among groups. For instance, if a researcher found three means such as those in the following example, a sampling confidence interval could be constructed around each mean. In this case, the dots in the centers of the distributions are the means and the lines extending up and down reflect a 95% confidence interval:

SPECIAL DISCUSSION 15-1
Interval Estimation Methods

If the width of the confidence interval around one mean is large enough to include the mean of another group, then there is no difference (in this case no difference at the .05 level, two-tailed). If the mean of a group is outside the confidence interval of another group, then there is a significant difference (p = .05). In our example, there is a significant difference between Group B and Group C, indicated by the fact that the means are outside the other's confidence interval (the confidence intervals may overlap, but that does not matter). But there is no difference between Group A and the other groups since the confidence interval of Group A is so large that it includes the means of Group B and Group C. Thus, the use of interval estimation methods has been advanced as a subtle way to identify the location and form of differences, just as point estimation methods attempt to reveal them directly.

---

the same as our previous example. Thus, there appear to be differences in satisfaction stemming from the three amounts of communication received by employees.

Trend analysis multiplies the means by weights (called *orthogonal polynomials*) to reflect linear and nonlinear trends. After weighing the means, simple analysis of variance is computed again. Thus, we can tell if the significant differences stem from a linear or nonlinear trend. The result of this analysis is a set of results as follows:[4]

Source of Variation	df	(between groups variance) Mean Square	F
Amount of Communication	2	250	10
Linear trend	1	125	5
Nonlinear trend	1	375	15
Within Groups	27	25	

mean square is a synonym for the variance

The term *mean square* is a synonym for the variance (shorthand for "the mean of the squared differences of scores from their mean"). The linear (straight line) and nonlinear (curved) effects are tested directly. These rows are indented to indicate that they are not new independent variables, but just the main effect examined for trends. If you look at Appendix C, you will find that for alpha risk at .05, the

---

[4] Though discussing these computation methods is beyond the scope of this book, they may be found in the discussion by Kirk (1982, pp. 150–161). In this case the linear effect orthogonal polynomial weights were −1, 0, and 1; the nonlinear weights were 1, −2, and 1. The formula used to compute the effect was

$$MS = \frac{\frac{n * [\Sigma \text{ weights} * \overline{X}]^2}{\Sigma \text{ weights}^2}}{\text{degrees of freedom}}.$$

critical value is 4.21 for 1 and 27 degrees of freedom (the degrees of freedom we use for examining the trends). As you can see, both the linear and nonlinear trends are significant. This finding means that although the linear effect exists, the nonlinear or curved trend really tells the tale. Thus, the best fit of a trend to the data is a curved one.

Obviously, trend analysis can help identify whether curved or linear effects exist in the data. This example had three groups—so only a simple nonlinear effect could be found. If we had more than three groups, we could examine additional types of trends in the data as well (such as cubic, quartic, or quintic trends). Thus, this method can help researchers identify fairly subtle patterns in the data.

Factorial Analysis of Variance

We often ask questions that involve more than one independent variable of interest, each one with two or more levels. Factorial analysis of variance is invited for these sorts of situations. The term **variable factor** is used to identify a variable that has been broken down into levels or groups. Thus, **factorial analysis of variance** is analysis of variance applied to multiple independent variables that have been broken down into levels or groups.

variable factor concept identified

Specifically, **factorial analysis of variance** is a test of statistical significance that identifies main and interaction effects between independent variables. **Main effects** are dependent variable effects from independent variables separately. In factorial designs, these main effects are identified by looking at differences between levels of each independent variable across levels of the other variables in the study. **Interaction effects** are dependent variable effects from independent variables taken together. These interaction effects involve variation in the dependent variable arising from special combinations of levels of independent variables.

factorial ANOVA

main effects identified

interaction effects identified

Rather than complete a bunch of studies on each independent variable separately, researchers may economize by sampling once and getting as much information as possible from the data. The language of factorial analysis of variance often describes the layout of a design. Figure 15.2 shows two designs. The first design is a

language of factorial analysis of variance

Single Factor Design

Independent Variable One

Low	Moderate	High

Two Factor Design

Independent Variable One

		Low	High
Independent Variable Two	Low		
	High		

FIGURE 15.2
Variable Factors and Cell Design

single factor design and the second is a two factor design. Since the first has only one independent variable with three levels, it often is called a "one by three" design. This sort of design can only identify a main effect since only one variable is included. Furthermore, the design invites use of a one-way analysis of variance as its statistical test.

layout of design

The second design features two independent variables, each of which has two levels. Depending on the preferences of the researcher, analysis of variance for this design is called a "two factor ANOVA," a "two-way ANOVA," a "two-by-two ANOVA," or a "two variable factorial ANOVA." The specific combinations of conditions are called "cells" of the design because they are framed by levels of independent variables. Though the figure shows only two independent variables, there is no limit to the number of independent variables that could be examined. Thus, you could have a "two-by-two-by-two design," a "three-by-six-by-two-by-four design," or any other combination of variable factors with different levels.

cells identified

Computing Factorial ANOVA

Once the design of the factorial analysis of variance is decided, researchers may collect dependent measure data for each condition. ANOVA is computed to determine where the differences in dependent measures are found in the design. Though designs can be extended for three or more factors, a two-factor design for equal sample sizes will be illustrated here (though, of course, the method can also be applied to unequal sample sizes). If a design has *radically* unequal sample sizes across cells, the researcher cannot really claim to have a balanced design and the statistics may not be robust to violations of the assumptions of normal distribution and homogeneous variances.

two factor ANOVA preferred if equal sample sizes maintained

Computing factorial analysis of variance is very much like one-way analysis of variance. An example may help. Let's look at a study to examine whether men and women differ in their scores of communication competence after taking a seminar on communication skills. The competence test has a possible range of scores from 1 to 50 (high scores indicate increased competence). Consider a study in which half of randomly selected groups of 42 men and 42 women at a large company are randomly assigned to take a standard training course in "Improving Interpersonal Communication," while the other half are not assigned to take it. Thus, the design has 21 subjects in each cell. Scores on the communication competence measure could be secured for each person. Table 15.4 shows the mean ($\overline{X}$) and variance (s^2) for each cell. We also have provided information about the column and row means ($\overline{\overline{X}}$—pronounced "X bar bar"). Furthermore, the **grand mean** or average of the averages is provided ($\overline{\overline{\overline{X}}}$—pronounced "X bar bar bar").

notation: grand mean identified

As Table 15.4 shows, formulae produce answers that are placed in a summary table. Start by computing the within groups variance (sometimes this line is called "error" for "error variance," or "residual" for "residual variance"). Names notwithstanding, the within groups variance is simply the pooled variance (s_p^2). When we have equal sample sizes, the pooled variance is just the average of the variances within each cell. In our case, this number is 40. Degrees of freedom are the number of events

computing within groups variance

TABLE 15.4 Data for the Communication Competence Study

Completion of Communication Class

	Completed Class	Did Not Take Class	
Men	$\bar{X} = 30$ $s^2 = 40$ (cell 1)	$\bar{X} = 24$ $s^2 = 34$ (cell 2)	$\bar{\bar{X}} = 27$
Women	$\bar{X} = 36$ $s^2 = 50$ (cell 3)	$\bar{X} = 26$ $s^2 = 36$ (cell 4)	$\bar{\bar{X}} = 31$
	$\bar{\bar{X}} = 33$	$\bar{\bar{X}} = 25$	$\bar{\bar{X}} = 29$

S E X

Table of Analysis of Variance with Computations

Source	df	Mean Square	F
Main Effects Training	(columns − 1)	$\dfrac{n \text{ in column} * s_{\bar{x}}^2 \text{column means}}{\text{degrees of freedom}}$	$\dfrac{\text{Mean Square}}{\text{Within Groups Mean Square}}$
Sex	(rows − 1)	$\dfrac{n \text{ in row} * s_{\bar{x}}^2 \text{row means}}{\text{degrees of freedom}}$	$\dfrac{\text{Mean Square}}{\text{Within Groups Mean Square}}$
Interaction Effects Sex × Training	(rows − 1) × (columns − 1)	$\dfrac{n \text{ in each cell} * (\text{each cell} - \text{row mean} - \text{column mean} + \text{grand mean})^2}{\text{degrees of freedom}}$	$\dfrac{\text{Mean Square}}{\text{Within Groups Mean Square}}$
Within Groups Variance	(total sample − number of cells)	s_p^2	

constructing the ANOVA summary table

in the study minus the number of cells (the number of mean parameters estimated from sample means within each cell to obtain a variance). For this example, there is a total sample of 84 minus 4 cells, for a total of 80 degrees of freedom.

Thus, the row for within groups variance may be filled in as follows:

ANOVA TABLE

Source	df	Mean Square	F
Within Groups	80	40	

computing between groups variance for sex variable

Now, you can look at the two main effects and the one interaction effect between the two variables. To compute the effect for the sex of the individuals who went through training

- Compute a variance using the two row means $(\overline{\overline{X}})$ for men and for women as our two pieces of data. The variance is 8.
- Multiply this variance by the number of events in each row. Multiply 8 by 42 (there were 42 men and 42 women—42 events in each row). The result of this step is 336, which is placed in the "mean square" column.

Degrees of freedom are the number of conditions (rows), minus 1. Here 2 rows minus 1 equals 1. This number is placed in the column marked df. To compute an F ratio

F ratio for the sex variable

- Divide between groups variance (mean square) by within groups variance (mean square). In this case divide 336 by 40. The result is 8.4. This number is placed in the column marked F, as follows:

Source	df	Mean Square	F
Sex	1	336	8.4
Within Groups	80	40	

To learn whether this difference is beyond chance alone, you need only look at the F table in Appendix C. For 1 degree of freedom in the numerator (column 1 on the table), and 80 degrees of freedom in the denominator (row 80), the critical F value for alpha risk at .05 is 3.96, as Figure 15.3 shows. Since the calculated F exceeds this critical value, our observed F statistic falls in the F distribution's critical region. Thus, you can reject the null hypothesis and conclude that there is a significant difference between the competence scores of men and women. Women in our sample score higher in communication competence than do men.

To identify any main effects from training, you can follow the same general process. Start by

computing between groups variance for the training variable

- Computing a variance from the 2-column means (across levels of the sex independent variable). With this step, you obtain 32.
- Multiplying by the number of events in each column (42). This action reveals the mean square for this source of variation: 1,344.
- Identifying degrees of freedom as the number of columns minus 1, yielding 1 degree of freedom in this example (2 − 1).

Portion of the *F* Table

95th Percentile Values
for the *F* Distribution
(d.f.$_1$ degrees of freedom in numerator)
(d.f.$_2$ degrees of freedom in denominator)

0.95

0.05

Between Groups Degrees of Freedom

Within Groups Degrees of Freedom

	1	2	3	4	5	6	7	8	9	10
1	161.4	199.5	215.7	224.6	230.2	234	236.8	238.9	240.5	241.9
2	18.51	19.00	19.16	19.25	19.30	19.33	19.36	19.37	19.38	19.39
3	10.13	9.55	9.28	9.12	9.01	8.94	8.89	8.85	8.81	8.79
80	3.96	3.11	2.72	2.48	2.33	2.21	2.12	2.05	1.99	1.95

F Distribution and Example Test Statistic

Critical
Value
3.96
d.f.: 1, 80

Test
Statistic
8.4

.95

.05

The *F* ratio is computed by dividing the treatment mean square by the within groups mean square, which produces a value of 33.6. When you enter it into the summary table, you get the following:

Source	df	Mean Square	F
Sex	1	336	8.4
Training	1	1344	33.6
Within Groups	80	40	

This *F* value also is statistically significant with 1 and 80 degrees of freedom (column 1 and row 80 on the *F* table). By looking at the means, you can observe that people who take the communication skills training score higher in competence than those who do not take the training.

The computation of the interaction is accomplished by

- Taking each cell mean, subtracting the corresponding row mean, subtracting the corresponding column mean, and then adding grand mean into the mix.[5]

**computing
interaction variance**

---

[5] If we had three independent variables, the three-variable interaction would be computed by taking the cell mean and subtracting the row mean, subtracting the column mean, subtracting the slice (that's what they call the third variable division) mean, and adding in the grand mean twice (to keep the numbers sensible).

For our example, we get the following numbers (cell 1 = −1; cell 2 = 1; cell 3 = 1; cell 4 = −1).

- Squaring the answer for each cell.
- Adding up these squared answers from all the cells (4 in this example).
- Multiplying this sum by the number of events in each cell; multiplying 4 by 21 (the number of events in each cell) produces 84, which is placed in the mean square column.
- Computing degrees of freedom by multiplying the degrees of freedom for each of the main effects of the variables in the interaction. Since each variable in the interaction had one degree of freedom, the total degrees of freedom are $1 \times 1 = 1$.
- Compute the F ratio by dividing this mean square by the within groups variance and placing the answer in the column indicated as F:

Source	df	Mean Square	F
Sex	1	336	8.4
Training	1	1344	33.6
Sex × Training Interaction	1	84	2.1
Within Groups	80	40	

As you can see, the interaction F ratio is smaller than the critical F ratio. Thus, no significant interaction effect can be claimed. Hence, it appears that women score higher in communication competence than men, and that those who attend the communication skills training score higher than those who do not take such training. Moreover, these effects are additive since there is no significant interaction between the two.

Examining Effect Patterns

main effects not interpreted if disordinal interactions present

As you recall from Chapter 11, main effects indicate the impact of one variable across levels of others in the design. As such, main effects can be interpreted as if a simple one-way analysis of variance had been completed. But there is a catch. If there are significant interactions, the researcher may or may not be permitted to interpret main effects for involved independent variables. If the interaction effect is shown to be a crossed interaction (disordinal), then the researcher should not interpret main effects for variables involved, since such information would be misleading. Yet, if the interaction effect is uncrossed (ordinal), main effects may be interpreted without fear of misleading the reader. Thus, the interactions must be teased out, often using multiple comparison tests and even formal diagrams.

As in one-way ANOVA, it is important for researchers to identify the size of the relationships observed. You can use the same eta statistic discussed previously. Thus, the comparative importance of each significant source of variation may be evaluated by the researcher.

BASIC NONPARAMETRIC TESTING

So far, this chapter has emphasized ways to compare the means of interval or ratio level dependent variables. But sometimes the data are simple frequency counts in categories and require different tools.

SPECIAL DISCUSSION 15–2
Bells and Whistles: A Reader's Guide to Advanced Statistical Methods

Many statistical methods go far beyond an initial understanding of statistical tools. This guide defines some advanced techniques for you and identifies some things to look for when you read reports of them.

Multiple Regression Correlation: (a.k.a. multiple correlation): produces a correlation of multiple predictors with a single output variable. **Beta weights** tell the contribution made by each predictor to the overall correlation. Predictors are supposed to be uncorrelated with each other (called absence of **multicollinearity**).

Multiple Discriminant Analysis: membership in particular groups from a knowledge of a number of predictor variables (measured on the interval or ratio level). Researchers report discriminant functions composed of linear combinations of variables which, in turn, are tested for significance. Prediction is also evaluated by using **canonical correlation** and hit ratio success.

Log-Linear Analysis: extension of chi-square testing for analysis of more than two variables measured on the nominal level. The method uses applications of maximizing methods (e.g., maximum likelihood estimation) to identify explanatory models and patterns.

Multivariate Analyses

Canonical Correlation: an extension of multiple regression correlating two sets of variables. Scholars interpret roots of canonical correlations (tested for significance using chi square) and identify components for each root (interpreted as meaningful the farther they are from zero). The redundancy index tells whether sets of variables should be interpreted differentially for additional canonical component roots (look for a redundancy index greater than .05).

MANOVA (Multivariate Analysis of Variance): extension of analysis of variance for multiple dependent variables. The method represents interrelated dependent variables (checked by a test of "sphericity") as a weighted linear combination. The method tests to determine if effects are on some dependent variables more than others (such as Wilks' lambda) or whether effects are shared across dependent variables (such as Pillai's trace).

Multivariate Multiple Correlation: extension of multiple regression for many interrelated dependent measures. Combined with canonical correlation, omnibus (Wilks') and trace (e.g., Pillai's) statistics to interpret results.

Multivariate Analysis of Covariance: extension of MANOVA to adapt analysis of covariance for multiple interrelated dependent variables (see MANOVA guides).

Hotelling's T^2: t test for intercorrelated dependent variables

---

SPECIAL DISCUSSION 15–2
(Continued)

Modelling Methods

Path Models: use correlational tools to interpret relationships to identify causal models with exogenous (input variable) sources, endogenous (mediating) variables, and dependent (output or criterion) variables. Tests of fit are often expected in acceptable models.

LISREL (Linear Structural Relations): a computer program to isolate relationships by examining covariances among variables. The method develops simultaneous equations (usually employing a method such as maximum likelihood estimation to maximize the degree of relationship found) to represent relations among variables. Tests of fit using residual mean square and chi-square tests are usually included.

The Nature of Nonparametric Tests: The Randomization Assumption

nonparametric tests identified

Nonparametric tests are statistical methods that do not make assumptions about population distributions or population parameters. Thus, these methods sometimes are called "distribution-free" statistics. But this statement does not mean that there are no assumptions made at all. On the contrary, there is one assumption made when using nonparametric tests: randomization. If you wish to examine how often a given set of categorical data or rankings could be found by chance, you must use randomization to begin figuring the odds of finding a set of results at random. Thus, as with parametric tests, randomization is a consistent requirement of statistical testing.

required for nominal or ordinal dependent measures

Nonparametric tests are required when researchers examine dependent measures on ordinal or nominal levels of measurement. Of course, the dependent variable data may originally have been measured on the interval level, but researchers can reduce the level of measurement to lower level data. For instance, a researcher might be interested in examining the impact of watching presidential debates on the credibility of candidates. People could fill out credibility scales before and after the debates. Instead of examining the degree of differences, researchers could simply count the number of people who rated the candidates more credible, less credible, or unchanged after the debate. Of course when you move to a lower level of measurement, you lose sensitivity contained in the original data. Thus, researchers tend to make such a choice only when practical matters of design and control demand it.

Tests for Nominal Level Dependent Variables

use of the chi-square statistic: count data

Nonparametric tests apply to situations in which the dependent measures are on the ordinal or nominal level. Though there are many formulae in these categories, the most popular ones in communication research are variations of chi square tests. Thus, we will focus on them for this introductory treatment. The **chi square test** is designed to deal with "count" data. That is, chi square allows us to use categories and determine if there are differences between the number of data that fall into each category. The "count" of the number of events in each category is analyzed by using the applications of chi square that we describe here: the one sample test and the test for independence of samples.

The One-Sample Chi Square Test

Sometimes inelegantly called the "goodness of fit" test, the one-sample chi square test allows a researcher to take a single independent variable that is broken down into nominal categories, and identify whether the arrangement among categories is beyond what would have been expected by chance alone.

    The chi square (χ^2) distribution is enlisted to help play the odds. This distribution may be considered as a probability distribution of squared differences of scores. Hence, it may be used to help assess differences among proportions and to identify when actual counts of data differ from counts that could have been expected by chance. As Figure 15.4 shows, this chi square distribution is not symmetrical, though it does tend to become more and more normal as degrees of freedom increase. This distribution's properties permit us to identify unusual differences by isolating the critical region, as we have with other distributions.

    The one-sample chi square test is often used when researchers gather data that they believe can be contrasted with theoretically expected patterns. For instance, it is known that the proportion of children with speech handicaps is about 7% of the population. Suppose a teacher noticed that a surprising number of her pupils seemed to have speech defects. She might randomly sample a group of 100 children and find this pattern:

	Speech Handicapped	Not Speech Handicapped
Number of Children	15	85

To test whether this pattern is statistically significant, you may use the chi square test with alpha risk set at .05. Using the symbol p for the probabilities or proportions of occurrence of events, the null hypothesis is

$$H_0 : p_1 = p_2 .$$

Since theory guides the teacher, those expectations can be compared against the actual observations. Since 7% of children have speech defects in the population, we could expect that 7 out of 100 children would have such defects, and 93 would not. This expectation would contrast with the observed frequencies as

	Speech Handicapped	Not Speech Handicapped
Number of Children	15	85
Theoretic expectation	7	93

The test statistic for this case is shown by the following formula:

$$\chi^2 = \sum \frac{(f_{observed} - f_{expected})^2}{f_{expected}} .$$

(margin notes)
one sample or "goodness of fit" chi square

the chi square distribution

one sample test used when contrasts with theoretically expected frequencies exist

Chi Square Distribution

Portion of the Chi Square Table

Alpha Risk Levels
(indicating the proportion of the chi
square distribution that lies to the right
of the critical value)

Degrees of Freedom	.95	.10	.05	.025	.01
1	.004	2.71	3.84	5.02	6.64
2	.10	4.61	5.99	7.38	9.21
3	.35	6.25	7.81	9.35	11.34
4	.71	7.78	9.49	11.14	13.28
5	1.15	9.24	11.07	12.83	15.09

FIGURE 15.4
Using the Chi Square
Distribution

**computation of chi
square**

The f stands for the frequency or count. To use the formula, you subtract the expected frequency from each observed frequency, square the difference (to get rid of minus signs since chi square has no negative numbers), and divide by the expected frequency. Then you repeat the process for all other groups. Finally we total the numbers and obtain a chi square test statistic. In this case, you get the following numbers:

$$\chi^2 = \frac{(15 - 7)^2}{7} + \frac{(85 - 93)^2}{93}$$

$$\chi^2 = 9.14 + .69$$

$$\chi^2 = 9.83$$

**degrees of freedom
for chi square**

Degrees of freedom are computed by looking at the number of groups −1. Thus, in this example, degrees of freedom are 2 − 1, or 1. As Figure 15.4 and Appendix D show, the critical chi square value for alpha risk at .05 and one degree of freedom is 3.84. Since our computed chi square of 9.83 is greater than 3.84, we enter the critical region—and the null hypothesis is rejected. It seems that the teacher's children have a higher rate of speech handicaps than found in the general population.

**the equal probability
hypothesis used**

Sometimes researchers do not have theory to go on. Thus, they make use of the **equal probability hypothesis** to form expected frequencies. For instance, suppose that you sampled 300 people to find out if there were differences among their preference for reading the weekly news magazines *Time, Newsweek,* and *U.S. News and World Report*. You might find the following:

	Time	**Newsweek**	**U.S. News and World Report**
Number of People Preferring	130	110	60

To find out if the observed pattern differs from what might be expected at random, you could hypothesize that if there were no preferences, each magazine would have an equal chance of selection. If each magazine were equally preferred, you would expect one-third of the sample to prefer each magazine. Thus, the equal probability hypothesis would lead you to the following comparisons:

	Time	Newsweek	U.S. News and World Report
Number of People Preferring	130	110	60
Expected Frequencies	100	100	100

The test statistic for this case is:

$$\chi^2 = \sum \frac{(f_{observed} - f_{expected})^2}{f_{expected}}$$

$$\chi^2 = \frac{(130 - 100)^2}{100} + \frac{(110 - 100)^2}{100} + \frac{(60 - 100)^2}{100}$$

$$\chi^2 = 9 + 1 + 16$$

$$\chi^2 = 26$$

Degrees of freedom are computed by looking at the number of groups − 1. Hence, the degrees of freedom are 3 − 1, or 2 degrees of freedom. Since at alpha risk of .05 the critical region of chi square begins at 5.99, the null hypothesis is rejected. Consequently, researchers would conclude that there is a difference in news magazine preferences.

degrees of freedom for the one-sample chi square

The Chi Square Test of Independence

If researchers have two or more ways to classify variables, they may create what are called "contingency tables" and see if there is a relationship between the variables that compose the framework of the table. For instance, suppose you wanted to find out whether teams of male or female college debaters won more or fewer debates than each other. You could find a sample of debate teams composed of males and a sample of debate teams composed of women. Then during the preliminary rounds of a tournament, you could count the number of debates each team won or lost. The null hypothesis in this case would be that the two classification variables are independent (unrelated to each other). After finding 150 debates by males and 150 debates by female debate teams (none involving the same pairs of debate teams debating against each other), the data might be found as follows:

using contingency tables with two classification variables

test of independence

	Number of Debates Won	Number of Debates Lost	Total Debates
Debates by Males	90	60	150 (50%)
Debates by Females	80	70	150 (50%)
Total	170	130	

The formula for this chi square test statistic is the same as the "goodness of fit" test. The only difference lies in the source of the expected frequencies. If the two classification variables are independent and unrelated of each other, then you expect to see a roughly equal distribution of counts across conditions. In this case, look at the row percentages and the column totals. As you can see, each row includes 50% of the

computing expected frequencies for the chi square test of independence

SPECIAL DISCUSSION 15–3
The Use of Factor Analysis in Measurement

Factor analysis is a commonly used statistical method that helps "the researcher discover and identify the unities or dimensions, called factors, behind many measures" (Kerlinger, 1986, p. 138). Largely because convenient computer programs are widespread, researchers routinely report results of factor analyses for scales as part of the report of reliability of measures. In fact, in communication research, this statistical tool most often is used as part of the reliability assessment of measures. Since reliability is computed for measures that deal with the same dimension, factor analysis is a useful way to learn which items really measure things on the same dimension. This discussion deals with factor analysis applied primarily to measurement reliability concerns.

Though factor analysis has some complicated applications, when it is used in measurement, researchers follow a rather consistent pattern. Factor analysis begins by a researcher giving the measure of interest to a group of subjects. Then, all the items on the measure are correlated with each other (sometimes using alternatives to correlations). Items that tend to be highly interrelated are identified as measuring common dimensions.

As a second step, factor analyses mathematically extract chief factors underlying the larger number of measures. Though there are other options, the most common method is the "Principal Components Solution," which attempts to identify the number of common centers of variation that underlie the variables. If one factor emerges as the center of variation for a set of test items, then the test items appear to measure only that one dimension. If two factors are found, the test items would appear to measure two different things. If three factors emerge, three dimensions would appear to underlie the test items. For each emerging factor, the association of the test items to the common factor are identified by a set of "item loadings," that reveal how closely the items are related to each factor.

data. Thus, if there were no relationship between classification variables (sex of team and win-loss record), you would expect to see 50% of each column total composed of male debate teams and 50% composed of female debate teams. Thus, researchers compute the row percentages, and use those percentages to identify the expected frequencies for each row.[6] Let's apply this logic to our example. The column for number of debates won was 170. Thus, we would expect to see 50% of this 170 on the row for women and 50% on the row for men. Similarly, the column indicating the number of debates lost was 130. Thus, we would expect to see 50% of this 130 on the row for women and 50% on the row for men. The result is shown in this revised table:

---

[6] There are other ways to get the expected frequency. For instance, to find it for a given cell you can multiply the column frequency by the row frequency and divide by the total frequencies in the study table.

As a third step, the factors are interpreted. To aid interpretation of factor loadings, the factors are "rotated" (contrary to popular confusion about the matter, "rotation" does not affect the factor analysis solution, but is only an aid in understanding factors). Rotations usually are made orthogonally so that the nature of factor loadings can be identified with greatest separation (i.e., a 90-degree rotation system is used). Next, one tries to decide what each factor really measures. The item loadings are checked to see which ones "load" or "define" each factor. As a protocol of sorts, researchers usually consider rotated item scores loaded on a factor if the item has a score of at least .60 and no loading on another factor of .40 or greater. The following example shows a typical loading pattern:

	Factor I	Factor II
Test Item 1	.80	.18
Test Item 2	.77	.22
Test Item 3	.45	.45
Test Item 4	.31	.66
Test Item 5	.28	.71
Test Item 6	.44	.62

As you can see, items one and two measure factor one, and items four and five measure factor two. These two dimensions then would be scored as separate measures for which reliability is assessed. By examining available theory and the properties shared by items on each factor, the researcher identifies an appropriate label to use to refer to the scores produced on each factor.

	Number of Debates Won	Number of Debates Lost	Total Debates
Debates by Males	90	60	150
expected frequency:	(85)	(65)	(50%)
Debates by Females	80	70	150
expected frequency:	(85)	(65)	(50%)
Total	170	130	300

The test statistic uses the standard formula for chi-square:

$$\chi^2 = \sum \frac{(f_{observed} - f_{expected})^2}{f_{expected}}$$

$$\chi^2 = \frac{(90 - 85)^2}{85} + \frac{(60 - 65)^2}{65} + \frac{(80 - 85)^2}{85} + \frac{(70 - 65)^2}{65}$$

$$\chi^2 = .29 + .38 + .29 + .38$$

$$\chi^2 = 1.34$$

degrees of freedom for the chi square test of independence

    Degrees of freedom are equal to the number of columns – one multiplied by the number of rows minus one. In this case, you have $(2 - 1)$ times $(2 - 1)$, which yields one degree of freedom. Since the critical chi square value is 3.84, it is clear that the test statistic does not fall into critical region of the chi-square distribution. Thus, the researcher fails to reject the null hypothesis and concludes that there is no difference indicated by the data. Hence, there did not appear to be a relationship between the sex of the debaters and the win-loss record.

Determining Effect Sizes

The chi square test permits you to identify whether chance can be eliminated to explain research findings. But the test does not identify how big the effects are. Thus, it is useful to assess effect size. Several are available, but among the most frequently employed is the contingency coefficient. This method involves taking the observed chi square value and computing the following formula:

$$C = \sqrt{\frac{\chi^2}{N + \chi^2}}.$$

This formula permits individuals to identify the size of relationships between variables equivalent to a correlation. Thus, the contingency coefficient is an important counterpart to significance testing.

SUMMARY

Analysis of variance involves the use of the F distribution to compare more than two means. Researchers may compute a variance using sample means as the data (between groups variance) and compare this variance to the kind of background variation that already exists within each group (within groups variance). This latter term is represented by the "pooled variance" (the squared pooled standard deviation used for the t test). To compare several means for one independent variable one uses one-way analysis of variance. Additional follow-up work must be completed after finding a significant F ratio. To identify the location of differences, multiple comparison tests may be used (these methods generally are computed so that alpha risk is stretched out across comparisons). Tukey's HSD is used to make all possible comparisons of means, when the means are taken two at a time. For complex comparisons Scheffe's critical S method is recommended. The researcher needs to supplement the measure of statistical significance with measures of effect size, such as eta (η) (also called the "correlation ratio") and eta squared (η^2).

To identify nonlinear relationships, researchers may follow-up by using trend analysis, a method that isolates the nature of linear and nonlinear effects by considering weighted means.

    A variable factor is a variable that has been broken down into levels or groups. Factorial analysis of variance is analysis of variance applied to multiple independent variables that have been broken down into levels or groups. This test of significance identifies main and interaction effects between independent variables. Main effects are dependent variable effects from independent variables separately. Interaction effects are dependent variable effects from independent variables taken together. If there is a crossed interaction (disordinal), then the researcher should not interpret main effects for variables involved, since such information would be misleading.

    Nonparametric tests are statistical methods that do not make assumptions about population distributions or population parameters. Yet, these methods make one assumption for use of these tests: randomization. The family of nonparametric tests applies to situations in which the dependent measures are on the ordinal or nominal level. The most popular ones in communication research are applications of chi square tests. The chi square test is designed to deal with "count" data. The one-sample chi square test allows a researcher to take a single variable that is broken down into nominal categories and identify whether the arrangement among categories is beyond what would have been expected by chance alone. It is often used when researchers gather data that they believe can be contrasted with theoretically expected patterns. At other times when researchers do not have theory to go on, they make use of the "equal probability hypothesis" to form expected frequencies. The chi square test of independence is used when there are two or more ways to classify variables that can be classed into "contingency tables." After finding a significant chi square, researchers follow-up by using a measure of effect size, such as the contingency coefficient.

TERMS FOR REVIEW

one-way analysis of variance
multiple comparison tests
Tukey's HSD
Scheffe's critical S
trend analysis
variable factors
factorial analysis of variance

main effects
interaction effects
grand mean
nonparametric tests
chi square test
equal probability hypothesis

Areas Under the Standard Normal Curve

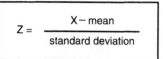

$$Z = \frac{X - \text{mean}}{\text{standard deviation}}$$

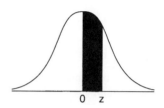

z	.00	.01	.02	.03	.04	.05	.06	.07	.08	.09
0.0	.0000	.0040	.0080	.0120	.0160	.0199	.0239	.0279	.0319	.0359
0.1	.0398	.0438	.0478	.0517	.0557	.0596	.0636	.0675	.0714	.0753
0.2	.0793	.0832	.0871	.0910	.0948	.0987	.1026	.1064	.1103	.1141
0.3	.1179	.1217	.1255	.1293	.1331	.1368	.1406	.1443	.1480	.1517
0.4	.1554	.1591	.1628	.1664	.1700	.1736	.1772	.1808	.1844	.1879
0.5	.1915	.1950	.1985	.2019	.2054	.2088	.2123	.2157	.2190	.2224
0.6	.2257	.2291	.2324	.2357	.2389	.2422	.2454	.2486	.2517	.2549
0.7	.2580	.2611	.2642	.2673	.2704	.2734	.2764	.2794	.2823	.2852
0.8	.2881	.2910	.2939	.2967	.2995	.3023	.3051	.3078	.3106	.3133
0.9	.3159	.3186	.3212	.3238	.3264	.3289	.3315	.3340	.3365	.3389
1.0	.3413	.3438	.3461	.3485	.3508	.3531	.3554	.3577	.3599	.3621
1.1	.3643	.3665	.3686	.3708	.3729	.3749	.3770	.3790	.3810	.3830
1.2	.3849	.3869	.3888	.3907	.3925	.3944	.3962	.3980	.3997	.4015
1.3	.4032	.4049	.4066	.4082	.4099	.4115	.4131	.4147	.4162	.4177
1.4	.4192	.4207	.4222	.4236	.4251	.4265	.4279	.4292	.4306	.4319
1.5	.4332	.4345	.4357	.4370	.4382	.4394	.4406	.4418	.4429	.4441
1.6	.4452	.4463	.4474	.4484	.4495	.4505	.4515	.4525	.4535	.4545
1.7	.4554	.4564	.4573	.4582	.4591	.4599	.4608	.4616	.4625	.4633
1.8	.4641	.4649	.4656	.4664	.4671	.4678	.4686	.4693	.4699	.4706
1.9	.4713	.4719	.4726	.4732	.4738	.4744	.4750	.4756	.4761	.4767
2.0	.4772	.4778	.4783	.4788	.4793	.4798	.4803	.4808	.4812	.4817
2.1	.4821	.4826	.4830	.4834	.4838	.4842	.4846	.4850	.4854	.4857
2.2	.4861	.4864	.4868	.4871	.4875	.4878	.4881	.4884	.4887	.4890
2.3	.4893	.4896	.4898	.4901	.4904	.4906	.4909	.4911	.4913	.4916
2.4	.4918	.4920	.4922	.4925	.4927	.2929	.4931	.4932	.4934	.4936
2.5	.4938	.4940	.4941	.4943	.4945	.4946	.4948	.4949	.4951	.4952
2.6	.4953	.4955	.4956	.4957	.4959	.4960	.4961	.4962	.4963	.4964
2.7	.4965	.4966	.4967	.4968	.4969	.4970	.4971	.4972	.4973	.4974
2.8	.4974	.4975	.4976	.4977	.4977	.4978	.4979	.4979	.4980	.4981
2.9	.4981	.4982	.4982	.4983	.4984	.4984	.4985	.4985	.4986	.4986
3.0	.4987	.4987	.4987	.4988	.4988	.4989	.4989	.4989	.4990	.4990
3.1	.4990	.4991	.4991	.4991	.4992	.4992	.4992	.4992	.4993	.4993
3.2	.4993	.4993	.4994	.4994	.4994	.4994	.4994	.4995	.4995	.4995
3.5	.4998									
4.0	.49997									
4.5	.499997									
5.0	.4999997									
6.0	.499999997									

Critical Values of *t*

Alpha risk for one-tailed tests

Alpha risk for two-tailed tests

	.05	.025	.01	.005
	.10	.05	.02	.01

Degrees of freedom:

d.f.	.10/.05	.05/.025	.02/.01	.01/.005
1	6.314	12.706	31.821	63.657
2	2.920	4.303	6.965	9.925
3	2.353	3.182	4.541	5.841
4	2.132	2.776	3.747	4.604
5	2.015	2.571	3.365	4.032
6	1.943	2.447	3.143	3.707
7	1.895	2.365	2.998	3.500
8	1.860	2.306	2.896	3.355
9	1.833	2.262	2.821	3.250
10	1.812	2.228	2.764	3.169
11	1.796	2.201	2.718	3.106
12	1.782	2.179	2.681	3.054
13	1.771	2.160	2.650	3.012
14	1.761	2.145	2.624	2.977
15	1.753	2.132	2.602	2.947
16	1.746	2.120	2.584	2.921
17	1.740	2.110	2.567	2.898
18	1.734	2.101	2.552	2.878
19	1.729	2.093	2.540	2.861
20	1.725	2.086	2.528	2.845
21	1.721	2.080	2.518	2.831
22	1.717	2.074	2.508	2.819
23	1.714	2.069	2.500	2.807
24	1.711	2.064	2.492	2.797
25	1.708	2.060	2.485	2.787
26	1.706	2.056	2.479	2.779
27	1.703	2.052	2.473	2.771
28	1.701	2.048	2.467	2.763
29	1.699	2.045	2.462	2.756
30	1.697	2.042	2.457	2.750
35	1.690	2.030	2.438	2.724
40	1.684	2.021	2.423	2.704
50	1.676	2.009	2.403	2.678
75	1.666	1.993	2.378	2.644
100	1.660	1.984	2.364	2.626
150	1.655	1.976	2.352	2.609
200	1.652	1.972	2.345	2.601
500	1.648	1.965	2.334	2.586
∞	1.645	1.960	2.326	2.576

(Number of events minus the number of new means computed in the numerator of the *t* statistic formula)

Example:

$$t = \frac{\bar{x} - \bar{x}}{s \, \text{diff}}$$

d.f. = n − 2

2.571 would have to go further out on base line to keep the 95% on the curve.

−1.96   +1.96

Critical Values of *F* with alpha risk = .05

between groups degrees of freedom

within groups degrees of freedom

	1	2	3	4	5	6	7	8	9	10	11	12	15	20	25
1	161.4	199.5	215.7	224.6	230.2	234	236.8	238.9	240.5	241.9	242.5	243.9	245.9	248.0	249.3
2	18.51	19.00	19.16	19.25	19.30	19.33	19.36	19.37	19.38	19.39	19.40	19.41	19.43	19.44	19.46
3	10.13	9.55	9.28	9.12	9.01	8.94	8.89	8.85	8.81	8.79	8.76	8.74	8.70	8.66	8.63
4	7.71	6.94	6.59	6.39	6.26	6.16	6.09	6.04	6.00	5.96	5.93	5.91	5.86	5.80	5.77
5	6.61	5.79	5.41	5.19	5.05	4.95	4.88	4.82	4.77	4.74	4.70	4.68	4.62	4.56	4.52
6	5.99	5.14	4.76	4.53	4.39	4.28	4.21	4.15	4.10	4.06	4.03	4.00	3.94	3.87	3.83
7	5.59	4.74	4.35	4.12	3.97	3.87	3.79	3.73	3.68	3.64	3.60	3.57	3.51	3.44	3.40
8	5.32	4.46	4.07	3.84	3.69	3.58	3.50	3.44	3.39	3.34	3.31	3.28	3.22	3.15	3.11
9	5.12	4.26	3.86	3.63	3.48	3.37	3.29	3.23	3.18	3.13	3.10	3.07	3.01	2.94	2.89
10	4.96	4.10	3.71	3.48	3.33	3.22	3.14	3.07	3.02	2.97	2.94	2.91	2.85	2.77	2.73
11	4.84	3.98	3.59	3.36	3.20	3.09	3.01	2.95	2.90	2.86	2.82	2.79	2.72	2.65	2.60
12	4.75	3.88	3.49	3.26	3.11	3.00	2.92	2.85	2.80	2.76	2.72	2.69	2.62	2.54	2.50
13	4.67	3.81	3.41	3.18	3.03	2.92	2.84	2.77	2.72	2.67	2.63	2.60	2.53	2.46	2.41
14	4.60	3.74	3.34	3.11	2.96	2.85	2.77	2.70	2.65	2.60	2.56	2.53	2.46	2.39	2.34
15	4.54	3.68	3.29	3.06	2.90	2.79	2.71	2.64	2.59	2.55	2.51	2.48	2.40	2.33	2.28
16	4.49	3.63	3.24	3.01	2.85	2.74	2.66	2.59	2.54	2.49	2.45	2.42	2.35	2.28	2.23
17	4.45	3.59	3.20	2.96	2.81	2.70	2.62	2.55	2.50	2.45	2.41	2.38	2.31	2.23	2.18
18	4.41	3.55	3.16	2.93	2.77	2.66	2.58	2.51	2.46	2.41	2.37	2.34	2.27	2.19	2.14
19	4.38	3.52	3.13	2.90	2.74	2.63	2.55	2.48	2.43	2.38	2.34	2.31	2.23	2.16	2.11
20	4.35	3.49	3.10	2.87	2.71	2.60	2.52	2.45	2.40	2.35	2.31	2.28	2.20	2.12	2.07
21	4.32	3.47	3.07	2.84	2.68	2.57	2.49	2.42	2.37	2.32	2.28	2.25	2.18	2.10	2.05
22	4.30	3.44	3.05	2.82	2.66	2.55	2.47	2.40	2.35	2.30	2.26	2.23	2.15	2.07	2.02
23	4.28	3.42	3.03	2.80	2.64	2.53	2.45	2.38	2.32	2.28	2.24	2.20	2.13	2.05	2.00
24	4.26	3.40	3.01	2.78	2.62	2.51	2.43	2.36	2.30	2.26	2.22	2.18	2.11	2.03	1.97
25	4.24	3.39	2.99	2.76	2.60	2.49	2.41	2.34	2.28	2.24	2.20	2.16	2.09	2.01	1.96
26	4.23	3.37	2.98	2.74	2.59	2.47	2.39	2.32	2.27	2.22	2.18	2.15	2.07	1.99	1.94
27	4.21	3.35	2.96	2.73	2.57	2.46	2.37	2.31	2.25	2.20	2.16	2.13	2.06	1.97	1.92
28	4.20	3.34	2.95	2.71	2.56	2.45	2.36	2.29	2.24	2.19	2.15	2.12	2.04	1.96	1.91
29	4.18	3.33	2.93	2.70	2.55	2.43	2.35	2.28	2.22	2.18	2.14	2.10	2.03	1.94	1.89
30	4.17	3.32	2.92	2.69	2.53	2.42	2.34	2.27	2.21	2.16	2.12	2.09	2.01	1.93	1.88
40	4.08	3.23	3.84	2.61	2.45	2.34	2.25	2.18	2.12	2.08	2.04	2.00	1.92	1.84	1.78
80	3.96	3.11	2.72	2.48	2.33	2.21	2.12	2.05	1.99	1.95	1.91	1.88	1.80	1.70	1.64
120	3.92	3.07	2.68	2.45	2.29	2.18	2.09	2.02	1.96	1.91	1.87	1.83	1.75	1.66	1.60
200	3.89	3.04	2.65	2.41	2.26	2.14	2.05	1.98	1.92	1.87	1.83	1.80	1.72	1.62	1.56
∞	3.84	3.00	2.61	2.37	2.21	2.10	2.01	1.94	1.88	1.83	1.79	1.75	1.67	1.57	1.51

Critical Values of Chi Square

	Alpha Risk Levels indicating the proportion of the chi square distribution that lies to the right of the critical value				
Degrees of freedom:	.95	.10	.05	.025	.01
1	.004	2.71	3.84	5.02	6.64
2	.10	4.61	5.99	7.38	9.21
3	.35	6.25	7.81	9.35	11.34
4	.71	7.78	9.49	11.14	13.28
5	1.15	9.24	11.07	12.83	15.09
6	1.64	10.64	12.59	14.45	16.81
7	2.17	12.02	14.07	16.01	18.48
8	2.73	13.36	15.51	17.53	20.09
9	3.33	14.68	16.92	19.02	21.67
10	3.94	15.99	18.31	20.48	23.21
11	4.57	17.28	19.68	21.92	24.72
12	5.23	18.55	21.03	23.34	26.22
13	5.89	19.81	22.36	24.74	27.69
14	6.57	21.06	23.68	26.12	29.14
15	7.26	22.31	24.99	27.49	30.58
16	7.96	23.54	26.30	28.85	32.00
17	8.67	24.77	27.59	30.19	33.41
18	9.39	25.99	28.87	31.53	34.81
19	10.12	27.20	30.14	32.85	36.19
20	10.85	28.41	31.41	34.17	37.57
21	11.59	29.62	32.67	35.48	38.93
22	12.34	30.81	33.92	36.78	40.29
23	13.09	32.01	35.17	38.08	41.64
24	13.85	33.20	36.42	39.26	42.98
25	14.61	34.38	37.65	40.65	44.31
26	15.38	35.56	38.89	41.92	45.61
27	16.15	36.74	40.11	43.19	46.96
28	16.93	37.92	41.34	44.46	48.28
29	17.71	39.09	42.56	45.72	49.59
30	18.49	40.26	43.77	46.98	50.89
40	26.51	51.81	55.76	59.34	63.69
50	34.76	63.17	67.50	71.42	76.15
75	56.07	91.06	96.21	100.83	103.60
100	77.93	118.50	124.34	129.56	135.81

GLOSSARY

absolute zero A score that indicates that the property measured is completely absent.

abstract bibliographic card Bibliographic cards featuring summaries of materials.

abstract calculus An element of theory, which is the logical structure of relationships (the word "calculus" refers to any deductive system).

accidental or convenience sampling Selection of events that are most readily available.

accretions Deposits of material left by some action.

act In Burke's dramatistic pentad, the symbolic action (the speech, for instance).

ad hoc rescue A fallacy of research in which support for a theory is claimed despite failed predictions.

advertising The study and practice of mass media methods of influence to promote a product, service, or cause.

agency In Burke's dramatistic pentad, the symbolic and linguistic strategies used to secure identification.

agent In Burke's dramatistic pentad, the actor or rhetor who performs the act.

alpha *See* Cronbach's coefficient alpha.

alpha risk (α risk) The probability of committing a Type I error.

alternate forms reliability A method of test reliability that constructs different forms of the same test from a common pool of measurement items, gives each to the same group of people, and determines the degree of consistency.

analogy *See* argument from analogy.

analysis of covariance A method of statistical control that determines the variation associated with each nuisance variable and then separates it from the remaining total variation in the experiment by use of analysis of variance methods.

analysis of variance A test of statistical significance that compares the means of two or more groups.

analytic inductions Methods that involve researchers starting with some tentative hypotheses that they apply in fieldwork. If these hypotheses are inadequate they may be abandoned or reformulated.

annotations Additional explanations, comments, evaluations, or criticisms that clarify the written material.

anonymity A method of protecting research participants by separating specific identities from the information given.

applied research Studies completed to develop a product or solve an immediate practical problem.

a priori Literally, "from the earlier part." A way of knowing that claims knowledge before having any experience with events.

argument A claim advanced on the basis of reasoning from evidence.

argumentation The study of reason-giving communication.

argument from analogy A method of reasoning that compares "two things known to be alike in one or more features and . . . suggests that they will be alike in other features as well" (McDonald, 1980, p. 164).

argument from definition A method of reasoning in which people submit that things do or do not belong in a certain class.

argument from example and generalization A method of reasoning that takes some particular cases and argues that what is true of instances is generally true in the population of events.

arithmetic mean The number computed by adding a set of scores and dividing by the number of scores.

arrangement The canon of rhetoric concerning the organization of ideas.

association   *See* correlation.

attenuation   A reduction in the size of observed effects because of errors in measurement.

authority   A way of knowing in which a claim is accepted because authority figures have accepted it.

averaging or reconstructive questions   Questionnaire items that ask respondents to report an average or to recall typical past behavior.

basic research   Studies completed to learn about relationships among variables, regardless of any immediate commercial product or service.

beta risk (β risk)   The probability of committing a Type II error.

beta weights   In multiple correlation, the contribution made by each predictor to the overall correlation.

bimodal   A condition in which a distribution possesses two modes.

blocking   Including a nuisance variable in the design as another independent variable of interest.

canonical correlation   An extension of multiple regression correlating two sets of variables.

canons of rhetoric   Five established major categories used to discuss communication.

case studies and interpretive studies   Intensive inquiries about single events, people, or social units (interpretive studies attempt to look for themes or stories that are helpful to "interpret" or understand the case).

categorical syllogism   A syllogism that starts with a categorical statement.

causal argument   A method of reasoning asserting that "a given factor is responsible for producing certain other results" (Reinard, 1991, p. 197).

CD–ROM   (Compact Disk–Read Only Memory) A compact disk that contains database records.

ceiling or floor effects   Occur when scores are so high (or so low) in

samples that the data are "crunched up" (or down) near the end of the measurement range. These effects understate the size of relationships observed.

central limit theorem   The statement that a sampling distribution of means tends toward normal distribution with increased sample size regardless of the shape of the parent population.

central tendency   A measure that reports averages.

check question   A check on test-taking behavior that involves asking the same question twice at different locations in the questionnaire, usually once positively worded and once negatively worded.

chi square distribution   A probability distribution of squared differences of scores.

chi square test of independence   Adaptation of chi square test to the analysis of contingency tables.

chronological summary   A summary strategy that reviews literature by considering studies in their order of publication from the oldest study through the most recent one.

circularity   A problem created when definitions simply repeat terms.

climate questions   Follow-up interview questioning that asks respondents to explain how they feel about the interview.

closed-ended questions   Questions to which people respond in fixed categories of answers.

cluster sampling   1. In content analysis, sampling in which groups of messages exist in a cluster (such as the cluster of articles that appears in a single newspaper). 2. Samples are defined based on the known proportions within the population, and random sampling is completed within each group.

code systems   The study of the uses of verbal and nonverbal symbols and signs in human communication.

coding units   In content analysis, categories used to count the communication forms in the examples chosen.

coefficient alpha   *See* Cronbach's coefficient alpha.

coefficient of determination   A number that shows the percentage of variation in one variable that can be explained by a knowledge of the other variable alone; the square of a correlation coefficient.

coefficient of reproducibility   In Guttman scales, a measure of reliability.

Cohen's *kappa*   A measure of intercoder reliability that compensates for the number of times rating categories are used.

communication   The process by which participants transact and assign meaning to messages.

communication disorders   *See* speech and hearing science.

communication education   *See* speech communication education.

communication policy   The study of public policy and regulation of mass media communication and freedom of speech.

communication research   "Research in speech-communication focuses on the ways in which messages link participants during interactions" (Kibler & Barker, 1969, p. 33).

communication technology   The study of the mechanisms and technologies of mass media.

complete observer   A view, in an observational study, that observes individuals in settings in which there is no contact between the observed and the observer.

complex questions   Questionnaire items that include extra qualifying words or phrases that render simple yes or no answers misleading.

complex statements   A research fallacy in which loaded or complicated statements are made that assume facts not in evidence.

concepts *See* hypothetical constructs.

conceptual (or constitutive) definitions Definitions that rely on other concepts to describe a term.

concurrent validity A method of test validity that involves correlating a new measure with a previously validated measure of the same construct.

conditional syllogism A form of syllogism whose major premise makes an "if-then" statement.

confidence intervals Numbers indicating the probability that sample statistics "capture" population parameters, within certain margins for error.

confidentiality The requirement that all information gathered from individual subjects is secret; the protection of the identity of research participants.

conflict management The study of the role of communication in the creation and control of conflict and disputes.

confounding Mixing (or confusing) variation from one source with variation from another source so that it is impossible to know whether effects are due to the impact of either variable separately or some combination of them.

consent *See* informed consent.

constant A symbol to which only one number may be assigned.

constitutive definition *See* conceptual definitions.

constructs "Generalizations about observables according to some common property" (Deutsch & Krauss, 1965, p. 9).

construct validity A method of test validity that involves correlating a new measure with at least two other measures, one of which is a valid measure of a construct that is known conceptually to be directly related to the new measure, and another one of which should be a valid measure of a construct that is known conceptually to be inversely related to the construct of interest.

content analysis "A systematic, quantitative study of verbally communicated material (articles, speeches, films) by determining the frequency of specific ideas, concepts, or terms" (*Longman Dictionary of Psychology and Psychiatry,* 1984, p. 176).

contingency coefficient A method to determine effect sizes following a significant chi-square test.

contingency questions "Questions asked only of respondents, determined by their responses to some other question" (Babbie, 1992, p. G2).

control 1. As a function of theory, the power to direct things; 2. In research design, methods researchers use to remove or hold constant the effects of nuisance variables.

convenience sampling *See* accidental or convenience sampling.

conversational analysis Content analysis that attempts to identify "turns" taken by people during exchanges.

conversational and discourse analyses Forms of content analysis in which the categories are suggested from naturally occurring conversations and their settings. Yet, these approaches do not produce numerical information. The structure or organization of conversations is examined along with functions that conversations perform for communicators. A distinction is often drawn between conversational analysis (which tends to analyze macroscopic message characteristics such as themes and stories and the rules they suggest) and discourse analysis (which tends to analyze microscopic message components in a pattern much like traditional linguistic analysis or translation).

correlation A measure of the coincidence of variables.

counterbalanced designs Quasi-experiments that introduce several different experimental treatments presented to the subjects in different orders or sequences.

counterbalancing Rotating the sequence in which experimental treatments are introduced to subjects in an effort to control for extraneous variables, such as fatigue or cumulative learning effects.

creative studies Use of the method of performance or demonstration to explore an aesthetic or creative experience.

criterion validity Methods, including concurrent and predictive validity, that assess a measure's worth by examining its relation to some outside criterion.

critical region In significance testing, the portion of the probability distribution that would cause rejection of the null hypothesis if it were the area in which the test statistic fell.

critical value The line that divides the critical region from the rest of the probability distribution.

criticism Message evaluation in which standards of excellence are announced (which, in turn, can be argued as relevant or irrelevant) for application. To the extent that a message meets the standards, it is evaluated positively. The further away from the standard the message is, the harsher is the negative evaluation.

Cronbach's coefficient alpha A formula for reliability, used when researchers want to determine the reliability of a measure that has no "correct" answer.

crossed interaction *See* disordinal interaction.

curvilinear relationship In correlations, relationships in which the best fit of a line to the data is not a straight line.

daily definitions Statements generally adopted by members of a society.

data The actual individual events in a sample.

data distributions Distributions of data actually collected.

debate The study of decision making in which adversaries present arguments for decision by a third party.

deductive reasoning A form of reasoning in which a valid conclusion necessarily follows from premises.

deductive summary A summary strategy that reviews literature by considering what is known in general categories, followed by increasingly specific categories that are related to the topic.

definitions Statements asserting that one term may be substituted for another.

degrees of freedom The number of events in a study minus the number of population parameters estimated from samples; used to enter probability distributions.

delivery The canon of rhetoric concerning the use of voice and gesture.

Delphi fallacy A special fallacy of research involving the use of vague predictions as research claims.

dependent variables Variables whose values or activities are presumed to be conditioned upon (variables that are consequent to) the independent variable in the hypothesis.

description The lowest level of theorizing in which behavior is characterized into different forms.

descriptive or observational surveys Direct observations of behavior by use of some measurement (the researcher does not manipulate or change any variables).

descriptive statistics Numbers that are designed to characterize some information in a data set.

determination *See* coefficient of determination.

direct classification variables Operational definitions that rely on simple identification or classification of observable characteristics of information.

directional material hypotheses Hypotheses that state the form of predicted differences.

direct questions Questionnaire items that ask for obvious reports.

direct relationship A correlation showing that as one variable increases, the other variable also increases.

discourse analyses Considerations of naturally occurring messages to examine "sequential and hierarchical organization, system and structure" using methods that are fairly "standard in phonology and linguistics" (Stubbs, 1981, p. 107).

discourse/conversational analyses Methods of examining utterances people exchange for the purpose of discovering the rules and strategies people use to structure, sequence, and take turns in speaking to learn how people manage their interactions with others.

discussion and conference The study of methods of decision making in which participants strive by consensus to discuss and explore an issue.

disinterestedness The norm of researchers, holding that "researchers must ban ulterior motives and be relatively free from bias" (Kerlinger, 1986, p. 9).

disjunctive syllogism A form of syllogism whose major premise makes an "either-or" statement.

disordinal interaction Dependent variable interaction effects that are not in the same direction as the main effects of the variables involved and that are diagrammatically revealed when lines drawn for each independent variable cross each other.

distributions Arrangements of scores along a continuum.

double-barreled questions Questionnaire items that include multiple objects of evaluation.

double interacts The combination of one person's conversation, a reaction by another, and the first person's response to the other's reaction.

Einstein syndrome A malady in which researchers fail to connect their "sudden breakthrough" with lessons from others.

elimination and removal A method of control that removes a nuisance variable from the experimental setting.

empirical Observable.

equal probability hypothesis A method of determining expected frequencies for the one-sample chi square test.

erosions Observations of evidence of the wear or use of objects.

error variance Another name for *within groups variance*.

eta (η) Also known as the "correlation ratio," it is directly interpreted as any correlation and is used to determine the size of effects following finding a significant "F". Eta also may be used to identify nonlinear as well as linear effects.

eta squared (η^2) A coefficient of determination computed from eta.

ethical and rhetorical theories Principles that describe good and effective communication respectively.

ethnography Research in which the investigator participates, overtly or covertly, in people's lives for an extended period of time, collecting whatever data are available to describe behavior.

ethnomethodology Also called the "new ethnography," originally developed by anthropologists to study societies of humans. An approach, rather than a rigorous method, in which researchers find an ethnic group, live within it, and attempt to develop insight into the culture. Emphasis is placed on the mundane and ordinary activities of everyday life, concentrating on the methods people use to report their common sense practical actions to others in acceptable rational terms.

ethos Sometimes called "ethical appeal," *ethos* is an element of the canon of invention (artistic proofs) referring to the speaker's credibility.

evidence Information used to support claims.

example *See* argument from example and generalization.

exemplary literature review Survey of only the most important contributions to the literature.

exhaustive literature review Survey that includes all material related to the subject.

experiment *See* experimental methods.

experimental independent variable An independent variable manipulated in an experiment.

experimental invalidity The presence of errors that prevent researchers from drawing unequivocal conclusions (*see also* internal invalidity; external invalidity).

experimental methods A method of studying the effect of variables manipulated by a researcher in situations where all other influences are held constant. Variables are manipulated or introduced by experimenters for the purpose of establishing causal relationships.

experimental mortality A source of internal invalidity involving biases introduced when subjects differentially (nonrandomly) drop out of the experiment.

expert jury validity A method of test validity that involves having a group of experts in the given subject matter examine a measurement device and judge its merit.

expert opinions Opinions from people who are experts in the field of inquiry.

explanation Taking an event and treating it as an instance of a larger system of things.

explication A literature review that makes an issue clear and comprehensive.

external invalidity The degree to which experimental results may not be generalized to other similar circumstances.

face validity A method of test validity that involves researchers' looking at the content of the measurement items on a test and advancing an argument that on its face the measure seems to identify what it claims.

factor analysis A statistical method that helps "the researcher discover and identify the unities or dimensions, called factors, behind many measures" (Kerlinger, 1986, p. 138).

factorial analysis of variance Analysis of variance applied to multiple independent variables that have been broken down into levels or groups.

factorial design Experimental design in which more than one independent variable is used.

factors Variables broken down into levels.

factual evidence Descriptions and characterizations of things.

fallacy of misplaced precision Attempts by researchers to claim precision that goes beyond the data.

false precision *See* fallacy of misplaced precision.

falsification The requirement that any theory must deal with statements that could be falsified by data and information if the theories were untrue.

fantasy theme analysis A method of analyzing collections of communication to determine underlying "world views" that people hold, judging by the messages they use.

F distribution In essence, a distribution of variances that have been divided into each other.

figurative analogy An analogy that compares something to a hypothetical situation.

focus group An interview style designed for small groups. Focus group interviews are either guided or unguided discussions addressing a particular topic of interest or relevance to the group and the researcher.

forced choice format A question system in which researchers give subjects two statements, one of which must be chosen.

full-participant observation research Fieldwork characterized by the investigator's gathering data while taking part in the activities of a group—and while concealing his or her research identity.

funnel questions A questioning strategy that starts with an open-ended question and follows up with increasingly narrow questions.

generalization *See* argument from example and generalization.

general questions Questions that ask about global evaluations.

general to specific A library search strategy in which one starts with general sources that lead to specific sources.

goodness of fit test *See* one-sample chi square test.

grand mean The average of the averages computed in factorial analysis of variance.

grounded theory A set of explanations that has immediate relevance to a specific field setting under investigation. Participant observers attempt to discover categories to describe their observations after they have entered the field. Then, researchers make additional observations to refine and modify these categories and potentially develop theory.

Guttman scalogram A scale involving series of statements dealing with one topic and arranged according to their level of intensity.

halo effect A special source of experimental invalidity in which strong positive or negative impressions of a source of communication may affect all other ratings that follow.

heuristic An ability of research to lead scholars to new inventions, ideas, explanations, or research avenues.

historical-critical methods Research designed to describe a period, person, or phenomenon for the purpose of interpreting or evaluating communication and its effects.

history A source of internal invalidity in which events not controlled by the researcher occur during the experiment between any pretest and post-test.

holding constant Controlling for other variables by limiting the range of intervening variables so that they are equal across studies (technically, all control methods involve taking nuisance variables and holding them constant).

homogeneous variances The parametric test assumption that any differences in variances should be within the limits of sampling error.

Hotelling's T *t* test for intercorrelated dependent variables.

hypothesis "An expectation about events based on generalizations of the assumed relationship between variables" (Tuckman, 1978, p. 27).

hypothetical constructs Concepts; constructs for which direct observations cannot be made.

identification The uniting of people by the use of ideas, images, and attitudes.

idiographic research Scholarship designed to develop a full understanding of "a particular event or individual" (English & English, 1958, p. 347).

impressionistic criticism Statements of opinion (or personal impression) made by reviewers.

independent variables Variables that predict outcomes (dependent variables) posited in hypotheses.

indirect questions Questionnaire items that ask respondents to react in ways that imply information.

inductive reasoning "The process by which we conclude that what is true of certain individuals is true of a class, what is true of part is true of the whole class, or what is true at certain times will be true in similar circumstances at all times" (Mill, in English & English, 1958, p. 259).

inductive summary A summary strategy that reviews literature by producing general propositions (laws or rules) that are demonstrated by each subcollection (studies are grouped largely by their findings, rather than their input variables).

inferential statistics Tools that help researchers draw conclusions about the probable populations from which samples did or did not belong.

informed consent The "procedure in which individuals choose whether to participate in an investigation after being informed of the facts that would be likely to influence their decision" (Diener & Crandall, 1978, p. 34).

infrequency index A measure of the inconsistency of response, indicative of a person giving random responses.

instrumentation A source of internal invalidity involving changes in the use of measuring instruments from the pretest to the post-test including changes in raters or interviewers who collect the data in different conditions.

interaction analysis A study that focuses on ways of tracking individual acts of communicators.

interaction and relational analyses Forms of content analysis designed to describe the continuing oral communication between people.

interaction effects Dependent-variable effects that result from independent variables taken together and involving variation arising from special combinations of levels of independent variables.

interaction of elements A source of internal invalidity involving effects created by the interaction of selection biases with differential levels of

maturation, history, or any other source of variation.

interaction of selection and the experimental variable Effects created by sampling groups in such a way that they are not representative of the population since they are more or less sensitive to the experimental variable than other subsamples from the same population (such as sampling college students in communication studies even though they may be more or less sensitive to the independent variable than the general population of people).

interaction of testing and the experimental variable Also called *pretest sensitization,* this source of experimental external invalidity is created when pretesting makes subjects either more or less sensitive to the experimental variable.

interacts The combination of one person's conversation and the reaction of another.

intercoder reliability Determines the consistency of different raters who respond to the same events by using some sort of check sheet.

intercultural communication The study and practice of communication among individuals of different cultural backgrounds.

internal invalidity The presence of contamination that prevents the experimenter from concluding that a study's experimental variable is responsible for the observed effects.

internal organizers In a written work, phrases that promote clarity by previewing, summarizing, and transitioning between main points.

interpersonal communication The study of communication interactions occurring in person-to-person and small group situations.

interpretive analysis of data A naturalistic approach that identifies communicators' interactions, uses of themes, and uses of stories to determine such things as the situations in which people find themselves, the structures within which they work, and the practical features of their world. (See also case studies and interpretive studies.)

intersubjectivity The degree to which different researchers with essentially different beliefs draw essentially the same interpretations of the meaning of observations.

interval level measurement Assigns numbers to items as a matter of degree ("the intervals between the numbers are *equal* in size" [Cozby, 1989, p. 149]).

interval sampling Sampling by selecting instances of communication at specific units (such as coding every third commercial during prime time for a month).

interview surveys The use of personal contacts between a questioner and respondent in which the questions and answers are exchanged orally.

invention The canon of rhetoric concerning the types and sources of ideas.

inventory questions Closed-ended questions that ask respondents to list all responses that apply to them.

inverse relationship A correlation showing that as one variable increases, the other variable decreases.

inverted funnel questions A questioning strategy that starts with a very specific question and expands by asking increasingly general questions.

isolate In network analysis, an individual who is not actively involved in any established communication network.

item to total reliability A method of assessing reliability that computes the correlation of items with the total test.

Jeanne Dixon fallacy A special fallacy of research that involves making multiple predictions and claiming partial support.

John Henry effect A special source of experimental invalidity in which subjects try to perform extra hard when they participate in an experiment.

journalism The study and practice of the methods of reporting and organizing news for presentation in print and electronic media.

kappa *See* Cohen's *kappa*.

keywords Terms under which information about a topic may be found.

known to unknown summary A summary strategy that reviews literature by considering what (little) is known separately about each variable in the research review question and then announces what remains to be learned.

K-R 20 Kuder-Richardson formula 20 for reliability, used when researchers want to determine the reliability of a measure that has items that are scored as correct or incorrect answers.

kurtosis A measure of the peakedness of a distribution.

law "A verbal statement, supported by such ample evidence as not to be open to doubt unless much further evidence is obtained, of the way events of a certain class consistently and uniformly occur" (English & English, 1958, p. 288).

law of large numbers A rule that holds that the assumptions of statistical method are best satisfied by large samples.

leading questions Questions that imply their answer.

leptokurtic A distribution that is tall, with a kurtosis above 3.

levels Categories of each factor.

liaison In network analysis, a person linking together people of different networks.

lie scale *See* MMPI lie (L) scale.

life-history or life story research Naturalistic study that involves "the autobiography of a person which has been obtained through interview and guided conversation" (McNeill, 1990, p. 85).

Likert scale A measurement tool composed of statements that reflect clear positions on an issue, for which subjects indicate their agreement on (typically) a 5-point scale.

line of regression In correlations, a line of "best fit" through the data.

LISREL (Linear Structural Relations) A computer program that isolates relationships by examining covariances among variables.

literal analogy An analogy that compares something to an event or object that really exists.

literature reviews *See* exhaustive literature reviews; exemplary literature reviews.

loaded language Questionnaire items worded to imply an evaluation.

log-linear analysis Extension of chi-square testing for analysis of more than two variables measured on the nominal level.

logos Treated by most critics as logical appeals, *logos* is an element of the canon of invention (artistic proofs) and refers to the use of rational appeals.

μ The Greek letter mu, representing the population mean.

macroaggregation To avoid breaching confidentiality, the process of constructing "average persons" from the data.

main effects Dependent-variable effects that result from independent variables separately.

manipulated independent variables Sometimes called "stimulus variables" because researchers introduce and control them in experiments.

manipulation check A researcher's measurement of a secondary variable to determine that an experimental variable actually was operating in a study.

MANOVA (multivariate analysis of variance) Extension of analysis of variance for multiple dependent variables.

matching   Pairing subjects on some variable on which they share equal levels and then assigning them to experimental or control conditions.

material hypothesis   *See* hypothesis.

matrix questions   Closed-ended questions that ask respondents to use the same categories to supply information.

maturation   A source of internal invalidity involving changes that naturally occur over time (including fatigue or suspicion), even if subjects are left alone.

maxmincon principle   A reminder to experimenters to follow procedures that "maximize systematic variance, control extraneous systematic variance, and minimize error variance" (Kerlinger, 1986, p. 284).

mean   *See* arithmetic mean.

measured/assigned variables   Variables not introduced or controlled by the researcher, but carefully observed and/or measured.

measurement   Assigning numbers to variables according to some system.

median   A score that appears in the middle of an ordered list of scores.

memory   The canon of rhetoric concerning the ability to recall passages and examples for utterance.

mesokurtic   A distribution that is neither very high nor very low, with a kurtosis close to 3.

message   The set of verbal and nonverbal cues communicators exchange.

meta-analysis   A statistical method that combines quantitative results from many studies to reveal the overall sizes of effects that exist among variables.

metatheories   Ways to think about theories (called *metatheory* to indicate notions "beyond the theories" themselves).

methodological studies   Inquiries that deal with the development and validation of new tools, measuring instruments, or research approaches.

mirror questions   A strategy of follow-up interview questioning that repeats previous responses to gain additional information.

misplaced precision   *See* fallacy of misplaced precision.

MMPI lie (L) scale   A scale to identify respondents who attempt to avoid being candid and honest in their responses (not a general personality disposition toward dishonesty).

mode   The most commonly occurring score.

model   An expression that not only states relationships but exhibits them.

moderator variables   Variables that mediate the independent variable's prediction of the dependent variable (in reality, moderator variables are just other independent variables that help input variables predict their effects).

mortality   *See* experimental mortality.

multicollinearity   In multiple correlation, the quality of predictors being uncorrelated with each other.

multimodal   A condition in which a distribution possesses many modes.

multiple-choice questions   Closed-ended questions that ask respondents to select a category response from a range of possible responses.

multiple comparison tests   Tests completed after finding a significant analysis of variance effect for the purpose of determining the location of differences among groups.

multiple discriminant analysis   A method that predicts membership in particular groups from a knowledge of a number of predictor variables (measured on the interval or ratio level).

multiple regression correlation (a.k.a. multiple correlation)   A method that produces a correlation of multiple predictors with a single output variable.

multiple treatment interference   A source of experimental external

invalidity in which subjects exposed to repeated additional experimental treatments react in ways that are not generalizable to subjects that are uncontaminated by such additional independent variables.

multistage cluster sampling   Sampling in which instances are selected sequentially (such as selecting commercials from one month, selecting one week from that month, selecting three hours from the days of the week, etc.).

multivariate analysis   Statistical analysis in which multiple dependent variables are treated as a common set.

multivariate analysis of covariance   Extension of MANOVA to adapt analysis of covariance for multiple interrelated dependent variables.

multivariate multiple correlation   Extension of multiple regression for many interrelated dependent measures.

mythic perspective   An approach to criticism that attempts to identify the underlying stories to which speakers appeal (a myth is defined as "a story about a particular incident which is put forward as containing or suggesting some general truth" [Sykes, 1970, p. 17]).

narrative fidelity   In the narrative paradigm, the consistency of new accounts with other stories people have heard.

narrative paradigm   An approach to criticism that analyzes messages by looking at them as stories.

naturalistic studies   Nonexperimental inquiries completed as subjects are involved in the natural course of their lives.

negative skew   Skewness in which the longest tail of the distribution lies to the left of the mean.

neo-Aristotelian criticism   Criticism using Aristotelian standards and involving the canons of rhetoric.

network analysis A method that obtains individuals' reports of their communication activities with others for the purpose of observing and describing the flow of information in a particular organizational system.

nominal level measurement Uses numbers as simple identifications of variables.

nomothetic research Scholarship designed to find general laws that apply to many instances.

nondirectional material hypotheses Hypotheses that state simply there will be some kind of relationship between variables (sometimes called *two-tailed hypotheses* because of the way statistics are used to test them).

nonlinear relationships Relationships between independent and dependent variables that are not simple straight line relationships, but curved.

nonparametric tests Statistical methods that do not make assumptions about population distributions or population parameters.

non sequitur A fallacy of reasoning in which a conclusion does not follow from premises because the necessary steps between them are omitted.

nonverbal cues Communication elements beyond the words themselves.

normative and prescriptive theories Theories whose principles involve defining the qualities that make communication meaningful or desirable.

normative science "A discipline that systematically studies man's attempts to determine what is correct, valuable, good, or beautiful" (English & English, 1958, p. 349), which has given rise to normative and prescriptive theories.

null hypotheses Statistical hypotheses that state that there is no relationship between variables.

O An abbreviation for an observation a researcher makes of the study's dependent variable.

observational surveys *See* descriptive or observational surveys.

one-across statement In relational control analysis, a statement in which one extends the discussion without increasing assertions or accepting others' statements.

one-down statement In relational control analysis, a statement in which one person submits to the opinions or definitional rights of another.

one-group pretest–post-test A pre-experimental design in which a pretest is added to a one-shot case study.

one-sample chi square test A test of statistical significance for nominal level variables for which frequency data are obtained.

one-sample test An application of the test that examines when a new sample mean differs from a known population mean under conditions when the population standard deviation is unavailable.

one-shot case study A pre-experimental design in which an experimental treatment is introduced and researchers look at effects on some output (dependent) variable.

one-tailed hypotheses or **one-tailed tests** *See* directional material hypotheses.

one-up statement In relational control analysis, a statement in which one person is dominant over another because he or she asserts one's "definitional rights."

one-way analysis of variance Analysis of variance in which the groups are levels for the independent variable.

open-ended questions Questions to which people respond in their own words.

operational definition Isolation of a concept by specifying the steps researchers follow to make observations (for example, of a variable).

opinions Interpretations of the meaning of collections of facts.

opinion surveys Assessments of reports from individuals about topics of interest.

oral interpretation The study of literature through performance involving the development of skilled verbal and nonverbal expression based on critical analysis of written texts (including aesthetics of literature in performance, criticism of literature in performance, group performance, oral traditions).

ordinal interaction Dependent variable interaction effects in the same direction as the main effects of the variables involved.

ordinal level measurement Uses rank order to determine differences.

organizational communication The study and practice of interrelated behaviors, technologies, and systems functioning within an organization.

organized skepticism The norm of researchers, holding that "researchers are responsible for verifying the results on which they base their work [Researchers do not accept claims blindly. They question research claims and offer criticism for each other.]" (Kerlinger, 1986, p. 9).

paired-comparison questions Questions that ask respondents to make a judgment between alternatives taken two at a time.

parameter A number computed from a population.

parametric tests Tests of statistical significance that make assumptions about populations from which the data were drawn.

parliamentary procedure The study and practice of the means used to handle deliberation in large, legislative bodies through the use of formal rules and procedures to regulate debate and discussion.

partial correlation A method of statistical control that determines the variation associated with each nuisance variable and then separates it from the remaining total variation in the correlation.

participant as observer methods Fieldwork in which the group to be studied is made aware of the researcher's role.

participant observation Fieldwork in which researchers study groups by gaining membership or close relationships with them (see Wax, 1968, p. 238).

patchwork quilt fallacy A special fallacy of research in which no predictions are made, but explanations are offered after the fact.

path models Use of correlational tools to interpret relationships to identify causal models with exogenous (input variable) sources, endogenous (mediating) variables, and dependent (output or criterion) variables.

pathos Sometimes called "pathetic appeals," *pathos* is an element of the canon of invention (artistic proofs) and refers to the use of emotional or motivational appeals.

Pearson product moment correlation A correlation method suitable for situations in which the independent and dependent variables (identified as X and Y respectively in most notation) are interval or ratio level measures.

periodic sampling A method by which researchers select respondents according to a predetermined schedule other than a random sequence.

persuasion The study of communication used to influence the choices made by others.

pi See Scott's *pi.*

pilot studies Studies usually involving small samples of people (sometimes as few as 10 or 20 people) who take part in an experiment as an aid in developing materials and protocols.

placebo effect A placebo is a stimulus containing no medicine or no experimental treatment at all; hence, a special source of experimental invalidity in which subjects show changes even in the absence of any treatments at all, in reaction to the mental suggestion that they may have been given some stimulus.

plagiarism "The act of using another person's ideas or expressions in your writing without acknowledging the source" (Gibaldi & Achtert, 1988, p. 20).

platykurtic A flat distribution with kurtosis under 3.

poetic definitions Statements that involve figurative interpretations of objects.

polarity rotation A check on test-taking behavior that avoids response set by (1) avoiding phrasing all items positively and (2) avoiding placing all positive adjectives on the same side of the measurement items.

polymodal *See* multimodal.

pooled standard deviation (s_p) The square root of the average of variances in subgroups involved in comparisons.

population The universe of events from which the sample is drawn.

positive skew Skewness in which the longer tail of the distribution lies to the right of the mean.

post-test only control group design A true experimental design that avoids pretest sensitization by deleting the pretest entirely.

power A statistical test's probability of rejecting the null hypothesis correctly.

pragmatic communication The study and practice of communication, the object of which is to influence or facilitate decision making.

prediction Descriptions of what can be expected in the future.

predictive validity The degree to which a measure predicts known groups in which the construct must exist.

premise A statement in a logical argument that is the foundation for others drawn from it.

presumptive questions Questions that assume information (e.g., "Have you stopped beating your spouse?").

pretest–post-test control group design A true experimental design that includes randomly selected

experimental and control groups, each of which is given a pretest and a post-test.

primary sources Reports provided by individuals who have firsthand experience with the events reported.

principal components solution In factor analysis, a method to identify the number of common centers of variation that underlie the manifest variables.

probability The tendency or likelihood with which an event occurs in a population.

probability distributions The theoretical patterns of expected sample data.

probability sampling Techniques that use randomization to identify samples.

probing questions A strategy of follow-up interview questioning that directly asks for elaboration and explanation.

problems Questions for which we expect to find answers through research.

problem-solution summary A summary strategy that reviews literature by considering a problem and its cause, followed by a research suggestion that might solve the problem.

professional responsibility The requirement that researchers follow accepted rules of conduct with thoroughness and attention to concerns of subjects.

public address The study of speakers and speeches, including the historical and social context of platforms, campaigns, and movements.

public relations The study and practice of methods of managing publicity and press relations for an organization, person, or cause.

purpose In Burke's dramatistic pentad, the intention of the rhetor.

purposive or known group sampling Selection of events from groups that are known to possess a particular characteristic under investigation.

qualitative methods Research methods of study that use descriptions of observations expressed in predominantly non-numerical terms.

qualitative observational studies Methods designed to use predominately attribute-type data when interpreting contemporaneous communication interactions.

quantitative methods Inquiries in which observations are expressed predominantly in numerical terms.

quasi-experiments Studies involving completion of experimental work where random assignment and control are not possible.

quasi-interval measures Interval-like measures that have enough properties of true interval measures to permit using statistical tools designed for them.

questionnaires Survey forms in which individuals respond to items they have read.

quota sampling Samples are defined based on the known proportions within the population, and nonrandom sampling is completed within each group.

quotation bibliographic card Bibliographic cards featuring quoted materials.

R 1. In experimental design, an abbreviation for randomization. 2. In statistics, an abbreviation for the coefficient of multiple correlation.

radio The study of the methods and uses of radio communication.

random assignment *See* randomization.

randomization Assigning subjects so that each event is equally likely to belong to any experimental or control condition.

random sampling Selection of data such that each event in the population has an equal chance of being selected.

range The difference between the highest and lowest scores.

ranking questions Closed-ended questions that ask respondents to rank a set of options.

ratio level measurement Assigns numbers to items as a matter of degree, including an absolute zero.

reactive arrangements A source of experimental external invalidity, consisting of elements in the experimental setting that make subjects react differentially to the experimental arrangements rather than to the experimental variable alone (such matters as awareness of participation in an experiment may alter normal reactions of people).

reciprocal pattern In network analysis, a pattern in which individuals share nearly an identical network pattern.

reconstructive questions *See* averaging or reconstructive questions.

redundancy index In canonical correlation, a coefficient that tells whether sets of variables should be interpreted differentially for additional canonical component roots.

regression 1. Statistical regression. 2. Line of regression. 3. Multiple regression correlation.

relational control analysis Studies that track message sequences to determine the relative patterns of position and control in the relationship.

reliability The internal consistency of a measure.

reliability coefficient Actually a correlation; a number indicating the degree of consistency of a measure.

replication The ability of other scholars to reproduce research.

report An account of what took place whether by a participant or by an outside observer.

representative sample Sampling that accurately reflects characteristics of the population from which it was drawn.

research 1. The systematic effort to secure answers to questions. 2. A way of knowing that makes claims by using the tools of scholarship and science.

research hypothesis *See* hypothesis.

research prospectus A complete proposal for a research activity to be completed at a future date.

response set A tendency for subjects to follow predictable patterns when responding to test items.

rhetor One who practices rhetoric.

rhetoric According to Aristotle, "The faculty of discovering in the particular case what are the available means of persuasion."

rhetorical and communication theory The study of the principles that account for human communicative experiences and behavior.

rhetorical criticism The use of standards of excellence to interpret and evaluate communication.

rhetorical visions Images of the way the world is organized as perceived by groups of people.

rhetorician One who studies rhetoric.

rotation In factor analysis, an aid in interpretation that helps reveal the items that are used to understand a factor.

rule "A theory that explains a pattern of effects by referring to human intentions, reasons, or goals" (M. J. Smith, 1988, p. 354).

rules of correspondence The degree to which a theory's constructs and abstract calculus can be applied to actual experience.

s A symbol that represents the standard deviation of a sample.

s^2 A symbol that represents the variance of a sample.

sacrifice groups A method to check the accuracy of respondent reports by interrupting groups during the interview or questionnaire process to see if they really understand what is meant by specific questions. Since these respondents have been distracted somewhat, they are "sacrificed" and their responses are used only to validate the survey question content.

sampling Selecting events from a population.

sampling error The degree to which a sample differs from the population on some measure.

scene In Burke's dramatistic pentad, the setting in which the act takes place.

Scheffe's critical S A multiple comparison test designed to contrast all possible comparisons of means, when the means are taken as part of complex comparisons.

scholarly definitions Highly specific statements that have technical meanings for a group of scholars.

science A way of testing statements by systematic application of the scientific method.

scientific method A method that involves collecting data and establishing "a functional relationship among these data" (Bachrach, 1981, p. 4); generally a method involving four steps: observation of facts, development of a working hypothesis or theoretical solution to guide the research, test of expectations against information, establishing a conclusion or functional relationship based on deciding whether the working hypothesis or theoretic solution is supported.

Scott's *pi* A measure of intercoder reliability that also compensates for the rates of agreement that would be expected by chance alone.

secondary sources Reports provided by individuals who do not have firsthand experience with the events reported.

selection A source of internal invalidity involving sampling biases in selecting or assigning subjects to experimental or control conditions (in essence rigging the study by taking samples capriciously).

semantic differential-type scales Scales (often 7-point intervals) bounded by pairs of bipolar adjectives.

separate sample post-test designs Quasi-experiments in which subjects in control conditions are selected to be close, but not assured to be equivalent to the experimental group.

serendipity Researchers' finding something of value while looking for something else.

significance A difference or relationship that is beyond what might be expected to occur by chance (sampling error) alone.

simple random sampling *See* random sampling.

single subject designs Also called *component search studies,* experimental designs that determine the effect of treatments by strategically repeated exposures for a single subject.

skewness A measure of the centeredness of distributions.

snowball sampling Selection of events based on referrals from initial informants.

social desirability A measure of the degree to which people attempt to describe themselves in ways that they think are acceptable, desirable, or approved by others.

Solomon four groups design A true experimental design that assesses the impact of pretesting by adding control groups.

sophists Teachers in ancient times who traveled around instructing people wherever there was a market.

Spearman rank order correlation A correlation method suitable for situations in which both the independent and dependent variables are ordinal level measures.

specific questions Questions that focus on individual activities.

specific to general A library search strategy in which one starts with a reference and writes down the citations to related research and theory identified in them. Then, the process is completed with the new sources until the information "snowballs" as one reference leads to others.

speech and hearing science The study of the physiology and acoustical aspects of speech and hearing (including biological, phonological, and physiological aspects of speech and hearing).

speech communication education The study of communication in pedagogical contexts (including communication development, oral communication skills, instructional communication).

speech pathology *See* speech and hearing science.

split half reliability A method of test reliability that divides a test into two parts, scores them separately, and checks consistency between the two scores.

standard deviation A measure of how far the average score deviates from the mean, symbolized for the sample standard deviation as s.

standard error The standard deviation of a distribution of elements other than raw scores.

standard error of the mean The standard deviation of a distribution of means.

standard normal curve A probability distribution that tells the expected value that would be obtained by sampling at random.

standard scores *See* z scores.

static group comparisons A pre-experimental design in which a control group is used, but the groups are not known to be comparable to begin with.

statistic A number computed from a sample.

statistical control Taking measures of nuisance variables and using statistical tools to hold them constant.

statistical regression A source of internal invalidity involving shifts produced when subjects are selected due to very high or very low scores on a test; statistical regression holds that people will "regress toward the mean" even if they simply are left alone.

statistics 1. Quantitative reports based on observations in a sample. 2. The study of quantitative information.

stimulus variables *See* manipulated independent variables.

stratification Sampling in which strata are identified (such as geographic region, type of radio station format, type of ad) and a random sample within each strata is proportionately selected.

stratified random sampling Population characteristics are identified (such as the number of men and women in the population); after deciding on the sample size to be drawn, a random sample is drawn from each level of the population stratification variable (using one of the methods of simple random sampling) to meet the proportion of the population in that sample subgroup.

structured interviews Interviews that use specific lists of questions.

studies of behavior, facts, and opinions Studies designed to determine the current status of conditions or attitudes by using questionnaires, interviews, or direct observations of communicators.

studies of status and development Intensive detailed studies of individual cases over time.

style The canon of rhetoric concerning the use of words.

subject tracings Keywords that list other subject headings under which a book is also listed.

subjects by treatments interactions *See* ceiling or floor effects.

survey Empirical study that uses questionnaires or interviews to discover descriptive characteristics of phenomena; opinion surveys.

syllogism A formal logical system in which the premises lead to a conclusion.

systematic sampling *See* periodic sampling.

telefocus session Focus group session completed by teleconferencing methods over the telephone.

tenacity A way of knowing in which we claim to know something because we have always believed it.

testing A source of internal invalidity involving alterations that occur when subjects are tested and made testwise or anxious in ways that affect them when they are given a second test.

test-retest reliability A method of test reliability that gives the measure twice and reports consistency between scores.

test statistic A number computed from a statistical formula to test the statistical hypothesis.

theoretic constructs Terms that are substituted into the abstract calculus of a theory (*see also* constructs).

theory "A body of interrelated principles that explain or predict" (*Longman Dictionary of Psychology,* 1984, p. 744).

Thurstone equal appearing interval scales A tool of measurement involving scales composed of statements with assigned point values.

time-budgeting studies Inquiries in which "the researcher asks the subjects of the research to keep a detailed diary over a given period" (McNeill, 1990, p. 88).

time series design A type of quasi-experiment that measures subjects at different times.

topical summary A summary strategy that reviews literature by reference to content categories into which the studies fall.

trend analysis A method that isolates the nature of linear and nonlinear trends in effects identified as significant by analysis of variance.

trial and error A way of knowing that claims knowledge by making repeated trials to eliminate unacceptable answers.

t **test** A test of statistical significance designed to assess the difference between the means of two groups.

t **test for dependent samples** An application of the test that compares the means of two sample groups in which subjects are matched or sampled twice.

t **test for independent samples** An application of the test that compares the means of two sample groups.

Tukey's HSD (John Tukey's Honestly Significant Difference test) A multiple comparison test designed to contrast all possible comparisons of means, when the means are taken two at a time.

two-tailed hypotheses or **two-tailed tests** *See* nondirectional material hypotheses.

Type I error Incorrectly rejecting the null hypothesis.

Type II error Failing to detect a relationship that is present; incorrectly failing to reject the null hypothesis.

unbiased estimator A sample statistic that is most likely to approximate the corresponding population parameter.

universalism The norm of researchers, holding that "scientific laws are the same everywhere" (Kerlinger, 1986, p. 9).

unobtrusive measurement Use of artifacts that do not hold the potential to influence the behavior being studied, including the use of accretions and erosions.

unstructured interviews Interviews that permit respondents to indicate their reactions to general issues without guidance from highly detailed questions.

urban archaeology Examination of modern artifacts of urban life (such as searching trash cans in a neighborhood to find evidence of alcoholism rates).

utterance In conversational analysis, what a person actually says in conversation.

validity 1. Test validity is the consistency of a measure with a criterion; the degree to which a measure actually measures what is claimed. 2. Experimental validity refers to the absence of errors that prevent researchers from drawing unequivocal conclusions.

variable A symbol to which numbers may be assigned.

variance A measure of the average of squared differences of scores from the mean, symbolized for the sample variance as s^2.

verbal cues Words people use in communication.

X An abbreviation for (1) a score from a continuous distribution, (2) the experimental variable used by researchers.

$\overline{X}$ "X bar," representing the sample mean.

z scores Scores represented as units under the standard normal curve.

WORKS CITED

Aczel, A. D. (1989). *Complete business statistics.* Homewood, IL: Irwin.

Adair, J. G., Dushenko, T. W., & Lindsay, R. C. L. (1985). Ethical regulations and their impact on research practice. *American Psychologist, 40,* 59–72.

Adair, J. G., & Spinner, B. (1981). Subjects' access to cognitive processes: Demand characteristics and verbal report. *Journal for the Theory of Social Behavior, 11,* 31–52.

Agar, M. H. (1988). *Speaking of ethnography.* Newbury Park, CA: Sage.

Allen, M. J., & Yen, W. M. (1979). *Introduction to measurement theory.* Monterey, CA: Brooks-Cole.

American Association for Public Opinion Research. (1954–1955). Propaganda analysis. *Proceedings,* 445–446.

Amidon, E. J., & Hough, J. B. (1967). *Interaction analysis: Theory, research, and application.* Reading, MA: Addison-Wesley.

Anastasi, A. (1968). *Psychological testing* (3rd ed.). New York: Macmillan.

Auer, J. J. (1959). *An Introduction to Research in Speech.* New York: Harper and Row.

Austin, B. A. (1986). Motivations for movie attendance. *Communication Quarterly 34,* 115–126.

Babbie, E. R. (1992). *The practice of social research* (6th ed.). Belmont, CA: Wadsworth.

Babbie, E. (1995). *The practice of social research* (7th ed.). Belmont, CA: Wadsworth.

Bachrach, A. J. (1981). *Psychological research: An introduction* (4th ed.). New York: Random House.

Baker, B. O., Hardyck, C. D., & Petrinovich, L. F. (1966). Weak measurements vs. strong statistics: An empirical critique of S. S. Stevens' proscriptions on statistics. *Educational and psychological measurement, 26,* 291–309.

Baker, D. C. (1990). A qualitative and quantitative analysis of verbal style and the elimination of potential leaders in small groups. *Communication Quarterly, 38,* 13–26.

Bales, R. F. (1950). A set of categories for the analysis of small group interactions. *American Sociological Review, 15,* 257–263.

Bales, R. F., & Cohen, S. P. (1979). *SYMLOG: A system for the multilevel observation of groups.* New York: Free Press.

Barnett, G. A., Oliveira, O. S., & Johnson, J. D. (1989). Multilingual language use and television exposure and preferences: The case of Belize. *Communication Quarterly, 37,* 248–261.

Baron, R. A. (1981). The "costs of deception" revisited: An openly optimistic rejoinder. *IRB: A Review of Human Subjects Research, 3*(1), 8–10.

Basch, C. E. (1987). Focus group interviews: An underutilized research technique for improving theory and practice in health education. *Health Education Quarterly, 14,* 411–448.

Beasley, D. (1988). *How to use a research library.* New York: Oxford University Press.

The beginner's guide to the Internet. (1995). Minneapolis, MN: Inst. Publishing.

Bello, R. (1996). A Burkean analysis of the "political correctness" confrontation in higher education. *Southern Communication Journal, 61,* 243–252.

Benoit, W. L. (1991). Two tests of the mechanism of inoculation theory. *Southern Speech Communication Journal, 56,* 219–229.

Berg, B. L. (1989). *Qualitative research methods for the social sciences.* Boston: Allyn and Bacon.

Berg, B. L. (1995). *Qualitative research methods for the social sciences* (2nd ed.). Boston: Allyn and Bacon.

Berg, B. L., Ksander, M., Loughlin, J., & Johnson, B. (1983, August). *Cliques and groups: Adolescent affective ties and criminal activities.* Paper presented at the Society for the Study of Social Problems Convention, Detroit.

Berger, C., & Calabrese, R. J. (1975). Some explorations in initial interaction and beyond: Toward a developmental theory of interpersonal communication. *Human Communication Research, 1,* 99–112.

Berlo, D. K. (1960). *The process of communication: An introduction to theory and practice.* San Francisco: Rinehart Press.

Berscheid, E. (1985). Interpersonal attraction. In G. Lindzey & E. Aaronson (Eds.), *Handbook of social psychology* (3rd ed.) (413–484). New York: Random House.

Best, J. W. (1981). *Research in education* (4th ed.). Englewood Cliffs, NJ: Prentice-Hall.

Bogardus, E. S. (1933). A social distance scale. *Sociology and Social Research, 17,* 265–271.

Bok, S. (1974, November). The ethics of giving placebos. *Scientific American,* 17–23.

Bokeno, R. M. (1987). The rhetorical understanding of science: An explication and critical commentary. *Southern Speech Communication Journal, 52,* 285–311.

Boneau, C. A. (1960). The effects of violations of assumption underlying the *t*-test. *Psychological Bulletin, 57,* 49–64.

Booth, W. C. (1964). *The rhetoric of fiction.* Chicago: University of Chicago Press.

Borg, W. R. (1963). *Educational research: An introduction.* New York: McKay.

Bormann, E. H. (1972). Fantasy and rhetorical vision: The rhetorical criticism of reality. *Quarterly Journal of Speech, 58,* 396–407.

Bormann, E. H. (1973). The Eagleton affair: A fantasy theme analysis. *Quarterly Journal of Speech, 54,* 143–159.

Bormann, E. H. (1982). Colloquy I: Fantasy and rhetorical vision: Ten years later. *Quarterly Journal of Speech, 68,* 288–305.

Bostdorff, D. M. (1967). Vice-presidential comedy and the traditional female role: An examination of the rhetorical characteristics of the vice presidency. *Western Journal of Speech Communication, 55,* 1–27.

Bowers, K. S. (1967). The effect of demands for honesty on reports of visual and auditory hallucinations. *International Journal of Clinical and Experimental Hypnosis, 15,* 31–36.

Brinson, S. L. (1995). The myth of white superiority in *Mississippi Burning. Southern Communication Journal, 60,* 211–221.

Brown, L. M. (1961). *A content analysis of anti-Catholic documents circulated through the mails during the 1960 presidential election campaign.* Unpublished master's thesis, University of Iowa, Iowa City.

Budd, R. W., Thorp, R. K., & Donohew, L. (1967). *Content analysis of communications.* New York: Macmillan.

Bullock, A., & Stallybrass, O. (Eds.). (1977). *The Harper dictionary of modern thought.* New York: Harper and Row.

Burgoon, M., Hall, J., & Pfau, M. (1991). A test of the "messages-as-fixed-effect fallacy" argument: Empirical and theoretical implications of design choices. *Communication Quarterly, 39,* 18–34.

Burke, K. (1945/1969). *A grammar of motives* (Reprint). Berkeley: University of California Press. (Original work published 1945.)

Burke, K. (1950/1969). *A rhetoric of motives* (Reprint). Berkeley: University of California Press. (Original work published 1950.)

Burkholder, T. R. (1989). Kansas populism, woman suffrage, and the agrarian myth: A case study in the limits of mythic transcendence. *Communication Studies, 40,* 292–307.

Burleson, B. R. (1980). The place of nondiscursive symbolism, formal characterizations, and hermeneutics in argument analysis and criticism. *Journal of the American Forensic Association, 16,* 222–231.

Byrne, D., Ervin, C. R., & Lamberth, J. (1970). Continuity between the experimental study of attraction and real-life computer dating. *Journal of Personality and Social Psychology, 16,* 157–165.

Campbell, D. T., & Stanley, J. C. (1963). *Experimental and quasi-experimental designs for research.* Chicago: Rand McNally.

Cappella, J. N. (1990). The method of proof by example in interaction analysis. *Communication Monographs, 57,* 236–240.

Cappella, J. N., & Palmer, M. T. (1990). Attitude similarity, relational history, and attraction: The mediating effects of kinesic and vocal behaviors. *Communication Monographs, 57,* 161–183.

Cathcart, R. (1981). *Post communication: Rhetorical analysis and evaluation* (2nd ed.). Indianapolis, IN: Bobbs-Merrill.

Cegala, D. J., Wall, V. D., & Rippey, G. (1987). An investigation of interaction involvement and the dimensions of SYMLOG: Perceived communication behaviors of persons in task-oriented groups. *Central States Speech Journal, 38,* 81–93.

Chaffee, S., Nass, C. I., Yang, S-M. (1990). The bridging role of television in immigrant political socialization. *Human Communication Research, 17,* 266–288.

Champion, D. J. (1970). *Basic statistics for social research.* Scranton, PA: Chandler.

Chaplin, J. P. (1985). *Dictionary of psychology* (2nd ed.). New York: Dell.

Chase, S. (1954). *The power of words.* New York: Harcourt Brace.

Christenson, P. (1992). The effects of parental advisory labels on adolescent music preferences. *Journal of Communication, 42,* 106–113.

Chung, K. L. (1975). *Probability theory with stochastic processes.* New York: Springer-Verlag.

Clark, R. D., & Word, L. E. (1974). Where is the apathetic bystander? Situational characteristics of the emergency. *Journal of Personality and Social Psychology, 29,* 279–287.

Coelho, C. A. (1990). Acquisition and generalization of simple manual sign grammars by aphasic subjects. *Journal of Communication Disorders, 23,* 383–400.

Cohen, J. (1960). A coefficient of agreement for nominal scales. *Educational and Psychological Measurements, 20,* 37–46.

Coke-Pepsi slugfest. (1976, July 26). *Time,* 64–65.

Copi, I. M. (1968). *Introduction to logic* (3rd ed.). New York: Macmillan.

Copi, I. M. (1986). *Introduction to logic* (7th ed.). New York: Macmillan.

Cozby, P. (1973). Self-disclosure: A literature review. *Psychological Bulletin, 79,* 73–91.

Cozby, P. C. (1989). *Methods in behavioral research* (4th ed.). Mountain View, CA: Mayfield.

Cragan, J. F., & Shields, D. C. (1981). *Applied communication research: A dramatistic approach.* Prospect Heights, IL: Waveland Press.

Craig, H. (1952). Woodrow Wilson as an orator. *Quarterly Journal of Speech, 38,* 145–148.

Crawford, J. E. (1980). *Taxonomy of questions in communication research.* Unpublished manuscript, Dept. of Communication, Arizona State University Tempe.

Cronbach, L. J. (1970). *Essentials of psychological testing* (3rd ed.). New York: Harper and Row.

Crowne, D. P., & Marlowe, D. (1960). A new scale of social desirability independent of psychopathology. *Journal of Consulting Psychology, 24,* 349–354.

Dahlstrom, W. G., Welsh, G. S., & Dahlstrom, L. E. (Eds.). (1972). *An MMPI handbook* (Vol. 1). Minneapolis: University of Minnesota Press.

Darroch, R. K., & Steiner, I. D. (1970). Role playing: An alternative to laboratory research? *Journal of Personality, 38,* 302–311.

Delia, J. G., & Grossberg, L. (1977). Interpretation and evidence. *Western Journal of Speech Communication, 41,* 32–42.

Denzin, N. K. (1983). Interpretive interactionism. In G. Morgan (Ed.), *Beyond method: Strategies for social research.* Newbury Park, CA: Sage.

DeStephen, R. S. (1983). Group interaction differences between high and low consensus groups. *Western Journal of Speech Communication, 47,* 340–363.

Deutsch, M., & Krauss, R. (1964). *Theories in social psychology.* New York: Basic Books.

DeVito, J. A. (1986). *The communication handbook: A dictionary.* New York: Harper and Row.

Dewey, J. (1910). Science as subject-matter as a method. *Science, 31,* 121–127.

Dickson, P., & Goulden, J. C. (1983). *There are alligators in our sewers and other American credos.* New York: Delacorte Press.

Diener, E., & Crandall, R. (1978). *Ethics in social and behavioral research.* Chicago: University of Chicago Press.

Dolin, D. (1995). An alternate form of teacher affinity-seeking measurement. *Communication Research Reports, 12,* 220–226.

Dominick, J. R., & Rauch, G. (1972). The image of women in network TV commercials. *Journal of Broadcasting, 16,* 259–265.

Dowling, R. E., & Ginder, G. A. (1995). An ethical appraisal of Ronald Reagan's justification for the invasion of Grenada. In E. Schiappa (Ed.), *Warranting assent: Case studies in argument evaluation* (pp. 103–124). Albany, NY: SUNY Press.

Duncan, O. D., & Lieberson, S. (1959). Ethnic segregation and assimilation. *American Journal of Sociology, 64,* 364–374.

Ellis, D. G. (1979). Relational control in two group systems. *Communication Monographs, 46,* 153–166.

Elms, A. C., & Janis, I. L. (1965). Counter-norm attitudes induced by consonant vs. dissonant conditions of role-playing. *Journal of Experimental Research in Personality, 1,* 50–60.

Emerson, R. (Ed.). (1983). *Contemporary field research.* Boston: Little, Brown.

Emerson, S., & Furman, J. (1991, November 18). The conspiracy that wasn't. *The New Republic,* pp. 12–15.

Emmert, P. (1989). Philosophy of measurement. In P. Emmert & L. L. Barker (Eds.), *Measurement of communication behavior* (pp. 87–116). New York: Longman.

Emmert, P., & Barker, L. L. (Eds.) (1989). *Measurement of communication behavior.* New York: Longman.

English, H. B., & English, A. C. (1958). *A comprehensive dictionary of psychological and psychoanalytical terms.* New York: McKay.

Erickson, B. H., & Nosanchuck, T. A. (1977). *Understanding data.* Toronto: McGraw-Hill Ryerson.

Errata note. (1995). *Western Journal of Communication, 59,* 355–356.

Feigl, H. (1945). Operationism and scientific method. *Psychological Review, 52,* 250–259.

Feller, W. (1968). *An introduction to probability theory and its applications* (2nd ed., Vol. 1). New York: Wiley.

Feller, W. (1971). *An introduction to probability theory and its applications* (3rd ed., Vol. 2). New York: Wiley.

Ferguson, M. (1983). *Forever feminine: Women's magazines and the cult of femininity.* London: Heinemann.

Fern, E. F. (1983). Focus groups: A review of some contradictory evidence, implications, and suggestions for future research. *Advances in Consumer Research, 10,* 121–126.

Festinger, L., Rieken, H. W., & Schachter, S. (1956). *When prophecy fails.* New York: Harper and Row.

Fisher, B. A., & Drexel, G. L. (1983). A cyclical model of developing relationships: A study of relational control interaction. *Communication Monographs, 50,* 66–78.

Fisher, B. A., Glover, T. W., & Ellis, D. G. (1977). The nature of complex communication systems. *Communication Monographs, 44,* 231–240.

Fisher, B. A., & Hawes, L. C. (1971). An interact system model: Generating a grounded theory of small groups. *Quarterly Journal of Speech, 57,* 444–453.

Fisher, W. R. (1987). *Human communication as narration: Toward a philosophy of reason, value, and action.* Columbia: University of South Carolina Press.

Fleiss, J. L. (1971). Measuring nominal scale agreement among many raters. *Psychological Bulletin, 76,* 378–382.

Fleiss, J. L. (1981). *Statistical methods for rates and proportions.* New York: Wiley.

Folger, J. P., & Poole, M. S. (1982). Relational coding schemes: The question of validity. In M. Burgoon (Ed.), *Communication yearbook 5.* New Brunswick, NJ: Transaction.

Foss, K. A., & Alexander, A. E. (1996). Exploring the margins of television viewing. *Communication Reports, 9,* 61–68.

Fox, D. J. (1969). *The research process in education.* New York: Holt, Rinehart and Winston.

Frankfort-Nachmias, C., & Nachmias, D. (1996). *Research methods in the social sciences* (5th ed.). New York: St. Martin's Press.

Freedman, J. L. (1969). Role playing: Psychology by consensus. *Journal of Personality and Social Psychology, 13,* 107–114.

Friedman, H. (1968). Magnitude of experimental effect and a table for its rapid estimation. *Psychological Bulletin, 70,* 245–251.

Gallup, G., & Rae, S. F. (1940). *The pulse of democracy.* New York: Simon and Schuster.

Gardner, R. J., and L. Zelevansky. (1975). The ten commandments for library customers. *Special Libraries, 66,* 326.

Gerbner, G. (1971). Violence in television drama: Trends and symbolic functions. In G. A. Comstock and E. A. Rubinstein (Eds.), *Television and social behavior: Vol. I, Media content and control.* Washington, DC: U.S. Government Printing Office.

German, K. M. (1995). Invoking the glorious war: Framing the Persian Gulf conflict through directive language. *Southern Communication Journal, 60,* 292–302.

Germond, J., & Witcover, J. (1989). *Whose broad stripes and bright stars?* New York: Time-Warner Books.

Gibaldi, J. (1995). *MLA handbook for writers of research papers.* New York: Modern Language Association of America.

Giere, R. N. (1979). *Understanding scientific reasoning.* New York: Holt Rinehart and Winston.

Ginsburg, G. P. (1979). The effective use of role-playing in social psychological research. In G. P. Ginsburg (Ed.), *Emerging strategies in social psychological research* (pp. 4–16). London: Wiley.

Glass, G. V., & Hopkins, K. D. (1984). *Statistical methods in education and psychology* (2nd ed.). Englewood Cliffs, NJ: Prentice-Hall.

Glass, G. V., Peckham, P. D., & Sanders, J. R. (1972). Consequence of failure to meet assumption underlying the fixed effects analysis of variance and covariance. *Review of Educational Research, 42,* 237–288.

Glossbrenner, A., & Glossbrenner, E. (1996). *Internet 101.* New York: McGraw-Hill.

Goldstein, R. (1981). On deceptive rejoinders about deceptive research: A reply to Baron. *IRB: A Review of Human Subjects Research, 3*(8), 5–6.

Gordon, W. I., & Infante, D. A. (1991). Test of a communication model of organizational commitment. *Communication Quarterly, 39,* 144–155.

Graham. W. K., & Dillon, P. C. (1974). Creative supergroups: Group performance as a function of individual performance on brainstorming tasks. *Journal of Social Psychology, 93,* 101–105.

Gravlee, G. J. (1981). Reporting proceedings and debates in the British Commons. *Central States Speech Journal, 32,* 85–99.

Greenberg, J., & Folger, R. (1988). *Controversial issues in social research methods.* New York: Springer-Verlag.

Guttman, L. (1944). A basis for scaling quantitative data. *American Sociological Review, 9,* 139–150.

Hadaway, C. K., Marler, P. L., & Chaves, M. (1993). What the polls don't show: A closer look at U.S. church attendance. *American Sociological Review, 55,* 243–254.

Haiman, F. (1949). An experimental study of the effects of ethos in public speaking. *Speech Monographs, 16,* 190–202.

Hale, J. L., Boster, F. J., & Mongeau, P. A. (1991). The validity of choice dilemma response scales. *Communication Reports, 4,* 30–34.

Hall, S., & Jefferson, T. (1975). *Resistance through rituals: Youth subcultures in post-war Berlin.* London, UK: Hutchinson.

Hammer, M. R. (1984). The effects of an intercultural communication workshop on participants' intercultural communication competence: An exploratory study. *Communication Quarterly, 32,* 252–262.

Hansen, C. H., & Hansen, R. D. (1990). The influence of sex and violence on the appeal of rock music videos. *Communication Research, 17,* 212–234.

Hawes, L. (1972). Development and application of an interview coding system. *Central States Speech Journal, 23,* 92–99.

Hayes, J. J., & Tathum, C. B. (1989). *Focus group interviews: A reader* (2nd ed.). Chicago: American Marketing Association.

Helmer, J. (1993). Storytelling in the creation and maintenance of organizational tension and stratification. *Southern Communication Journal, 59,* 34–44.

Hensley, C. W. (1975). Rhetorical vision and the persuasion of a historical movement: The Disciples of Christ in nineteenth century American culture. *Quarterly Journal of Speech, 61,* 250–264.

Herson, M., & Barlow, D. H. (1976). *Single case experimental designs: Strategies for studying behavior change.* New York: Pergamon.

Hill, Forbes I. (1972). Conventional wisdom—traditional form: The President's message of November 3, 1969. *Quarterly Journal of Speech, 58,* 373–386.

Homans, G. C. (1961). *Social behavior: Its elementary forms.* New York: Harcourt, Brace and World.

Hoogestraat, W. E. (1960). Memory: The lost canon? *Quarterly Journal of Speech, 46,* 141–147.

Hoover, K. (1979). *The elements of social scientific thinking* (2nd ed.). New York: St. Martin's Press.

Hopkins, K. D., & Glass, G. V. (1978). *Basic statistics for the behavioral sciences.* Englewood Cliffs, NJ: Prentice-Hall.

Hsu, T. C., & Feldt, L. S. (1969). The effect of limitations on the number of criterion score values on the significance of the *F* test. *American Educational Research Journal, 6,* 515–527.

Hubbard, R. C. (1985). Relationship styles in popular romance novels, 1950–1983. *Communication Quarterly, 33,* 113–125.

Huesmann, L. (1982). Violence and aggression. In D. Pearl, L. Bouthilet, & J. Lazar (Eds.), *Television and behavior: Ten years of scientific progress and implications for the eighties.* Washington, DC: U.S. Government Printing Office.

Huff, D. (1954). *How to lie with statistics.* New York: Norton.

Humphreys, L. (1970). *Tearoom trade: Impersonal sex in public places* (Enlarged ed.). Chicago: Aldine.

Isaac, S., & Michael, W. B. (Eds.) (1981). *Handbook in research and evaluation: For education and the behavioral sciences* (2nd ed.). San Diego, CA: EdITS.

Jablin, F. M., Seibold, D. R., & Sorenson, R. (1977). Potential inhibitory effects of group participation on brainstorming performance. *Central States Speech Journal, 28,* 113–121.

Jackson, D. N. (1973). *The IPA.* San Francisco: Psychological Research Organization.

Jacobs, S., & Jackson, S. (1979a, November). *Collaborative aspects of natural argument.* Paper presented at the Speech Communication Association Convention, San Antonio, TX.

Jacobs, S., & Jackson, S. (1979b, November). *Routes for the expansion of influence attempts in conversation.* Paper presented at the Speech Communication Association Convention, San Antonio, TX.

Jones, R. (1973). The Nature of Research. In R. H. Jones (Ed.), *Methods and techniques of educational research.* Danville, IL: Interstate.

Judd, C. M., Smith, E. R., & Kidder, L. H. (1991). *Research methods in social relations* (6th ed.). Fort Worth, TX: Holt, Rinehart and Winston.

Kaplan, A. (1964). *The conduct of inquiry: Methodology for behavioral science.* Scranton, PA: Chandler Publishing.

Kardas, E. P., & Milford, T. M. (1996). *Using the Internet for social science research and practice.* Belmont, CA: Wadsworth.

Katz, W. A. (1982). *Introduction to reference work* (Vol. 1). New York: McGraw-Hill.

Kazmier, L. J. (1988). *Business statistics* (2nd ed.). New York: McGraw-Hill.

Kelman, H. C. (1967). The human use of human subjects: The problem of deception in social psychological experiments. *Psychological Bulletin, 67,* 1–11.

Kerlinger, F. N. (1986). *Foundations of behavioral research* (3rd ed.). New York: Holt, Rinehart and Winston.

Klofas, J. M., & Cutshall, C. R. (1985). The social archeology of a juvenile facility: Unobtrusive methods in the study of institutional culture. *Qualitative Sociology, 8,* 368–382.

Kibler, R. J., & Barker, L. L. (Eds.). (1969). *Conceptual Frontiers in Speech-Communication.* New York: Speech Communication Association.

Kiefer, M. (1992, June 17–23). A question of class: What we have here is a failure to communicate. *New Times,* 8, 10.

Kirk, R. E. (1982). *Experimental design: Procedures for the behavioral sciences* (2nd ed.). Belmont, CA: Brooks/Cole.

Kline, S. L., & Floyd, C. H. (1990). On the art of saying no: The influence of social cognitive development on messages of refusal. *Western Journal of Speech Communication, 54,* 454–472.

Knutson, J. F., & Lansing, C. R. (1990). The relationship between communication problems and psychological difficulties in persons with profound acquired hearing loss. *Journal of Speech and Hearing Disorders, 55,* 656–664.

Koenker, R. (1961). *Simplified statistics.* Bloomington, IL: McKnight and McKnight.

Krantz, D. C. (1979). Naturalistic study of social influence on meal size among moderately obese and nonobese subjects. *Psychosomatic Medicine, 41,* 19–27.

Kratochwill, T. R. (Ed.) (1978). *Single subject research: Strategies for evaluative change.* New York: Academic Press.

Kraut, R. E., & Johnston, R. E. (1979). Social and emotional messages of smiling: An ethological approach. *Journal of Personality and Social Psychology, 37,* 1539–1553.

Krejcie, R. V., & Morgan, D. W. (1970). Determining sample size for research activities. *Educational and Psychological Measurement, 30,* 607–610.

Krippendorff, K. (1980). *Content analysis: An introduction to its methodology.* Beverly Hills: Sage.

Kruglanski, A. W. (1973). Much ado about the "volunteer artifacts." *Journal of Personality and Social Psychology, 28,* 350.

Lamm, H., & Trommsdorf, G. (1973). Group versus individual performance on tasks requiring ideational proficiency (brainstorming): A review. *European Journal of Social Psychology, 3,* 361–388.

Lannon, J. M. (1986). *The writing process: A concise rhetoric* (2nd ed.). Boston: Little, Brown.

Larson, S. G. (1991). Television's mixed messages: Sexual content on all my children. *Communication Quarterly, 39,* 156–163.

Lazarsfeld, P. (1959). Problems in methodology. In R. K. Merton (Ed.), *Sociology today.* New York: Basic Books.

Leedy, P. D. (1989). *Practical research: Planning and design* (4th ed.). New York: Macmillan.

Lengua, L. J., Roosa, M. W., Schupak-Neuberg, E., Michaeles, M. L., Berg, C. N., & Weschler, L. F. (1992). Using focus groups to guide the development of a parenting program for difficult-to-reach, high risk families. *Family Relations, 41,* 163–168.

Leno, J. (1991). *Headlines III: Not the movie, still the book.* New York: Warner Books.

Levine, M. (1988). *Effective problem solving.* Englewood Cliffs, NJ: Prentice-Hall.

Levinson, S. C. (1983). *Pragmatics.* Cambridge, UK: Cambridge University Press.

Li, C. (1975). *Path analysis: A primer.* Pacific Grove, CA: Boxwood Press.

Libresco, J. D. (1983, August/September). Focus groups: Madison Avenue meets public policy. *Public Opinion,* 51–53.

Lindey, A. (1952). *Plagiarism and originality.* New York: Harper.

Lofland, J., & Lofland, L. H. (1984). *Analyzing social settings.* Belmont, CA: Wadsworth.

Longman dictionary of psychology and psychiatry: A Walter D. Glanze book. (1984). New York: Longman.

Manusov, V. (1992). Mimicry of synchrony: The effects of intentionality attributions for nonverbal mirroring behavior. *Communication Quarterly, 40,* 69–83.

Marks, D., & Kammann, R. (1981). The nonpsychic powers of Uri Geller. In K. Frazier (Ed.), *Paranormal borderlands of science* (pp. 113–121). Buffalo, NY: Prometheus Books.

Marshall, J. C., & Powers, J. M. (1969). Writing neatness, composition errors, and essay grades. *Journal of Educational Measurement, 6,* 97–101.

Martin, W. (1988). Emily Dickinson. In E. Elliott (Gen. Ed.), *Columbia literary history of the United States* (pp. 609–626). New York: Columbia University Press.

Marwell, G., & Schmitt, D. R. (1967). Dimensions of compliance gaining behavior: An empirical analysis. *Sociometry, 30,* 350–364.

Mason, E. J., & Bramble, W. J. (1989). *Understanding and conducting research: application in education and the behavioral sciences* (2nd ed.). New York: McGraw-Hill.

Matlon, R. J., & Ortiz, S. P. (Eds.). (1992). *Index to journals in communication studies through 1990.* Annandale, VA: Speech Communication Association.

Matsumoto, D. (1991). Cultural influences on facial expression of emotion. *Southern Communication Journal, 56,* 128–137.

McBath, J. H., & Jeffrey, R. C. (1978). Defining speech communication. *Communication Education, 27,* 181–188.

McCroskey, J. C. (1966). Scales for the measurement of ethos. *Speech Monographs, 33,* 65–72.

McCroskey, J. C. (1967). *Studies of the effects of evidence in persuasive communication.* East Lansing, MI: Michigan State University, Speech Communication Research Laboratory, SCRL 4-67.

McCroskey, J. C. (1972). *An introduction to rhetorical communication* (2nd ed.). Englewood Cliffs, NJ: Prentice-Hall.

McCroskey, J. C. (1977). Oral communication apprehension: A summary of recent theory and research. *Human Communication Research, 4,* 78–96.

McCroskey, J. C. (1978). Validity of the PRCA as an index of oral communication apprehension. *Communication Monographs, 45,* 192–203.

McCroskey, J. C. (1982). *An introduction to rhetorical communication* (4th ed.). Englewood Cliffs, NJ: Prentice-Hall.

McCroskey, J. C. (1992). Reliability and validity of the willingness to communicate scale. *Communication Quarterly, 40,* 16–25.

McCroskey, J. C., & Young, T. J. (1981). Ethos and credibility: The construct and its measurement after three decades. *Central States Speech Journal, 32,* 24–34.

McDonald, D. (1980). *The language of argument* (3rd ed.). New York: Harper and Row.

McGuire, M. (1977). Mythic rhetoric in *Mein Kampf:* A structuralist critique. *Quarterly Journal of Speech, 63,* 1–13.

McNeill, P. (1990). *Research methods* (2nd ed.). London: Routledge.

McQuail, D. (1984). With the benefit of hindsight: Reflections on uses and gratifications research. *Critical Studies in Mass Communication, 1,* 177–193.

McQuail, D., Blumler, J., & Brown, R. (1972). The television audience: A revised perspective. In D. McQuail (Ed.), *Sociology of mass communications.* Harmondsworth, UK: Penguin.

Mechling, E. W. (1979). Patricia Hearst: MYTH AMERICA 1974, 1975, 1976. *Western Journal of Speech Communication, 43,* 168–179.

Meehl, P. E., & Hathaway, S. R. (1946). The K factor as a suppressor variable in the Minnesota Multiphasic Personality Inventory. *Journal of Applied Psychology, 30,* 525–564.

Merton, R. K. (1987). The focused interview and focus groups. *Public Opinion Quarterly, 51,* 550–566.

Milavsky, J. R., Kessler, R. C., Stipp, H. H., & Rubens, W. S. (1982). *Television and aggression: A panel study.* New York: Academic Press.

Miller, G. R., & Berger, C. R. (1978). On keeping the faith in matters scientific. *Western Journal of Speech Communication, 42,* 44–57.

Millham, J., & Jacobson, L. I. (1978). The need for approval. In H. London & J. E. Exner (Eds.), *Dimensions of personality* (pp. 365–390). New York: Wiley.

A million random digits with 100,000 normal deviates. (1955). New York: Free Press.

Mohrmann, G. P., Leff, M. C. (1974). Lincoln at Cooper Union: A rationale for neo-classical criticism. *Quarterly Journal of Speech, 60,* 459–467.

Monge, P. R. (1987). The network level of analysis. In C. R. Berger & S. H. Chaffee (Eds.), *Handbook of communication science* (pp. 239–270). Newbury Park, CA: Sage.

Monge, P. R., & Miller, G. R. (1985). Communication networks. In A. Kuper & J. Kuper (Eds.), *The social science encyclopedia* (pp. 130–131). London, UK: Routledge & Kegan.

Morgan, D. L. (1989). *Focus groups as qualitative research.* Newbury Park, CA: Sage.

Morris, W., & Morris, M. (Eds.). (1985). *Harper dictionary of contemporary usage* (2nd ed.). New York: Harper and Row.

Mortensen, C. D. (1972). *Communication.* New York: McGraw-Hill.

Motley, M. T. (1990). On whether one can(not) communicate: An examination via traditional communication postulates. *Western Journal of Speech Communication, 54,* 1–20.

Motley, M. T., & Reeder, H. M. (1995). Unwanted escalation of sexual intimacy: Male and female perceptions of connotations and relational consequences of resistance messages. *Communication Monographs, 62,* 355–382.

Myers, M. T., & Myers, G. E. (1982). *Managing communication: An organizational approach.* New York: McGraw-Hill.

Nachmias, D., & Nachmias, C. (1987). *Research methods in the social sciences* (3rd ed.). New York: St. Martin's Press.

Naisbitt, J., & Aburdene, P. (1982). *Megatrends.* New York: William Morrow.

Nelson, J., & Flannery, M. A. (1990). The sanctuary movement: A story of religious confrontation. *Southern Communication Journal, 55,* 372–387.

Newhagen, J. E., Cordes, J. W., & Levy, M. R. (1995). Nightly@nbc.com: Audience scope and the perception of interactivity in viewer mail on the Internet. *Journal of Communication, 45* (3), 164–175.

Nicotera, A. M., & Rancer, A. S. (1994). The influence of sex on self-perception and social stereotyping of aggressive communication predispositions. *Western Journal of Communication, 58,* 283–307.

Nisbett, R. E., & Wilson, T. D. (1977a). Telling more than we can know. Verbal reports on mental processes. *Psychological Review, 84,* 231–259.

Nisbett, R. E., & Wilson, T. D. (1977b). The halo effect: Evidence for unconscious alteration of judgments. *Journal of Personality and Social Psychology, 35,* 250–256.

Nunnally, J. (1978). *Psychometric theory* (2nd ed.). New York: McGraw-Hill.

Orne, M. T. (1970). Hypnosis, motivation, and the ecological validity of the psychological experiment. *Nebraska Symposium on Motivation, 18,* 187–265.

Osgood, C. E., Suci, G. J., & Tannenbaum, P. H. (1957). *The measurement of meaning.* Urbana: University of Illinois Press.

Ott, L., & Hildebrand, D. K. (1983). *Statistical thinking for managers.* Boston: PWS Publishers.

Paradis, A. A. (1966). *The research handbook: A guide to reference sources.* New York: Funk and Wagnalls.

Parrella, G. C. (1971). Projection and adoption: Toward a clarification of the concept of empathy. *Quarterly Journal of Speech, 57,* 204–213.

Pavitt, C. (1990). The ideal communicator as the basis for competence judgments of self and friend. *Communication Reports, 3,* 9–14.

Pearson, K. (1924). Historical note on the origin of the normal curve of errors. *Biometrika, 16,* 402–404.

Peirce, C. (1955). *Philosophical writings of Peirce* (J. Buchler, Ed.). New York: Dover.

Perse, E. M. (1996). Sensation seeking and the use of television for arousal. *Communication Reports, 9,* 37–48.

Pfau, M., & Burgoon, M. (1988). Inoculation in political campaign communication. *Human Communication Research, 15,* 91–111.

Pomerantz, A. (1990). Conversation analytic claims. *Communication Monographs 57,* 231–235.

Popper, K. R. (1968a). *Conjectures and refutations: The growth of scientific knowledge* (2nd ed.). New York: Harper Torchbooks.

Popper, K. R. (1968b). *The logic of scientific discovery* (2nd ed.). New York: Harper Torchbooks.

Popper, K. R. (1972). *Objective knowledge.* Oxford, UK: Oxford University Press.

Pramualratana, A., Havanon, N., & Knodel, J. (1985, February). Exploring the normative basis for age at marriage in Thailand: An example from focus group research. *Journal of Marriage and the Family, 47,* 203–271.

Publication manual of the American Psychological Association (4th ed.). (1995). Washington, DC: American Psychological Association.

Quine, W. (1946). Truth by Convention. In O. H. Lee (Ed.), *Philosophical essays for Alfred North Whitehead.* New York: Longmans Greens.

Randi, J. (1981). New evidence in the Uri Geller matter. In K. Frazier (Ed.), *Paranormal borderlands of science* (pp. 122–127). Buffalo, NY: Prometheus Books.

Ransford, H. E. (1968). Isolation, powerlessness, and violence: A study of attitudes and participants in the Watts riots. *American Journal of Sociology, 73,* 581–591.

Ray, J., & Zavos, H. (1966). Reasoning and argument: Some special problems and types. In G. R. Miller & T. R. Nilsen (Eds.), *Perspectives on argumentation* (pp. 80–109). Chicago: Scott, Foresman.

Ray, W. J., & Ravizza, R. R. (1988). *Methods: Toward a science of behavior and experience* (3rd ed.). Belmont, CA: Wadsworth.

Reinard, J. C. (1991). *Foundations of argument: Effective communication for critical thinking.* Dubuque, IA: W. C. Brown.

Reinard, J. C., & Boster, F. J. (1978, May). *Information processing under stress: Developments on a theory of stress coping to communication.* Paper presented at the Speech Communication Association Convention, Minneapolis, MN.

Rescourla, L. (1989). The language development survey: A scoring tool for delayed language in toddlers. *Journal of Speech and Hearing Disorders, 54,* 587–599.

Reynolds, P. D. (1971). *A primer in theory construction.* Indianapolis: Bobbs-Merrill.

Reynolds, P. D. (1979). *Ethical dilemmas in social science research.* San Francisco: Jossey-Bass.

Reynolds, R. A., & Burgoon, M. (1983). Belief processing, reasoning, and evidence. In R. Bostrom (Ed.), *Communication yearbook 7* (pp. 83–104). Beverly Hills, CA: Sage.

Richardson, L. S. (1970). Stokely Carmichael: Jazz artist. *Western Speech, 34,* 212–218.

Ring, K., Wallston, K., & Corey, M. (1970). Mode of debriefing as a factor affecting subjective reaction to a Milgram-type obedience experiment: An ethical inquiry. *Representative Research in Social Psychology, 1,* (67) 67–88.

Rivlin, A. M., & Timpane, P. M. (Eds.). (1978). *Ethical and legal issues of social experimentation.* Washington, DC: Brookings Institution.

Robinson, J. P., Shaver, P. R., & Wrightsman, L. S. (Eds.). (1991). *Measures of personality and social psychological attitudes* (Vol. 1). San Diego: Academic Press.

Rogers, L. E., & Farace, R. V. (1975). Analysis of relational communication in dyads: New measurement procedures. *Human Communication Research, 1,* 222–239.

Rosenfeld, L. B., & Bowen, G. L. (1991). Marital disclosure and marital satisfaction: Direct-effect versus interaction-effect models. *Western Journal of Speech Communication, 55,* 69–84.

Rosenthal, R., & Rosnow, R. L. (1969). The volunteer subject. In R. Rosenthal & R. L. Rosnow (Eds.), *Artifact in behavioral research* (pp. 59–118). New York: McGraw-Hill.

Rowland, R. C. (1987). Narrative: Mode of discourse or paradigm? *Communication Monographs, 54,* 264–275.

Rubin, R. B., Palmgreen, P., & Sypher, H. E. (1994). *Communication research measures: A sourcebook.* New York: Guilford Press.

Rubin, R. B., Rubin, A. M., & Piele, L. J. (1990). *Communication research: Strategies and sources* (2nd ed.). Belmont, CA: Wadsworth.

Rubin, Z., & Shenker, S. S. (1978). Friendship, proximity, and self-disclosure. *Journal of Personality, 46,* 1–22.

Rushing, J. H. (1986). Mythic evolution of "the new frontier" in mass mediated rhetoric. *Critical Studies in Mass Communication, 3,* 265–296.

Sachs, D., & Stair, H. (1996). *Hands-on Netscape.* Upper Saddle River, NJ: Prentice-Hall.

Sanbonmatsu, A. (1971). Darrow and Rorke's use of Burkean identification strategies in *New York vs. Gitlow* (1920). *Speech Monographs, 37,* 36–48.

Sandberg, C. (1954). *Abraham Lincoln: The prairie years and the war years, One-volume edition.* New York: Galahad Books.

Sapolsky, B. S., & Tabarlet, J. (1991). Sex in primetime television: 1979 versus 1989. *Journal of Broadcasting and Electronic Media, 35,* 505–516.

Scheidel, T. M., & Crowell, L. (1964). Idea development in small group communication. *Quarterly Journal of Speech, 50,* 140–145.

Schmid, J., & Fiedler, K. (1996). Language and implicit attributions in the Nuremberg trials. *Human Communication Research, 22,* 371–398.

Schutt, R. K. (1996). *Investigating the social world: The process and practice of research.* Thousand Oaks, CA: Pine Forge Press.

Scott, W. (1955). Reliability of content analysis: The case of nominal scale coding. *Public Opinion Quarterly, 17,* 321–325.

Siler, T. (1975, April 18). Best of the best. *Knoxville News-Sentinel,* p. 18.

Simpson, C. (1994). *Science of coercion: Communication research and psychological warfare 1945-1960*. New York: Oxford University Press.

Singer, E. (1983). Informed consent procedures in surveys: Some reasons for minimal effects on response. In R. F. Boruch & J. S. Cecil (Eds.), *Solutions to ethical and legal problems in social research* (pp. 183–211). Orlando, FL: Academic Press.

Smith, H. W. (1991). *Strategies of social research* (3rd ed.). Orlando, FL: Holt, Rinehart and Winston.

Smith, M. J. (1988). *Contemporary communication research methods*. Belmont, CA: Wadsworth.

Snow, M. (1985). Martin Luther King's "letter from Birmingham jail" as Pauline epistle. *Quarterly Journal of Speech, 71,* 318–334.

Sobal, J. (1984). The content of survey introductions and the provisions of informed consent. *Public Opinion Quarterly, 48,* 788–793.

Spitzberg, B. H. (1988). Communication competence: Measures of perceived effectiveness. In H. Tardy (Ed.), *A handbook for the study of human communication* (pp. 67–106). Norwood, NJ: Ablex Publishing Corp.

Stanovich, K. E. (1986). *How to think straight about psychology*. Glenview, IL: Scott, Foresman.

Stevens, J. (1986). *Applied multivariate statistics for the social sciences*. Hillsdale, NJ: Lawrence Erlbaum Associates.

Stevens, S. S. (1951). Scales of measurement. In S. S. Stevens (Ed.), *Handbook of experimental psychology* (pp. 23–30). New York: Wiley.

Stewart, C. J., & Cash, W. B. (1988). *Interviewing: Principles and practices* (5th ed.). Dubuque, IA: W. C. Brown.

Stewart, D. W., & Shamdasani, P. M. (1990). *Focus groups: Theory and practice*. Newbury Park, CA: Sage.

Stinchcombe, A. L. (1968). *Constructing social theories*. New York: Harcourt, Brace and World.

Strickland, B. R. (1977). Approval motivation. In T. Blass (Ed.), *Personality variables in social behavior* (pp. 315–356). Hillsdale, NJ: Erlbaum.

Strunk, W., Jr., & White, E. B. (1979). *The elements of style* (3rd ed.). New York: Macmillan.

Stubbs, M. (1981). Motivating analyses of exchange structure. In M. Coulthard, & M. Montgomery (Eds.), *Studies in discourse analysis*. London: Routledge and Kegan Paul.

Stuckey, M. E., & Antczak, F. J. (1994). The battle of issues and images: Establishing interpreting dominance. *Communication Quarterly, 42,* 120–132.

Student. (1908). On the probable error of the mean. *Biometrika, 6,* 1–25.

Sussman, S., Burton, D., Dent, C. W. Stacy, A. W., & Flay, B. R. (1991). Use of focus groups in developing an adolescent tobacco use cessation program: Collection norm effects. *Journal of Applied Social Psychology, 21,* 1772–1782.

Swenson, W. M., Pearson, J. S., & Osbourne, D. (1973). *An MMPI sourcebook: Basic item, scale, and pattern data on 50,000 medical patients*. Minneapolis: University of Minnesota Press.

Sykes, A. J. M. (1970). Myth in communication. *Journal of Communication, 20,* 17–31.

Tanaka-Matsumi, J., & Kameoka, V. A. (1986). Reliabilities and concurrent validities of popular self-report measures of depression, anxiety, and social desirability. *Journal of Consulting and Clinical Psychology, 54,* 328–333.

Tardy, Charles H. (Ed.). (1988a). *A handbook for the study of human communication: Methods and instruments for observing, measuring and assessing communication processes*. Norwood, NJ: Ablex Publishing.

Tardy, Charles H. (1988b). Interpersonal interaction coding systems. In C. H. Tardy (Ed.), *A handbook for the study of human communication: Methods and instruments for observing, measuring and assessing communication processes*. Norwood, NJ: Ablex Publishing.

Tatsuoka, M. (1969). *Validation studies: The use of multiple regression equations*. Champaign, IL: Institute for Personality and Ability Testing.

Thergerge, L. J. (Ed.). (1981). *Crooks, conmen and clowns: Businessmen in TV entertainment*. Washington, DC: The Media Institute.

Thill, J. V., & Bovee, C. L. (1991). *Excellence in business communication*. New York: McGraw-Hill.

Thomas, S., & LeShay, S. V. (1992). Bad business? A reexamination of television's portrayal of businesspersons. *Journal of Communication, 42,* 95–105.

Troester, R., & Meister, C. S. (1990). Peace communication: A survey of current attitudes, curricular practice, and research priorities. *Western Journal of Speech Communication, 54,* 420–428.

Trujillo, N., & Dionisopoulos, G. (1987). Cop talk, police stories, and the social construction of organizational drama. *Central States Speech Journal 38,* 196–209.

Tucker, R. K., Weaver, R. L., II, Berryman-Fink, C. (1981). *Research in speech communication*. Englewood Cliffs, NJ: Prentice-Hall.

Tuckman, B. W. (1978). *Conducting educational research* (2nd ed.). New York: Harcourt Brace Jovanovich.

Tuttle, L. P., Terry, D., & Shinedling, M. M. (1977). Note on increase of social interacting of mental patients during a camping trip. *Psychological Reports, 33,* 72–74.

Typing and improved academic performance. (1976, July). [Brochure]. Smith-Corona.

Vancil, D. L., Pendell, S. D. (1987). The myth of viewer-listener disagreement in the first Kennedy-Nixon debate. *Central States Speech Journal, 38,* 16–27.

Vanlear, C. A., Jr., & Zeitlow, P. H. (1990). Toward a contingency approach to marital interaction: An empirical integration of three approaches. *Communication Monographs, 57,* 202–218.

Veloso, K., Hall, J. W., III, & Grose, J. H. (1990). Frequency selectivity and comodulation masking release in adults and in 6-year-old children. *Journal of Speech and Hearing Research, 33,* 96–102.

Wagner, S. F. (1992). *Introduction to statistics.* New York: HarperCollins.

Wallas, G. (1926). *The art of thought.* New York: Harcourt, Brace.

Walther, J. B. (1992). Interpersonal effects in computer-mediated interaction: A relational perspective. *Communication Research, 19,* 52–90.

Wartella, E., Heintz, K. E., Aidman, A. J., & Mazzarella, S. R. (1990). Television and beyond: Children's video media in one community. *Communication Research, 17,* 45–64.

Warwick, D. (1975, October). Deceptive research: Social scientists ought to stop lying. *Psychology Today,* pp. 38–40.

Watzlawik, P., Beavin, J. H., & Jackson, D. D. (1967). *Pragmatics of human communication.* New York: Norton.

Wax, R. H. (1968). Participant observation. *International encyclopedia of social sciences* (p. 238). New York: Macmillan.

Webb, E., Campbell, D. T., Schwartz, R. D., Sechrest, L., & Grove, J. B. (1981). *Nonreactive measures in the social sciences.* Boston: Houghton Mifflin.

Weber, K. D., & Patterson, B. R. (1996). Construction and validation of a communication based emotional support scale. *Communication Research Reports, 13,* 68–76.

Weick, K. E. (1969). *The social psychology of organizing.* Reading, MA: Addison-Wesley.

Weinberg, M. S. (1965). Sexual modesty, social meanings, and the nudist camp. *Social Problems, 12,* 311–318.

Whately, R. A. (1844). *Elements of logic.* London: B. Fellows.

Wheeler, M. (1977). *Lies, damn lies, and statistics: The manipulation of public opinion in America.* New York: Dell.

White, P. (1980). Limitations on verbal reports of internal events: A refutation of Nisbett and Wilson and of Bem. *Psychological Review, 87,* 105–112.

White, S. E. (1995). A content analytic technique for measuring the sexiness of women's business attire in media presentations. *Communication Research Reports, 12,* 178–185.

Whitney, F. L. (1950). *The elements of research* (3rd ed.). New York: Prentice-Hall.

Wiemann, J. M. (1977). Explication and test of a model of communicative competence. *Human Communication Research, 3,* 195–213.

Willard, C. A. (1981). The status of the non-discursiveness thesis. *Journal of the American Forensic Association, 17,* 190–214.

Williams, F. (1991). *Reasoning with statistics: How to read quantitative research* (4th ed.). Fort Worth, TX: Harcourt Brace Jovanovich.

Wilson, T. D., & Nisbett, R. E. (1978). The accuracy of verbal reports about the effects of stimuli on evaluation and behavior. *Social Psychology, 41,* 118–131.

Wimmer, R. D., & Dominick, J. R. (1983). *Mass media research: An introduction.* Belmont, CA: Wadsworth.

Wimmer, R. D., & Dominick, J. R. (1997). *Mass media research: An introduction* (5th ed.). Belmont, CA: Wadsworth.

Woal, M. (1987). Listening to monotony: All-news radio. *Central States Speech Journal, 38,* 28–34.

Wright, M. H. (1994). Burkean and Freudian theories of identification. *Communication Quarterly, 42,* 301–310.

Yamane, T. (1967). *Elementary sampling theory.* Englewood Cliffs, NJ: Prentice-Hall.

NAME INDEX

SUBJECT INDEX